CHANGING PARADIG
AND SYSTEMATIC THEOLOGY

General Editors
Sarah Coakley   Richard Cross

ORTHODOX READINGS OF AQUINAS

This book is the first exploration of the remarkable odyssey of Thomas Aquinas in the Orthodox Christian world, from the Byzantine to the modern era. Aquinas was received with astonishing enthusiasm across the Byzantine theological spectrum. By contrast, modern Orthodox readings of Aquinas have been resoundingly negative, routinely presenting Aquinas as the archetype of as a specifically Western form of theology against which the Orthodox East must set its face. Basing itself primarily on a close study of the Byzantine reception of Thomas, this study rejects such hackneyed dichotomies, arguing instead for a properly catholic or universal construal of Orthodoxy-one in which Thomas might once again find a place. In its probing of the East-West dichotomy, this book questions the widespread juxtaposition of Gregory Palamas and Thomas Aquinas as archetypes of opposing Greek and Latin theological traditions. The long period between the Fall of Constantinople and the Russian Revolution, conventionally written off as an era of sterility and malformation for Orthodox theology, is also viewed with a fresh perspective. Study of the reception of Thomas in this period reveals a theological sophistication and a generosity of vision that is rarely accounted for. In short, this is a book which radically re-thinks the history of Orthodox theology through the prism of the fascinating and largely untold story of Orthodox engagement with Aquinas.

Marcus Plested is Associate Professor, Department of Theology, Marquette University.

CHANGING PARADIGMS IN HISTORICAL AND SYSTEMATIC THEOLOGY

General Editors: Sarah Coakley (Norris-Hulse Professor of Divinity, University of Cambridge) and Richard Cross (John A. O'Brien Professor of Philosophy, University of Notre Dame)

This series sets out to reconsider the modern distinction between 'historical' and 'systematic' theology. The scholarship represented in the series is marked by attention to the way in which historiographic and theological presumptions ('paradigms') necessarily inform the work of historians of Christian thought, and thus affect their application to contemporary concerns. At certain key junctures such paradigms are recast, causing a reconsideration of the methods, hermeneutics, geographical boundaries, or chronological caesuras which have previously guided the theological narrative. The beginning of the twenty-first century marks a period of such notable reassessment of the Christian doctrinal heritage, and involves a questioning of the paradigms that have sustained the classic 'history-of-ideas' textbook accounts of the modern era. Each of the volumes in this series brings such contemporary methodological and historiographical concerns to conscious consideration. Each tackles a period or key figure whose significance is ripe for reconsideration, and each analyses the implicit historiography that has sustained existing scholarship on the topic. A variety of fresh methodological concerns are considered, without reducing the theological to other categories. The emphasis is on an awareness of the history of 'reception': the possibilities for contemporary theology are bound up with a careful re-writing of the historical narrative. In this sense, 'historical' and 'systematic' theology are necessarily conjoined, yet also closely connected to a discerning interdisciplinary engagement.

This monograph series accompanies the project of *The Oxford Handbook of the Reception of Christian Theology* (OUP, in progress), also edited by Sarah Coakley and Richard Cross.

RECENT SERIES TITLES

Calvin, Participation, and the Gift
The Activity of Believers in Union with Christ
J. Todd Billings

Newman and the Alexandrian Fathers
Shaping Doctrine in Nineteenth-Century England
Benjamin J. King

Orthodox Readings
of Aquinas

MARCUS PLESTED

OXFORD
UNIVERSITY PRESS

OXFORD
UNIVERSITY PRESS

Great Clarendon Street, Oxford OX2 6DP
United Kingdom

Oxford University Press is a department of the University of Oxford.
It furthers the University's objective of excellence in research, scholarship,
and education by publishing worldwide. Oxford is a registered trade mark of
Oxford University Press in the UK and in certain other countries

© Marcus Plested 2012

The moral rights of the author have been asserted

First published 2012
First published in paperback 2015

Impression: 1

Published in the United States of America by Oxford University Press
198 Madison Avenue, New York, NY 10016, United States of America

British Library Cataloguing in Publication Data
Data available

ISBN 978-0-19-965065-1 (Hbk.)
ISBN 978-0-19-870889-6 (Pbk.)

For Mariamni

Acknowledgements

This has been very much a Princeton project. My initial researches were conducted during the Spring Semester of 2008 at the Center of Theological Inquiry (CTI). I am most grateful to CTI for its provision of an exceptionally stimulating environment for theological endeavour. The bulk of the work was carried out as the George William Cottrell, Jr. Member of the Institute for Advanced Study (IAS) in the academic year 2010–11. IAS is an academic Elysium without par and it was perfectly exhilarating to work in the company of so many prodigiously talented scientists, mathematicians, and historians. I am particularly grateful to Caroline Bynum for graciously mentoring those of us in the medieval history section of the School of Historical Studies. The librarians and support staff of IAS were always exceptionally helpful. Thanks are also due to the Institute for Orthodox Christian Studies and to its Principal, David Frost, for being willing to grant me extended bouts of research leave in short succession. Likewise to the Faculty of Divinity of the University of Cambridge for a grant towards the cost of the index which was prepared by Johannes Börjesson. Elements of this book have been presented at the American Academy of Religion, Fordham University, Princeton University, the University of Notre Dame, IAS, CTI, Holy Cross Greek Orthodox School of Theology, and the Institut St-Serge. Discussion following these papers has invariably been to the betterment of this book. Thanks also to those scholars who have read and commented on portions of this book: Brian Daley, Thomas Guarino, Nadieszda Kizenko, and Assaad Kattan. Philip Steer read through the text with a careful eye for infelicities of style and language. My editors, Richard Cross and Sarah Coakley have also, together with the Press' anonymous readers, provided some invaluable suggestions and advice. The remaining errors are of my own devising.

Cambridge
6 August 2012
Feast of the Transfiguration

Table of Contents

Abbreviations

BZ	*Byzantinische Zeitschrift*
CCSG	Corpus christianorum series graeca
CEG	Thomas Aquinas, *Contra errores graecorum*
CPG	*Clavis patrum graecorum*
CSEL	Corpus scriptorum ecclesiasticorum latinorum
DS	*Dictionnaire de spiritualité*
DTC	*Dictionnaire de théologie catholique*
ECR	*Eastern Churches Review*
EO	*Échos d'orient*
GCS	Die griechischen christlichen Schriftseller der ersten drei Jahrhunderte
JEH	*Journal of Ecclesiastical History*
JÖB	*Jahrbuch der Österreichischen Byzantinistik*
JTS	*Journal of Theological Studies*
OCA	Orientalia christiana analecta
OCP	*Orientalia christiana periodica*
PG	Migne, Patrologia graeca
PL	Migne, Patrologia latina
PLP	*Prosopographisches Lexikon der Palaiologenzeit*
PO	Patrologia orientalis
PTS	Patristische Texte und Studien
REB	*Revue des études byzantines*
SC	Sources chrétiennes
SCG	Thomas Aquinas, *Summa contra gentiles*.
ST	Thomas Aquinas, *Summa theologiae*.
SVQ	*St Vladimir's Theological Quarterly*
TLG	*Thesaurus linguae graecae*
TRE	*Theologische Realenzyklopädie*
TU	Texte und Untersuchungen
VC	*Vigiliae christianae*

Introduction: 1354 and all that

At three o'clock in the afternoon of 24 December 1354, Demetrios Kydones put the final touch to his translation of Thomas Aquinas' *Summa contra gentiles*, a task that had taken him a year to complete amid his many other pressing concerns as chief minister of the Byzantine Empire.[1] 1354 was also, by unhappy coincidence, the year of the Ottoman capture of Gallipoli. On 2 March a massive earthquake had devastated much of Thrace, hitting Gallipoli especially hard. The survivors of the catastrophe picked up their bags and left, leaving this once beautiful city desolate. The Ottoman Turks, quick to seize an opportunity, crossed the Hellespont in force and established themselves in the ruins. In short order, the walls were rebuilt and a fortress established. Thus the Turks gained their first permanent foothold in Europe in a strategic position that afforded control of the Dardanelles and of the crossing between Asia and Europe. This event, more than any other, sealed the fate of the dwindling and embattled Empire.[2]

That the Turks were in a position to take such swift advantage of this disaster was to some degree the fault of the Byzantines themselves. Turkish soldiers had been employed on both sides of

---

[1] Demetrios gives us this information in autograph at the end of MS *Vaticanus graecus* 616. The colophon is reproduced in Alexander Turyn, *Codices Graeci Vaticani saeculis XIII et XIV scripti annorumque notis instructi*, 197. The MS also contains, again in his own hand, the Latin collect to St Thomas: 'Deus, qui Ecclesiam tuam beati Thomae Confessoris tui mira eruditione clarificas, et sancta operatione fecundas: da nobis, quaesumus, et quae docuit intellectu conspicere, et quae egit imitatione complere.'

[2] The recapture of Gallipoli in 1366 by Count Amadeus of Savoy and its fleeting return to the Byzantine fold could not reverse the gains made by the Turks in Europe by virtue of this strategic foothold.

the bitter civil war between John VI Kantakuzene and the guardians of his nephew, John V Palaiologos. In that time, the Turks had had ample opportunity to dwell in and scout out the lands they were soon to claim for their own. John VI had won the first phase of this civil war (1341–7)—partly thanks to his Turkish troops—but the loss of Gallipoli precipitated his abdication on 10 December 1354. He took the monastic habit at that point, assuming the name Joasaph. Demetrios Kydones had been his chief minster (μεσάζων) and shared in his master's fall, retiring for a time to the same monastery— St George of the Mangana.[3] It was at that monastery that the translation of the *Summa contra gentiles* was completed.

The contemporary Greek philosopher and theologian, Christos Yannaras also homes in on 1354 as a pivotal and epoch-making year in his *Orthodoxy and the West in Modern Greece*. But for Yannaras, it is not the loss of Gallipoli or the abdication of John VI that most concerns him but rather Kydones' translation. For Yannaras, the translation of the *Summa contra gentiles* marks the beginning of the extinction of what he calls 'real Hellenism', the start of a process that saw the living tradition of the Gospel and the Greek Fathers submitted to and eventually subsumed by the West: 'the great historical cycle which started motion in 1354 with Demetrios Kydones as its symbolic marker seems to be coming to a conclusion in the shape of Greece's absorption by Europe—the final triumph of the pro-unionists'.[4] The problem with Aquinas, for Yannaras, is that scholastic methodology makes God into a definable and knowable entity, breaking the connection between Creator and creation. The consequences of this scholastic approach are frankly appalling:

> Man in the Western scholastic tradition does not participate personally in the truth of the cosmos. He does not seek to bring out the meaning,

---

[3] John-Joasaph spent only a matter of weeks at the monastery of St George, moving more permanently to the monastery of Nea Peribleptos, also known as Charsianites (or Charsianitou) after its founder, John Charsianites. As a monk, and having made peace with his nephew, John VI remained a major player in the affairs of the Empire. Kydones too was not long in the political wilderness and went on to serve as μεσάζων to John V and Manuel II—a quite unparalleled distinction.

[4] ' Ὀρθοδοξία καὶ Δύση στὴ Νεώτερη Ἑλλάδα, 489 [ET 61]. I refer in the first instance to the original Modern Greek, but also refer to the excellent translation of Norman Russell and Peter Chamberas. This is in deference to Yannaras, who has taken exception to the English translation. Thanks to Norman Russell himself for this information. See also Andrew Louth, 'Some Recent Works by Christos Yannaras in English Translation', 333.

the logos of things, the disclosure of the personal activity of God in the cosmos, but seeks with his individualistic intellect to dominate the reality of the physical world. This stance truly forms the foundation of the entire phenomenon of modern technology.[5]

Precisely the opposite conclusions have been reached by another contemporary Greek thinker, Stelios Ramphos. In his alternative 'grand narrative', it is the triumph of Hesychasm and the theology of St Gregory Palamas which represents the real disaster of this period. In this narrative, it is not 1354 that is the turning-point but rather 1351, the year of the Council of Constantinople which definitively canonized the theology of St Gregory Palamas. Ramphos characterizes this event as the triumph of a world-denying and anti-rational faith and a decisive turn away from history.[6] Orthodoxy has eschewed the linear and logical thought patterns of Aristotle and favoured instead a broadly neo-Platonic orientation, divorced from the world, suspicious of the body, and dismissive of reason. By this act, Orthodoxy rejected Western Christianity's more world-affirming and distinctly rational faith—as exemplified by Aquinas.[7] The victory of Hesychast asceticism and rejection of Western Christianity, per-petuated by that great anthology of Hesychast sources, the *Philokalia*, has sown the seeds of Greece's subsequent woes. These include: the surrender of the Byzantine Empire to the Turks in 1453, the result of a fatalistic acceptance of the rule of the Sultan over any accommodation with Latin Christianity that might bring military aid; a yearning for impossible metaphysical solutions and a neglect of day-to-day-reality; an endemic antipathy to hard work; and a lack of societal conscious-ness. Even the bursts of extremism and violence that punctuate modern Greek life, such as in the fall-out from the financial crisis of 2008, are directly attributable to the void that has opened up the Greek soul as a result of the victory of a world-denying form of Christianity.[8]

---

[5] Christos Yannaras, 'Orthodoxy and the West', 287.

[6] Stelios Ramphos, *Τὸ ἀδιανόητο τίποτα: Φιλοκαλικὰ ριζώματα τοῦ νεοελληνικοῦ μηδενισμοῦ. Δοκίμιο φιλοσοφικῆς ἀνθρωπολογίας*, 400f.

[7] Aquinas is presented as the decisive figure in the West's use of Aristotle to provide an intellectually coherent defence of the faith—something the East with its anti-rational orientation has failed to secure. *Τὸ ἀδιανόητο τίποτα*, 462.

[8] See especially *Τὸ ἀδιανόητο τίποτα, passim* and «Τὸ μηδέν σαν μακρόβιος ἐπιθανάτιος ρόγχος».

To put it in a nutshell, for Yannaras, Greece's problem is that it is too Western. For Ramphos, its problem is that it is too Eastern. In both cases, medieval Western scholasticism serves as a symbol of that which Greece either most needs or must always decisively reject. For each, Aquinas typifies and exemplifies all that is meant by 'the West'.

These examples from modern Greece, while doubtless deeply obscure to many outside that country, serve as a useful sign of the extent to which Aquinas remains a figure of the utmost moment and importance for the Orthodox today. Such debates are only one recent manifestation of a long history of fascination with Thomas in the Orthodox world. Aquinas has impressed, intrigued, and appalled Orthodox theologians from the time of Kydones' first translations to the present day, serving as a perennial interlocutor for the articulation of Orthodox theology and identity. Indeed, Aquinas has consistently enjoyed in the Orthodox East the kind of normative and pre-eminent status as the archetypal representative of Catholic theology that he has only intermittently enjoyed in the West.

Orthodox responses to Aquinas have, naturally, varied greatly over the years. But the most startling development in the Orthodox reception of Aquinas is that while his first emergence into the Byzantine world after 1354 was met with remarkable enthusiasm across the political and theological spectrum, the majority of modern Orthodox commentators have, by contrast, united in proclaiming Aquinas a *very bad thing*. In many of these writers, Gregory Palamas is held up as an alternative archetype, a mystical and experiential Easterner to be contrasted with a rationalistic and scholastic Westerner. Thus Orthodox neo-Palamism emerges as a counter to Catholic neo-Thomism. This book exists to explore the strange divergence between Byzantine and modern Orthodox readings of Aquinas and, more generally, to probe the whole question of East *versus* West in modern Orthodox theology.

It should already be clear that the study of the Orthodox reception of Thomas is to some extent the study of Orthodox theology itself, so central and enduring is his role as both friend and fiend. This is an instance of reception history that reveals much about the pattern and shape of Orthodox theology while also offering an unfamiliar perspective on Thomas himself. This book represents a first attempt at a comprehensive account of this deeply formative encounter, taking the story from the Byzantine era to the present day.

The book opens (Chapters 1–2) with a call for a paradigm shift, an 'exercise in multiple perspective'. It aims to show that the Christian East is not quite as 'Eastern', nor the West as 'Western', as is generally assumed, even when it comes to their supposed archetypes, Thomas Aquinas and Gregory Palamas. The Byzantine chapters (Chapters 3–4) form the heart of the book with the modern Orthodox chapter (Chapter 6) serving as an instructive counterpoint. Considerable attention has, however, also been paid to the intervening early modern period (Chapter 5), an era routinely written off as one of 'Babylonian captivity' or 'pseudomorphosis' of Orthodox theology. The last chapter (Chapter 7) reflects on the contribution Orthodox readings of Aquinas make to Thomas studies more generally and concludes with an exploration of the possibility for an Orthodox re-appropriation of Aquinas.

Part I

Greek East and Latin West:
An Exercise in Multiple Perspective

1

Thomas Aquinas and the Greek East

Many readers will be familiar with the term 'reverse perspective', widely used to characterize the artistic principles and visual impact of the Orthodox icon by contrast with the linear perspective that has become standard in Western art since the Renaissance. Rather than inviting the gaze of the viewer to rest on some imagined point in the distance through the use of convergent sight-lines, the perspective of the icon springs from within and moves outwards, arresting the attention with its sheer immediacy. Notions of distance collapse as certain objects are rendered larger the further away they are. The absence of an outside light source militates against any sense of mere spectating. The light comes, rather, from within the icon. The persons depicted emerge to impress themselves upon the viewer and to invite a response, whether of veneration or of rejection. *Theoria*, in this case, is inescapably participatory, ineluctably relational. The very nature of the icon confounds any attempt to treat it simply as an object. Indeed, as a function of this non-linear perspective, the icon becomes, in a sense, the active subject and the viewer the viewed.[1]

What we call reverse perspective is, however, only one of the modalities of the Orthodox icon. Indeed, 'reverse perspective' is

---

[1] The notion of 'reverse perspective' was introduced by Oskar Wulff in his 1907 article 'Die umgekehrte Perspektive und die Niedersicht'. The term has gained currency in Orthodox circles principally through the work of Fr Pavel Florensky; see especially the 1920 lecture on reverse perspective translated in his *Beyond Vision: Essays on the Perception of Art*. In the broader sphere of art history, Erwin Panofsky's famous essay of 1925, 'Die Perspektive als symbolische Form' remains the key work. All of these writers treat reverse perspective as only one element in the modes of spatial representation employed in the Orthodox icon. A most useful and perceptive discussion of current research in the area may be found in Clemena Antonova's 'On the Problem of "Reverse Perspective": Definitions East and West' and *Space, Time, and Presence in the Icon*.

something of a misnomer in that the technique long predates the linear perspective of which it is supposedly the reverse. Icons also routinely combine a bird's eye view with a face-on presentation, or a two-dimensional figure with a three-dimensional background, or interior space with exterior features: there is no single perspective, reverse or otherwise. In the icon, we also encounter a challenge to our received notions of time as non-simultaneous events are depicted on the same plane. In the icon it is always 'now'. In short, the icon operates on what we would do better to call a multiple perspective, both spatially and temporally.[2]

The notion of multiple perspective strikes me as a very salutary one for any undertaking that involves the reading of texts. If *Rezeptionsgeschichte*, reception history, has taught us anything it is that texts are never received as raw data, as neutral archive material. When a given author reads another, there is always an ongoing and very present dynamic of interpretation and selection, negotiation and dialogue. Aquinas himself was certainly aware of this interactive and synchronic dynamic and makes this apparent in his own sensitive treatment of Church tradition. An analogous sensitivity is incumbent upon anyone seeking to assess the legacy of Aquinas in the Orthodox world. We must be under no illusions that we are somehow outside the picture, looking in and capable of purely objective analysis of what we observe in the past. We are, rather, part of the picture, responding and relating to Aquinas within a rich and ever-expanding vista.

This, then, is the primary benefit of a multiple perspective: the realization that our sources are not simply inanimate objects from the past to be observed and analysed from a safe distance. Our sources are as much active subjects as objects of enquiry—better approached, in other words, as icons than as paintings of the conventional Western type.

A secondary benefit may be accrued from a further development of the idea of a multiple perspective: that is through the simple expedient of beginning this book on the Orthodox reception of Thomas not (as one might expect) with early examples of that reception but, conversely, with Thomas' reception of the Orthodox. A further

---

[2] Many of these features are, of course, shared by pre-Renaissance Western art. A change begins to set in with the pioneering work of Giotto, famously credited by Vasari in his *Lives of the Artists* as having 'completely shed the clumsy style of the Greeks'.

multiplication of perspective will be provided through an analysis of St Gregory Palamas' reception of the Latin West in the following chapter.

1.1. A NEW IMAGE OF THOMAS

In examining Thomas' reception of the Greek patristic and Byzantine tradition we are helped immeasurably by the huge advances in Aquinas studies over the last half-century and more. The picture of Thomas that emerges in recent scholarship is barely recognizable from the Thomas of Analytical, Transcendental, or even Existential Thomism, still less from the Thomas of the great commentators, or the Thomas of neo-scholasticism. Perhaps the decisive shift has been the widespread abandonment of any attempt to make of Thomism a coherent system ready to oppose or to meet (according to one's disposition) the philosophical challenges of the modern world.[3] The critical factor here has been the 'historical turn' in Aquinas studies encouraged in the early to mid-twentieth century by figures such as Pierre Mandonnet, Martin Grabmann, Étienne Gilson, and Marie-Dominique Chenu.[4] This approach was given great stimulus in Catholic circles by Vatican II with its effective de-emphasis of Thomism as a uniquely privileged theological and philosophical system.[5] This de-emphasis was certainly a change of tack from the

---

[3] Not that all such attempts have been abandoned: witness David Berger's *Tho-mismus: grosse Leitmotive der thomistischen Synthese und ihre Aktualität für die Gegenwart* (2001). For Berger, a philosophico-theological Thomist synthesis is both essential and inescapable. The 'historical turn' is thus a pernicious phenomenon, detracting from the true import and urgency of Thomism. Having said that, the 'historical turn' should not be taken to obscure the undoubted coherence and systematic quality of Thomas' philosophical achievement. These virtues are well articulated in Robert Pasnau and Christopher Shields, *The Philosophy of Aquinas*.

[4] While Gilson is rightly associated with Existential Thomism, he was also a leading figure in the historical retrieval of Thomas. Chenu, for his part, pointedly begins his *Introduction à l'étude de saint Thomas d'Aquin* with a chapter on 'L'œuvre dans son milieu'. In 1950, this was still by no means the obvious place to start a book on Thomas. Having previously been in very bad odour for his alleged historicism, Chenu's approach was substantially vindicated at Vatican II.

[5] This stimulus, I should note, took some time to take effect. The immediate impact of Vatican II was rather to inhibit extensive scholarly reflection on Aquinas within Catholic circles.

programme seemingly envisaged in the papal encyclical of 1879, *Aeterni Patris*.[6] The move away from syntheses and systems has opened the way for a deeper appreciation of Thomas as a theologian working in a specific historical context and within a tradition: scriptural, patristic, liturgical, spiritual, and philosophical. This deeper appreciation has been particularly well expressed in the work of Jean-Pierre Torrell and Gilles Emery.

Of course, I cannot possibly do justice here to all the nuances and dimensions of this fuller and more historically grounded picture of Thomas.[7] But I can at least sketch its lineaments. Firstly, Thomas' status as first and foremost a theologian (as opposed to a philosopher) is now widely affirmed. Here we may think of works such as Thomas O'Meara's *Thomas Aquinas: Theologian*, Gilles Emery's *The Trinitarian Theology of Saint Thomas Aquinas*, or the collected volume *The Theology of Thomas Aquinas*.[8] Hand-in-hand with this theological emphasis has been an increased awareness of the scriptural basis of Thomas' work, very evident in works such as the *Commentary on John* but also underpinning the great *Summae*.[9] He remained above all else a *magister in sacra pagina* (master of the sacred page), charged with the exposition, interpretation, and proclamation of scripture. Thomas' Dominican context is ably fleshed out in the collected volume *Christ among the Medieval Dominicans*, a work which includes, among many fine contributions, some illuminating reflections on Thomas' liturgical compositions.[10] Recognition of the

---

[6] By way of reaction, Pope John Paul II's 1998 encyclical *Fides et ratio* expressly re-affirms Leo XIII's 'insistence upon the incomparable value of the philosophy of Saint Thomas' (§57) while simultaneously upholding the value of the historical retrieval of Thomas (§58).

[7] It is quite impossible to keep fully abreast of the many thousands of works on Thomas to have been published in recent years. In the 1930s, G. K. Chesterton invoked with awe the sheer outpouring of publications on Thomas. Doubtless, the volume of such publications can probably now be magnified by a factor of ten or more. Some guidance on recent developments may be sought in Jean-Pierre Torrell's essays on 'Saint Thomas et l'histoire' and 'Situation actuelle des études thomistes', both available in his *Nouvelles recherches thomasiennes*. Fergus Kerr's occasional pieces on 'Recent Thomistica' are also most useful.

[8] Rik van Nieuwenhove and Joseph Wawrykow (eds.).

[9] On the *Commentary on John*, see Michael Dauphinais and Matthew Levering (eds.), *Reading John with St Thomas Aquinas: Theological Exegesis and Speculative Theology*. On the commentaries in general, see Thomas Weinandy et al. (eds.), *Aquinas on Scripture: An Introduction to his Biblical Commentaries*.

[10] Kent Emery and Joseph Wawrykow (eds.). On liturgy, see Robert Wielockx's 'Poetry and Theology in the *Adore te devote*: Thomas Aquinas on the Eucharist and

Dominican context has not wholly obscured the abiding monastic influences within the pattern of life of the Order of Preachers.[11] Thomas' place as a great spiritual teacher, even a mystic, has been magisterially dealt with by Jean-Pierre Torrell.[12] The importance of the principle of deification in Thomas has recently been given prominence in such works as Luc-Thomas Somme's *Thomas d'Aquin, la divinisation dans le Christ*, Anna Williams' *Ground of Union*, and Antoine Lévy's superb *Le créé et l'incrée*. Finally, the nature of Thomas' philosophical debts has lately been substantially nuanced. Long gone is the image of a Thomas intellectually enslaved to Aristotle.[13] Concomitant with this emancipation from the supposition of uncritical Aristotelianism is the widespread acknowledgement of the substantial Platonic (and especially neo-Platonic) current in Thomas' work. A broadly Platonic reading of Aquinas is fundamental to Radical Orthodoxy's contention for a participatory metaphysic in Aquinas.[14] Aquinas' neo-Platonic inheritance has also been energetically declaimed by, amongst others, Wayne Hankey.[15]

This is not to say that there is any univocal and unchallenged presentation of Thomas emerging, nor to dismiss the value of the various Thomisms mentioned,[16] nor yet to suggest that there is no longer any room for purely metaphysical or philosophical explorations of Thomas.[17] Many elements of this fuller picture are, of course,

---

Christ's Uniqueness', 157–74. Aquinas' authorship of this hymn is disputed, but accepted by Wielockx with good cause. Thomas certainly produced many of the texts for the feast of Corpus Christi, including the famous *Pange lingua*. There are excellent treatments of Thomas's sacramental teaching by John Yocum in Weinandy et al. (eds.), *Aquinas on Doctrine* and by Liam Walsh in van Nieuwenhove and Wawrykow (eds.), *The Theology of Thomas Aquinas*.

[11] See, for example, Jean Leclercq, 'Tradition patristique et monastique dans l'enseignement de saint Thomas sur la vie contemplative'.

[12] *Saint Thomas Aquinas: Spiritual Master*. This volume is in part the outworking of Torrell's entry on Thomas in the *Dictionnaire de spiritualité*.

[13] See, for example, Eric Mascall's 'Guide-Lines from St. Thomas for Theology Today' or Mark Jordan's *The Alleged Aristotelianism of Thomas Aquinas* (re-worked in his *Rewritten Theology: Aquinas after his Readers*, Chapter 4).

[14] See John Milbank and Catherine Pickstock, *Truth in Aquinas*.

[15] See his *God in Himself: Aquinas' Doctrine of God as Expounded in the Summa theologiae*.

[16] Here I would again underline the historical sensitivities of such great proponents of a renewed Thomism as, in particular, Étienne Gilson.

[17] For some examples of largely philosophical approaches to Aquinas, see the *Cambridge Companion to Aquinas* edited by Norman Kretzmann and Eleonore Stump and also the latter's *Aquinas*. Brian Davies' *The Thought of Thomas Aquinas*

not new but rather a matter of emphasis or re-emphasis. The importance of the principle of deification in Aquinas, for instance, has long
been established.[18] Equally, the neo-Platonic dimension of Thomas'
work (and of medieval scholasticism in general) was vigorously
affirmed by François Picavet as long ago as 1905.[19] A small flurry of
books went on to take up aspects of this theme quite independently of
one another during and immediately after the Second World War.[20]

It should, however, be clear from this brief survey that any presentation of Thomas that paints him as an out-and-out rationalist,
philosophizing about God without due recourse to scripture, outside
the context of the worshipping Church, and with scant regard for
spiritual experience, will fall short of the truth.[21] It should also be
obvious that many of the elements of the fuller picture I have
sketched have the potential to enhance Thomas' generally dismal
reputation amongst the Orthodox. This fuller picture will also aid
our investigation into the reasons behind Thomas' popularity in the
late Byzantine period. But I have deliberately left to last the one factor
that most emphatically expresses the rootedness of Thomas in the

appears content to examine Aquinas' thought with little reference to *Sitz im Leben* or
historical sources. This is, however, a potential imbalance substantially corrected in
his *Aquinas: An Introduction*.

[18] Dating from 1957, the article 'Divinisation' in the *Dictionnaire de spiritualité*
ascribes to Thomas an unusually robust, convincing, and detailed doctrine of deification (vol. 3 1426–32). Yves Congar, writing in 1974, proclaims deification 'dans toute
la vérité de l'expression' to be an established feature of Thomas' theological vision.
'"Ecclesia" et "populus (fidelis)" dans l'ecclésiologie de S. Thomas', 170.

[19] *Esquisse d'une histoire générale et comparée des philosophies médiévales*. See, on
this work, the perceptive comments of Anselme Catoire, 'Philosophie Byzantine et
philosophie scolastique'. Catoire also provides a very pregnant critique of Théodore
de Régnon's deeply influential but unduly dichotomous *Études de théologie positive
sur la sainte Trinité*, querying his 'affirmations parfois un peu solennelles et fantai-
sistes'. Ibid., 193.

[20] See Cornelio Fabro, *La nozione metafisica di partecipazione secondo S. Tommaso
d'Aquino*; Louis-Bertrand Geiger, *La participation dans la philosophie de S. Thomas
d'Aquin*; Josef Santeler, *Der Platonismus in der Erkenntnislehre des Heiligen Thomas
von Aquin*; and Arthur Little, *The Platonic Heritage of Thomism*. Little puts his thesis
in pithy and quasi-Chestertonian terms: 'Thomism owes to Aristotle its firm foundation in reality, but to Plato its skiey grain.' Ibid., xiv. Also worth noting are the slightly
later works of Robert Henle, *Saint Thomas and Platonism* and Klaus Kremer, *Die
neuplatonische Seinsphilosophie und ihre Wirkung auf Thomas von Aquin*.

[21] *In nuce*, it would not be wholly just to say that he theologizes Ἀριστοτελικῶς
ἀλλ᾽ οὐκ ἁλιευτικῶς.

universal tradition of the Church and his affinity with the Christian East: his love for and grounding in the Greek Fathers.

1.2. AQUINAS AND THE GREEK FATHERS

Research into Thomas' patristic sources remains a work in progress. Gustave Bardy wrote that it had 'à peine commenceée' in 1923, a judgement Godefroid Geenen was able reproduce word for word in 1946. In 1965, Ceslaus Velecky christened it the 'Cinderella' of Thomist studies. Things have certainly improved since then but it remains a domain that is, as Carmelo Conticello put it in 2004, 'encore assez peu exploré'.[22] That said, this emerging field is one of the most exciting arenas of contemporary Thomist scholarship, most especially in terms of his indebtedness to the Greek East.

Aquinas expresses an extraordinary and unusual devotion to the Greek Fathers.[23] A telling anecdote has him express his preference for a copy of St John Chrysostom's commentary on Matthew over the whole city of Paris.[24] This tale nicely encapsulates Thomas' debt to the patristic revival of the twelfth century. The Golden Mouth was among the Greek Fathers translated in the middle of that century by Burgundio of Pisa, a great bridge-builder between Greek East and Latin West.[25] Burgundio is one of the key figures in the remarkable

---

[22] Bardy, 'Sur les sources patristiques grecques de saint Thomas', 493; Geenen, 'Saint Thomas et les Pères', 738; Velecky, 'Following the Fathers', 131; Conticello, 'Théophylacte de Bulgarie, source de Thomas d'Aquin (*Catena aurea in Ioannem*)', 62. Ceslao Pera's *Le fonti del pensiero di S. Tommaso d'Aquino nella Somma teologica* deserves an honourable mention at this point. A pioneering study when first published in 1952, it was re-issued in expanded form in 1979 with lavish praise by Chenu in his preface.

[23] The term 'Greek', for Thomas, denotes anyone writing in that language, hence it is used interchangeably of classical philosophers, Church Fathers, and contemporary Byzantines. Thomas himself prefers the term 'doctors' to 'fathers' in obedience to scriptural precept (*Contra errores Graecorum* 2.41).

[24] Torrell, *Saint Thomas Aquinas: The Person and His Work*, 140.

[25] This accomplished individual accompanied Anslem of Havelberg to Constantinople in 1136 and took part in the famous dialogue between Anselm and Nicetas of Nicomedia—perhaps the most far-reaching and sophisticated of East–West debates in the early Middle Ages. A contemporary chronicler (Robert of Mons, *Continuation of the Chronicle of Sigebert of Gembloux*) tells us that he had translated many works of St John Chrysostom and that he brought with him to the Third Lateran Council (1179) translations of the commentary on John. At that time Burgundio reported that

recovery of Greek patristic material in the Latin West at this time, producing excellent translations of such seminal works as St John of Damascus' *Exact Exposition of the Orthodox Faith* and Nemesius of Emesa's *On the Nature of Man*.[26] These were significant projects, the former done at the behest of Pope Eugenius III and the latter dedicated to the Emperor Frederick Barbarossa. Peter Lombard was able to correct a number of his citations of the Damascene in the *Sentences* from Burgundio's translation, having previously used the less accomplished partial version of Cerbanus. Cerbanus had also, in the early twelfth century, produced a translation of Maximus the Confessor's *Chapters on Love*. This fruitful century also saw a revival of interest in existing translations of the Greek Fathers, notably the Carolingian translations of Dionysius and Maximus produced by John Scotus Eriugena. A revised version of Eriugena's translation of Dionysius was produced by John Sarrasin in the latter part of the twelfth century and served as an important element in the Dionysian revival of the period.[27]

Enthusiasm for the Greek Fathers could sometimes take surprising forms. One pair of enthusiasts, Hugh of Honau and Master Peter of Vienna, requested from Hugh Etherian a set of Greek patristic translations concerning certain Christological and Trinitarian matters.[28] They did so principally to find support for various positions associated with Gilbert of Poitiers, above all the necessity of the distinction between nature and person. Hugh Etherian was a Pisan resident in Constantinople, an accomplished Hellenist and sometime adviser of Emperor Manuel I. The request is couched in the most adulatory terms, Hugh proclaiming that 'from the Greeks has flowed the source of all wisdom' and voicing the desire 'to cut off the

---

he had also translated part of the commentary on Genesis. These translations were evidently very popular, and are the basis of many of the medieval Latin manuscripts of Chrysostom.

[26] Robert of Mons gives 1151 as the date of the translation of John of Damascus. Burgundio is also widely credited with the earliest Greek–Latin translation of Aristotle's *Nicomachean Ethics* and *On Generation and Corruption*.

[27] For an excellent survey of Greek patristic translations in the twelfth century, see Marie-Thérèse d'Alverny, 'Translations and Translators', in Robert Benson and Giles Constable (eds.), *Renaissance and Renewal in the Twelfth Century*, 430–3. See also Martin Grabmann, *Die Geschichte der scholastischen Methode* (vol. II), 81–94.

[28] The texts are provided by Nicholas Haring, 'The "Liber de Differentia naturae et personae" by Hugh Etherian and the letters addressed to him by Peter of Vienna and Hugh of Honau'.

dangerous doubts of the Latins [. . .] by means of the authority of the Greek doctors, who have spoken more expressly than ours about these issues'. Hugh Etherian produced his *Liber de differentia naturae et personae* by 1179. The sources chosen are interesting in themselves, including not only the Cappadocian Fathers and Cyril of Alexandria but also later writers such as Anastasius of Sinai, John of Damascus, and Theodore Abu Qurra.[29]

In short, if it is indeed correct to speak of a Twelfth-Century Renaissance, then it should be acknowledged that the recovery/discovery of Greek patristic sources played a significant role in this renaissance.[30] The spirit of the time is perhaps best encapsulated by William of St-Thierry who, in 1144, famously lauded the *orientale lumen*, the light of the Eastern monastic tradition now illuminating the dark and dank places of the West.[31]

Thomas' work is bathed in this *orientale lumen*. He makes very extensive use of the Greek Fathers available to him, favouring original sources over florilegia wherever possible.[32] What is more, he took steps to increase the volume of Greek patristic and Byzantine literature available in Latin. His interest in the Greek Fathers seems to come to the fore from the 1260s being especially evident in that massive work of patristic erudition, the *Catena aurea*. Composed at papal command between 1262/3 and 1267/8, this collection of patristic commentaries on the four Gospels neatly indicates the seamless connection between scriptural and patristic authority: the Fathers are

---

[29] This appears to be the first appearance in Latin of this fascinating Arab Christian theologian, a Chalcedonian writer of the early ninth century and sometime bishop of Harran. Hugh Etherian also produced, in 1177, a work defending the procession of the Holy Spirit from the Son, *De sancto et immortali Deo* (PL 202 233C–369D, given there as *De haeresibus quas graeci in latinos devolvunt*). Hugh makes extensive use of Greek patristic authorities and also cites explicitly anti-*filioque* sources such as Photios, Nicholas of Methone, Nicetas of Thessalonica, and Theophylact of Ochrid.

[30] Charles Haskins' *Renaissance of the Twelfth Century* launched the concept in 1927. The various contributions to Robert Benson and Giles Constable (eds.), *Renaissance and Renewal in the Twelfth Century* give a fine idea of some of the problems and enduring value of Haskins' work. Giles Constable, for example, puts the emphasis not so much on 'renaissance' as 'reformation' in his 'Renewal and Reform in Religious Life', a line of enquiry pursued further in his *The Reformation of the Twelfth Century*. For a trenchant critique of Haskins' narrative, see Marcia Colish's 'Haskins's *Renaissance* Seventy Years Later: Beyond Anti-Burckhardtianism' and *Remapping Scholasticism*.

[31] *Epistola ad fratres de Monte Dei* 1 (SC 223 144).

[32] Torrell, 'St Thomas et l'histoire', 162–3; *Saint Thomas Aquinas: The Person and his Work*, 140.

valued above all else as guides in the reading of scripture. Chrysostom is the single most often cited author, pushing even Augustine (usually Thomas' preferred patristic source) into second place.[33] Among other Greek authorities, a substantial place is given to Origen, with smaller contributions from Athanasius, Eusebius, Basil, the two Gregories (of Nazianzus and of Nyssa), Cyril of Alexandria, Dionysius the Areopagite, John of Damascus, and others (in total, 57 Greek writers are cited alongside 22 Latin). But the most striking feature of the *Catena* for our purposes is the prominence given to Theophylact of Ochrid, also known as Theophylact of Bulgaria (*c*.1050/60–*c*.1125).[34] Theophylact was one of Byzantium's finest scholars, bishops, and exegetes but was virtually unknown in the West. It was Thomas who ordered the translation of his biblical commentaries.[35] The evident admiration Thomas had for a near-contemporary Byzantine author speaks eloquently of his irenic attitude towards the Greeks of his own time.[36]

Production of the *Catena* was to provide Thomas with a wealth of material to draw upon in later works.[37] It is also in the 1260s that Thomas begins making extensive use of the *acta* of the Ecumenical

[33] With, according to the *Index Thomisticus*, 2689 as against 2075 mentions. Mere numbers are, of course, a crude indicator of esteem but do serve to give an idea of the sheer scale of the work. It should also be acknowledged that not all citations of a given author will be authentic.

[34] In dating, I rely upon Christian Hannick's entry in the *TRE*.

[35] The *Index Thomisticus* gives 1033 mentions of which 362 *in Marcum*, 423 *in Lucam*, and 248 *in Joannem*. Matthew, the first volume completed (by October 1264) contains no references to Theophylact. In the subsequent volume, on Mark, Thomas specifies that he has had various translations undertaken. Presumably, these were not available to him at the time of the composition of *In Matthaeum*. These translations also included the commentary-catena of Victor of Antioch (C5/C6) on Mark and the catena of Nicetas of Heraclea on Luke (C11/C12): see Conticello, 'San Tommaso ed i Padri: la *Catena aurea super Ioannem*', 55–7.

[36] It must be noted that Thomas' express citations of Theophylact do not appear to extend far beyond the *Catena aurea*. He mentions him by name only once outside elsewhere, in the *Commentary on John* 11 l.2 1490. In this work, dated by Torrell to 1270–2, he is introduced almost off-hand as 'quidam Graecus, scilicet Theophylactus'. On at least one other occasion in the *Commentary on John* he attributes to a gloss a comment he had previously correctly attributed to Theophylact (1 l.14 259). Given that Theophylact was something of a synthesizer of earlier exegetical authorities (especially St John Chrysostom), one might surmise that he was simply not of any great utility outside the context of a compilation such as the *Catena aurea*. That said, Conticello has demonstrated that much of the *Commentary on John* is a re-working of material from the *Catena aurea*—including considerable (and unattributed) chunks of Theophylact. 'San Tommaso ed i Padri', 79–86.

[37] See Bataillon, 'Les sermons de Saint Thomas et la *Catena aurea*' and 'Saint Thomas et les pères: de la *Catena* à la *Tertia pars*'. As we have noted, parts of the

Councils. Here again we see Thomas as something of a pioneer: none
of his immediate predecessors had made substantial use of this
material, still less made it so central to their Christology. His first
frame of reference is to Ephesus-Chalcedon, evident, for example, in
Summa contra gentiles IV 24–25 or the *Contra errores graecorum* 32.
Thomas was here most likely making use of the *Synodicon* of the
deacon Rusticus (also known as the *Collectio Casinensis*). The error of
Eutyches was of particular concern to Aquinas, receiving repeated
attention. But, as Geenen points out, whereas works from 1259 or
before generally report Eutyches' positions at second hand, later
works instead report plainly 'Eutyches dixit [...]'.[38] Thomas' concern to make his case through direct use of conciliar sources is
striking testimony to his commitment to a mode of theologizing
within the context of Church tradition. Indeed, this is a commitment
that appears to have grown and intensified throughout the 1260s and
into the 1270s. Martin Morard has demonstrated Thomas' use of the
acta of Constantinople II (553)—a wholly new development in medieval Latin theology. He dates Thomas' first acquaintance with this
material to between 1264 and 1265.[39] He has also, in a more recent
work, drawn attention to Thomas' knowledge of Constantinople III
(681), evident from around 1271.[40]

Thomas' increasing use of conciliar material went hand-in-hand
with a thoroughgoing and ever-intensifying engagement with the
Greek Fathers not only in his exegetical works but also in his more
overtly theological works.[41] The prominent role of Dionysius the

Commentary on John are also effectively re-workings of material gathered in the
Catena aurea.

[38] The first major study of this aspect of Thomas' work is Ignaz Backes, *Die
Christologie des heilige Thomas von Aquin und die griechischen Kirchenväter*. Godefroid Geenen takes the question further in his 'En marge du Concile de Chalcédonie.
Les textes du Quatrième Concile dans les œuvres de Saint Thomas'. Geenen extends
the frame of reference beyond the two *Summae* dealt with by Backes.
[39] 'Une source de saint Thomas d'Aquin: Le deuxième concile de Constantinople
(553)'.
[40] 'Thomas d'Aquin, lecteur des conciles'. His findings corroborated by Torrell:
*Somme Théologique. III*ᵃ, *q.1–26: Le Verbe incarné*, 422–32. Elsewhere, Torrell
charmingly observes of Thomas' concern for patristic and conciliar documentation:
'il n'était pas seulement un *thinker*, mais aussi un grand *scholar*'. 'St Thomas et
l'histoire', 173.
[41] Gilles Emery has made a particularly fine contribution to the study of Thomas'
Greek patristic inheritance. See his *The Trinitarian Theology of Saint Thomas Aquinas*; 'Le photinisme et ses précurseurs chez Saint Thomas', and the marvellous 'A note

Areopagite has long been recognized. Dionysius represents the central conduit of the substantial neo-Platonic current in Thomas. His legacy is abundantly evident not only in the *Commentary on the Divine Names* but throughout the *corpus thomisticum*, patent in its apophatic dimension and in its various treatments of liturgy. John of Damascus (in Burgundio's translation) also impacted decisively on Thomas' theology, opening to him by way of constructive synthesis virtually the whole Greek patristic tradition.[42] Coupled with his ongoing engagement with conciliar material, Thomas' Christology emerges as distinctly Greek in character and emphasis: from its resolute dismissal of Nestorianism and Monophysitism to its keen apprehension of the hypostatic union and the instrumentality of Christ's humanity. Taken in the round, Thomas' profound commitment to Greek patristic and conciliar sources and the practical steps he took to extend the volume of such material available in Latin stand out by comparison with his contemporaries. One might even go so far as to characterize his theology as being *ad mentem patrum*.[43]

Thomas is, of course, far from being a synthesizer or compiler of patristic tradition.[44] He is also careful not to elevate patristic authority above that of scripture but rather uses the Fathers in order to

on St. Thomas and the Eastern Fathers' in *Trinity, Church, and the Human Person: Thomistic Essays*, 193–207. See also Leo Elders' 'Thomas Aquinas and the Fathers of the Church'.

[42] Richard Cross puts it well when he observes that John of Damascus was, notwithstanding (and indeed partly due to) his status as an 'an unashamed encyclopedist', 'almost the sole means whereby the most theologically vital Patristic tradition was passed on to Western theologians of the Middle Ages'. 'Perichoresis, Deification, and Christological Predication in John of Damascus', 69.

[43] The phrase *ad mentem patrum* ('in the sprit of the Fathers'/'according to the mind of the Fathers') was used by Fr Georges Florovsky to sum up the essential quality of his envisaged 'neo-patristic synthesis'. He lighted upon this phrase in what looks like a deliberate counterpoint to a theology *ad mentem sancti Thomae Aquinatis* envisaged by the Encyclical *Aeterni Patris* and instantiated in numerous products of the subsequent scholastic revival.

[44] Pera has a rather fine sense of the dynamic creativity of Thomas' reception of tradition, evoking the 'movimento spiraliforme' set up by the interaction of reason and tradition, opening ever-expanding possibilities of ascent and development 'in una mirabile e continuamente rinnovata primavera spirituale'. *Le fonti del pensiero di S. Tommaso d'Aquino*, 106. Similar sentiments regarding reception are expressed by Mark Jordan in the conclusion of his *Rewritten Theology*: authorities received alive by Thomas, generating new questions and new forms. Jordan does, however, weaken his position by intruding a subversive and anti-establishment current in Thomas that, to my mind, can be squared with the author's *intentio* only with great *inventio*.

understand and explicate scripture correctly. Reason only ever holds a third place behind the authority of, strictly in that order, scripture and the doctors of the Church.[45] He will also not hesitate to disagree with a patristic authority when he deems it appropriate. For all its traditional character, his was a blindingly original theology. But it was original in the best sense of the word, plumbing the depths of the tradition, reaching back to the sources and origins of faith in order to underpin a truly creative, truly original, theological vision.

1.3. AQUINAS AND THE LATIN–GREEK SCHISM

An appreciation of Thomas' patristic (and especially Greek patristic) roots is essential if one is to understand his attitude to the Greeks of his own time. He has an acute sense of the shared tradition of Greek East and Latin West and it is this sense of commonality that undergirds the relative equanimity with which he views the situation. The question is not so much one of competing heterogeneous ideologies but of competing interpretations of a shared tradition: in other words, a question of reception.

At this point it is worth noting that Thomas' approach to the Greek–Latin dilemma is very like that of one of own his favoured sources, Theophylact of Ochrid. Theophylact had, in 1112, composed a treatise on the errors of the Latins.[46] In this disquisition, Theophylact displays rare and remarkable restraint in limiting the essential

---

[45] Thomas makes this taxonomy crystal clear in *ST* I^a q.1 a.8. In the *Commentary on the Divine Names* (ch.2, l.1) he specifies that the Fathers are to be received above all as guides in the proper interpretation of scripture: 'Oportet enim non solum conservare ea quae in sanctis Scripturis sunt tradita, sed et ea quae dicta sunt a sacris doctoribus, qui sacram Scripturam illibatam conservaverunt.' I have this reference from Conticello, 'San Tommaso ed i Padri', 32.

[46] Προσλαλιά τινι τῶν αὐτοῦ ὁμιλητῶν περὶ ὧν ἐγκαλοῦνται Λατῖνοι (Gautier (ed.), *Theophylacte d'Achrida: Discours, traités, poesies*, 247–85). Tia Kolbaba provides a fine treatment of Theophylact in her 'The Orthodoxy of the Latins in the Twelfth Century', presenting Peter III of Antioch as a parallel instance of a 'moderate' approach. See also the excellent portrait of Theophylact in Sir Dimitri Obolensky's *Six Byzantine Portraits*, 34–82. Theophylact has, amazingly, very little to say on the matter of the papacy. Obolensky follows Sir Steven Runciman (*The Eastern Schism*, 76–7) in drawing an intriguing comparison between Theophylact and Anselm of Canterbury. At Bari in 1098, Anselm had exhibited a similarly conciliatory and generous approach to the problem.

difference between Greeks and Latins strictly to the matter of the
filioque and not piling up accusation upon accusation as many of his
contemporaries on both sides of the debate were prone to do. And
while lamenting the Latin position on the procession of the Spirit, he
is loath to attribute the error to deliberate heresy but rather to a
regrettable ignorance, compounded by the inferiority of the Latin
language. 'They err', he says, 'not so much from wickedness of judgement as from ignorance of what is right'. They are, in particular,
impeded by the incapacity of Latin to distinguish between (eternal)
procession and (temporal) mission.[47] While I can find no evidence that
Thomas was aware of this work (at least *in toto*), it is striking to note the
parallels to it in his own direct discussion of the errors of the Greeks.
Like Theophylact, Thomas limits the area of real contention: in his case
to the *filioque* and the organically related question of papal primacy. He
steadfastly refrains from designating the Greeks as heretics, preferring
rather to speak of their errors born of ignorance or stubbornness.[48] He
also notes the inability of the Greek language to distinguish properly
between 'cause' and 'principle' (both rendered by the term ἀρχή). But
the spirit of his approach is very much that of Theophylact: in neither
case is there any doubt as to the substantial orthodoxy of the other side,
for all their wrong-headedness and linguistic impedimenta.

Closer to home, Thomas' irenic approach was very plausibly
fostered by Humbert of Romans, Provincial of France from 1244–
54 and Master of the Dominican order from 1254–63.[49] Humbert will
have had oversight of Thomas' early studies and teaching in Paris,
and indeed over much of his later career. Humbert will presumably
have been involved in soliciting Thomas' defence of the mendicant
way, the *Liber contra impugnantes Dei cultum et religionem* in 1256. It
was also Humbert who commissioned Thomas to report (with Albert
the Great) in 1259 on educational reform (including use of the
so-called 'new learning' associated with the Aristotelian revival). In
later history, Humbert has, of course, been much eclipsed by the fame

---

[47] Προσλαλιά, 253–5.
[48] Bonaventure, for one, had no such compunction and labelled the Greeks as both
heretics and schismatics (*Commentary on the Sentences* I d.11, a. un., q.1). Peter
Lombard himself had taken a more conciliatory line, anticipating Thomas in his
affirmation of agreement between Latins and Greeks 'in sensu, et differentia in verbis'
(*Book of Sentences* I d.11, ch.2). I have these references from Emery, *The Trinitarian
Theology of Saint Thomas Aquinas*, 294–6.
[49] On Humbert, see Edward Brett, *Humbert of Romans*.

of his subordinates in the Order but it would be difficult to dissociate his approach to the Latin–Greek schism from that of Thomas. Humbert's thoughts on the question are gathered together in his *Opusculum tripartium* (1272–3), composed in preparation for the reunion Council of Lyons.

Humbert's position is astonishingly even-handed, recognizing culpability for the schism on both sides. He too refuses to call the Greeks heretics and acknowledges that they are fathers in the faith to the Latins, lamenting that they have been subjected to scandalous mistreatment by Latins in the East. The Greeks deserve both respect and help. A systematic programme of translations ought to be instituted in order to increase mutual knowledge of the respective traditions. The Pope ought to be willing to travel to the East and even to recognize that papal primacy might be exercised differently in the East than in the West. Thomas does not go as far as this, nor does he discuss the question in such practical detail, but he does certainly partake of the same spirit of reconciliation voiced so emphatically by his sometime Master-General.

Thomas addresses the question of differences with the Greeks in a series of works datable to 1263–5: *Contra errores graecorum* (1263–4), *Summa contra gentiles* IV (1264–5), *Quaestiones disputatae de potentia* (1264–5), and the *De rationibus fidei ad Cantorem Antiochenum* (1265).[50]

The *Contra errores graecorum* (*CEG*) is not, as might appear from the title, a systematic treatise by Thomas on the question.[51] It is, rather, Thomas' expert opinion on a rather poor collection of texts (many of which are distorted or of dubious authenticity) produced by Nicholas of Cotrone, a native of what is now Durrës in Albania. Nicholas, a unionist bishop, produced the collection at the request of the Emperor Theodore Laskaris (1254–8). Very likely, he drew on earlier florilegia.[52] Pope Urban IV requested Thomas' judgement on the *Libellus de fide sanctae Trinitatis*, about which he evidently harboured suspicions. It is much to be regretted that Thomas did

---

[50] In dating Thomas' works, here and elsewhere, I rely on Jean-Pierre Torrell, *Saint Thomas Aquinas: The Person and his Work*.

[51] See, on this work, Mark Jordan's excellent 'Theological Exegesis and Aquinas's Treatise "Against the Greeks"'.

[52] The history of patristic florilegia remains one of the most unexplored, but vitally important, areas of scholarship. We may speculate (but no more) that Hugh Etherian's *De sancto et immortali Deo* fed into Nicholas' confection.

not exercise his customary care for the accuracy of his sources in analysing this tawdry work; it may be that he took such a task to be outside his brief.[53] But for all the textual inaccuracies, the text does furnish some insight into Thomas' approach to the schism.

The prologue to the *CEG* offers some crucial pointers as to the proper reading of the Fathers. They are to be expounded in a reverential manner, *exponere reverenter*, recognizing that the challenges posed by various heresies will elicit different responses at different times. He also recognizes that linguistic differences can exacerbate the apparent divergences between Greeks and Latins but affirms 'Latins and Greeks professing the same faith do so using different words'. Translations therefore must adhere to the meaning (*sententia*) and not merely to the verbal forms of the original and always operate with a hermeneutic of orthodoxy. Attention is also paid to the differing possibilities of the Greek and Latin languages, for instance the capacity of Latin to distinguish between 'principle' and 'cause' (*CEG* I 1). In the epilogue, he has some harsh words about the infelicities of Nicholas' translations, remarks that speak for a finer knowledge of Greek than that with which he is commonly credited. In the *CEG* we can see a double front operating: Thomas is concerned not only to convince the Greeks of the traditional character of the Latin position but also to persuade modern Latins of the indispensability of the Greek patristic tradition, for all the thin support the Greek Fathers give to the doctrine of the *filioque*. This is a properly catholic enterprise, concerned to encompass the universal patristic tradition.

In a later work, *Quodlibet* IV (9.3), Thomas specifies that in arguing with Greeks (whom he plainly terms schismatics), one must rely (in addition to Scripture) on 'those doctors they accept' and not on 'our holy ones'. This is the precisely the practice of the *CEG*: all the sources (however bastardized) are Greek sources. Thomas is attempting to argue for the *filioque* from Greek sources (or at least trying to show that the Greek sources do not rule out the *filioque*). Part I of the work is intended to remove any doubts (presumably on the part of contemporary Latins) as to the orthodoxy of the sources adduced. Only in Part II does he proceed from possible *errores*

---

[53] Someone able to detect the Proclan character of *Liber de causis* falsely attributed to Aristotle will surely have had some doubts about the authenticity of much of the material gathered by Nicholas. What Torrell calls his 'flair du chercheur' ('Saint Thomas et l'histoire', 165) appears to have deserted him here.

Latinorum to *errores Graecorum.* These embrace the procession of the spirit, papal primacy, the use of azymes, and purgatory. Thomas is concerned not to multiply the differences between Greeks and Latins and to maintain a due sense of order. Thus only the first two issues pertain to matters 'necessary to salvation'. The Greeks are certainly in error when it comes to the inadmissibility of the use of unleavened bread in the eucharist or the non-existence of purgatory, but these are not treated as essential matters. But even in the matter of the *filioque* and the related question of papal primacy, it is not that the Greeks are in heresy as such but rather unable—for some mystifying reason—to recognize the testimony of their own tradition. This approach is far from crude mudslinging.

The *De potentia* (*DP*) confirms this estimation. Here we encounter the crucial affirmation that: 'If we take careful note of the statements of the Greeks we shall find they differ from us more in words than in meaning.'[54] Like Theophylact, and indeed Maximus the Confessor before him, Thomas is concerned to penetrate beyond the inevitable limitations of language and to read his opponents with a hermeneutic of orthodoxy.[55] This does not mean that he reads them indulgently. The Greeks fail to affirm clearly the procession of the Spirit 'either through ignorance, obstinacy or sophistry or some other cause'. Thomas is so vexed precisely because there is in the Greek theological tradition an undeniable connection between the Son and the procession of the Holy Spirit:

> and yet they acknowledge that the Holy Spirit is the Spirit of the Son, and that he is of the Father through the Son, which would not be true if the procession of the Holy Spirit were entirely independent of the Son. Hence we may infer that even the Greeks themselves understand that the procession of the Holy Spirit has some connection with the Son. (*DP* 10 a.5 co.)

Thomas has even John of Damascus in view here, maintaining that he allows that the Spirit proceeds from the Son 'in some way' by accepting that he is the 'Spirit of the Son' (*DP* 10 a.5 ad 14). This is somewhat wishful thinking in that John can easily be interpreted

---

[54] There is no question but that he is speaking of *contemporary* Greeks here.

[55] Maximus' *Letter to Marinus* expresses essentially the same hermeneutic of orthodoxy notwithstanding the differing possibilities of the respective tongues (PG 91 136A–D).

as speaking only of the temporal procession of the Spirit (and explicitly denies eternal procession elsewhere) but is further testimony of Thomas' conviction of the fundamental orthodoxy of the Greeks—including the Greeks of his own time.[56]

A similar approach is evident in the *Summa contra gentiles* (*SCG*) IV. Again, the argument for the procession of the Spirit from the Son is very deliberately made with reference to both Latin and Greek Fathers (*SCG* IV 24).[57] Aquinas has harsh words for 'some who are pertinacious in their wilful resistance to the truth' (*SCG* IV 25), specifically those who take John 15:26 to *exclude* procession from the Son. On the use of azymes, Thomas does not argue against the use of leavened bread but rather for the legitimacy of the Latin practice against Greek objections, observing very sensibly that 'different churches have different customs in this matter, but each of the two can be in harmony with the significance of the sacrament' (*SCG* IV 69.2). On purgatory, he is content with a brief mention of the 'error of certain Greeks' who deny purgatory (*SCG* IV 91.11). This error is also mentioned, and refuted, in his *De rationibus fidei ad Cantorem Antiochenum*. This letter to an unidentified cantor of Antioch deals with the procession of the Spirit in limpid fashion and without any anti-Greek polemic.

In closing, we must take account of the *Summa theologiae* (*ST*). This crowning achievement confirms the position established in the works already discussed, adding little that is new. We encounter the same regard for the Greek Fathers and the contention that they do indeed recognize that the procession of the Spirit has something (*aliquem ordinem*) to do with the Son (*ST* Iᵃ q.36 a.2 co.). We also find in this article further reflections on the implicit nature of the

---

[56] Of course, for Thomas orthodoxy means accepting the *filioque* (and, with it, papal primacy). But here we must recall that in his historical and theological context, failure to do so meant opening the door to Sabellianism (by failing to distinguish adequately between Son and Spirit) and Arianism (by detracting from the dignity of the Son). Sabellianism has some claim to be the archetypal heresy of the West whereas Arianism, although initially stronger in the East, had had a far more threatening *Nachleben* in the West. Indeed the various councils in the West that affirmed the *filioque* invariably did so in response to resurgent Arianism (see Peter Gemeinhardt, *Die Filioque-Kontroverse zwischen Ost- und Westkirche im Frühmittelalter*). Thomas' full awareness that the Greeks were neither Sabellian nor Arian only heightened his frustration at their inability to embrace what he saw as an essential banner of orthodoxy.

[57] He appeals here to (pseudo-)Athanasius, Cyril of Alexandria, and Didymus.

filioque doctrine within Church tradition (especially as manifested in the Ecumenical Councils), and the admission that John of Damascus is simply not to be followed *if* he did indeed deny the doctrine— and Thomas does not quite grant that he did. We also find an expanded treatment of the inability of the Greek language to distinguish between 'cause' and 'principle' (Iᵃ q.33 a.1 ad 1). But in many ways it is his discussion of liturgical diversity that is most revealing. In the crowning part of this crowning achievement, the end of the Third Part, Thomas makes a series of comparisons with contemporary Greek liturgical practices that leave us in no doubt as to their sacramental validity. He discusses varying customs with regard to baptism, especially the use of the formula 'the servant of Christ *N.* is baptized' by the Greeks rather than the Latin 'I baptize you', affirming that 'both confer the sacrament validly'.[58] The case is similar with the eucharist: the Greek use of leavened bread is deemed both reasonable and appropriate.[59] In each case it is clear that the customs of the respective traditions are equally legitimate and equally valid.[60]

1.4. CONCLUSION

Aquinas' reception of the Greek East is deeply instructive for the broader programme of this book. By virtue of his deep and searching engagement with the 'doctors of the Greeks', both patristic and Byzantine, Thomas came to a profound conviction of the fundamental orthodoxy of the Greek tradition as a whole. Certainly the Greeks are seen to be in schism, but not in heresy. Their unity with Rome was impaired, and with this their own capacity to refute heresy. For some unfathomable reason they were refusing to recognize the united witness of ecclesial tradition, both Latin and Greek, on the principal issues of contention: the *filioque* and papal primacy. There was to be no room for relativism, no mincing of words, on such matters. But the

---

[58] IIIᵃ q.60 a.8 s.c. See also IIIᵃ q.65 a.5 and 67 a.6.
[59] IIIᵃ q.74 a.4. By contrast, Thomas believes the Greek practice of giving communion to infants is misguided but stops short of condemning it (IIIᵃ q.80 a.9).
[60] Similar observations are made of differing marriage customs (with regard to priests) in the *Commentary on the Sentences* IV d.37, q.1, a.1–2.

Greeks were undoubtedly to be seen as Church, possessed of grace and inheritors of a shared tradition.

It would, of course, be fruitless to speculate on what might have happened had Thomas reached the Council of Lyons in 1274, instead of dying *en route*. Leo XIII's contention that he nonetheless 'took part and presided over' the Council was, at best, an exaggeration and in any event there was no substantial theological debate at Lyons. But in the broader arena of the Latin–Greek schism, Thomas is a fine example of one who, without doctrinal compromise, sought to bridge the gap between the competing traditions through greater knowledge, understanding, and respect—very much in the manner envisaged by Humbert of Romans. The conscious pursuit of catholicity and consistent hermeneutic of orthodoxy evidenced in Aquinas provides a paradigm for any serious approach to healing the ongoing schism. It is a paradigm that will also be operative in the coming examination of the reception of Thomas by the Orthodox.

2

Gregory Palamas and the Latin West

A further multiplication of perspective may be attained through an investigation of St Gregory Palamas' reception of the Latin West. As with Thomas' reception of the Greek East, this is an aspect of his theology that has come to the fore only in relatively recent scholarship. Palamas' reception of the Latin West is, it must be acknowledged, both less thoroughgoing and more controverted than the reverse phenomenon in Aquinas. But it does represent a significant dimension of his thought, recognition of which not only runs counter to the dominant neo-Palamite narrative of modern Orthodox theology but also calls into question some of the presuppositions of Palamas' Western critics.

2.1. PALAMAS AND AUGUSTINE

The key development in recent scholarship has been the widespread recognition of a significant encounter with Augustine in Palamas' works. Martin Jugie was the first to draw attention to this possibility. In his painfully excoriating article on Palamas, Jugie observes some interesting parallels between Gregory and Augustine, most notably in the *One Hundred and Fifty Chapters* (*Capita*).[1] Jugie's claims were somewhat sweeping and never fully substantiated, and found

---

[1] On *Capita* 36, Jugie exclaims: 'Fait remarquable dans l'histoire de la théologie grecque et byzantine, et à notre connaissance, inouï jusque-là, Palamas expose sur le mystère des processions divines une théorie identique a celle de saint Augustin et de saint Thomas.' 'Palamas, Grégoire', 1766. The association with Aquinas is unlikely since it would require knowledge of Aquinas well before the completion of Kydones' 1354 translation of the *Summa contra gentiles* (Jugie had taken the *Capita* to be

little purchase in immediately subsequent scholarship. Indeed, the classic twentieth-century accounts of Palamas positively preclude the possibility of any significant Augustinian element in his thought. According to the dominant neo-Palamite narrative, there is a great gulf fixed between Latin (essentialist) and Greek (personalist-existentialist) doctrines of the Trinity.[2] The Latins, in this view, have fallen prey to a static ontology in which abstract notions of being have obscured the mystery of actual existence. The Greeks, on the other hand, have remained fully alive to the primacy of personal existence. These polar positions are found to be expressed in, on the one hand, Augustine and Aquinas and, on the other, the Cappadocian Fathers and Palamas. This narrative is marked out in 1944 in Vladimir Lossky's *Essai sur la théologie mystique de l'Église d'Orient*.[3] Georges Florovsky had also

among the last works of the Hesychast doctor). The case with Augustine is, as we shall see, considerably more certain.

[2] The personalist-existentialist reading of Palamas mirrors the analogous retrieval of Aquinas by Étienne Gilson, Jacques Maritain, and others. Indeed, there was something of a veiled competition afoot as to who was to be deemed the better personalist or existentialist: Aquinas or Palamas. Lossky had immense admiration for Gilson who was to furnish a moving tribute to his sometime pupil in the preface to Lossky's posthumously published thesis on Meister Eckhart: *Théologie négative et connaissance de Dieu chez Maître Eckhart*.

[3] Thus the opponents of Palamas are 'Eastern theologians who had been strongly influenced by Thomism' and who took the essence–energies distinction to be a 'derogation of the simplicity of God'. 'Having become alienated from the apophatic and antinomical spirit of Eastern theology, they set up against it a conception of God which perceived him, primarily at any rate, as a simple essence, in which even the hypostases assumed the character of relations within the essence.' They were thus incapable of conceiving God other than as 'pure act'. Barlaam and Akindynos are the targets here and as evidence for their supposed Thomism, Lossky adduces Barlaam's training in Italy and Akindynos' (*sic*) translation of Aquinas' *Summa theologiae*. *Essai sur la théologie mystique de l'Église d'Orient*, 74 [cf. ET 76–7]. In fact, Barlaam's theological culture was predominately Byzantine and expressly anti-Thomist. Akindynos, for his part, was a deeply traditional theologian who never translated a word of Aquinas. The English translation amends the claim to the effect that Akindynos 'quotes the Greek translation of the *Summa theologiae*' but the text Lossky has in view here was the *De essentia et operatione* by Prochoros Kydones, incorrectly ascribed to Akindynos in Migne's *Patrologia graeca* and elsewhere. Lossky could, however, be considerably more subtle when dealing with Western theology *in se*. In 1950, in his review of Eric Mascall's *Existence and Analogy*, he paid tribute to Gilson's 'existentialist' retrieval of the 'authentic Thomism of S. Thomas and his immediate predecessors' while wisely cautioning, 'But we must be careful not to make this primacy of existence in S. Thomas seem too much like the existentialism which is now spread everywhere and even coming into theological thought. We must not form parties of the existentialists and the essentialists; these would both be equally far in one-sidedness from any sane theology.' His 'La notion théologique de la

suggested a basic incompatibility between Eastern personalism (represented by Palamas) and Western essentialism (represented by Augustine).[4] The finest twentieth-century student of Palamas, John Meyendorff, also follows this line closely. From his classic *Introduction à l'étude de Grégoire Palamas* onwards, this polarity is a given in Meyendorff's work.[5] As one of his later articles puts it:

> Indeed, as all scholars today would agree the real difference between the Latin—Augustinian—view of the Trinity, as a single Essence, with personal characters understood as 'relations', and the Greek scheme, inherited from the Cappadocian Fathers, which considered the single divine Essence as totally transcendent, and the Persons, or *hypostaseis*— each with unique and unchangeable characteristics—as revealing in themselves the Tri-personal divine life, was the real issue behind the debates on the *Filioque*.[6]

personne humaine' of 1955 also has some very positive remarks on Gilson and Thomas.

[4] While otherwise deeply attached to Augustine (albeit embracing him as a kind of honorary Easterner), Florovsky berates the Bishop of Hippo for his inability to acknowledge distinction within the divine simplicity and claims, 'Already S. Augustine diverged at this point from the Eastern tradition.' 'Under Augustinian presuppositions', he continues, 'the teaching of S. Gregory is unacceptable and absurd.' While cautious on the use of the 'existentialist' label, Florovsky portrays Gregory as the foe of all 'essentialist' theologies' and as the champion of the 'metaphysics of persons'. 'Saint Gregory Palamas and the Tradition of the Fathers', 175–6. Florovsky was, however, never quite as categorical as Lossky on the division between East and West and could be considerably more nuanced when so minded. See below, pp.197–204.

[5] The closing paragraph of the *Introduction à l'étude de Grégoire Palamas* resumes Palamas' achievement as a 'théologie personnaliste et existentielle'. Ibid., 327. Chapter 5 characterizes the essence–energies distinction as an 'existential theology' while Chapter 6 goes on to contrast the respectively personalist and essentialist characters of the Trinitarian theologies of East and West. Note that I refer to the original French version of this book, as opposed to the rather less substantial English version, *A Study of Gregory Palamas*.

[6] 'Theology: East and West', 674 (In lightly revised later versions of his article, Meyendorff backtracks slightly by modifying 'all scholars' to 'most'.) Like Lossky, Meyendorff was conscious of his indebtedness to the basic schema of Théodore de Régnon (the East proceeds from the three to the one, the post-Nicene West from the one to the three). Indeed, de Régnon's *Études de théologie positive sur la sainte Trinité* is the only source mentioned in support of this claim. Meyendorff is guilty of some hyperbole, but he is not wrong in observing the basic schema of de Régnon to be the dominant paradigm for Trinitarian theology in the twentieth century. On the general hegemony of de Régnon, see Michel René Barnes, 'Augustine in Contemporary Trinitarian Theology' and 'De Régnon Reconsidered'.

And he rounds off with a note of triumph:

> The Orthodox side, however—from Blemmydes, to Gregory of Cyprus and to Palamas—was gradually transcending a purely defensive stand, by discovering that the real problem of the *Filioque* lies not in the formula itself, but in the definition of God as *actus purus* as finalized in the *De ente et essentia* of Thomas Aquinas, vis-à-vis the more personalistic trinitarian vision inherited by the Byzantines from the Cappadocian Fathers.[7]

Thus Augustine's essentialism reaches its apogee in Aquinas, just as the personalism of the Cappadocian Fathers receives its perfect expression in Palamas.

The great irony here is that many of the most potent critiques of Palamas in recent years have berated him precisely for his essentialism, for his inability to distinguish properly the personal existence of the three divine hypostases. Catherine LaCugna finds the real distinction between the imparticipable essence and participable energies in God not only philosophically incoherent but positively dangerous, going so far as to assert that it 'breaks the back of orthodox trinitarian theology'. She finds particularly troubling the affirmation that the multiple energies of God are the single operation of the Trinity, concluding that this erases the particular characteristics of the persons, breaks the properly inseparable connection between economic and immanent Trinity, and overall 'sounds suspiciously similar to Augustine and Aquinas'.[8] Here she sides with Dorothea Wendebourg, for whom Palamas emerges as a functional modalist quite unable to account for the distinction of persons. Wendebourg too finds Palamas deeply reminiscent of Augustine and characterizes the triumph of Palamism as the 'defeat of Trinitarian theology'.[9] Robert

---

[7] 'Theology: East and West', 678. No indication is given as to how and when and by whom this 'discovery' was made. Meyendorff's perception of Aquinas is woefully anachronistic, reading back a definitive character to his theology that in fact only obtained between *Aeterni patris* and Vatican II. He is also mistaken in supposing the *filioque* to have anything to do with the notion of God as *actus purus*. Its theological genealogy is quite different.

[8] *God for Us*, 194. There is a certain incoherence in LaCugna's presentation of Palamas' thought here: in contiguous paragraphs she asserts that the imparticipable essence lies beyond the distinction of persons and that the distinction of persons belongs to the imparticipable essence.

[9] Wendebourg, *Geist oder Energie* and 'From the Cappadocian Fathers to Gregory Palamas: The Defeat of Trinitarian Theology. LaCugna also cites Christoph von

Jenson has also attacked Palamas along similar lines. While he finds much to admire in Palamas' teaching on *theosis*, Jenson finds the essence–energies distinction on which it is based a 'disaster', taking it to disconnect the Trinity from the world thereby amounting to a 'bluntly modalist' doctrine.[10]

A further irony is that those who criticize Palamas for his essentialism persist in taking him as archetypal of an Eastern theological tradition quite distinct from that of the West. LaCugna, for example, presents Palamas and Aquinas as exemplars and culminations of the 'central ethos' of their respective traditions of East and West.[11] These traditions are, she maintains, separated by a great gulf: 'on nearly every significant doctrinal point [. . .] the differences between East and West are decisive and probably irreconcilable'. The West sees the persons of the Trinity as relations within the essence while the East, after Palamas, restricts the divine persons to the imparticipable essence. In both cases the creation is cut off from the immanent Trinity. She is disinterested as to the relative merits of Palamism and Thomism, allowing them to be 'two legitimate albeit divergent systems of thought'.[12] This relativism is doubtless to be explained by her conviction that both systems are complicit in the defeat of the doctrine of the Trinity, and thus similarly redundant and equally deficient.[13]

It should not have escaped notice that LaCugna's vision of East and West is uncannily akin to that of Lossky and Meyendorff: Palamas and Aquinas presented as the twin peaks of their mutually opposing traditions, with the West tainted with essentialism and the East (at least until Palamas) more sensible of the distinction of persons. There are, of course, serious differences. LaCugna has no stake in Palamas or neo-Palamism and takes Palamas to be the champion not of personalism but of essentialism. She sees no real continuity between Palamas and the Cappadocian Fathers in respect

---

Schönborn's critique of Palamas and his detection of a strong parallel with Aquinas in *Capita* 132 where Palamas affirms that the name 'Father' may be used of the Holy Trinity in relation to the creation. Von Schönborn, 'Immanente und ökonomische Trinität', 251–2. See below, n.35.

[10] *Systematic Theology* I, 152–3.   [11] *God for Us*, 143–4.

[12] Here LaCugna references de Halleux, 'Palamisme et scholastique'. De Halleux's approach is in fact rather more sophisticated than the apparent relativism embraced by LaCugna.

[13] See *God for Us*, 97–8.

of the essence–energies distinction, a continuity strenuously defended
by virtually all Orthodox theologians engaged in the retrieval
and reaffirmation of Palamite theology. LaCugna is happy to find
Palamas reminiscent of Augustine or Aquinas, not because of any
actual connection but because of an analogous process of breakdown
in Trinitarian doctrine in the otherwise opposing traditions of
East and West. She will also poke fun at Lossky for his unwitting
neo-scholasticism, but again without this detracting from the fundamental divergence of East and West.[14] This dichotomy between East
and West is virtually an article of faith for LaCugna, as it is for Lossky
and Meyendorff. Such a dichotomy would certainly seem to preclude
any but merely adventitious parallels between Gregory and Augustine. But substantive parallels, and direct citations, there certainly are.
It is time now to examine these more closely.

Meyendorff knew well that in Chapter 36 of the *One Hundred and
Fifty Chapters* (*Capita*) there is a striking 'psychological' image of the
Trinity, with the Holy Spirit presented as the mutual love of Father
and Son. This image he described as 'unparalleled' elsewhere in
Byzantine theological literature and even 'somewhat similar' to that
of Augustine, allowing this to be a sign of Gregory's general openness
to the West.[15] A later estimation, however, ruled out any direct
acquaintance with Augustine and downgraded the parallelism to
merely 'quite superficial'.[16] But in either case, any substantial connection was deemed out of the question.[17]

---

[14] *God for Us*, 196. In similar vein, Jenson speaks of Lossky's theology 'as a vision of
God as frozen as any we have encountered, and a new evacuation of trinitarianism'.
Systematic Theology I, 152.

[15] *Introduction à l'étude de Grégoire Palamas*, 316 ('assez semblable'). Lossky, for
his part, had previously declared such images to be unheard of in the East. *Essai sur la
théologie mystique de l'Église d'Orient*, 78 [ET 81].

[16] 'Theology: East and West', 673 and 679 n.11. He states quite categorically that,
'The Greek translation of Augustine's *De Trinitate* by Maximos Planoudes (†1310)
remained the work of an isolated humanist, whose work was hardly ever used
by Byzantine theologians.' Here he is responding to Edmund Hussey, 'The Palamite
Trinitarian Models'. Hussey, for his part, tentatively suggests that Didymus the
Blind may be Palamas' immediate source here.

[17] Meyendorff had no particular animus against Augustine and observes that in his
insistence on the absolute necessity of grace, Gregory is 'l'un des auteurs les plus
"augustiniens" de l'Orient chrétien'. *Introduction à l'étude de Grégoire Palamas*, 175.
But here too no substantial connection between the twin paragons of East and West is
envisaged.

But more recent work in this area has demonstrated that Gregory's encounter with Augustine was considerably more extensive than Meyendorff, or others, could allow.[18] Reinhard Flogaus, in particular, has put forward a persuasive case for Palamas' having made free and frequent use of Augustine, drawing directly and at times verbally on the translation of the *De Trinitate* made by Maximos Planoudes in *c.*1280.[19] This contention fits well within Flogaus' broader neo-Platonic reading of Palamas.[20] Gregory's encounter with Augustine is especially evident in Chapters 34–37 and 125–35 of the *Capita* (*c.*1349–50) and in other works from the mid to late 1340s onwards such as Homily 16 (*Discourse on the Economy of Christ*) and *To Xena*.[21] Further investigation may yet yield further points of contact. The instances uncovered thus far encompass a wide range of subjects: from the motives of the incarnation (Homily 16), to the meaning of death (*To Xena*), the four kinds of *logos* within man, and God's possession of goodness and wisdom not as quality but as essence (*Capita* 34–35). In one very revealing case from the late 1350s, Palamas introduces a quotation from Augustine with the words, 'For as one of the wise and apostolic men has said, "dispositions and states and places and times and suchlike things are not properly

---

[18] Robert Sinkewicz was deeply sceptical, warning of the need to avoid the 'temptation' of reading Augustine's ideas into Palamas. Idem (ed.), *The One Hundred and Fifty Chapters*, 18. Jacques Lison is rather more open, but still cautious as to the extent of direct influence. See his *L'Ésprit répandu: la pneumatologie de Grégoire Palamas* and 'L'Ésprit comme amour selon Grégoire Palamas: une influence augustinienne?' Sinkewicz has, more recently, come to accept that Palamas both cites and draws on Augustine: 'Gregory Palamas', 163–4.

[19] See his 'Der heimliche Blick nach Westen: zur Rezeption von Augustins *De Trinitate* durch Gregorios Palamas'; *Theosis bei Palamas und Luther*; 'Palamas and Barlaam Revisited: A Reassessment of East and West in the Hesychast Controversy of 14th Century Byzantium'; and 'Inspiration–Exploitation–Distortion: The Use of St Augustine in the Hesychast Controversy'. The examples given in this paragraph are all owed to Flogaus. See also John Demetracopoulos, Αὐγουστῖνος καὶ Γρηγόριος Παλαμᾶς. Τὰ προβλήματα τῶν Ἀριστοτελικῶν κατηγοριῶν καὶ τῆς Τριαδικῆς ψυχοθεολογίας; Josef Lössl, 'Augustine in Byzantium' and 'Augustine's *De Trinitate* in the 150 Chapters of St Gregory Palamas'.

[20] In emphasizing the neo-Platonic roots of Palamism, Flogaus follows in the footsteps of Nikephoros Gregoras (*Historia Romana* (Bekker and Schopen eds.) III 481–2), Martin Jugie ('Palamas, Grégoire', 1761), and Endre von Ivánka (*Plato Christianus*, 389–445).

[21] For the dating of the *Capita*, I follow Sinkewicz (ed.), *The One Hundred and Fifty Chapters*, 49–55. Meyendorff had opted for a slightly earlier date of 1344–7 (*Introduction à l'étude de Grégoire Palamas*, 373–4). For Homily 16, Meyendorff's dating of 1347–51 seems very likely (ibid. 391). For *To Xena*, see below n.46.

but only metaphorically to be ascribed to God; but to create and to act should be said to belong most truly only to God".'[22] This reluctance to name the source speaks volumes, not only of his conviction of the authority of Augustine but also of the need for a certain discretion in appealing to that authority.[23]

Given the prevalence of essentialist *versus* personalist paradigm in Palamas scholarship, it is intriguing to find Palamas himself countenancing Augustine even at his most 'essentialist'. This calls for some further discussion, beginning with *Capita* 36. Here, the Holy Spirit is likened to 'an ineffable love (ἔρως)' of the Begetter towards the Begotten. The Son 'possesses this love as co-proceeding (συμπροελθόντα) from the Father and himself and as resting connaturally (συμφυῶς) in him'. The Spirit is not only 'of the Father' but also 'of the Son', who possesses him 'as the Spirit of truth, wisdom, and word'. The Spirit is, moreover, intimated in Proverbs 8:30 in which the Logos declares: 'I was she who rejoiced together with (συνέχαιρον) him.' This verse leads Palamas to conclude that, 'This pre-eternal rejoicing of the Father and the Son is the Holy Spirit who is, as has been said, common to both.' But this does not, he is careful to note, detract in any way from the fact that the Spirit 'proceeds from the Father alone according to his being' (παρ' αὐτοῦ μόνου ἐκπορεύεται καθ' ὕπαρξιν). Palamas thus maintains a strict sense of the monarchy of the Father as the single principle of the Godhead.[24]

Palamas is clearly precluding here any hint of the Latin *filioque* in respect of origination. But he is equally clearly not confining co-procession to the temporal mission of the Spirit: he is certainly speaking of the immanent eternal life of the Divine Trinity. There are antecedents for this kind of language in the Byzantine tradition: Maximus the Confessor's intuition of the fundamental congruity of procession 'through' and 'from' the Son; John of Damascus' eternal

---

[22] *Against Gregoras* 2.43 (Chrestou IV: 296) (cf. *De Trinitate* 5.8.9). The passage is reproduced in *Capita* 133, without even a guarded attribution.

[23] See below, p.59.

[24] Augustine himself preserves a definite sense the monarchy of the Father, noting that the Holy Spirit proceeds 'principaliter' from the Father (*De Trinitate* 15.17.29) and that the Father is principle in relation both to the Son and to the Spirit (*De Trinitate* 5.13.14–5.14.15). Medieval Western theologies of the Trinity invariably have some means of retaining something of the monarchy of the Father, albeit with nothing like the emphasis that would be required to satisfy the majority of Orthodox theologians.

'resting' of the Spirit in the Son; or Gregory of Cyprus' eternal 'shining forth' of the Spirit through the Son.[25] But such precedents cannot explain away the astonishing parallels with Augustine's notion of the Spirit as the 'mutual love' of Father and Son.[26] The fact that Palamas proceeds immediately to propose a Trinitarian image in man in terms of the operation of mind, knowledge, and love only serves to make the connection with Augustine unmistakable.[27]

This sympathetic but not uncritical reception of some key features of Augustine's Trinitarian teaching is, at first sight, puzzling. Palamas is known to have been a staunch opponent of the Latin *filioque* and it seems very strange to find him embracing some of the key images of Augustine, the foremost progenitor of that doctrine. In his distinctly anti-Latin *Apodictic Treatises* (*c*.1336), Palamas indeed insists in no uncertain terms on procession from the Father alone. But on closer inspection, Palamas reveals himself to be rather more than an unbending monopatrist, unable to think beyond the purely temporal mission or sending of the Spirit by the Son. Perfectly aware that some Greek patristic texts, such as Cyril of Alexandria's *Thesaurus*, involve the Son in the eternal procession of the Spirit in some way, Palamas produces a remarkably constructive approach to the whole problem.[28]

Palamas insists that there can be no talk of procession of the hypostasis of the Spirit from the hypostasis of the Son. The Spirit has his particular mode of being from the hypostasis of the Father alone. To claim otherwise, as do the Latins, is to make a single

---

[25] Maximus the Confessor, *Letter to Marinus* (PG 91 136A–D); John of Damascus, *Exact Exposition of the Orthodox Faith* 8.173 (Kotter II: 25); Gregory of Cyprus, *Tomos* of 1285 (PG 142 240C).

[26] *De Trinitate* 15.6.10, 15.17.29, 15.19.37, 15.26.47.

[27] *Capita* 37. Cf. *De Trinitate* 9 (*passim*).

[28] Palamas' sources are exclusively Greek. Latin positions are referred to *en bloc*, with no specific citations. St Cyril of Alexandria's *Thesaurus* is of special interest with its indications of some form of eternal co-procession. This was, naturally, a key text for Latin appeals to the Greek patristic tradition in support of the *filioque*. Palamas recognizes (not unlike Thomas) the need to read the Fathers in context if one is to read them aright: thus much of what Cyril has to say about the relation of the Father and the Son is to be understood within the framework of his anti-Arian programme (*On a Saying of Cyril* 1. Chrestou IV: 102). Palamas shows a rare historical intuition here given that later Western affirmations of the *filioque* were invariably motivated by anti-Arian considerations (See Peter Gemeinhardt, *Die Filioque-Kontroverse*). On Cyril's *Thesaurus*, see the useful note in Norman Russell, *Cyril of Alexandria*, 214 n.96.

hypostasis of Father and Son. But we can speak of the Spirit's being from the Father and the Son, or from the Father through the Son, in terms of nature. Because of the consubstantiality of Father and Son, the Spirit may be said to be 'naturally from the Son and from his essence', manifesting thereby the Spirit's own consubstantiality with the Father and the Son.[29] This eternal divine movement has its temporal counterpart: 'The Spirit eternally flows-forth from the Father into the Son and becomes manifest in the saints from the Father through the Son.'[30] Similarly, 'The Holy Spirit is naturally and eternally of the Father and in the Son, and goes forth and is manifest from the Son to the saints.'[31] Palamas is careful to underline that this temporal manifestation and going-forth pertains to the uncreated *energeia* of the Holy Spirit, and not to his nature or hypostasis.

The distinction between divine essence and divine *energeia* (energy, activity, or operation) adds an important dimension to what we might call an 'Orthodox *filioque*'. Since, for Palamas, *energeia* pertains to nature and not to hypostasis, there is necessarily a single *energeia* of Father, Son, and Holy Spirit. The consubstantiality of the triune God is thus expressed and revealed in the divine operation. We may certainly speak of the Spirit being from the Father and Son, or from the Father through the Son, when we speak of the extension to human beings of the uncreated grace of the Spirit. There is an order to be observed here: the divine *energeia* may be single but it is not undifferentiated. There is, maintains Palamas, a real sense in which we may speak of the Father and the Son 'giving' the Spirit, if we understand by this not nature or hypostasis but the uncreated *energeia* of God communicated in and through the Holy Spirit.[32]

Thus the Spirit proceeds from the Father alone according to hypostasis, but is united essentially to the Son, 'resting in him, proper to him, and abiding eternally in him, for he is the dispenser of the Spirit'. Thus it is 'nothing new' to say that 'the Spirit goes forth (προϊέναι) from the Son and from his nature'. Concomitant with this procession from the nature of the Son, the Spirit is also 'given,

---

[29] *Apodictic Treatise* 2.67 (Chrestou I: 138–9).
[30] *Apodictic Treatise* 2.58 (Chrestou I: 131).
[31] *Apodictic Treatise* 2.71 (Chrestou I: 143–4).
[32] *Apodictic Treatise* 2.69 (Chrestou I: 141).

sent, poured out, and goes out' 'through and from' the Son to the worthy. In respect of this temporal mission of the Spirit, Palamas will even use the verb 'proceed from' (ἐκπορεύεσθαι). This is, of course, the term used of the Spirit in the Creed of Nicaea-Constantinople and usually reserved by Palamas for the eternal procession of the Spirit from the hypostasis of the Father alone.[33] The fact that he is prepared to use such a heavily-loaded term for the temporal procession of the Spirit from the Son only serves to underline the fact that, for Palamas, temporal and eternal procession are inseparably, if inscrutably, connected.

While scarcely sympathetic to (or indeed especially well-informed about) the contemporary Latin position on the *filioque*, Palamas nonetheless offers in his *Apodictic Treatises* a very constructive Orthodox take on this vexed question. He allows for an 'Orthodox *filioque*' both in respect of the eternal divine life and the manifestation of the divine *energeia* among creatures. But he remains adamant that the hypostasis of the Father is the sole originating principle of the divinity. While there can certainly be no question of adding the offending word to the Creed, or of accepting the *filioque* in terms of origination, Palamas' capacity to embrace co-procession on both eternal and temporal planes will have prepared the ground for the remarkably positive reception of Augustine's Trinitarian teaching evident in subsequent works such as the *Capita*. *Capita* 36 is, in short, perfectly congruous within the Palamite corpus in its treatment of the co-procession of the Spirit, for all that it has taken up some distinctly Augustinian themes.

This is not a case of a benighted Easterner being so bedazzled by Augustine as to embrace some of his ideas at the expense of the coherence of his own doctrine. Augustine appealed to Palamas precisely because of the underlying congruity of their approaches to the mystery of the Trinity. Palamas has an acute sense of the unity of the Godhead that is quite as 'essentialist' as anything one might find in Augustine but which remains, like Augustine's, duly alive to the distinction of persons.[34] In *Capita* 132, for example, he embraces an Augustinian formulation in affirming: 'The hypostatic properties in God are referred to as mutual relations and differ from one another

---

[33] *Apodictic Treatise* 2.73 (Chrestou I: 144).
[34] The question of the distinction of persons was also a matter of high importance within Latin scholasticism. See above, Chapter 1.2.

in hypostasis but not in substance.'[35] This kind of language also has a foundation in the East, witnessed most notably in Gregory the Theologian.[36] Such formulations also dovetail with the Eastern concept of the divine *perichoresis*, as articulated above all by John of Damascus. Palamas is certainly in John's line here, declaring in *Capita* 104: 'God himself is within himself since the three divine hypostases connaturally and eternally possess one another and co-inhere in one another unmixedly.'[37] Again, what we see here is not the intrusion of a foreign element into Palamas' oeuvre but rather his recognition of the compatibility of Augustine, *mutatis mutandis*, with his own theological tradition and trajectory.

This compatibility is also evident in their respective treatments of the divine wisdom. *Capita* 34, as we have noted, specifies that God's wisdom pertains to his essence. 'The supreme mind, says Palamas, 'is itself wisdom'. Such an affirmation plainly does not fit Meyendorff's presentation and indeed puzzles more recent observers such as Flogaus for whom it serves as a sign of the anomalous nature of the Augustinian elements in Palamas.[38] Wisdom is indeed most commonly treated by Palamas as a divine *energeia*, by which God

---

[35] Cf. *De Trinitate* 5.11.12 (Flogaus, 'Das heimliche Blick', 285). The passage goes on to speak of the Father as principle in relation to the Son and Spirit, and to creation. The Son is also called principle in relation to the creation, but Palamas is careful to specify that they are 'not two principles but one'. He goes on to conclude, 'therefore Father and Son, together with the Spirit are one principle in relation to the creation'. This is very much what we read in Augustine: the Father and the Son are 'one principle in respect to the creation, and since the Holy Spirit is one with them we must affirm that God is spoken of as one principle in relation to the creation, not as two or three principles' (*De Trinitate* 5.13.14). This is precisely the passage to which von Schönborn takes exception: 'Immanente und ökonomische Trinität', 251–2. See above, n.9.

[36] Gregory of Nazianzus, *Oration* 31.9: the names of the divine persons express the 'mutual relations' or 'difference of manifestation' within the divinity.

[37] Similar language is found in *Capita* 112. For *perichoresis* in John of Damascus see, for example, *Exact Exposition* 1.8, 1.14 (Kotter II 29.262–4, 42.11–16).

[38] Meyendorff seems not to acknowledge such statements at all, claiming blithely that Palamas avoids identifying wisdom with the divine essence, so avoiding the error of the Russian Sophiologists (*Introduction à l'étude de Grégoire Palamas*, 304). Sergius Bulgakov, for Meyendorff the Sophiologist-in-chief, had indeed staked a claim for Palamite theology as an 'incomplete sophiology' 'in its inner sense' (*Le buisson ardent*, 181 [ET 156]). Flogaus expresses himself quite perplexed here: 'The idea is actually foreign to Palamas' theology, since he would normally identify these predications with God's *energy* and consider God's essence as beyond all names and knowledge'. 'Inspiration–Exploitation–Distortion', 76.

reaches across the ontological gulf to unite creatures to himself. He is 'the wisdom of the wise' (*Triads* 3.2.25).[39] This participable *energeia* is, naturally, common to the Holy Trinity: 'the divine wisdom allows herself to be shared by those who show themselves wise [...] I speak now of the wisdom contemplated in the Father, the Son, and the Holy Spirit'.[40]

But *Capita* 34 is not isolated in also associating wisdom with the essence of God. In the *Triads* (1338–41), in a passage closely following Dionysius, Palamas asserts that as the source of being, wisdom, and life: 'the superessential and singular hiddenness is properly conceived and named God and wisdom and life, and not only essence' (*Triads* 3.2.23).[41] Dionysius is also behind the further explanation given in *Capita* 78: God both is and is not wisdom, just as he is and is not nature, or goodness, or being. In his energetic condescension to the created world, he manifests himself as the nature of natures, the wisdom of the wise, the being of beings, the good of the good, and so forth. Yet he remains utterly other in his essential nature, wisdom, being, and goodness: of which we may not say or know anything.[42] In each case, the same terms are predicated both of the imparticipable divine essence and the participable divine *energeia*. Thus wisdom does indeed, properly understood, pertain both to essence and to *energeia* in Palamas' oeuvre—and not only in *Capita* 34.

The fact that Palamas associates wisdom primarily with God's Trinitarian being is deeply significant.[43] The association of the Son

---

[39] For further examples, see *Capita* 78, 82, 83, 87.

[40] *Apology* cited Meyendorff, *Introduction à l'étude de Grégoire Palamas*, 304. Meyendorff takes this passage to preclude identification of wisdom with the essence of God. In fact, Palamas is simply denying that the energetic manifestation of the divine wisdom is a manifestation of the divine essence.

[41] Cf. *Divine Names* 5.2 (PG 3 816C). Dionysius distinguishes between the 'goodness, essence, life, and wisdom of the self-superessential deity', of which we may not speak, and the providential action of that deity as cause of all such qualities in the created order (and so also properly named goodness, essence, life, and wisdom).

[42] Even his most radically apophatic statements (e.g. *Capita* 144, 145) do not preclude the naming of God as wisdom, they rather require a simultaneous un-naming. As Gregory himself makes plain in *Capita* 123, the apophatic and cataphatic ways are not opposites but rather complementary approaches to the divine mystery: 'Apophatic theology does not oppose or do away with cataphatic theology but shows rather that cataphatic statements about God are true and made in an orthodox manner but God does not possess such things in the way that we do.'

[43] He will also speak of the 'common wisdom' of Father, Son, and Holy Spirit made known in the creation (*Dialogue with Gregoras* 25: Chrestou IV: 226–7). Recognition

with wisdom remains secondary, a function of the Son's essential and energetic character *qua* wisdom.[44] This primary association of wisdom with the Trinitarian being of God is distinctly uncommon in the patristic tradition but is, of course, a prominent trait in Augustine and in later Latin theology.[45] For Augustine, wisdom is primarily to be understood in terms of the divine unity: 'the Father is wisdom, the Son is wisdom, and the Holy Spirit is wisdom, and together not three wisdoms, but one wisdom' (*De Trinitate* 7.3.6). We may also note that for both Augustine and Palamas, the gift of divine wisdom is understood in terms of the realization of the *imago Dei*. In the context of his discussion of the trinity that is the mind remembering, understanding, and loving God, Augustine asserts that it is only when the mind has attained wisdom that the *imago Dei* is realized (*De Trinitate* 14.12.15). In the *Triads* (1.1.22), Palamas likewise claims that only the gift of divine wisdom (what he calls 'our theosophy') realizes the image of God within us.

The treatments of wisdom in Palamas and Augustine share much in common: the primary association of wisdom with the Trinitarian nature of God and the sense that participation in the divine wisdom realizes the *imago Dei*. Of course there is also much which divides them, most notably the whole dimension of the distinction between divine essence and energies, scarcely conceivable from an Augustinian standpoint. But without supposing any direct connection or borrowing here, the respective treatments of wisdom serve as a further demonstration of the congruity of approach in these supposed archetypes of East and West: one that is in neither case reducible to personalism or essentialism. This underlying congruity, evident not only in the *Capita* but also in the *Triads*, helps explain how Gregory could be quite so positively receptive of

of this 'common wisdom' is deemed perfectly compatible with recognizing the Son as self-hypostasizing Wisdom (*Against Akindynos* 6.25.96: Chrestou III: 458).

[44] Palamas routinely ascribes scriptural references to wisdom to the Son, recognizing him as hypostatic Wisdom (e.g. *Triads* 1.1.5, 1.1.17, 2.3.55). Augustine similarly allows that scriptural references to wisdom to refer chiefly to the Logos: 'When anything concerning wisdom is declared or narrated in the Scriptures, whether as itself speaking, or where anything is spoken of it, the Son chiefly is intimated to us' (*De Trinitate* 7.3.5). Augustine's treatment of wisdom is motivated in part by his concern regarding the proposition that the Son thinks for the Father, *De Trinitate* 15.7.2.

[45] Maximus is a partial exception: see my 'Wisdom in St Maximus the Confessor'.

Augustine when he encountered the Planoudes translation of the *De Trinitate* in the early to mid-1340s.[46]

In sum, Palamas' patent use of Augustine emerges as perfectly consistent with his broader theological programme. Before his encounter with Augustine, Palamas had already established a highly constructive approach to the *aporia* of the *filioque* that enabled him to adopt a remarkably tolerant approach to the Latin tradition and formulae when viewed outside the context of East–West disputation. Allowing for some form of co-procession in terms both of essence and of *energeia* and sharing a similar conceptualization of wisdom, Palamas was predisposed to look favourably on Augustine. This sympathetic reading does not amount to any sort of decisive influence and still less did it effect any form of doctrinal compromise: Palamas' theological vision was well developed and articulated before he happened upon the Planoudes translation. The *De Trinitate* served, rather, as a confirmation of aspects of his own theological vision— even including, with some essential caveats, the disputed matter of the *filioque*.

This remarkable encounter stands not only as a sign of an under-lying congruity but also as a marker of the openness of Palamas to Latin theology. In this respect, the encounter serves to foreshadow the capacity of many Palamites (and anti-Unionists) to be ardent admirers of Thomas Aquinas, one of Augustine's most prominent epigones. But the basic fact that an 'archetypal Easterner' should embrace an 'archetypal Westerner', as Palamas does Augustine, is strange only if one begins with the assumption of an East–West dichotomy (with attendant archetypes) in the first place. What is really puzzling is the fact that so many observers across the

---

[46] The earliest treatise which clearly draws directly on Augustine is *To Xena*. Meyendorff plumps for a date of around 1345–6 (*Introduction à l'étude de Grégoire Palamas*, 386) whereas Chrestou opts for early 1342 (Chrestou V: 138). The text is written after the death of Andronikos III (1341) and in the midst of the civil war (1341–7). Palamas refers to his current mistreatment and the maligning of his writings. He speaks of his own synodal condemnation, likening his plight to that of Chrysostom: excommunicated and condemned to exile on a baseless charge (*To Xena* 3–6. Chrestou V: 194–5). Palamas suffered synodal condemnations in the summer of 1342 and in November 1344: his writings condemned at the first, himself excommuni-cated at the second. The analogy with Chrysostom seems to fit the second condem-nation better, thus 1345–6 seems the more likely *terminus ad quem*. Palamas may have come across the text during his period of imprisonment in the imperial Palace (four years from April/May 1343).

theological spectrum have approached the issue under precisely such an assumption. A serious engagement with Augustine is thus simply out of the question for virtually all critics and admirers of Palamas alike.[47] But a serious engagement there was, and one which must press us to question further the hackneyed dichotomy of East and West.

2.2. THEOLOGICAL METHODOLOGY IN PALAMAS: A SCHOLASTIC INHERITANCE

Another way in which the opposition between East and West is commonly presented is in terms of a methodological incompatibility. This particular dichotomy has Gerhard Podskalsky as its prime exponent. For Podskalsky, the triumph of Palamism represents the displacement of reason and the defeat of any properly systematic or even coherently ordered approach to theology. Byzantine theology becomes at best an *ad hoc* response to particular problems based on monastic experience. Most commonly, it consists in little more than the assemblage of patristic testimony, not infrequently geared to patriotic assertions of national identity. Faced with the more sophisticated Latin theological tradition, the Byzantines had only two options before them: amazed wonder or complete rejection.[48]

---

[47] To the critics already mentioned (LaCugna, Wendebourg, Jenson) we may add Gerhard Podskalsky, for whom Palamas' acquaintance with Augustine barely impinges on his broader scheme of methodological opposition between East and West (*Theologie und Philosophie*, 176–7 and *passim*). Podskalsky's review of Flogaus' *Theosis bei Palamas und Luther* consists largely of filling bibliographical lacunae and has precious little to say on the implications of the Augustine connection. To the admirers (Lossky, Meyendorff) we may add David Bradshaw who characterizes Palamite theology as a reaction to Barlaam's alleged Augustinianism and seems barely to register Palamas' own use of Augustine. *Aristotle: East and West*, 222. Bradshaw appears to follow John Romanides, for whom any taint of Augustinianism (which he associates squarely with Barlaam) in Palamas is wholly inadmissible. See Romanides' 'Notes on the Palamite Controversy and Related Topics'. A similar basic incompatibility between Augustine and Palamas is assumed throughout Christos Yannaras' 'Orthodoxy and the West' and ' Ὀρθοδοξία καὶ Δύση στὴ Νεώτερη Ἑλλάδα. Even Flogaus, the chief exponent of the connection between Augustine and Palamas, seems unsure quite what to make of it.

[48] Here I summarize Podskalsky's conclusions in *Theologie und Philosophie*, 238–44. It should be noted that he adopts a more moderate account of East–West difference in his later work *Von Photios zu Bessarion*.

The idea of a methodological impasse is not peculiar to Podskalsky. Many Orthodox writers have found such an approach (minus the assumption of Western superiority) deeply congenial, happily contrasting the apophatic and mystical East with the rational and scholastic West. This approach was unforgettably delineated by Vladimir Lossky and widely embraced by writers such as John Meyendorff, Philip Sherrard, and Christos Yannaras.[49] Some more nuanced voices, those of Kallistos Ware and André de Halleux for example, have questioned this sense of a stark opposition between the theological methodologies of East and West but without seriously questioning the methodological otherness of the two traditions.[50] It is this assumed otherness that I intend to probe in this section, beginning with an account of the shape of the Byzantine theological tradition inherited by Palamas.

The question of the methodological otherness of East and West turns on the issue of the innovatory and unwontedly rationalistic

[49] Lossky declares in typically categorical fashion that, 'for all its richness, the religious thought of the East has never had a scholasticism'. *Essai sur la théologie mystique de l'Église d'Orient*, 99 [ET 104]. By scholasticism, Lossky understands an alliance with philosophy in the interests of doctrinal synthesis. Naturally, he does not deny the liberal use of philosophy in the East 'for apologetic purposes' but asserts that the East never set much store by such 'relative and changing truths' (ibid.). That said, in less guarded moments he will in practice acknowledge elements of scholasticism in the East. Praising the liturgical character of John of Damascus' theology, he declares that, 'Even his most scholastic statements give rise to poetic flights.' *Orthodox Theology: An Introduction*, 14. The same might be said of Thomas—like John no mean liturgical compositor. Lossky admits that an untutored observer might see in debates of the Palamite controversy a 'scholastic subtlety' (with the understanding that this would be a misapprehension). *In the Image and Likeness of God*, 60. Scholasticism is never a positive label in Lossky and is certainly to be contrasted with the resolutely mystical and soteriological character of theology in the Christian East. Meyendorff, similarly, assumes an essential difference between the theological methodologies of East and West. His *Introduction à l'étude de Grégoire Palamas* presents Palamism as a counterpoise to the scholasticism of the Latin West, for all that he very carefully denies any inherent anti-Latinism in Palamas and his immediate followers (the real opposition is perceived to be between Palamism and a chain of later Western developments: nominalism, Renaissance humanism, and modern secularism). His 'Theology East and West' puts the methodological otherness in especially plain terms. The methodological gap is presented in categorical terms in Sherrard's *The Greek East and Latin West* and in Yannaras' various contributions on the theme of Orthodoxy and the West.

[50] Ware, 'Scholasticism and Orthodoxy: Theological Method as a Factor in the Schism'. Ware is here commenting on Yannaras' 'Orthodoxy and the West'. De Halleux, 'Palamisme et Scolastique: exclusivisme dogmatique ou pluriformité théologique?'

character of Western scholasticism as opposed to the apophatic and experiential traditions of the Christian East. This is a contrast that has been much overblown. If by scholasticism we understand not some caricature of untrammelled reason but rather the careful and ordered use of reason to explicate and define revealed truth, bolstered by an appeal to patristic and philosophical authority (strictly in that order), then it is undeniable that this method is perfectly proper to and indeed rooted in the Byzantine East. Byzantine theology has never been the preserve of apophaticism and mysticism alone but has frequently exemplified all the tedious dryness so lamented by detractors from scholasticism in East and West alike. A discernible shift sets in between the more immediately scriptural, expansive, and rhetorical style of the Fathers of the third and fourth century and the distinctly more forensic and authority-led character of theological endeavour from the time of the Christological controversies of the fifth century onwards. In the fourth century, appeal to the authority of non-scriptural writers is still almost negligible as a criterion of theological truth.[51] Only in the fifth century does the appeal to the authority of 'the Fathers' become normative, above all through the labours of Cyril of Alexandria.[52]

A theological heavyweight, devastating polemicist, and ruthless political operator, Cyril mustered all the forces at his disposal in his various battles. Within his ample armoury lay a mode of theologizing quite as dry and analytical as many a later scholastic production. His anti-Arian works on the Trinity of the early 420s have been aptly characterized as 'perhaps the earliest Christian works composed in a completely academic, dialectical style which still exist'.[53] His most able adversary from the opposing Christological tradition of Antioch,

---

[51] This is not to say that it is unheard of: Athanasius, for example, produces a lengthy collection of ecclesiastical testimonies in the latter part of his *On the Decrees of the Council of Nicaea* (*Athanasius Werke* 2.1: 33–42). Similarly, Basil in his *On the Holy Spirit* (SC 17bis: 29.71–3) demonstrates the traditional character of his teaching with an appeal to a series of pre-Nicene figures esteemed not only for their antiquity but for the exactness of their teaching (Clement of Rome, Irenaeus of Lyons, and Origen are among those mentioned).

[52] See Thomas Graumann, *Die Kirche der Väter: Vätertheologie und Väterbeweis in den Kirchen des Ostens bis zum Konzil von Ephesus (431)*.

[53] Brian Daley, 'Boethius' Theological Tracts and Early Byzantine Scholasticism', 167. Daley refers here to the *Thesaurus* (PG 75 9–356) and *Dialogues on the Trinity* (SC 213, 237, 246) and sees the same method carried over into his later Christological works.

Theodoret of Cyrrhus, was capable of similar rational detachment
and intellectual rigour, as witnessed especially in his *Eranistes*. Both
he and Cyril used syllogisms freely.[54] Theodoret was also to provide a
systematic presentation of the Christian faith in his *Healing of Greek
Maladies*, the first such presentation since Origen's *De Principiis*
some two hundred years earlier.[55] In addition to a number of
more straightforward commentaries on scripture, Theodoret also
set himself quite deliberately to tackle various problematic passages
of the Old Testament.[56] A similar deliberate wrestling with thorny
problems is evident in the *Questions and Responses to the Orthodox* of
the Pseudo-Justin, a work roughly contemporary with and from
a similar geographical milieu as Theodoret (and indeed often ascribed
to him). The *eratopokriseis* (question and response) format here
is unlike that which we find in Basil the Great or Macarius-Symeon
or Barsanuphius and John of Gaza where the responses tend to
be fairly definitive answers to specifically monastic questions.[57]
Rather, these are questions for discussion, to be handled dialectically,
with due credence to be given to the various possible positions on
the matter at hand—all in accordance with Aristotelian rules of
argumentation. The text is distinctly Aristotelian in tone and content
and may justifiably be characterized as a forerunner of scholastic
methodology.[58]

   The Christological controversies brought with them a concern for
careful definition that rivals in its minuteness and philosophical
sophistication any debate of the high scholastic period. Whether

[54] The *Eranistes* pursue a consistent methodological programme, using syllogistic
demonstration to indicate conformity of his teaching with scriptural testimony (ed.
Ettlinger, 62.29–32). For Cyril's sophisticated grasp of Aristotelian logic, and especially of the syllogism, see Marie-Odile Boulnois, *Le paradoxe trinitaire chez Cyrille
d'Alexandrie*.
[55] Theodoret himself gives an intriguing alternative title: *Knowledge of Gospel
Truth [as distinct] from Greek Philosophy*. Prologue, 16 (SC 57 103).
[56] *Quaestiones in Octateuchum* (Fernández Marcos and Sáenz-Badillos, eds.) and
Quaestiones in libros Regnorum et Paralipomenon (PG 80 528–858.).
[57] Basil's *Longer* and *Shorter Rules* (PG 31 890–1305) are composed in response to
questions. The genre is also frequent in Macarius-Symeon; see my *The Macarian
Legacy*, 48. The wisdom of the 'Great Old Man' and the 'Other Old Man' of Gaza is
preserved in their responses to 848 questions (SC 426–7, 450–1, 468).
[58] Thus Martin Grabmann, *Die Geschichte der scholastischen Methode* (vol. 1), 94.
On the genre of 'questions and responses', see Hermann Dörries, 'Eratopokriseis
(Christlich)' and Gustave Bardy, 'La littérature patristique des "Quaestiones et
Responsiones" sur l'Écriture sainte'.

this be Leontius of Byzantium on the enhypostasization of the human nature of Christ, or the anti-Chalcedonian but similarly Aristotelian John Philoponos on the composite single nature of Christ, or indeed Maximus the Confessor on the gnomic will, there is a care for terminological exactitude that can scarcely be denied the label 'scholastic'.[59]

The post-Chalcedonian period also witnesses an increasing reliance on patristic authority. Cyril's global appeal to 'the Fathers' served, naturally, to encourage the appeal to the authority of particular Fathers. Many of the decisive moments of the Christological Controversies were to hinge around the interpretation of particular patristic utterances.[60] Thus Dionysius the Areopagite's alleged reference to 'one theandric energy' provided much of the fuel for the Monoenergist position in the early seventh century.[61] The proper interpretation of this and other problematic patristic citations constitutes the entirety of Maximus the Confessor's weighty *Aporiai* (or *Ambigua*).[62] Application to such difficult patristic utterances was to be a cornerstone of the training of the medieval schoolmen, exemplified in the tradition of commenting upon the *Sentences* of Peter Lombard. Maximus was also to produce a set of responses to difficulties in scripture in his *Quaestiones ad Thalassium* and to difficulties both scriptural and patristic in his *Quaestiones et dubia*.[63] A younger contemporary of Maximus, Anastasius of Sinai, produced a set of *Questions and Responses* on an extraordinary range of spiritual and topical matters that enjoyed great popularity and a wide circulation,

---

[59] Sergius Bulgakov has no hesitation in so doing: 'Along with Boethius in the West and John of Damascus in the East, Leontius is one of the founders of scholastic theology, which seeks to surmount dogmatic difficulties through its definitions.' *Du verbe incarné*, lxiii [ET 63–4]. The definitions and controversies engaged in by Maximus are also deemed scholastic by Bulgakov. *Du verbe incarné*, lxxiv–lxxv [ET 76–7].

[60] Cyril himself famously made use of what he took to be Athanasius' (in fact Apollinarius') 'one nature of God the Word incarnate': *Against Nestorius* 2, prologue (ACO 1.1.6 p.33.6–7) and *Letters* 45 and 46 (*To Succensus*) (ACO 1.1.6 153.23; 159.9, 11–12; 160.1–2, 7–8, 19–20; 161.26–162.1). In these texts, Cyril does not introduce the phrase as an utterance of Athanasius but rather 'as the Fathers have said' or simply 'as it is said'. Patristic authority remains principally a collegiate not an individual affair for Cyril.

[61] *Letter 4: To Gaius* (ed. Ritter 161; PG 3 1072C). All extant MSS read 'new' not 'one' here.

[62] CCSG 18, 48.

[63] CCSG 7, 22; 10.

albeit often in adulterated form. Like the Pseudo-Justin, Anastasius' approach has a distinctly scholastic flavour with its probing of objections and possible solutions, its careful definitions, and appeal to authority.[64] Such works foreshadow the whole system of questions and disputations so fundamental to medieval Western scholasticism.

The appeal to patristic authority encouraged in its turn the production of patristic florilegia. This was not a new phenomenon: the digest of Origen known as the *Philokalia* serves as an early instance of the compilatory instinct.[65] The Council of Ephesus received a collection of patristic extracts from Cyril of Alexandria while the Councils of Chalcedon, Constantinople II and III, and Nicaea II also gave great (and increasing) weight to such collections.[66] From the seventh century onwards, florilegia begin to proliferate and to play a decisive role in the mediation of patristic tradition. The most substantial and earliest surviving dogmatic florilegium is the *Doctrina patrum de incarnatione verbi* of the late seventh or early eighth century: a vast collection of nearly a thousand extracts bearing largely on Christology. This was also a period that witnessed a great flourishing of *catenae*, collections of extracts from patristic commentaries on scripture. Such compilations continued to shape Byzantine theology down to and beyond the fall of the City in 1453.

The theological shift of the post-Chalcedonian period is perhaps best exemplified in the person of John of Damascus: a powerful and immediate authority for Palamas as for Aquinas. In John, the philosophical

---

[64] CCSG 59. Anastasius' *Viae Dux* (or *Hodegos*) (CCSG 8) and *In Hexaemeron anagogicarum contemplationum* (OCA 278) also display a thoroughly Aristotelian character. Georges Florovsky criticizes the *Questions and Responses* for being insufficiently rigorous and disappointingly unsystematic: 'True, St. Anastasius unmasks the spirit of petty, abstruse questioning; however, he himself looks into petty difficulties and permits perplexing questions. For the historian there are many important details in this work, especially in the explanation and application of the texts from Scripture. His references to the ancients are also very important. But the spirit of a system vanishes, coherence weakens, and attention becomes lost in a labyrinth of *aporias*.' *The Byzantine Fathers of the Sixth to Eighth Century*, 30.

[65] SC 226, 302.

[66] For an unbeatable overview of the use and production of florilegia in the Christological controversies from Ephesus to the beginnings of Iconoclasm, see Alois Grillmeier, *Christ in Christian Tradition* II.1, 51–77. For the place of florilegia at the Iconoclast and Iconophile councils of the eighth and ninth centuries, see Paul van den Ven, 'La patristique et l'hagiographie au concile de Nicée en 787'; Paul Alexander, 'Church Councils and Patristic Authority: the Iconoclastic Councils of Hiereia (754) and St. Sophia (815)'; and Daniel Sahas, *Icon and Logos: Sources in Eighth-Century Iconoclasm*.

preponderance of Aristotle within the Greek theological tradition is both complete and assured. John's work stands as an ordered and systematic compendium of the whole patristic tradition, a distillation of the wisdom of the Fathers that was to be of inestimable value to later theologians down to and including the present day. Palamas fittingly conveys John's brilliant achievement of synthesis, hailing him as the 'inspired and common tongue of the divine theologians' (*Capita* 80). Like Caesar's Gaul, John's *chef d'oeuvre*, the *Fount of Knowledge*, is divided into three parts. The first, the *Philosophical Chapters* or *Dialectic* gives a potted version of Aristotelian logic, a kind of introductory summary of the philosophical tools and terminology underpinning and facilitating Christian theology. The second part, *On Heresies*, reproduces and sup-plements earlier collections of heresies while the third part, *The Exact Exposition of the Orthodox Faith*, offers a systematic presentation of the Christian faith beginning with the incomprehensibility of the divine and proceeding to demonstrate the existence of God and his oneness. John then turns to speak of the Trinity, the creation, the incarnation, the sacraments, and many other subjects closing with the resurrection. It is the first systematic presentation of the Christian faith since Theodoret and irrefutably a forerunner of the great *Summae* of Latin scholasticism. John is also plausibly credited with the production of the vast *Sacra Parallela* or *Hiera*, a collection of biblical and patristic extracts arranged in parallel (hence the name) and ordered by topic.[67] The fact that the Damascene was steeped in the monastic traditions of the Christian East and a fine liturgical poet to boot should in no way inhibit us from characterizing his theology as scholastic and as an important forerunner of the developed scholasticism of the Latin Middle Ages.[68]

---

[67] Karl Holl (ed.), *Die Sacra Parallela des Johannes Damascenus*.

[68] A scholastic approach to theology does not rule out the liturgical, mystical, and ascetic context: indeed, at least in hands such as John's and Thomas', it assumes and requires such a context. Thomas' great *Summae* may certainly, like John's *Fount of Knowledge*, be read as a conscious inculcation into wisdom ordered upon the vision of God, and not merely as some sort of academic textbook. Such a reading is a prominent feature of the retrieval of Thomas led by Jean-Pierre Torrell (see his *Saint Thomas Aquinas: The Person and his Work*, 150–8). In John's regard, I differ from Andrew Louth who, having emphasized the original arrangement of the Damascene's work in the 'centuries' format favoured in monastic literature of the Evagrian tradition, draws the conclusion that, '*The Fountain Head of Knowledge* is not really a proto-scholastic summary, as it is often taken to be; rather, it is concerned with shaping and moulding the monastic vocation of its readers, or, more widely, with defining what it is to be a Christian, understood less as a set of beliefs (despite the high doctrinal content) than

Space does not permit examination of the many other exponents of Byzantine scholasticism that might be mentioned.[69] But it will already be apparent that the theological shift delineated in these paragraphs came very much under the aegis of Aristotle, his influence being especially felt in the philosophical underpinnings of the post-Chalcedonian Christology and in the widespread adoption of Aristotelian modes of argumentation. The very extensive tradition of Byzantine commentary on and study of the works of the Stagirite provides further testimony to his central place in the Byzantine thought-world.[70] Aristotle's displacement of Plato as the prime philosophical resource for theology was to obtain throughout the Byzantine and into the Ottoman era. To display too keen an interest in Plato could even land one in hot water. In the eleventh century, the prominent philosopher John Italos was indicted for heresy on a number of charges including his adherence to Platonic concepts such as the reality of the realm of Ideas. He had, it seems, expressed himself too freely in his responses to the questions posed by his students. While Italos was also deeply versed in Aristotle, it was his penchant for Platonic metaphysics and apparent willingness to

as a way of life.' *St John Damascene*, 37. I have no quibble with this typically limpid and acute presentation of the monastic dimension in John, but doubt the claim that this dimension necessarily precludes a 'proto-scholastic' designation. Scholasticism, too, can be a 'way of life'. Bonaventure's *Itinerarium mentis in deum* serves as a further example of the inherent compatibility of scholastic theology and a life oriented on ascetic and mystical experience.

[69] Two further examples will have to suffice: Theodore the Studite's *Logoi antirritikoi* (PG 99 328–436) and Photios of Constantinople's *Amphilochia* (Basil Laourdas and Leendert Westerink (eds.), *Photii Patriarchae Constantinopolitani Epistulae et Amphilochia*). Kallistos Ware remarks of Theodore's work, 'Few texts [. . .] could be more elaborately (not to say, tediously) syllogistic than the three *Logoi Antirritikoi* of St Theodore the Studite.' 'Scholasticism and Orthodoxy: Theological Method as a Factor in the Schism', 20 n.7. Photios' *Amphilochia* is a huge and somewhat diffuse collection of questions and responses to various difficulties in scripture.

[70] Here we may mention Photios of Constantinople, Michael Psellos, Eustratios of Nicaea, Michael of Ephesus, and Nikephoros Blemmydes. Eustratios of Nicaea (a controversial figure in his own time) was to be of particular importance for the medieval West, being used by Robert Grosseteste, Albert the Great, and Thomas Aquinas. On Aristotle in Byzantium, see Basile Tatakis, *La philosophie byzantine* (*passim*); Klaus Oehler, 'Aristotle in Byzantium' and *Antike Philosophie und byzantinisches Mittelalter*; Linos Benakis, 'Commentaries and Commentators on the Logical Works of Aristotle in Byzantium' and 'Commentaries and Commentators on the Works of Aristotle (except the Logical Ones) in Byzantium'; Charles Barber and David Todd Jenkins (eds.), *Medieval Greek Commentaries on the Nicomachean Ethics*; and Katerina Ierodiakonou, *The Byzantine Reception of Aristotle's Categories*.

subordinate theology to philosophy that attracted censure. Elements of this condemnation live on in the anathemas of the *Synodikon of Orthodoxy* still recited, at least in theory, in Orthodox churches around the globe on the first Sunday of Lent.[71] Even in this most anti-philosophical of texts, allowance is made for the pedagogical value of introductory studies in philosophy, studies that will naturally have relied largely on Aristotle. The sense that Aristotle is somehow safer as resource for theology was dramatically vindicated in the fifteenth century when George Gemistos Plethon's embrace of Plato seems to have propelled him back into paganism. By the eighteenth century, it was even possible to be condemned by Orthodox Church authorities for *not* adhering to the 'salutary philosophy' of Aristotle.[72]

In speaking of the dominance of Aristotle in the Byzantine theological tradition some caveats are necessary. Firstly, no one seriously opposed Plato and Aristotle until the very last days of the Empire: they were viewed as complementary and not as antagonistic. Furthermore, when I speak of 'Aristotle' or 'Plato' this is shorthand for a more or less Platonized Aristotelianism or Aristotelianized Platonism. Aristotle was still chiefly encountered through the neo-Platonic prism of Porphyry's *Eisagoge* while neo-Platonism itself was decisively shaped by Peripatetic principles. Eclecticism was the norm. That said, it remains possible to distinguish a preponderance of Aristotelian elements in the philosophical backdrop of Byzantine theologians. These elements consist for the most part in studies relating to logic, that is, to the initiatory stages of the classical curriculum, with less rein given to the heady pleasures of metaphysics.[73] Most importantly, the Aristotelian current in Byzantine theology remains above all a Christian Aristotelianism. For Leontius of Byzantium as for Anastasius of Sinai or John of Damascus, Aristotle is a resource to be used

---

[71] This is a text that has been much expanded and adapted over the centuries following its introduction at the time of the restoration of icons in 843. My comments are based on the standard text given in the printed editions of the Greek *Triodion*.

[72] Here I refer to the sad case of Methodios Anthrakites. See Gerhard Podskalsky, *Griechische Theologie in der Zeit der Türkenherrschaft (1453–1821)*, 312–17. See further below, pp.161–2.

[73] Aristotle's *Physics* and *Metaphysics* play very little part in the Aristotelianism of Leontius or John.

on strictly practical grounds and absolutely to be contradicted or dispensed with where disconsonant with revealed truth.[74] Palamas is heir to this long tradition of Byzantine scholasticism as much as he is heir to the earlier patristic tradition and to the whole mystical, apophatic, and monastic edifice of the Christian East. Praised for his mastery of Aristotle in his youth and instructed in logic by none other than Theodore Metochites,[75] Palamas went on to draw on that philosophical expertise in his dispute with Barlaam of Calabria, the first in a series of able critics of certain of the beliefs and practices of the Hesychast monks of Mount Athos. The dispute began not over techniques of prayer or the vision of divine light but over the correct application of Aristotle. Taking exception to the Calabrian's theological agnosticism (expressed in an anti-Latin context), Palamas asserted in unmistakably Aristotelian terms the propriety of apodictic (demonstrative) argumentation in the theological realm.[76] Palamas assuredly blasts philosophy in the most graphic terms when removed from its proper subservient status but embraces it with alacrity when rightly ordered in the service of theology.[77] Much of what Palamas has to say negatively about philosophy orbits around his sharp denigration of the fallen wisdom of the pagan Greeks and his repeated contention that the errors of his opponents, especially Barlaam, are rooted in this false philosophy.[78] It would, however, be wholly wrong

---

[74] All three are very vocal in their criticism. Leontius seldom mentions Aristotle save to criticize him; for Anastasius the Church always teaches οὐκ ἀριστοτελικῶς, ἀλλὰ θεολογικῶς, basing itself first and foremost not on philosophy but on scripture (*Viae Dux* 8.1.10–13); John of Damascus ascribes the errors of the Miaphysites to their adherence to Aristotle, taxing them with having made of him a 'thirteenth apostle' (*Contra Jacobitas* 10. Kotter IV: 113–14.12–14).

[75] The incident is preserved in Philotheos Kokkinos' *Encomium* (PG 151 559D–560A) and in Palamas' own *Against Gregoras* 1.14 (Chrestou IV: 242). See also Meyendorff, *Introduction*, 46–9.

[76] See his *Apodictic Treatises* and *Letters to Barlaam* (Chrestou I: 23–153, 225–95).

[77] For example, *Triads* 1.1.12: such pretended wisdom is actually an 'abortion of wisdom'. In another vivid image, he argues that we should use Aristotelian logic against the philosophers much as we extract venom from snakes to produce antidotes: *First Letter to Barlaam* 37 (Chrestou I: 281).

[78] Palamas consistently refers to Barlaam as 'the philosopher' and does not intend this as a compliment. His *Letters to Barlaam* (Chrestou I: 225–95) ram home time and time again the charge that Barlaam prefers the Greek philosophers over the witness of Fathers. Barlaam complains of this calumnious treatment in his own *Second Letter to Palamas* (whose own philosophical inclinations he deliberately highlights) (ed. Fyrigos, 298–368). Meyendorff fully embraces Palamas' characterization of Barlaam, accepting the premise of his primarily philosophical motivations, labelling him a

to set Palamas up as an obscurantist on this count. He is at pains to point out that this wisdom is not wisdom properly so-called. There is, Palamas explains, a natural wisdom which is a gift of God and which is implanted in the rational creation.[79] This is a wisdom which can be cultivated through application and learning, including by means of the standard classical curriculum in which Gregory himself was educated.[80] This sort of wisdom has a vital role to play in the proclamation and defence of spiritual truths manifest in scripture and witnessed in the lives of the saints. Gregory is quite frank about his own use of certain methods of Greek philosophical argumentation in this regard.[81] And in his non-polemical works such as the *Capita* he reveals an acute interest in topics of natural science. The role of philosophy must, however, Gregory cautions, always be strictly restricted to that of an ancillary. When properly subordinated in this way, philosophy is transposed and transformed by theology.[82]

In fact, it is Gregory's opponents who exhibit the anti-logical theological mentality all too commonly associated with him and his supporters. Barlaam, although no mean student of logic himself, was deeply sceptical about the possibility of any rational argumentation in relation to the divine and scornful of the Latin dependence on syllogisms.[83] Barlaam was especially dismissive of Aquinas, decrying

humanist for the quasi-autonomy he allowed the human reason, and even a nominalist (*Introduction* 43, 85, 173–5, 221 n.115). Meyendorff's pejorative use of the term 'nominalist' doubtless owes much to Gilson's relentlessly negative take on nominalism. For a more sympathetic treatment of Barlaam, see Podskalsky, *Theologie und Philosophie*, 126–50; Juan Nadal Cañellas, *La résistance d'Akindynos à Grégoire Palamas*, 4–28; Antonio Fyrigos, *Dalla controversia palamitica all polemica esicastica*; Robert Sinkewicz, 'The Doctrine of the Knowledge of God in the Early Writings of Barlaam the Calabrian'.

[79]   *Triads* 1.1.19; 2.1.25.

[80]   *Triads* 1.1.22; 3.1.37.

[81]   *Triads* 2.1.6.

[82]   Ibid. See also *Triads* 1.1.9: profane learning must be joined by love and transformed by grace. *Triads* 2.1.6: in the truly good, the not truly good becomes good.

[83]   Barlaam is probably the stricter Aristotelian here in that Aristotle had denied the possibility of apodictic demonstration of first principles. Palamas is, however, more in line with the Christian Aristotelianism outlined above in employing Aristotle in support of revealed truths—however drastically this might depart from Aristotelianism in the strict sense. The debate here revolves around some of the same issues debated by Thomas in *ST* I^a q.1 a. 8: whether theology (*sacra doctrina*) be subject to demonstration (*argumentiva*). On Barlaam's conception of theology, see Sinkewicz, 'The Doctrine of the Knowledge of God in the Early Writings of Barlaam the Calabrian'. I follow Sinkewicz in seeing only minimal direct acquaintance with

his reliance on reason and rejecting outright his use of the syllogism, most particularly the apodictic syllogism.[84] In stark contrast, Palamas not only defends the apodictic syllogism but also explicitly defends the *Latin* use of the syllogism, declaring that 'we have in truth been taught by the Fathers to syllogize about [theological matters], and no one would write even against the Latins because of this'.[85] Palamas insists on the necessity of rational discourse and will not hesitate to use the syllogism in the defence of revealed truth, after the pattern of the Fathers.[86] His radical apophaticism in no way entails an abandonment of cataphatic theology.[87] Gregory Akindynos attacks Palamas in strictly traditional terms, berating him for departing from patristic tradition (which he cites *ad nauseam*) and deploying the hoary tactic of associating the innovations of his opponent with a panoply of heresies of old.[88] His methodology is decidedly pedestrian with none of the philosophical dexterity or sophisticated text-reception of Palamas.[89] Nikephoros Gregoras, the third of our prominent anti-Palamites, displays a positive allergy to Aristotle and refuses all

Western scholasticism (including Thomas) in Barlaam's works of this period. What he knew of Thomas was, Sinkewicz suggests, largely restricted to material supplied by his Latin interlocutors. See below, p.67 n. 18.

[84] See his *Opere contro i Latini* (ed. Fyrigos), B, V, 21.266–73; B, V, 30.382–92; *Legatus* 164–7; A, IV, 21.183–204. A, IV, 8–11, 58–104 has some especially choice invective against Thomas, speaking of his ravings, fantasies, and demonic inspiration.

[85] *First Letter to Akindynos* 8 (Chrestou I: 211.3–5). Palamas finds patristic support for the syllogism, as employed by the Latins, in Basil the Great and Euthymios Zigabenos. This is one of the very few occasions on which Palamas gives any hint of an acquaintance with contemporary Latin theology. The context here is the aftermath of the debates between Barlaam and the papal legates Richard of England and Francesco da Camerino sent to Constantinople to negotiate reunion in 1334. Barlaam's subsequent defeat by Palamas in the Hesychast controversy did not stop his anti-logical take on Latin Christianity gaining the ascendancy in the Orthodox world over and against Gregory's more benign estimation of the virtues of Latin scholasticism.

[86] See, for example, *First Letter to Akindynos* 9 (Chrestou I: 212–13).

[87] 'Apophatic theology does not oppose or do way with cataphatic theology but rather demonstrates that cataphatic statements about God are made in a true and orthodox manner, and that God does not possess these things as we do' (*Capita* 123).

[88] Meyendorff presents Akindynos as a proponent of a 'medieval byzantine scholasticism', content simply to repeat the formulae of the past. While he recognizes Akindynos' patristic conservatism and attachment to Hesychast spirituality, he does not baulk (notwithstanding the almost total lack of supporting evidence) to tar him with the brushes of humanism, nominalism, and even (confusingly) realism (*Introduction*, 85–6).

[89] For an extremely sympathetic estimation of Akindynos, see Juan Nadal Cañellas, *La résistance d'Akindynos à Grégoire Palamas*. Cañellas does a great a service in highlighting the existence of a learned monastic culture in Byzantium, the Hesychast credentials of Akindynos, his reluctant entry into the controversy, and his strictly

utility to the syllogism, seeing it as tool fit only for feeble minds, such as those of the Latins.[90] There is indeed a certain irony in the fact that the chief legacy of the anti-Palamites is precisely the anti-rational obscurantism that Podsklasky deems the defining characteristic of Palamism. In the hands of Palamas' opponents this theological obscurantism was to take on an increasingly anti-Latin character.

Reason and philosophy have an integral place in Palamas' methodology, albeit strictly in the service of the revelation of God manifested in scripture and in the lives and teaching of the saints. In appealing to the tradition, Palamas does not simply pile up patristic citations but demonstrates a capacity to sift, deploy, critique, and expand upon his sources that show him to be a thinker both creative and properly original, much in the same way that I have characterized Aquinas.[91] Palamas' approach to theological argumentation may be considerably

patristic mode of argumentation. But his presentation of Palamas is woefully distorted—even more so than Meyendorff's own overly negative presentation of Akindynos, to which this book is a conscious counterblast. Cañellas develops (91–4, 172–7) a frankly bizarre thesis as to the Messalian/Macarian roots of Palamite 'neo-Hesychasm' that seems innocent of any knowledge of developments in Macarian studies since Louis Villecourt and Irénée Hausherr. There is no awareness that Villecourt's thesis of 1920 as to the straightforwardly Messalian character of the Macarian writings has been shattered in recent scholarship (see Columba Stewart, *Working the Earth of the Heart*; Klaus Fitschen, *Messalianismus und Antimessalianismus*; and also my own *The Macarian Legacy*). Particularly troubling is his perpetuation of Hausherr's horrendously simplistic distinction made in 1935 between the intellectualist (Evagrian) and affective (Macarian) 'grands courants' of Eastern spirituality, a distinction Cañellas extends to explain the opposition between (Evagrian) humanists and (Macarian) Palamites in the fourteenth century. This is precisely the schema with which Meyendorff himself had worked: Cañellas has simply reversed the heroes of this particular dichotomy, producing a book that is a mirror image of Meyendorff. For a critique of this schema in Hausherr and Meyendorff, see my *The Macarian Legacy*, Chapter 4. Cañellas goes on (315–19) to treat the *Imiaslavie* heresy of the early twentieth century as a natural outworking of the mystical and antirational theology of Palamas, demonstrating here his absolute allegiance to the false methodological dichotomy of Lossky, Podskalsky, et al.

[90] See Katerina Ierodiakonou, 'The Anti-Logical Movement in the Fourteenth Century', 221–4. Such sentiments did not, of course, save him from the recurring charge of being motivated by profane learning in his opposition to Palamas (see Philotheos Kokkinos, *Antirrhetikos IV against Nikephoras Gregoras* (PG 151 827D–828A, cited programmatically by Podskalsky in his *Theologie und Philosophie*, 1). That said, Palamas also attacks Gregoras for his illogical and ineffective use of the syllogism. *Against Gregoras* 16–17 (Chrestou IV: 349).

[91] We have already discussed at length his critical but sympathetic use of Augustine and noted his sense of historical context when reading Cyril of Alexandria (above, n.28). To these we may add his dextrous handling of the differences between Macarius-Symeon, Gregory of Nyssa, and others in the matter of the physical locus of the intellect

less structured, limpid and implacably rigorous than that of Aquinas, more *ad hoc* and often *ad hominem*, but there is no absolute methodological impasse between them. In terms of the use of reason and the appeal to patristic authority there is precious little to separate them. In overall tone, strategies, and conclusions they are very different, to be sure, but the fundamental methodological presuppositions are not. Given that both are heirs to the long tradition of Byzantine scholasticism, things could hardly be otherwise.

None of this is intended to undermine Palamas' deserved reputation as an apophatic and experiential theologian but rather to emphasize that this picture does not tell the whole story. The fact that he was a monastic theologian in no way precluded his embrace of the methods and presuppositions of Byzantine scholasticism. Indeed it is one of his chief glories that he recapitulates so much of the Eastern Christian tradition: Macarius and Evagrius, Dionysius and Maximus, Athonite Hesychasm and Aristotelian scholasticism. This section has attempted to sketch Palamas' roots in this long tradition of Christian Aristotelianism and his own disciplined use of reason and logic to bolster his appeal to scriptural and patristic authority. In this respect, there is something distinctly scholastic about him too. Less has been said about the other, more familiar, aspects of his make-up. To conclude, there is no sense in which in his theology may justifiably be characterized as a defeat of reason (*pace* Podskalsky), or as the triumph of an anti-scholastic mystical theology (*pace* Lossky et al.), or even as anti-Latin. It is this scholastic current in Palamas and his own positive but duly critical disposition towards Latin theology that was to pave the way for the sympathetic reception of Thomas by a surprising number of Palamites.

Having cast some doubt on the suggestion that Palamite theology represents some sort of antithesis to the scholasticism of the Latin West, I turn now briefly to the attitude of Palamas and his circle to the Latin–Greek schism. Here again we shall see that it is not Palamas but rather his opponents that exhibit most open hostility to the Latin West.

(head, heart, or without bodily locus): *Triads* 2.2.2 (cf. *Triads* 1.2.3 and the *Tomos of the Holy Mountain* 3 (Chrestou II: 572)).

2.3. PALAMAS AND THE LATIN–GREEK SCHISM

Few slurs in Byzantium were more deadly than the charge of being *Latinophrone* (Latin-minded).[92] Memories of the atrocities of the Fourth Crusade and, still more, the forced policy of reunion pursued by Michael VIII Palaiologos remained vivid and unhealed. To be in theological sympathy with the Latins could be seen as tantamount to treason, a betrayal both political and cultural of the embattled Empire. But while charges of Latin-mindedness and Latin sympathies were certainly thrown around with some abandon in the course of the Hesychast Controversy, the dispute was never a question of East *versus* West, but rather an internal dispute conducted largely within the traditional parameters of Byzantine theology.

Barlaam first found fame on the Orthodox side of the Constantinopolitan debates of 1334 opposing the papal legates Richard of England and Francesco da Camerino. He showed himself to be an implacable opponent of the papal claims, the *filioque*, and Latin theological methodology in general. As we have seen, he reserved especially harsh criticism for the Latin use of the syllogism exemplified by Aquinas.[93] Akindynos, for his part, betrays no sympathy with or indeed much interest in the contemporary Latin West, of which he appears to knows little.[94] Gregoras, by contrast, was actively and implacably hostile throughout his career, making a mark alongside Barlaam in 1334 with his denunciation of Aristotelian reasoning directed against the same papal legates. For Gregoras, logic has no place in the higher realms of theology and represents a departure from strictly patristic theology. Any debate with the Latins, even within the setting of an ecumenical council, was bound to be futile given their persistent heresy and pernicious reasoning.

---

[92] The charge goes back to the days of Michael VIII Palaiologos and his Patriarch John Bekkos. Barlaam is the chief victim of this particular slur in the fourteenth century, suffering it even at the hands of anti-Palamites: see, for example, Gregoras *Historia Romana* (ed. Bekker and Schopen II: 905.19–20). Palamas uses it of Bekkos and his ilk in respect of the *filioque*, but not (so far as I have seen) otherwise (*Against Bekkos* 1, 9, 10, 11 (Chrestou I: 163.3, 170.9, 172.16, 174.9)). For Barlaam he coins the term 'Latinohellene', targeting here his Italian origins and penchant for pagan philosophy rather than any sympathy with Latin theology as such (*Triads* 3.3.10, 16).

[93] See above, n.84.

[94] He does, however, know something of the Latin Fathers, citing Augustine by name and great reverence ('the wise and wonderful Augustine'). *Refutation of Two Works of Gregory Palamas* II.9 (ed. Cañellas, 96).

Gregoras' intervention was, by his own account, sufficient to scupper this particular scheme of reunion.[95] Palamas displays no such animosity. While he attacked certain of their theological conclusions, he maintained noticeably friendly relations with the Latins. During his captivity in the Blachernae palace, he fostered contacts with the Latins of Galata in Pera and sent his works to the Grand Master of the Knights Hospitaller of Rhodes and to other Latins on that island—facts that Akindynos turns against him.[96] Such sympathy could be dangerous given the prevailing atmosphere of antipathy towards the Latins. This general antipathy may well have encouraged Palamas to be discreet about his own use of Augustine.[97] Palamas and his supporters (notably Patriarch Philotheos Kokkinos) consistently supported John Kantakuzene in his various overtures to the West and, in particular, his repeated calls for an ecumenical council to settle the doctrinal disputes between Constantinople and Rome.[98] Palamas himself had no sense that his teaching was in any way contradictory to the theology of the Latin West, holding it to be simply a development of patristic teaching.[99] Only in the debate of 1355 between Gregoras and Palamas at the imperial palace before John V and the papal legate, Paul of Smyrna, does any sense of East–West tension become apparent, and this not in Palamas' attitude but in that of the legate.[100] Paul was to remain convinced that Palamite theology is inconsistent

---

[95] See his *Historia Romana* (ed. Bekker and Schopen I: 507–8).

[96] *Ep.* 44 to Gregoras (ed. Hero, 192.70–4).

[97] The fact that Augustine was not seen as an unimpeachable authority for some Byzantines (by reason of his association with the *filioque*) may have militated against any explicit appeal to him.

[98] John called for an ecumenical council in 1350 (as Emperor) and 1367 (on behalf of his nephew, John V). See Donald Nicol, 'Byzantine Requests for an Oecumenical Council in the Fourteenth Century'; Meyendorff, 'Projets de concile oecuménique en 1367: Un dialogue inédit entre Jean Cantacuzène et le légat Paul'. Barlaam, to give him credit, had also suggested to Pope Benedict XII that an ecumenical council was the only way to gain general accord to reunion among the Greeks (*Oratio pro unione*. PG 151 1331–42).

[99] At the Constantinopolitan council of 1351, Palamas described his teaching as a 'development' (ἀνάπτυξις) of the teachings of the Sixth Ecumenical Council on the two energies of Christ. *Synodal Tome* (PG 151 722B). See Meyendorff, *Introduction à l'étude de Grégoire Palamas*, 142.

[100] See Meyendorff, *Introduction*, 164–6 and Candal 'Fuentes Palamíticas: Dialogo de Jorge Facrasi sobre el contradictorio de Palamas con Niceforo Gregoras'. A letter purporting to be Paul's unfavourable report to Urban V is given in Migne (PG 154 835–8). Meyendorff believes there is good reason to doubt its authenticity (ibid., 166 n.54).

with the teachings of Rome, notwithstanding Palamas' own irenic stance vis-à-vis the Latins and the best efforts of John Kantakuzene to persuade him otherwise.[101]

2.4. *CODA:* PALAMAS AND AQUINAS

I do not intend to pursue any detailed comparison of Palamas and Aquinas, being content to fall back on the medieval maxim, *non sunt adversi sed diversi*.[102] While comparisons between the two are not profitless, they are inevitably somewhat abstract, not least due to the basic fact that neither knew the other's works. Such comparisons also invariably work within the framework of some sort of East–West dichotomy, supposing the two to be the twin peaks of their respective traditions and drawing their various conclusions within this framework.[103] It has, rather, been the burden of this opening 'exercise in multiple perspective' to suggest that Palamas is not as 'Eastern', nor Aquinas as 'Western', as has previously been generally supposed. Each has substantial interests in the other's tradition, shares a complementary approach to theological endeavour, and displays an unusually irenic attitude to the Latin–Greek schism. In each case they stand out among their contemporaries for the breadth, depth, and openness of their theological vision. The implications of these conclusions will, I trust, become clear as we embark upon a detailed study of the Orthodox reception of Aquinas.

---

[101] Meyendorff, *Introduction*, 166, rightly notes that Paul's opinion was not to become papal policy: Palamism was not seen as a bone of contention at the reunion council of Ferrara–Florence. The correspondence between John Cantacuzene and Paul of Smyrna is now edited: Edmond Voordeckers and Franz Tinnefeld, *Iohannis Cantacuzeni. Refutationes duae prochori cydonii et disputatio cum Paulo Patriarcha Latino epistulis septem tradita* (CCSG 16).

[102] 'Not adverse but diverse'. This is not to be read as a species of relativism but as an affirmation that these are different ways of approaching and articulating the same reality. On the maxim, see Joseph de Ghellinck, *Le mouvement théologique du XIIe siècle*, 517–23 and Henri de Lubac, 'À propos de la formule: "diversi, sed non adversi"'.

[103] Here we may think of Anna Williams' *Ground of Union: Deification in Aquinas and Palamas* or Édouard Divry's, *La transfiguration selon l'orient et l'occident: Grégoire Palamas, Thomas d'Aquin: vers un dénouement oecuménique*. In his *Le créé et l'incréé. Maxime le confesseur et Thomas d'Aquin: aux sources de la querelle palamienne*, Antoine Lévy takes the wise course of approaching Aquinas and Palamas not by way of comparison but by means of a common source: Maximus the Confessor.

Part II

Byzantine Readings of Aquinas

3

The First Phase

3.1. DEMETRIOS KYDONES (c.1324/5–1397/8)

Demetrios Kydones was a man of great parts. One contemporary hailed him as supreme in wisdom, a paradigm of virtue, the celebrated right-hand of emperors, one who rendered the tongue of Aeneas into that of the Achaeans. Another lauded him as a pinnacle of wisdom, a supreme rhetor, an unusually exact translator from the language of the Romans into that of the Greeks, and a fine exponent of humility and chastity. There is, of course, more than a tincture of hyperbole in both estimations, but what is more interesting is the source of the praises. The first is Manuel Kalekas, a disciple who was to the follow his master into communion with Old Rome and even to join the Dominican Order.[1] The second is Joseph Bryennios, an eminent Byzantine scholar and scholastic theologian implacably and vociferously opposed to union with the Latins.[2] Demetrios' ability to inspire such praise in such different figures is a fitting testament to the broadness of his vision and the scope of his achievement.

---

[1] Manuel's praise is couched in the form of an epitaph. The text is given and discussed in Giovanni Mercati, *Notizie di Procoro e Demetrio Cidone, Manuela Caleca e Theodore Meliteniota ed altri appunti per la storia della teologia e della letteratura bizantina del secolo XIV*, 109–11.

[2] Joseph Bryennios expresses his sentiments in his Letter 4, 'To the most wise of men, Demetrios Kydones' (ed. Tomadakes 292.47–52). The letter puts Kydones in Venice, in which city he had extended sojourns in 1370–1, 1390–1, and 1396. One of the latter two dates must be preferred in view of the established friendship assumed and Bryennios' age (b. c.1350). Bryennios does not, of course, miss the chance to encourage Demetrios to return to the Orthodox fold.

Demetrios served as chief minister ($\mu\epsilon\sigma\acute{a}\zeta\omega\nu$) to three emperors:
John VI Kantakuzene, John V Palaiologos, and Manuel II Palaiologos:
a quite unprecedented record.[3] His consistent policy in office was to
minimize accommodation with the Ottoman Turks and instead to
seek help and support from the Latin West to shore up the embattled
empire.[4] His interest in Aquinas came as a direct consequence of his
political and diplomatic activities.[5] Demetrios recounts the story in
an elaborate *Apology*.[6] Growing dissatisfied with the need to rely
on official interpreters of uncertain ability in his negotiations with
Westerners, he took it on himself to learn Latin. He engaged as
teacher a Dominican from Pera, the Genoese colony across the
Golden Horn from Constantinople proper, installing him in the
palace and devoting the small hours to his studies.[7] Having achieved
a measure of fluency, he was given to study Thomas' *Summa contra
gentiles*, just as one might give a student in Greek Homer or Hesiod

---

[3] The function of the $\mu\epsilon\sigma\acute{a}\zeta\omega\nu$ (literally the 'intermediary' between the emperor and
his subjects and diplomatic partners) was somewhat fluid, depending on the wishes of
the emperor of the time. See Raymond-Joseph Loenertz, 'Le chancelier impérial à
Byzance au XIVe et au XIIIe siècle'.

[4] On Demetrios' life and times, see *PLP* 13876; Raymond-Joseph Loenertz, 'Démé-
trius Cydonès I: de la naissance à l'année 1373' and 'Démétrius Cydonès II: de 1373 à
1375'; Frances Kianka, 'The Apology of Demetrius Cydones: A Fourteenth-Century
Autobiographical Source', 'Byzantine-Papal Diplomacy: The Role of Demetrius
Cydones', and 'Demetrius Cydones: Intellectual and Diplomatic Relations between
Byzantium and the West'; Franz Tinnefeld, *Demetrios Kydones: Briefe* I.1 4–62 and
Judith Ryder, *The Career and Writings of Demetrius Kydones*.

[5] Sources on Demetrios' engagement with Aquinas are very numerous. See, for
example: Michael Rackl, 'Demetrius Kydones als Verteidiger und Übersetzer des
heiligen Thomas von Aquin', 'Die ungedruckte Verteidigungsschrift des Demetrios
Kydones für Thomas von Aquin gegen Neilos Kabasilas', and 'Thomas von Aquin im
Werturteil eines byzantinische Theologen'; Martin Jugie, 'Démétrius Cydonès et la
théologie latine a Byzance'; Stylianos Papadopoulos, $'E\lambda\lambda\eta\nu\iota\kappa\alpha\grave{\iota}$ $\mu\epsilon\tau\alpha\phi\rho\acute{a}\sigma\epsilon\iota\varsigma$
$\theta\omega\mu\iota\sigma\tau\iota\kappa\tilde{\omega}\nu$ $\check{\epsilon}\rho\gamma\omega\nu$. $\Phi\iota\lambda o\theta\omega\mu\iota\sigma\tau\alpha\grave{\iota}$ $\kappa\alpha\grave{\iota}$ $\grave{a}\nu\tau\iota\theta\omega\mu\iota\sigma\tau\alpha\grave{\iota}$ $\grave{\epsilon}\nu$ $B\upsilon\zeta\alpha\nu\tau\acute{\iota}\omega$; Thomas Tyn,'Prochoros und Demetrios Kydones: der byzantinische Thomismus des XIV Jahrhun-
derts'; Frances Kianka, 'Demetrius Cydones and Thomas Aquinas'; Norman Russell,
'Palamism and the Circle of Demetrius Cydones'.

[6] *Apology* I (*Ai Greci Ortodossi*). Giovanni Mercati (ed.), *Notizie di Procoro e
Demetrio Cidone, Manuela Caleca e Theodore Meliteniota ed altri appunti per la
storia della teologia e della letteratura bizantina del secolo XIV*, 359–403. The *Apology*
is, predictably, somewhat self-serving and disingenuous. Many of the same themes are
also taken up in *Apology* II (*Difesa della propria sincerità*: ibid., 403–25) and *Apology*
III (*Il testamento religioso*: ibid., 425–35).

[7] This tutor is sometimes identified as Philip de Bindo Incontri. See Raymond-
Joseph Loenertz, 'Fr Philippe de Bindo Incontri, O.P. du convent de Pera, Inquisiteur
en Orient'. Demetrios refers to the Domincans as the 'Society of Thomas'. *Apology*
I 364.34.

for his delectation. Demetrios was hooked: 'Having tasted of the lotus, I could restrain myself no longer, but immersed myself utterly in the Latin language.'[8] In short order, the translation of the *Summa contra gentiles* was complete and Aquinas transposed into the tongue of the Achaeans.[9]

This was the first full translation into Greek of a major work of Aquinas, but certainly not the first time his voice had sounded in the Eastern Empire.[10] For all its hideously shameful origins, the Latin occupation of Constantinople from 1204 was to open a cross-cultural conduit that was never to be closed. From then on, the Byzantines could no longer entertain even an illusion of splendid isolation from the barbarous West. Through the many diplomatic and theological exchanges of the period, and especially through the prominent Dominican presence in the City, Thomas' reputation and teachings had begun to percolate into Byzantium well before Demetrios' first translations.[11]

The Dominicans were first established in Constantinople before 1233 and soon began to make their presence felt in the Latin-occupied

---

[8] *Apology* I, 361–3.

[9] The colophon to MS *Vaticanus graecus* 616 expresses Demetrios' excusable sense of accomplishment: 'Finito libro sit laus et gloria Chr[ist]o. Istum librum transtulit de latino in grecu[m] demetrius de thesalonicha, servus Ihe[s]u Ch[rist]i; laboravit aut[em] tr[an]sfere[n]do p[er] unu[m] annum et fuit [com]pletus anno mccclv, indictione octava, xxiiii me[n]sis decebris, ora post meridium t[er]tia.' The MS itself was the work of an assistant, Manuel Tzykandyles, but this colophon appears to be an autograph of Demetrios. It is reproduced in Alexander Turyn, *Codices Graeci Vaticani saeculis XIII et XIV scripti annorumque notis instructi*, 197. Use of the *Anno Domini* dating system was unusual in Byzantium, which maintained the *Annus mundi* system of reckoning. Demetrios gives 1355 for what we know as 1354 since all Byzantine years, however reckoned, began on 1 September. The translation was completed at the monastery of St George of the Mangana, the same monastery to which his patron John VI Kantakuzene had retired on 10 December 1354, taking the monastic name Joasaph.

[10] There is precious little evidence to support the contention of the eighteenth-century Dominican historians Jacques Echard and Bernard de Rubeis that Maximos Planoudes had translated the *Summa theologiae*. Edmond Bouvy rejects this contention while allowing (without further explanation) that he may have translated the first 49 questions of the *Prima pars*. 'Saint Thomas: Ses traducteurs byzantins', 403 n.1.

[11] On the Dominican establishments and activities in Constantinople, see Raymond-Joseph Loenertz, 'Les établissements dominicains de Péra-Constantinople'; Marie-Hélène Congourdeau, 'Notes sur les Dominicains de Constantinople au début du 14 siècle'; and Claudine Delacroix-Besnier, *Les dominicains et la chrétienté grecque aux XIVe et XVe siècles*.

city. A significant piece of anti-Greek polemic dates from this period: the *Tractatus contra graecos* of 1252.[12] It is unclear whether the foundation survived the Byzantine *reconquista* of 1261—much depends on whether it was in Pera (where it might have been protected by prior arrangement with the Genoese) or the City proper. The latter seems by far the most likely option.[13] The Dominican William Bernard de Gaillac is known to have acquired a house in Constantinople itself in 1299, which remained open until 1307 when it was closed at the instigation of the fiercely anti-Latin Patriarch Athanasios.[14] At that point, the friars removed to Pera which was then under Genoese control. By this time, Thomas had become an indispensable part of the Dominican armoury in discussion with the Greeks. The *Tractatus contra graecos* of 1252 was also reworked in 1305 so as to incorporate arguments from Thomas' *Summa theologiae*.[15] De Gaillac made use of his time to learn Greek, to translate extracts from Thomas, and to engage in anti-Greek polemic. Several other Constantinopolitan Dominicans indulged in polemic, among whom are Simon of Constantinople and Philip de Bindo Incontri, both authors of treatises on the procession of the Holy Spirit.[16] The treatises and activities of the Dominicans of Pera generated discussion and rebuttals by figures such as Manuel Moschopoulos from the early years of the fourteenth

[12] See Antoine Dondaine, '*Contra Graecos*. Premiers écrits polémiques des Dominicains d'Orient'. Dondaine establishes that the ascription to Bartholomew of Constantinople represents a later working of the text. See also Raymond-Joseph Loenertz, 'Autour du traité de fr. Barthélemy de Constantinople contre les Grecs'. The treatise (a version of which is given in PG 140 487–574) contains long extracts from Hugh Etherian's *De sancto et immortali Deo*. Thomas' own *Contra errores graecorum* is based in part on materials produced by his confrères in Constantinople.

[13] See Raymond-Joseph Loenertz, 'Les établissements dominicains de Péra-Constantinople', 334–5.

[14] Donald Nicol memorably describes Athanasios as a kind of Byzantine John Knox 'who expected everyone to live up to his own high standards of unhappiness' and celebrates the irony that his relics are now housed in the Church of San Zaccaria in Venice and much venerated as a symbol of Christian unity. *Church and Society in the Last Centuries of Byzantium*, 12, 29–30.

[15] See Dondaine, '*Contra Graecos*. Premiers écrits polémiques des Dominicains d'Orient', 326–7.

[16] See Marie-Hélène Congourdeau, 'Frère Simon le Constantinopolitain OP (1235?–1325?)'; Antoine Dondaine, '*Contra Graecos*. Premiers écrits polémiques des Dominicains d'Orient', 405–6; Raymond-Joseph Loenertz, 'Fr Philippe de Bindo Incontri, O.P. du convent de Pera, Inquisiteur en Orient'. Simon was a survivor of the original Constantinopolitan house who had taken refuge on Venetian Euboea in the interim.

century onwards.[17] The discussions initiated in 1334 by the arrival in Constantinople of two Dominican papal representatives, Richard of England and Francesco da Camerino, generated a furious response from Barlaam the Calabrian that included a direct critique of Aquinas. Thomas became archetypal for Barlaam as a proponent of a form of theology that is insufficiently scriptural, non-patristic, and inadmissibly syllogistic.[18]

But while Thomas was known to some extent in Byzantium prior to 1354, none of this compares to Demetrios' work in impact or importance. Demetrios' was the first complete translation and the work not of a despised foreigner but of one of the Empire's finest scholars and foremost statesmen. Demetrios was able to gain the support and patronage of John VI for his endeavours, the emperor predicting that the translations would avail much to the good of the Greek commonwealth and having copies made at his own expense.[19] This imperial support, coupled with the extreme interest the translations generated, helps explain the sheer profusion of extant manuscripts.[20] Allowing for some exaggeration, it was not wholly

---

[17] Moschopoulos very likely composed his anti-Latin treatise in response to the activities and arguments of the Dominicans of Pera, in particular the treatise of Simon of Constantinople. See Ioannis Polemis, 'An Unpublished Anti-Latin Treatise of Manuel Moschopoulos'. Polemis concludes that 'Moschopoulos is probably the first Byzantine author who came into contact with the theology of scholasticism, and more particularly of Thomas Aquinas, and tried to refute it'. Ibid., 254.

[18] It seems likely that Barlaam had no great acquaintance with Thomas but was relying rather on the material supplied by his interlocutors. Here I depend on the estimation of Robert Sinkewicz, 'The Doctrine of the Knowledge of God in the Early Writings of Barlaam the Calabrian', 195 n.56: 'A careful reading of the *Antilatin Treatises* leaves little doubt that Barlaam's acquaintance with the works and the theology of Thomas Aquinas was minimal and restricted entirely to what was provided to him by his Latin (and Dominican) opponents.'

[19] *Apology* I, 363.22–3, 364.48–52. John Meyendorff sagely affirms that with figures such as the emperor, Neilos Kabasilas, and Gennadios Scholarios, the Byzantines 'pouvaient parler aux Latins avec infiniment plus d'information sur la pensée de leurs interlocuteurs que les Latins n'en possédait sur la pensée grecque. He goes on to argue that this theological rapprochement might have produced a result had circumstances been otherwise and had the days of the Empire not been numbered. 'Projets de concile oecuménique en 1367: un dialogue inédit entre Jean Cantacuzène et le légat Paul', 163.

[20] Several dozen MSS of his translations survive. One intriguing example (MS *Vaticanus graecus* 613) is in Ottoman style and belonged at one time to Sultan Mehmet II the Conqueror: a striking sign of the translation's reach. See Julian Raby, 'Mehmed the Conqueror's Greek Scriptorium'. Thanks to Garth Fowden for this reference.

implausible for Demetrios to claim that, by the 1360s, 'Everyone today knows Thomas for the wealth of his writings, the loftiness of his thought, and the rigour of his syllogisms.'[21]

Making the riches of Latin learning available in Greek became a passionate vocation for Demetrios. Like many of his compatriots, he had not expected much from the Latins who were generally to be encountered as merchants and seamen. But through his study of Thomas, it had become clear to him that the Latins too had people of the highest intellectual attainments.[22] He pours scorn on the apparently common assumption of Roman superiority, especially the enduring belief that the world is divided between Greeks and barbarians, that is, between the Romans and the rest. In this scenario, the Romans are the heirs of Plato and Aristotle and the Latins barely recognizable as human, fit only for menial activities such as inn-keeping.[23] He acknowledges the estrangement and mutual ignorance that has built up between Romans and Latins over time.[24] His translations are clearly intended to stand in the breach. The great virtue of Latin writers, for Demetrios, is the enticing exactness of their arguments and their expert use of classical philosophy: 'these are men who have by great labour plunged themselves into the intricacies of Plato and Aristotle which our own had never yet wrestled with'.[25]

Demetrios believes that it is principally language that divides East and West.[26] Turning away from contemporary disagreements to the witness of the ancient Fathers of East and West he finds that they are in complete harmony, formed by and founded upon the same scripture and guided by the same Spirit.[27] He decries those who reject

---

[21] *Apology* I, 362.2–4. It is thanks to Demetrios' efforts that Thomas merits an entry in the *Prosopographischen Lexikon der Palaiologenzeit*: PLP 7795.

[22] *Apology* I, 364.37–41.

[23] *Apology* I, 365.77–84.

[24] *Apology* I, 365.86–366.87. A little later (*Apology* I, 386.51–2) he estimates the gap between the two nations to have existed for nearly 500 years, thus pointing to the Photian era as the origin of the schism.

[25] *Apology* I, 366.88–9, 95–6. Note the emphasis on demonstrative theological method: ἡ γὰρ τῶν ἀποδείξεων ἀκρίβεια. This runs precisely counter to Barlaam's objections to Latin scholastic methodology and tallies much more closely with Palamas' embrace of the apodictic method.

[26] This was view shared by some anti-unionists, for example Metropolitan Anthimos of Athens (later of Crete) (d. c.1370). See his treatise on the Holy Spirit edited by Konstantinos Dyobuniotes, «᾽Ανθίμου Ἀθηνῶν λόγος ἀνέκδοτος περὶ τῶν τοῦἉγίου Πνεύματος προόδων».

[27] *Apology* I, 367.46–368.51.

this harmonious testimony, rejecting the Latin Fathers and accepting only that of those who hail from the East. Such men are guilty not only of absurdity but also of blasphemy, falling ultimately into the errors of Arius and Sabellius.[28] This is a theme he returns to after a long discussion of primacy and of the various merits of New and Old Rome, condemning those who follow 'Athanasius, Basil, Gregory, John, and Cyril' but refuse to pay heed to the teachings of Fathers long venerated liturgically by the Church, 'Hilary, Jerome, Ambrose, Augustine, Leo, and Gregory', purely on the grounds of language.[29] Such a contumely attitude is to make of an accident of geography a theological divide ('as far as the East is from the West') that simply is not there.[30] Those who campaign now against Latin theology should be prepared, says Demetrios, to reject these Fathers outright and give up any pretence of honouring them.[31] This absurd conflation of geography and theology, he writes, represents a manifest betrayal of the truth, truth being the property neither of Asia nor of Europe.[32] Demetrios is certainly aware of a tendency to make the geographical West into a theological category but he resists any such notion with all the forces at his disposal.

In his Letter 333, Kydones expands on his reasons for admiring Thomas.[33] Writing to Maximos Chrysoberges, he praises his dedication to 'the blessed Thomas', 'for the treasury of divine ideas in this man is really great, and you would not find any difficult question in the dogmas of the faith which he in his treatises does not either investigate in itself or demonstrate in his other questions and answers'. Demetrios singles out the sheer discipline and limpidity of Thomas' theological method as his most characteristic feature: 'he presents the arguments opposed to the question as if they were spoken by opponents. After resolving these arguments in no ordinary way, but so that they have no effectiveness left, he then binds fast the

---

[28] *Apology* I, 368.62–79. Kydones faithfully follows Aquinas in seeing the *filioque* as an essential guard against both Arianism and Sabellianism. He also composed a separate treatise in defence of the Latin Fathers, on which see Frances Kianka, 'A Late Byzantine Defence of the Latin Church Fathers'.

[29] *Apology* I, 382.35–40, citing Psalm 102(3):12.

[30] *Apology* I, 383.53–7.

[31] *Apology* I, 383.61–70.

[32] *Apology* I, 399.83.

[33] Loenertz II: 266–8. Here I use the English translation of Frances Kianka, 'Demetrius Cydones and Thomas Aquinas', 285.

object of enquiry with proofs from all sides, using evidence from scripture, which takes precedence in all his works, and also using proofs from reasoning and from philosophy, in order that thus we might abound in strong proofs of the faith.' In his *Defence of Thomas Aquinas against Neilos Kabasilas* he pithily sums up the virtues of 'the blessed Thomas' as 'wisdom, exactitude, and holiness'.[34] All this at a time when Thomas' authority in the West was still far from fully assured.[35]

In his enthusiastic embrace of Thomas, Demetrios was not welcoming in an alien culture to which he felt inferior; indeed he expressly denies any such sentiment.[36] Rather, he embraces Thomas as, essentially, 'one of us'. Aquinas represents for Kydones the undivided faith of the Church: founded upon the common scriptures, proclaimed in the united witness of the patristic tradition, and expressed according to the best traditions of Greek philosophy.[37] This sense of affinity is in large measure a sign of Aquinas' own continuity with Eastern scholasticism and rootedness in the Greek patristic tradition. His mastery of Plato and Aristotle set the seal on what was really a kind of homecoming. He was, in effect, ushered into Byzantium as an honorary Hellene and a true Roman, bringing to the City, in the words of the Divine Liturgy, 'thine own of thine own'.

For all that he had 'tasted of the lotus', Demetrios did not forget his homeland and conceived his task of translation as a means towards the healing of the schism—and, as a consequence, the assurance of substantial military aid. He shows a rare perspicacity in treating the schism not at the level of doctrinal disputes but rather as the result of a long process of cultural and linguistic estrangement. Here he

---

[34] The *Defence* is as yet unedited. This extract is given from *Vaticanus graecus* 1103 and 614 by Michael Rackl, 'Die griechische Übersetzung der Summa Theologiae des hl. Thomas von Aquin', 49–50. Rackl gives substantial extracts in 'Die ungedruckte Verteidigungsschrift des Demetrios Kydones für Thomas von Aquin gegen Neilos Kabasilas' and 'Der hl. Thomas von Aquin und das trinitarische Grundgesetz in byzantinische Beleuchtung', the latter also giving a summary version in German. Podskalsky gives his own précis in *Theologie und Philosophie*, 196–204. In Podskalsky's account (204), Demetrios and Neilos are presented as types of the opposing theological methodologies of East and West.

[35] See further below, pp.137–8.

[36] *Apology* I, 384.71–4.

[37] Hans-Georg Beck expresses this perfectly by affirming that Demetrios, in his polemic with Neilos Kabasilas, stood for 'die alte Orthodoxie in neuem Gewande'. 'Der Kampf um der thomistischen Theologiebegriff in Byzanz', 17.

anticipates the judgement of many a learned later commentator: Yves Congar's 'progressive estrangement', Paul Lemerle's 'collapse of a primitive Christian universalism', and Georges Florovsky's 'process of the Christian disintegration'.[38] The schism is rightly to be seen as a process, not an event.

Demetrios was also to translate several other works of Aquinas, including much of the *Summa theologiae*, in which task he was joined by his brother, Prochoros.[39] He also translated the *Ad cantorem Antiochenum* and *De articulis fidei et ecclesiae sacramentis ad archiepiscopum Panormitanum*, together with various works of Augustine, Boethius, Anselm, and Ricoldo da Monte Croce.[40] He shows no particular interest in the more narrowly philosophical works of Aquinas, being consistently more interested in the use of philosophy in theology rather than philosophy *per se*.[41] Demetrios' translations themselves are done with a good deal of skill and care, including frequent correction of Thomas' citations of Aristotle against the original Greek.[42] But in matters theological he finds little, if anything,

[38] Congar, 'Neuf cents ans après: notes sur le "Schisme oriental"', 37; Lemerle, 'L'Orthodoxie byzantine et l'œcuménisme médiéval: les origines du "schisme" des Églises', 239; Florovsky, 'The Tragedy of Christian Divisions', 31.

[39] Only the *Secunda Secundae* 1–79 has yet been edited: Georgios Leontsinis and Athanasia Glycofrydi-Leontsini et al., Δημητρίου Κυδώνη, Θωμᾶ Ἀκυινάτου: Σούμμα Θεολογική, ἐξελληνισθεῖσα. Demetrios produced versions of the *Prima pars* and the *Prima* and *Secunda secundae*, Prochoros much of the *Tertia pars*. The *Prima pars* translation appears to have been in an advanced form by at least 1363—the date of the death of Neilos Kabasilas who draws on it in his work *On the Procession of the Holy Spirit*. Dating of the remainder of the translation remains uncertain. See Tinnefeld, *Demetrios Kydones: Briefe* I.1, 71.

[40] For a complete list of his translations, see Tinnefeld, *Demetrios Kydones: Briefe* I.1, 68–72. On the translations of Augustine, see Michael Rackl, 'Die griechischen Augustinusübersetzungen'; Dionysios Kalamakes, Ἀνθολόγιον ἐκ τῶν ἔργων Αὐγουστίνου Ἱππῶνος ἐξελληνισθὲν ὑπὸ Δημητρίου τοῦ Κυδώνη (edition of the translation of the *Liber sententiarum Sancti Augustini* compiled by Prosper of Aquitaine); and Frances Kianka, 'The Letters of Demetrios Kydones to Empress Helena Kantakouzene Palaiologina'.

[41] Demetrios is in no doubt of the superiority of Christian over Hellenic wisdom, averring that had Aquinas debated with Aristotle and Plato he would surely have persuaded them to close the Academy and join the Church. Letter 33 (Loenertz I: 66). This conviction is also displayed in his rendering of the title *Summa contra gentiles* as Κατὰ Ἑλλήνων (*Against the Pagans*).

[42] See Michael Rackl 'Die griechische Übersetzung der Summa Theologiae'; Evangelos Moutsopoulos, 'L'hellénisation du Thomisme au XIVe siècle'; Photios Demetracopoulos, 'Demetrius Kydones' Translation of the Summa Theologica'; and Athanasia Glycofrydi-Leontsini, 'Demetrius Cydones as a Translator of Latin Texts'. The partial edition of the translation of the *Summa theologiae* contains some excellent

to critique. Indeed he came to accept Thomas' teaching on papal primacy and the *filioque* and was in due course (most likely in 1357) received into communion with the Church of the elder Rome. Demetrios was, of course, largely disappointed in his hopes that theological and political rapprochement with Rome would ensure the long-term survival of the Empire. He was also, according to some reports, to contemplate a return to the Orthodox communion late in life, perhaps having found the Catholic Church, caught in its own schism from 1378, not quite the unassailable bastion he had envisaged.[43] Demetrios also had to contend throughout his career with the deeply ingrained hostility to the Latins in Byzantium itself. Too few were prepared to accept the commonality of Old and New Rome and to heed his plaintive cry: 'what closer allies have the Romans than the Romans?'[44] But while his diplomatic schemes were to achieve small success, and his own conversion prove less than smooth, his translations unleashed something of great power and incalculable impact onto the Byzantine and post-Byzantine world.[45] Things would never be the same again.

introductory material by Moutospoulos: the first volume reproduces the article just cited; the second has 'Influences aristotéliciennes dans les traductions des œuvres de saint Thomas par Démétrius Cydonès'; the third, 'La technique de reconstitution des citations aristotéliciennes chez Démétrius Cydonès'. As a further sign of the care with which he operated, in Letter 333 (Loenertz II: 268), Demetrios regretted the fact that he had only one MS of the *Summa contra gentiles* at his disposal at the time of his translation and was consequently unable to check for scribal and other errors. Albert Erhard expresses a high opinion of Demetrios' literary flair in Karl Krumbacher, *Geschichte der byzantinischen Literatur*, 204–7.

[43] See the discussion in Mercati, *Notizie*, 441–50. He is dubious, as is Tinnefeld, *Demetrios Kydones: Briefe* I.1, 49–50.

[44] *Oratio pro subsidio latinorum* (PG 154 977D).

[45] Works attempting some general assessment of the impact of Thomas in the Byzantine world include Edmond Bouvy, 'Saint Thomas: Ses traducteurs byzantins'; Martin Jugie, 'Démétrius Cydonès et la théologie latine à Byzance'; Hans-Georg Beck, 'Der Kampf um der thomistischen Theologiebegriff in Byzanz'; Carmine Buda 'Influsso del Tomismo in Bisanzio nel XIV'; Stylianos Papadopoulos, Ἑλληνικαὶ μεταφράσεις θωμιστικῶν ἔργων. Φιλοθωμισταὶ καὶ ἀντιθωμισταὶ ἐν Βυζαντίῳ and 'Thomas in Byzanz. Thomas Rezeption und Thomas Kritik in Byzanz zwischen 1354 und 1435'; Thomas Tyn, 'Prochoros und Demetrios Kydones: der byzantinische Thomismus des XIV Jahrhunderts'; Apostolos Karpozilos, 'St. Thomas Aquinas and the Byzantine East'; Emmanuel Moutsopoulos, 'Thomisme et Aristotélisme à Byzance'; Hugh Barbour, *The Byzantine Thomism of Gennadios Scholarios*; Linos Benakis, «Ἡ Παρουσία τοῦ Θωμᾶ Ἀκινάτη στό Βυζάντιο»; Gerhard Podskalsky, *Theologie und Philosophie*, 180–230.

3.2. PROCHOROS KYDONES (*c.*1335–*c.*1369/70)

Prochoros was of a different stamp to his elder brother. While sharing the same patrician upbringing and outlook, Prochoros was to opt for a life of monastic seclusion rather than a career at the heart of the Byzantine state. A greater theologian than Demetrios, Prochoros was also a much poorer diplomat. As the most prominent anti-Palamite in the years following the death of Gregoras in *c.*1360, Prochoros drew on Thomas in a struggle against Palamite theology that was as unrelenting as it was unwise. He was condemned for his pains in 1368 and died excommunicate.[46]

Demetrios had long harboured reservations concerning Palamite theology but wisely kept his own counsel for the most part, speaking out publicly only after his brother's condemnation. In his one treatise on the subject, Demetrios attacks these 'new dogmas' in firm but courteous terms, taking the real distinction between essence and energies as a grave assault on the divine simplicity and denying any possibility of its justification by analogy with the hypostatic differentiation of Father, Son, and Holy Spirit which he takes to be a quite different distinction that in no way impinges on the divine unity.[47] For Demetrios, the essence–energies distinction is warranted neither by scripture, nor by the witness of the Fathers (Gregory of Nazianzus being his chief authority), nor by reason. There are certainly important elements of Thomas in Demetrios' arguments—God's nature as pure act, the identity of his essence and his existence (and goodness,

---

[46] Prochoros (*PLP* 13883) has received considerably less scholarly attention that his elder brother. The best single article is Norman Russell's 'Prochoros Cydones and the Fourteenth-Century Understanding of Orthodoxy'. See also Thomas Tyn, 'Prochoros und Demetrios Kydones'; Franz Tinnefeld, *Demetrios Kydones: Briefe* I.1, 237–44; and Gerhard Podskalsky, *Theologie und Philosophie*, 207–9.

[47] *De personarum proprietatibus in Trinitate ad Constantinum Asanem.* Manuel Candal (ed.), 'Demetrio Cidonio y el problema trinitario palamitico'. He could be more forthright in other writings, complaining to John V of the 'wrongful cutting-up of the Deity and scattering aboard of the supremely united unity; the levels of divinity; the division between imparticipable and participable God; between the invisible and that susceptible (as they maintain) to bodily vision; between the higher and the lower; between the one honoured with the most venerable of names but cast out from the government of all there is and the invented other having the dominion of all there is, as if he were its creator and father'. *Ad Ioannem Palaeologum oratio* 17 (Loenertz I: 18–19). John remained faithful to his μεσάζων, assuring him protection in what might otherwise have been a very perilous situation.

wisdom, life)—but no significant use of the distinctive methodology he had found so enthralling.[48] Overall there is little that here is not precedented in Akindynos or Gregoras and the treatise is for the most part a typical product of Byzantine scholasticism.[49] Prochoros' approach was rather different.

Prochoros entered the monastery of the Great Lavra on Mount Athos as a youth, receiving much of his education there and being ordained a hieromonk (priest-monk) in 1364. It seems that at the Lavra he had ample opportunity to develop his obvious intellectual talents. In his *Synodal Tome* of 1368, Patriarch Philotheos Kokkinos speaks of Prochoros as the foremost of those who had 'madly applied themselves to the vanity of Greek letters and imbibed deeply of their erroneous opinions'.[50] It seems clear that Athos was very much a centre of learning at this time. How he learned Latin on Athos is something of a mystery but however he did so, he achieved a great fluency, collaborating with his brother on the *Summa theologiae* (translating large portions of the *Tertia pars* and the *Supplementum*) and also translating Aquinas' *Quaestiones disputatae de potentia*, *De mundi aeternitate* and the prooemium (at least) to the *Sententia libri Metaphysicae*, along with various works by Augustine, Jerome, Boethius, and Hervaeus Natalis.[51]

---

[48] *De personarum proprietatibus* 10, 18 (Candal (ed.), 96, 109).

[49] In *De personarum proprietatibus* 6, Demetrios produces a citation from 'one of the theologians' confuting any notion of duality or multiplicity in the unorginate. This is, in fact, from Maximus' *Ambigua* (PG 91 1188AB), although it is likely that Demetrios' immediate source was Akindynos, *Refutatio* I 66.8–10 (CCSG 31 82).

[50] *Synodal Tome (Against Hieromonk Prochoros Kydones who thinks like Barlaam and Akindynos)* PG 151 694B. An improved edition has been made available by Antonio Rigo, *Gregorio Palamas e oltre: studi e documenti sulle controversie teologiche del XIV secolo bizantino* 99–134. This *Tome*, together with several letters of Demetrios, represent the chief sources on the controversy surrounding Prochoros.

[51] On the translations of Prochoros, see Mercati, *Notizie* 28–40. Some have since been edited: Herbert Hunger, *Prochoros Kydones, Übersetzung von acht Briefen des Hl. Augustinus*; idem. Prochoros Kydones' *Übersetzungen von S. Augustinus, De libero arbitrio I 1–90, und Ps.-Augustinus, De decem plagis Aegyptiorum*; Demetrios Nikitas, *Boethius*, De topicis differentiis καὶ οἱ βυζαντινὲς μεταφράσεις τοῦ Μανουὴλ Ὀλοβώλου καὶ τοῦ Προχόρου Κυδώκη*Prochoros also translated Augustine's *De vera religione* and *De beata vita*, together with some of Jerome's prefaces to his biblical translations. Hervaeus Natalis (d. 1323) was Master of the Dominican order and an ardent advocate of Thomas' cause against Durandus of Saint-Pourçain and other detractors (not that Hervaeus was immune to drawing on Scotus when it suited him: see Isabel Iribarren, *Durandus of St. Pourçain: A Dominican Theologian in the Shadow of Aquinas*). Prochoros translated selections from Hervaeus' *Commentary on the Sentences*. Taken together, these translations attest to a remarkable level of scholarly

Prochoros was not long to enjoy his life of priestly service and scholarly *hesychia*. Athos was evidently still in some ferment in the 1350s and 1360s. Notwithstanding the victory at the Council of 1351, the Palamite party had suffered a setback with the retirement of John VI Kantakuzene in December 1354 and the deposition of Patriarch Philotheos Kokkinos soon after.[52] Philotheos' return to the patriarchal throne in 1364 represented a swing back towards the Palamite cause, albeit in a deal brokered by Demetrios Kydones on condition that he leave the anti-Palamites in peace.[53] Philotheos, however, scented the possibility of a final resolution and was not long to honour the bargain. Prochoros had been gaining notoriety on Athos and beyond for his very public doubts concerning the Palamite theology. In 1365 or 1366, a group of Athonite monks denounced Prochoros to the Patriarch. With the reputation of the Lavra on the line, its abbot also wrote to the Patriarch asking for a copy of the *Synodal Tome* of 1351. This was duly despatched and Prochoros required to read it out and sign before the whole community of the Lavra. This he did, but the matter did not end there. Prochoros withdrew his affirmation of the *Tome* of 1351 in emulation, Philotheos recounts, of the ever-changing Euripus and the Chameleon.[54] This act of insubordination prompted the abbot to search his cell where he was to discover what are described as 'heretical writings'. From that point on, Prochoros was shunned by the community of the Lavra and soon after expelled.[55]

Prochoros took his case straight to the top, writing to the Patriarch concerning the unjust treatment meted out to him. But he did so with

activity and contacts at the Lavra in the 1350s–60s—including knowledge of very recent developments in Western theology.

[52] For the biography of Philotheos (*PLP* 29887), see Tinnefeld *Demetrios Kydones: Briefe* I.2, 398–404. Born *c.*1300, he was a hieromonk of Athos by 1340, when he signed the *Tome of The Holy Mountain* composed by Gregory Palamas (Chrestou II: 577). Soon after, he became abbot of the Great Lavra until appointed to the Metropolitan see of Herakleia in 1347 in which capacity he played an important role at the Council of 1351.

[53] Demetrius Kydones, *Contro Philotheo dopo la morte di Prochoro* (Mercati, *Notizie*, 322.14–20) and Letter 129 (Loenertz I: 165.18–22).

[54] The Euripus is the narrow strait separating Euboea from Boeotia on the Greek mainland. Its tides are said to change direction seven times a day. An apocryphal tale has Aristotle throwing himself into the swift-flowing waters in his frustration at being unable to discern their pattern.

[55] Philotheos Kokkinos, *Synodal Tome*, PG 151 695A–696B.

scant regard for diplomatic or ecclesiastical norms. According to
Philotheos, Prochoros complained to him of tradesmen, cooks, and
actors trespassing onto the hallowed grounds of theology with their
new dogmas.[56] This must have been a calculated insult, given
that Philotheos was precisely of such humble stock.[57] The Kydones
brothers thought little of this plebeian patriarch, with Demetrios
rubbing in the fact that he had worked as a lower servant in the
kitchens of Thomas Magistros in order to pay for his education.[58] He
also very pointedly draws attention to the Patriarch's Jewish origins.[59]
Prochoros blithely enclosed a selection of his writings for the Patriarch to study and soon presented himself in person to argue his case.
A commission was established to examine the writings but Prochoros
then committed a catastrophic error of judgement, denouncing the
veneration of Palamas in a *pittakion* (formal document) addressed to
the abbot of the Lavra. This intervention provoked a furious response
on Athos, where a council under the local bishop, the Metropolitan
of Ierissos, anathematized Prochoros.[60] Proceedings in the capital
then took the form of a trial, beginning in April 1368, at which
Prochoros and his writings were subjected to fierce probing. Prochoros was rebuked for his temerity in engaging in theology since this
was properly the preserve of bishops alone. Philotheos expressed his
exasperation at this recalcitrant monk insisting on solutions being
given to the difficulties he had raised, rather than dutifully submitting
to the teachings of scripture and the Fathers.[61] His understanding
of the light of the Transfiguration proved a particular bone of contention, with Christological deviancy being detected in his replies.[62] The
pittakion was dismembered and the veneration of Gregory upheld.[63]

---

[56] *Synodal Tome* 696C.
[57] See Norman Russell, 'Prochoros Cydones and the Fourteenth-Century Understanding of Orthodoxy', 78.
[58] *Apologia di Prochoro nell'imminenza della condanna* (ed. Mercati, *Notizie*,
302–3). Gregory Akindynos was also a student of Magistros, a teacher who was
evidently given to taking in boys of small means but great talent.
[59] Demetrios refers to Philotheos' Jewish roots in an angry letter of 1368 and
expresses the hope that he will soon once more be seeking sanctuary in Hagia Sophia
as he had done on John V's entry into the City on the night of 29 November 1354.
Letter 129 (Loenertz I: 164–6). See also Tinnefeld, *Briefe* I.2, 401 n.4.
[60] *Synodal Tome* 704AB.
[61] *Synodal Tome* 705CD.
[62] *Synodal Tome* 705D–710C, 715A.
[63] *Synodal Tome* 710D–712B.

Prochoros was slated as a worse heretic than Barlaam and Akindy-nos.[64] He was also taken to task for his alleged preference for the light of Aristotelian syllogisms over revealed truth and his subjection of scripture and patristic tradition to rational interrogation.[65] After failing to appear before subsequent sessions of the synod, he was anathematized, forbidden all priestly service, and excommunicated.[66] He died within a few years—but without ever renouncing the Church of his birth.

In all this, there is no hint of an anti-Latin stance on the part of the Palamite accusers of Prochoros. Indeed, Philotheos even gets the better of the defendant in terms of the correct interpretation of Augustine, whom he clearly regards as fully authoritative.[67] Even the attack on Prochoros' use of reason and syllogisms has no anti-Latin character. It is not the syllogism itself that is attacked but the use Prochoros makes of them.[68] Much the same had been alleged of Eustratios of Nicaea in the early twelfth century. It is also striking that while Prochoros is clearly associated with the condemned heret-ics Barlaam and Akindynos, the essence–energies distinction does not loom as large as might be expected in the proceedings. Instead it is the whiff of Christological heresy and the impugning of the *cultus* of Gregory Palamas that did for Prochoros.

This lack of any anti-Latin element is intriguing given that Prochoros was so steeped in Latin theology. It is time now to look more closely at some of his own writings.[69] The chief of these is his work in six books *On Essence and Energy* (*De essentia et opera-tione*).[70] This was, in whole or in part, known to Philotheos and informs many of his strictures against Prochoros.[71] We also have a

---

[64] *Synodal Tome* 712CD, 714A.
[65] *Synodal Tome* 713AB, cf. 698B, 699BC.
[66] *Synodal Tome* 713C–714B, 716B.
[67] *Synodal Tome* 707AB.
[68] In his defence of the syllogism, Prochoros is indeed much more confident as to the potentialities of human reason than is Aquinas, and much less guarded as to its necessary subordination to scriptural and patristic authority. See Franz Tinnefeld, 'Ein Text des Prochoros Kydones in Vat. gr. 609 über die Bedeutung der Syllogismen für die theologische Erkenntnis'.
[69] Merctai lists these in *Notizie*, 19–28.
[70] *De essentia et operatione* 1–2 (PG 151 1191–1242) (attributed to Akindynos); 6 (ed. Manuel Candal), 'El libro VI de Prócoro Cidonio [sobre la luz tabórica]'.
[71] Philotheos cites the headings of chapters 11, 10, 15, 16, and 17 of Book 2 in *Synodal Tome* 699B: 'That the intelligible activity of God is his essence, that the intelligible power of God is his essence, that the wisdom of God is his essence, that the

version of his *Refutation of the Misuse of Citations in the Tome against [Metropolitan Matthew] of Ephesus and Gregoras*. This is, in effect, a repudiation of the decisions of the Council of 1351 and again known to and attacked by Philotheos.[72] Other works include a treatise *On the Cataphatic and Apophatic Ways in Theology and on the Theophany of the Lord on the Mountain*.[73]

The *De essentia et operatione* is Prochoros' most decidedly Thomist work. In point of fact, much of it is Thomas, Books I–V being largely composed of assembled translations from the *Summa contra gentiles*, *Summa theologiae*, and *De potentia*. Book I shows that there is no potentiality in God and that God's essence is identical with his being. Book II contends that the intelligible activity, intelligible power, wisdom, truth, will, life, blessedness, and goodness of God are identical with his essence and demonstrates that names are not applied to God and to creatures by homonymy but rather by analogy. Books III–V continue with various other extracts from Thomas bearing on the distinction between essence and energy. But Book VI, while keeping closely to Thomas' methodology appears to be largely an original composition. It is this Book, *On the Light of Thabor*, that is the central target of the Patriarch and indeed of subsequent refutations. The Book proceeds very much after the pattern of the *Summa theologiae* using many of its familiar tags:

(§1) *Prooemium*: the problem of the divine light.

(§2) *Question* (Ζητητέον τοίνυν πότερον): whether the divine light exists within God, inherent to the divine essence, and is therefore to be seen as uncreated.

It seems so (Καὶ δοκεῖ ναί). *Videtur quod*: eleven patristic citations, all Greek, indicating that the divine light is uncreated.

---

truth of God is his essence, that the will of God is his essence and these things he demonstrates not from divine scripture, nor by bringing forward sayings of the saints, but through his own reasonings, using Aristotelian syllogisms in his demonstrations.'

[72] Philotheos gives the title and prooemium in *Synodal Tome* 697CD. A substantial extract has been edited by Franz Tinnefeld, 'Ein Text des Prochoros Kydones in Vat. gr. 609 über die Bedeutung der Syllogismen für die theologische Erkenntnis'. There is also a smaller extract in Ioannis Polemis, *Theophanes of Nicaea: His Life and Works*, 79–80.

[73] *Vaticanus graecus* 678 ff. 31–59r. See Mercati, *Notizie*, 22–3. Podskalsky gives a brief summary in *Theologie und Philosophie*, 208–9. Prochoros accuses the Palamites of disrupting and distorting the traditional understanding of the two modes of theology and claiming (impossibly) to know and name the divine directly.

Again (*Ἔτι*). *Praeterea*: here and in other sections used to introduce successive witnesses.

(§3) *But against that* (*Ἀλλὰ τοὐναντίον*). *Sed contra*: five arguments, including citations from Dionysius and Augustine.

(§4–24) *Response* (*Ἀπόκρισις. Ῥητέον ὅτι*). *Respondeo dicendum quod*: twenty-four sections, with many patristic citations (from Dionysius in particular, also Gregory of Nazianzus and Basil). The light of Thabor is to be understood in terms of analogy and not as uncreated.

(§25–35) *Against the objections* (*Πρὸς τὸ πρῶτον* [κτλ.] *οὖν ῥητέον ὅτι*). *Ad primum* [etc.] *ergo dicendum quod*: replies to the eleven witnesses cited in §2.

(§36) *Epilogue*: Prochoros submits his treatise to the judgement of the Church.

But while the pattern is similar—albeit with a 'response' section much longer than anything we find in Aquinas—actual connections with Aquinas on the specific matter of the Transfiguration are few.[74] Prochoros' response begins with the principle of analogy, using Aristotle's description of the operation of the intellect as light as an example of an analogical usage. Reiterating a key theme of Book II, Prochoros insists that terms applied to God and creatures are never homonyms or synonyms, but analogies (§4). He discusses God's own essence as light (§5–7) and demonstrates that God cannot be the accidental cause of anything (§8). He goes on to decry all those who would claim that the light of Thabor is the light of the essence, a theophany of the divine *ousia*, concluding that the light cannot be the essence (§9–14). The light is rather to be understood allegorically, as a natural symbol or type of a divine mystery (§15). A long treatment of the Fall follows, with Prochoros adopting an unusually sombre account of the organic transmission of original sin to the whole human race that is more reminiscent of Augustine than Aquinas— and Augustine at his bleakest too. Prochoros' account becomes positively dualistic in the opposition it sets up between inherited sin and inherited righteousness (§16–18). Christ must, for Prochoros, be excepted from this gloomy narrative, hence the novel conclusion that since the Lord assumed human nature, and not a human person, he is free of both natural and inherited sin, assuming only natural

---

[74] Response sections in later scholastic writers (such as Duns Scotus or Henry of Ghent) tended to be much larger, eventually displacing the disputation sections altogether.

righteousness (§19).[75] He concludes with a treatment of the general resurrection and concludes that sinners and righteous alike will see God—but in very different ways.[76] The righteous will see the essence of God and shine in varying degrees of created glory whereas the sinners will see God in a lesser fashion and be punished, their bodies being rendered as dark as their misdeeds (§20–3). The last section reaffirms the created nature of the light of Thabor. This created light, says Prochoros, shone forth from the body of Christ representing by analogy the interior light of the soul (§24).

All this is very different to what we find in Aquinas.[77] This is very puzzling since Aquinas' most developed treatment of the question is in *Summa theologiae* III[a] q.45, precisely one of the texts translated by Prochoros.[78] This particular text shows Thomas at his most rooted in the Greek patristic tradition—indeed he comes across as considerably more consonant with the Greek patristic tradition than does Prochoros. Certainly, Thomas has none of the curious Christological speculations that were to prove so deadly to Prochoros' cause at his trial. Of course, Thomas does not address the question of the Transfiguration in terms of a choice between created and uncreated light, still less in terms of an essence–energies distinction. He does, however, have a good deal to say on the subject notwithstanding the near complete absence of the theme from textbook treatments of his theology.

Thomas' reflection on the Transfiguration emerges out of his deep immersion in scripture and the Fathers. This is especially evident in

[75] In his trial Prochoros is, oddly, accused of having produced a wholly new heresy by denying the sinlessness of the flesh of Christ, *Synodal Tome* 715A, with the pertinent citation in 701D–702A. This position would seem to contradict what he says in *De essentia et operatione* VI.19 (ed. Candal, 280). Prochoros' position is clarified somewhat in Demetrios' *Apologia di Prochoro nell'imminenza della condanna* (ed. Mercati, *Notizie*, 308).

[76] Philotheos takes him to task for this assertion in *Synodal Tome* 707B.

[77] On the Transfiguration in Aquinas, see Édouard Divry, *La transfiguration selon l'orient et l'occident: Grégoire Palamas, Thomas d'Aquin: vers un dénouement oecuménique*, 251–99.

[78] In translating the *Tertia pars*, Prochoros focused on texts bearing on the nature of the divine light. Indeed, he re-ordered Thomas' work to give precedence to the theme, with III[a] q.45 a.1–2 and a.3–4 forming the opening and concluding sections respectively. See Mercati, *Notizie*, 34. The fact that Prochoros tops and tails his translation of the *Tertia pars* with q.45 in this fashion only serves to underline how puzzling it is that he should plough a quite different furrow in his own treatment of the question.

the *Catena aurea* in Luke. John of Damascus is his chief witness for the Transfiguration narrative in Luke 9:28–31, being cited on the crucial question of the nature of the light as follows:

> Moses indeed was arrayed with a glory, which came from without; our Lord, with that which proceeded from the inherent brightness of Divine glory (ex innato gloriae divinae fulgore). For since in the hypostatic union there is one and the same glory of the Word and the flesh, he is transfigured not as receiving what he was not, but manifesting to his disciples what he was [...] And his raiment was white and glistening; that is, lighted up by its participation of the divine light (illustratus scilicet per divinae lucis participationem).[79]

The immense patristic labour represented by the *Catena aurea* bore splendid fruit in the *Summa theologiae*. The *Summa* is often understood (following Chenu) in terms of the neo-Platonic schema of procession and return (Latinized as *exitus-reditus*): procession (I[a]), return (II[a]) in Christ (III[a]).[80] If we broadly accept this schema, it is surely not amiss to note that the mid-point of the return in Christ, question 45 of the 90 questions of the *Tertia pars*, is the Transfiguration. Granted that this is an accident attendant upon the abandonment of the project in its closing stages, it is nonetheless a felicitous indicator of the axial character of the Transfiguration in Thomas.

The account in *ST* III[a] q.45 begins with a demonstration of the fittingness of the Transfiguration as a showing of Christ's inner glory and as foretaste of the glory to which his disciples will be configured at the resurrection. This was to stiffen their sinews for the trials and tribulations ahead and to show them their goal, much as one might show an archer his target. It proceeds in article 2 to consider the

---

[79] *Catena in Lucam* 9 l.6 [ET 319–20]. The text from John may be found in his *Oration on the Transfiguration* 10–13 (Kotter V: 449–52). The extract given here extract corresponds to lines 449.39–43; 450.13–15, 17–19; 452.36, 41–2.

[80] For a critique of this widely accepted schema (and an alternative linear model), see Rudi te Velde, *Aquinas on God: The 'Divine Science' of the Summa theologiae*, 11–18. Thomas gives a clear statement of his own structural vision in the prooemium to *ST* I[a] q.2: 'Because the chief aim of sacred doctrine is to teach the knowledge of God, not only as he is in himself, but also as he is the beginning of things and their last end, and especially of rational creatures, as is clear from what has been already said, therefore, in our endeavour to expound this science, we shall treat: first of God; second of the rational creature's advance towards God; and third of Christ who, as man, is our way to God.' By this account, the structure of procession and return certainly informs the overall schema, but is by no means an exhaustive explanation thereof.

nature of the light: whether this light (*claritas*) was the light of glory.[81] He concludes that this light was:

> the light of glory as to its essence, but not as to its mode of being. For the light of the glorified body is derived from that of the soul, as Augustine says in his *Epistle to Dioscorus*. And in like manner, the light of Christ's body in his transfiguration derived from his divinity, as the Damascene says, and from the glory of his soul.

The temporary showing-forth of this permanent state of inner glory was due to a divine dispensation. Thomas argues that this temporary revelation is to be distinguished from the resurrection glory of the saints, whose bodies are permanently glorified in the outpouring of the glory of their souls.[82] This glorification represents a change in state, whereas Christ's transfiguration was a revelation of his inner state:

> But in Christ's transfiguration light overflowed from his divinity and from his soul into his body, not as an immanent quality affecting his very body, but rather after the manner of a transient passion, as when the air is lit up by the sun.

Thomas is concerned here to refute the notion of Hugh of St Victor that this brilliance was somehow acquired by Jesus at his Transfiguration (*ST* III[a] q.45 a.2 co.). He does, however, allow that Christ's shining garments serve as a prefiguration of the resurrection glory of the saints (*ST* III[a] q.45 a.2 ad 3). The *Quaestio* concludes with a powerful affirmation of the interconnectedness of baptism and transfiguration:

> Just as in the Baptism, where the mystery of the first regeneration was proclaimed, the operation of the whole Trinity was made manifest, because the Son incarnate was there, the Holy Spirit appeared under the form of a dove, and the Father made himself known in the voice; so also in the Transfiguration, which is the mystery of the second regeneration, the whole Trinity appears—the Father in the voice, the Son in the

---

[81] The Latin term 'claritas' denotes clearness, brilliance, splendour, brightness. I render it here simply as 'light' to facilitate comparison with Greek sources.

[82] Kallistos Ware observes that in his evocations of the outpouring of the soul's glory onto the body at the resurrection, Aquinas 'writes in similar terms' to Macarius-Symeon. 'The Transfiguration of the Body', 29. Macarius had also developed his teaching on the resurrection glory in the context of his discussion of the Transfiguration. See further my *The Macarian Legacy*, 33–4, 220.

man, the Holy Spirit in the bright cloud; for just as in baptism he confers
innocence, signified by the simplicity of the dove, so in the resurrection
will he give his elect the light of glory and relief from all evil, which things
are signified by the bright cloud. (*ST* III[a] q. 45 a. 4 ad 2)

This connection between Christ's Baptism and Transfiguration,
between the restoration of fallen man and the further gift of participation in the divine light, beautifully encapsulates Thomas' vision of
the return of man to God.

Little of all this seems to have come through to Prochoros. At his
trial, he seems to have abandoned his contention that the light of the
Transfiguration is simply created adopting instead the position that it
is both created and uncreated, since Christ is dual—both God and
man.[83] This wavering position has none of Thomas' Christological
clarity and rigour, founded upon his close readings of the decrees and
acts of the ecumenical councils and, especially, on John of Damascus'
presentation of the hypostatic union and the instrumentality of
Christ's humanity. In fact, by virtue of their common roots in
Greek patristic and conciliar tradition, it is Philotheos who is far
closer to Aquinas here in his apprehension of the perfect union of
divinity and humanity of Christ.[84] All this opened up Prochoros to
the most deadly of charges: concealed Arianism.[85] Prochoros is also
said to have likened the light that shone from Christ with that which
shone from Moses, holding that both were temporary phenomena
and simply came and went. Again, this is in direct contradiction to
what we find in Aquinas. Kokkinos, like Aquinas, draws on the same
passage from the Damascene to show that Moses' light was exterior to
him whereas Christ's divine light came from within.[86]

---

[83] *Synodal Tome* 709D–710A. Philotheos astutely notes that this is a departure
from the position maintained in his writings, 710B.

[84] Prochoros has only the vaguest apprehension of the *communicatio idiomatum*,
the exchange of attributes between the divinity and the humanity on account of the
one hypostasis, *De essentia et operatione* VI.34 (ed. Candal, 294). Even when speaking
of the one hypostasis, his account of the union remains deeply inadequate. Philotheos
seems to have sensed the superficiality of Prochoros' Christology very early on,
recommending at a meeting in 1367 that he go away and read the acts of the Sixth
Ecumenical Council, Maximus the Confessor's *Dialogue with Pyrrhus*, and John of
Damascus' 'dogmatic book'—presumably the *Exact Exposition of the Orthodox Faith*.
Synodal Tome 703D.

[85] *Synodal Tome* 710B.

[86] *Synodal Tome* 706BC. Prochoros has only two short extracts from John's
Oration on the Transfiguration, and these in the 'it seems so' (καὶ δοκεῖ ναί) section:

There are certainly borrowings from Thomas in Book 6 of the *De essentia et operatione*, but these are largely a matter of methodology and general principles. In fact, Prochoros emerges as considerably less profoundly shaped by Thomas' theology than is Demetrios. Prochoros strikes out on his own in this work and comes a cropper accordingly. Had he stuck to Thomas, to the theology of passages he himself had translated, he would have been on considerably surer ground at the trial. As it is, the weakest portions of Prochoros' disquisition on Thabor are very much his own invention. The condemnation of 1368 can therefore in no way be represented as anti-Latin, anti-scholastic, or anti-Thomas. This was very much an intra-Byzantine affair with Prochoros condemned for what students today are invited to attest is 'all their own work'.

3.3. JOHN VI KANTAKUZENE (*c.*1295–1383)

The Emperor John VI (reigned 1347–54) was intimately involved in the emergence of Aquinas into the Byzantine world. He was also the pivotal figure in the triumph of Palamite theology at the Council of 1351. A man of great culture, John was, as we have seen, very favourably impressed by the translations of his chief minister Demetrios Kydones, commenting on their great value for the common weal of the Greeks and paying for numerous copies to be made.[87] Even after his abdication and profession as the Monk Joasaph in December 1354, he remained a figure of note in the ecclesiastical affairs of the Empire, a rallying point for the Palamite cause and a chief spokesperson in reunion negotiations with the Latins.[88] Perhaps

testimonies appearing contrary to his own position and awaiting elucidation or qualification. *De essentia et operatione* VI.2.8, 10 (ed. Candal, 260, 262).

[87] See above, p.67. By his own account, John was conversant in both Latin and Turkish—if true, a most unusual accomplishment. He was certainly able to sign himself in Latin and did so as, 'Iohannes in Christo Deo fidelis imperator et moderator Romanorum Canthcusinos'. See Donald Nicol, *The Reluctant Emperor: A Biography of John Cantacuzene, Byzantine Emperor and Monk*, 3, 163.

[88] The name 'Joasaph' is intriguing. Presumably this choice was in emulation of another monk-emperor who had fallen foul of the Palaiologoi, John IV Laskaris, Emperor of Nicaea from 1258–61. John IV was deposed and blinded (on his eleventh birthday) by Michael VIII Palaiologos, first of his line, shortly after his recapture of Constantinople. He spent the remainder of his life as the Monk Joasaph. St Joasaph,

only in Byzantium might we find a retired emperor in monastic habit maintaining his imperial styling and acting as an *ad hoc* minister for ecclesiastical affairs. Be that as it may, once relieved of his many administrative cares, John-Joasaph was able to give free rein to his consuming interest in theology. He composed treatises against both Jews and Muslims, the latter largely dependent upon another of Demetrios' translations, the *Refutatio Alcorani* of Ricoldo da Monte Croce.[89] To Demetrios' bitter disappointment, the Monk-Emperor was to dedicate much of his theological energy to the defence of Palamite theology, with Prochoros the primary target.[90]

Prochoros has the dubious and perhaps unique distinction of having attracted theological rebuttals on the part of both a patriarch and an (ex-)emperor. Philotheos himself did not compose a systematic refutation of Prochoros' works, leaving that task to his imperial patron and to his erstwhile student, Theophanes of Nicaea. Philotheos had, during John's reign and at his command, composed a lengthy set of refutations of Nikephoros Gregoras in traditional Byzantine scholastic mode.[91] John's undertaking of the refutation of

---

according to the hagiographical sources, is the son of a prince who eventually achieves martyrdom. The *Life of Barlaam and Joasaph*, once attributed to John of Damascus, has long been noted for its incorporation of elements from the *Life of the Buddha*— another prince who found a higher calling than earthly governance.

[89] Anti-Jewish works in Soteropoulos (ed.), ' Ἰωάννου ΣΤ Καντακουζηνοῦ Κατὰ ' Ἰουδαίων Λόγοι Ἐννέα. Anti-Islamic works in PG 154 372–692.

[90] In *Letter* 400, Demetrios rebukes the ex-emperor in stern terms, lamenting his patronage of the 'new theology' of Palamas and much regretting the wide dissemination of the *Refutations* (Loenertz II: 355–6). The emperor had also composed refutations of Isaac Argyros (*Parisinus graecus* 1242 and other MSS) and John Kyparissiotes (*Laurentianus* VIII.8 being the sole witness).

[91] Demetrios Kaïmakes (ed.), Φιλοθέου Κοκκίνου δογματικὰ ἔργα I. These solid and rather relentless treatises dissect and demolish Gregoras' various positions in methodical fashion, principally by means of appeal to and discussion of patristic citations. These 15 *Antirrhetikoi* are composed in the high Attic style taught him by Thomas Magistros, with occasional classical allusions to underline the extent of his learning. Gregoras is characterized as a wilful opponent of the united witness of scripture and patristic tradition whose errors, are, predictably, deemed to be rooted in philosophy. Philotheos claims the authority of an ecumenical council (some MSS indicate the sixth) for the assertion of the incompatibility of Aristotelian arguments with those of the Gospels and apostles (VI 176.319–23). Gregoras is repeatedly rebuked for his love for the syllogism, without regard for his frequent denigrations of the same (VI 176.308). This attack on syllogisms does not stop Philotheos from out-syllogizing his opponent: he evidently takes some delight in showing the logical inadequacies of his opponent (VI 178.371–6). Anti-rationalism here seems to be

Prochoros in his monastic retirement may have been something of a return favour.

John's talents as a theologian have rarely been judged highly. Hans-Georg Beck treats him as a dilettante, remarking that his 'passion for theology was greater than his *acumen mentis*'. Gerhard Podskalsky is similarly cutting, complaining of his 'verbose but ultimately vacuous polemic'. But the editors of his refutations of Prochoros rightly discern a greater interest than such supercilious dismissals would allow.[92] In John's by no means negligible theological contributions we gain a valuable insight into the sheer complexity of the Byzantine reception of Aquinas. As patron of the Palamite cause and a keen reader of Aquinas, as pro-union (in the right circumstances) and devotedly Orthodox, John embodies in himself many of the currents of the late fourteenth century.[93] But for all his enthusiasm for Thomas and regard for Demetrios, John could hardly be expected to refrain from taking a stance in the Prochoros affair. Prochoros had, after all, explicitly called into question the decisions of the Council of 1351 over which John had presided. He had also attacked the veneration of Gregory Palamas, whom John had so publicly championed.

The refutations followed on swiftly from the condemnation of 1368, being completed in 1369–70. They tackle Prochoros' assault on the *Tome* of 1351, including his defence of the syllogism and thoughts on the ecclesiastical hierarchy. But above all, they attack Book VI of the *De essentia et operatione*. This is noteworthy: John will surely have known perfectly well that Books I–V were largely

something of a rhetorical trope. The dispute is conducted solely within traditional Byzantine parameters with minimal reference to the Latin world.

[92] See Beck, *Kirche und theologische Literatur im Byzantinischen Reich*, 329 (where he is unfavourably constrasted with Palamas); Podskalsky, *Theologie und Philosophie*, 165 (the same judgement applying equally to Philotheos Kokkinos); and Edmond Voordeckers and Franz Tinnefeld, *Iohannis Cantacuzeni. Refutationes duae prochori cydonii et disputatio cum Paulo Patriarcha Latino epistulis septem tradita*, xxxviii–xliv.

[93] Some of these complexities are conveyed by the MS *Parisinus graecus* 135. Caroline Alcalay has put forward a fascinating case that this illustrated Book of Job (with patristic commentary) may have been a gift commissioned within the circles of papal legates to the East for John-Joasaph. While the thesis remains unproven, the depiction of Job's resignation in the face of misfortune, conformity with Aquinas' commentary on Job, and use of Gothic and Byzantine architectural styles, would certainly have made it a suitable gift. 'Le *parisinus graecus* 135: un hommage à Jean Cantacuzène? Étude historique d'un livre de Job du XIVe siècle.'

composed of selections from Thomas.[94] Having been intimately connected with Demetrios' translation work, this fact can hardly have escaped him. Instead, it is principally Book VI that John has in his sights—precisely that part of the work we have distinguished as Prochoros' own. While Thomas does not wholly escape criticism in this work, it may by no means be construed as a general attack on his theology or method.

Refutation I devotes much attention to Prochoros' defence of the syllogism.[95] John adopts the position that the syllogism is a product of Greek philosophy and thus of no theological utility. Revelation alone is the source of theological truth. Neither the prophets nor the great spiritual teachers of recent times have had need of syllogisms (I 7–9). John produces a series of patristic testimonies on the inadequacies of worldly logic (I 12–14).[96] Needless to say, he does not mention Palamas' explicit defence and use of the syllogism. On the contrary, his strictures against the syllogism draw directly on Barlaam the Calabrian.[97] And as if, he writes, patristic testimony were not enough, he will bring even Aquinas to bear against Prochoros: 'I bring before you the witness of Thomas, teacher among the Latins, who breathes syllogisms rather than air, and against whom it would not be right for you to object.'[98] Thomas is then cited with evident approbation. John reproduces a long extract from the *Summa contra gentiles* 1.9, making use of the translation of Demetrios which he himself had sponsored (I 16).[99] This well-known passage speaks of the twofold truth of divine things, distinguishing 'one which reason is competent to

[94] Mercati points out that the translations are largely Prochoros' own and not those of his elder brother (*Notizie*, 15–18).

[95] Franz Tinnefeld (ed.), 'Ein Text des Prochoros Kydones in Vat. gr. 609 über die Bedeutung der Syllogismen für die theologische Erkenntnis'.

[96] Here he appeals to Basil of Caesarea, Gregory of Nyssa, Dionysius the Areopagite, and Maximus the Confessor—an array of the most philosophically cultured of the Fathers.

[97] See Ioannis Polemis, *Theophanes of Nicaea*, 167–8. Polemis argues that it is John's espousal of Barlaam's anti-logical arguments that opened the way for their widespread adoption in Palamite circles.

[98] In a nice example of Byzantine 'intertextuality', this comment appears to be lifted from Neilos Kabasilas, *Refutation of the Syllogisms of the Latins* §64 (ed. Candal, 238). To 'breathe syllogisms' need not necessarily be a jibe but rather a recognition of the profoundly philosophical orientation of Thomas' life. Thanks to Peter Brown and Christian Wildberg for comments on this point.

[99] In another incident of interconnectedness, the *Refutations* and the translations were copied by the same scribe: Manuel Tzykandyles.

investigate, the other which escapes all human intellectual prying'.[100] The former (pertaining to such things as God's existence) is susceptible of demonstrative argumentation while the latter (pertaining to such things as God's triune nature) wholly transcends such rational demonstration. John continues the citation to encompass Thomas' assertion of the harmony between reason and faith, the primacy of scriptural revelation, and the overarching methodological considerations of the *Summa contra gentiles*. Prochoros is here squarely condemned for failing to heed his supposed master on the strict limits of rational enquiry and for trespassing onto areas where even the angelic doctor feared to tread.

This astonishing use of Aquinas against Prochoros only serves to underline the fact that the Prochoros affair did not amount to a condemnation of Western theology in general, nor of Thomas in particular. The bulk of the remainder of *Refutation* I is devoted to a systematic demolition of Book VI of Prochoros' *De essentia et operatione* while *Refutation* II deals with some further patristic extracts adduced by Prochoros in support of his theses. Books I–V escape virtually without comment. The only direct citation is the prooemium to Book I, Prochoros' introduction to the series of extracts from Thomas that follow, couching the whole as a rejoinder to the essence–energies distinction (*Refutation* I 4). Here it is not Thomas who is under attack but rather Prochoros' use of Thomas for his own purposes. The other references to Books I–V listed by the editors are, at most, oblique.[101]

It goes beyond our purpose here to rehearse all of John's arguments against Prochoros' understanding of the light of Thabor. Suffice it to say that he proceeds methodically through Book VI (of which he cites, in time-honoured fashion, large chunks) addressing each and every element. He very consciously dissects Prochoros' case, fully accepting its scholastic approach but seeking to outdo his opponent in forensic skill and correct interpretation of patristic authority—including a correction of Prochoros' appeal to Augustine (I 31). He builds up a weighty case for the essence–energies distinction,

---

[100] The translation here is, for obvious reasons, from the Greek text as reproduced by John and not from the original Latin.

[101] Edmond Voordeckers and Franz Tinnefeld, *Iohannis Cantacuzeni. Refutationes duae prochori cydonii et disputatio cum Paulo Patriarcha Latino epistulis septem tradita*, 275.

the uncreated nature of the light of Thabor, and reality of human deification. It would be foolish to claim that John's theology is easily harmonized with that of Aquinas or that his works amount to a wholesale approbation of Thomas: that is not the point. What is significant is that they are not in any way a repudiation of Aquinas. John remains broadly true to his original positive estimation of the value of Thomas' works. He eschews direct criticism of the material culled from Thomas in Books I–V, calls into question Prochoros' manipulation of Thomas for anti-Palamite purposes, and uses Thomas against Prochoros.[102] In effect, Prochoros is reproached not so much for his Thomism but for being insufficiently Thomist.

3.4. THEOPHANES OF NICAEA (d. 1380–1)

As if patriarchal condemnation and imperial refutation were not enough, Prochoros was also subject to the attentions of Theophanes III, Metropolitan of Nicaea.[103] A protégé of Patriarch Philotheos, Theophanes was raised to the see of Nicaea on his patron's reinstatement in 1368.[104] Theophanes was certainly of the Palamite party but not without some equivocation.[105] His absence from the Synod of 1368 had been pointedly noted by Demetrios Kydones and Theophanes may have found it expedient to provide a testimonial of his

---

[102] Like Julian the Apostate lamenting the Christians' use of Hellenic learning against the pagans, Prochoros would have had cause to complain, 'for in the words of the proverb, we are stricken by our own arrows. For from our own writings they take the weapons wherewith they engage in the war against us' (*Shorter Fragment 7, The Works of the Emperor Julian* (Loeb volume III), 299).

[103] *PLP* 7615. See also the fine study of Ioannis Polemis, *Theophanes of Nicaea: His Life and Works*, to which I am much indebted in what follows.

[104] Nicaea was by that time *in partibus infidelium* and Theophanes seems never to have visited his see, sending in his stead letters of pastoral support and counsel to his flock, PG 150 288–350. Theophanes was also *locum tenens* of the see of Ancyra from c.1370.

[105] Meyendorff speaks of him as only 'nominally Palamite' in *Introduction à l'étude de Grégoire Palamas*, 261 n.21 and again in 'Le thème du "retour en soi" dans la doctrine palamite du XIVe siècle', 99–100. For him, Theophanes falls decidedly into the Evagrian-intellectualist school. Jugie had offered an analogous judgement in 'Palamite (Controverse)', 1797: 'Théophane minimise la distinction Palamite, mais non au point de la rendre acceptable pour un catholique.'

orthodoxy in the form of a written denunciation of Prochoros.[106] Theophanes' refutation differs from that of the Monk-Emperor in that whereas John's is a typical product of Byzantine scholasticism, Theophanes makes deliberate and extensive use of the method and theology of Thomas Aquinas.

Theophanes' discourses *On the Light of Thabor* were composed sometime between 1368 and 1376.[107] The very fact of their composition shows the ongoing heat of the controversy, even after Prochoros' condemnation. Theophanes acknowledges the need to address various outstanding *aporiae* relating to the question of the divine light, admitting that the 'heresy of Barlaam and Akindynos' has not yet been fully extinguished.[108] Theophanes proceeds in fine scholastic style, distinguishing various questions in need of response, weighing witnesses and arguments for and against, methodically examining textual sources, carefully defining his terms, and producing demonstrations and solutions. In all this, Theophanes shows himself well versed in Aristotelian argumentation and terminology. The methodological clarity and rational discipline with which he operates is not readily paralleled elsewhere in the Byzantine scholastic tradition.

Questions for investigation include why it was that Judas was allowed to commune at the Last Supper, but not to witness the Transfiguration, what Maximus meant by describing the divine light as a symbol, whether the light were in any way apprehensible by the senses, or experienced differently by different persons.[109] Theophanes produces an uncompromising assertion of the uncreated character of the divine light, experience of which varies according to

---

[106] Demetrios Kydones tells us Theophanes had been the chair of the commission appointed to examine Prochoros' writings but adds that as a man of sense, he distanced himself from the trial proper, *Contro Philotheo dopo la morte di Prochoro* (Mercati, *Notizie*, 322.2–3, 21–4). Theophanes did in fact have a good excuse for his absence, being on official business in Serbia at the time.

[107] Charalambous Soteropoulos (ed.), Θεοφάνους Γ' ἐπισκόπου Νικαίας περὶ Θαβωρίου φωτός, λόγοι πέντε. Polemis offers some corrections to this edition in his *Theophanes of Nicaea*, 208–14.

[108] *On the Light of Thabor* II 5–7.

[109] The argument surrounding Judas emerged as an attack on Philotheos' explanation of why only certain disciples came with Jesus onto the Mountain. Theophanes argues that whereas Judas could commune with Christ's body at the Last Supper, he could not participate in its deifying energies—and nor could he have witnessed the Thaboric light at any level beyond the sensory.

capacity and requires for full realization a change by grace of the operation of the senses. John of Damascus' *Homily on the Transfiguration* is quoted at length, operating as a kind of benchmark text as it does for Philotheos and for Thomas.[110] Ioannis Polemis has made a convincing case that Theophanes has Prochoros as his primary target at a number of points in the treatises: the contention that the light could not be uncreated if it represented that which is above intellect and reason, or was seen by sinners, or was merely a symbol, or was mediated by angels.[111] To these instances may be added his assertion that Jesus assumed not only universal human nature, but also particular human nature.[112]

As with the critiques of the Monk-Emperor and Patriarch, the attacks on Prochoros relate principally to his own conclusions and not to ideas derived from Thomas. On the contrary, Theophanes draws directly from Thomas in his defence of Palamite theology. This connection was first noted by Polemis who draws attention to a number of distinct parallels.[113] For instance, Theophanes puts forward an account of the threefold division of knowledge: from creation through the senses, from faith based on revelation, and from direct apprehension of God 'as he is' (I John 3:2).[114] This triplex model is presented in strikingly similar fashion to that given in *Summa contra gentiles* IV.1, down to the citation from I John. Theophanes also proposes, on grounds of the divine simplicity, the identity of God's essence with his intellect, intellectual activity (τὸ νοεῖν), and self-existence as wisdom.[115] Here again, an unmistakable connection with Aquinas may be detected, in particular *Summa contra gentiles* III.53 with which it exhibits some very close verbal parallels.[116] This is a proposition that sits uneasily with the more usual Palamite position that such things are to be counted among the

---

[110] See, for example, *On the Light of Thabor* IV 291–314.

[111] *Theophanes of Nicaea* 74–86. Polemis also notes a number of instances where John Kyparissiotes or Isaac Argyros may be targeted.

[112] *On the Light of Thabor* I 479–516. Cf. Prochoros Kydones, *De essentia et operatione* VI.19.

[113] *Theophanes of Nicaea* 92–109. I mention here the parallels I consider to be the strongest.

[114] *On the Light of Thabor* II 840–926

[115] *On the Light of Thabor*, II 1029–41.

[116] Theophanes: ταὐτὸν ἔσται ταύτῃ τὸ νοεῖν καὶ τὸ εἶναι; cf. Thomas: ταὐτὸν εἶναι τό τε εἶναι καὶ τὸ νοεῖν (tr. Demetrios Kydones: *Vaticanus graecus* 613 f.82).

divine energies, and still more uneasily with the fact that this notion was specifically condemned in association with Prochoros.[117]

Theophanes is also the author of a number of other extant texts. In 1369–70, he composed a *Letter to the Archbishop Paul* on behalf of the ex-emperor, clarifying further the Palamite position to the papal legate.[118] Theophanes makes extensive reference to the works of Prochoros, chiefly Book VI of the *De essentia et operatione*, and remains closely tied to the official Palamite teaching.[119] A more expansive approach is evident in his treatise *On the Eternity of Beings*.[120] This is a curious text for a Palamite theologian in that it distinguishes a created energy of God, by which the world is established. Theophanes appears to be defending Palamite theology from the charge that the doctrine of the uncreated energies necessarily entails the eternity of creation. But to deal with this accusation by positing a created creative operation appears quite contrary to Palamas' assertion that all energies of God are to be understood as uncreated. But while the text is largely shaped by specifically Byzantine concerns, Theophanes certainly knows of Aquinas' treatise *De mundi aeternitate*, translated by Prochoros. In that treatise, Thomas was concerned to demonstrate the logical possibility of the eternity of creation, while affirming through faith that the creation did indeed have a beginning. While his main concern is to demonstrate that the creation is not in any way eternal, actually or logically, Theophanes shows awareness of Thomas' basic contention and refrains from ruling out the purely theoretical possibility of the world's eternity.[121]

Theophanes calls the created creative energy of God a 'passive movement' or 'passive power' ($\pi\alpha\theta\eta\tau\iota\kappa\dot{\eta}$ $\kappa\dot{\iota}\nu\eta\sigma\iota\varsigma/\delta\dot{\upsilon}\nu\alpha\mu\iota\varsigma$).[122] This 'passive power' or 'relative energy' ($\sigma\chi\epsilon\tau\iota\kappa\dot{\eta}$ $\dot{\epsilon}\nu\dot{\epsilon}\rho\gamma\epsilon\iota\alpha$) is a feature or

---

[117] Philotheos Kokkinos, *Synodal Tome*, 699B.

[118] The best MS of this and several other texts of Theophanes is *Oxoniensis Baroccianus graecus* 193 (C14). For the MSS tradition, see Polemis, *Theophanes of Nicaea*, 31–41.

[119] Polemis, *Theophanes of Nicaea*, 67–8, argues that Paul's questions were to some extent generated by his acquaintance with anti-Palamite circles, and with Prochoros' works in particular—hence the need for specific rebuttal.

[120] Polemis (ed.), $\Theta\epsilon o\phi\dot{\alpha}\nu o\upsilon\varsigma$ $N\iota\kappa\alpha\dot{\iota}\alpha\varsigma$ $\dot{A}\pi\dot{o}\delta\epsilon\iota\xi\iota\varsigma$ $\dot{o}\tau\iota$ $\dot{\epsilon}\delta\dot{\upsilon}\nu\alpha\tau o$ $\dot{\epsilon}\xi$ $\dot{\alpha}\ddot{\iota}\delta\dot{\iota}o\upsilon$ $\gamma\epsilon\gamma\epsilon\nu\dot{\eta}\sigma\theta\alpha\iota$ $\tau\dot{\alpha}$ $\dot{o}\nu\tau\alpha$ $\kappa\alpha\dot{\iota}$ $\dot{\alpha}\nu\alpha\tau\rho o\pi\dot{\eta}$ $\tau\alpha\dot{\upsilon}\tau\eta\varsigma$. See also idem, *Theophanes of Nicaea*, 113–25.

[121] *On the Eternity of Beings* §30 22.26–23.3. See Polemis, *Theophanes of Nicaea*, 125.

[122] *On the Eternity of Beings* §36 37.7, 40.5.

quality of the creation by means of which creatures are united to the uncreated energy of God.[123] Similar distinctly Aristotelian terminology is used by Thomas to denote the receptive power instilled within the creation, a power absolutely distinct from God's wholly active power which is identical with his essence.[124] Granted the very different understandings of the relation between divine essence and operation, Theophanes' use of the concept of 'passive power' to act as median between God (*qua* energy) and the creation may very plausibly be seen as emerging out of his reading of Aquinas.

Theophanes' method in this treatise is also most striking. As we have noted, *On the Light of Thabor* proceeds in an unusually precise fashion: heading each treatise with a question and producing witnesses and arguments for and against. He introduces his own response section with the formula 'In response it should be said [...]' (Πρὸς δὴ τὰ τοιαῦτα ῥητέον [...]), a formula corresponding to Aquinas' *Respondeo dicendum* ('I respond by saying' [...]).[125] *On the Eternity of Beings* makes even greater use of such tags. He begins by enumerating the arguments of his opponents, proceeds to a long response section, then tackles the objections one by one with the formula, 'In response to the nth [objection] it should be said that [...]' (Πρὸς δὲ τὸ $ν^{ον}$ ῥητέον ὅτι [...]).This corresponds closely to the formula used in the Greek translation.[126] It is difficult to explain how Theophanes, who himself seems to have known no Latin, came to adopt such tags and methodology without reference to the translation of the *Summa theologiae*.[127]

---

[123] *On the Eternity of Beings* §37 43.4–8.
[124] This is a recurrent theme in Thomas. See, for example, *SCG* II.8, 22 and *De potentia, passim*.
[125] *On the Light of Thabor* I 221, 457; II 28; III 555–6; IV 107–8, 642–3, 933; V 45–6. Demetrios Kydones habitually translates *Respondeo dicendum* by Ἀπολογουμένοις ῥητέον [...]. See Δημητρίου Κυδώνη, Θωμᾶ Ἀκυινάτου: Σούμμα Θεολογική, ἐξελληνισθεῖσα II 15, 31.10 and *passim*.
[126] Kydones renders the formula thus: Πρὸς δὲ τὸ $ν^{ον}$ λεκτέον ὅτι [...]. See Δημητρίου Κυδώνη, Θωμᾶ Ἀκυινάτου: Σούμμα Θεολογική, ἐξελληνισθεῖσα II 15, 31.28 and *passim*.
[127] The influence may conceivably be indirect. Another prominent anti-Palamite, John Kyparissiotes, had also adopted a similar schema with enumerated arguments, but does so less systematically and with little verbal reminiscence of the Aquinas translation by contrast with either Prochoros or Theophanes. See Manuel Candal, 'Juan Ciparisiota y el problema trinitario palamítico'. It remains, however, much more likely that Theophanes should have this direct from the Greek translation rather than by means of any anti-Palamite text.

But while Theophanes' acquaintance with Aquinas seems indubitably to have impacted on his method and various points of his doctrine, he is in no doubt as to the error of the Latin position on the procession of the Holy Spirit. Like Aquinas and Palamas, he refrains from multiplying the errors of the opposing side and focuses his attention rather on the cardinal issue of the *filioque*. His four discourses *Against the Latins* (after 1368) tackle the question from a variety of angles, rehearsing many of the familiar topics and themes of this hoary debate.[128] What is most interesting for our purposes are the repeated swipes at positions held by Demetrios Kydones, the espousal of Barlaam's anti-logical arguments, and the influence of Neilos Kabasilas. In all cases, Aquinas is in the background as a decisive source for Demetrios and a target of the anti-Latin polemic of Neilos and Barlaam.[129] In the matter of the *filioque* any positive appreciation of Aquinas is, naturally, out of the question. What is perhaps more surprising is that Theophanes has, in practice, sided with Barlaam over Palamas in respect of the place of reason in theology. One may also note that this work eschews the distinctive tags of Latin scholasticism employed in *On the Light of Thabor* and *On the Eternity of Beings*. This was doubtless a nod, however inconsistent, to its avowed anti-logical prescriptions.

Like his doctrine of the divine energies, Theophanes' doctrine of the Trinity exhibits some unusual characteristics. In particular, he contends that there is an order within the immanent Trinity. Polemis takes this to be a sign of a departure from the mainstream Byzantine tradition in which order is confined to the economic Trinity, citing Photios as his chief example. Polemis also takes this to be a departure from Palamas, whom he regards as taking Gregory of Cyprus' notion of the 'shining-forth' of the Spirit through the Son to refer solely to the distribution of the energies to the creation. Leaving aside the question of how representative Photios is of the Byzantine tradition

---

[128] These treatises were valued after their composition. Gennadios Scholarios makes a point of praising them in the C15 while in the C18 Dositheos of Jerusalem describes the publication of the works of 'Palamas, Theophanes of Nicaea, and Kanatakuzene' as being of particular importance. See Andronikos Demetrakopoulos, ' Ορθόδοξος Ελλὰς, 84–5.

[129] See Polemis, *Theophanes of Nicaea*, 126–69. Much of the work is, in fact, lifted straight from Neilos. Polemis also obverses that Theophanes made indirect use of a pro-Latin florilegium composed by the unionist Patriarch John Bekkos—again taking his cue from Neilos.

in toto, the point regarding Palamas is worth pursuing. As we have laboured at some length to demonstrate, Palamas does in fact allow for order within the immanent Trinity in his treatment of what we have termed an 'Orthodox *filioque*'.[130] In this respect, therefore, Theophanes may be closer to Palamas than Polemis allows.

Other works of Theophanes need not detain us long. The treatise *Against the Jews* contains little that cannot be paralleled in earlier anti-Jewish literature.[131] The homily *On the Mother of God* is of greater interest in its evocations of the piety, sinlessness, and purity of the Virgin.[132] This is one of the rare Byzantine texts to have earned the unalloyed praise of Martin Jugie, its editor. The homily works its way through the various titles of the Virgin and goes on to speak of her in the most elevated of terms: she is the neck of the body of which Christ is head; she takes to herself the divinity of Christ as the Father takes to himself his humanity; she is ineffably united to the Holy Spirit and archetype of the deified life; and she is mediatrix of grace. An extraordinary homily, but not one which even Jugie regards as having any particular connection with the West.

In Theophanes, we are presented with the arresting phenomenon of a Palamite anti-unionist drawing to a significant degree on the Greek Thomas in both doctrine and methodology. His use of the distinctive methodology of the Latin scholastics is patent in *On the Light of Thabor* and *On the Eternity of Beings*. It is also in these treatises that we see some significant points of doctrine being forged under the influence of certain positions of Thomas, in particular the triplex model of knowledge, the identity of essence and noetic activity in God, and the notion of the created energy of God as a 'passive power'. But Theophanes is by no means the only Palamite anti-unionist to draw on Aquinas. For another outstanding example, we may turn to Palamas' successor as Archbishop of Thessalonica, Neilos Kabasilas.

---

[130] See above, pp.37–9.

[131] See Polemis, *Theophanes of Nicaea*, 170–84. Polemis detects a response to Prochoros in Theophanes' defence of the sinlessness of Christ's body.

[132] Martin Jugie (ed.), *Theophanes Nicaenus († 1381). Sermo in sanctissimam Deiparam*. On this text, see Polemis, *Theophanes of Nicaea*, 185–90, including a fascinating if unproven suggestion of a connection between this text and Nicholas Kabasilas' *The Life in Christ* in respect of the Virgin as a type and exemplar of the deified life.

3.5. NEILOS KABASILAS (d. 1363)

Born in the latter years of the thirteenth century, Neilos rose to be one of the most respected men of his time, admired and courted by Palamites and anti-Palamites alike.[133] Despite having been a layman for much of his life, he was a candidate for the patriarchal throne in 1353 and was appointed to the see of Thessalonica as Gregory's successor in 1361. His baptismal name appears to be have been Nicholas, hence the frequent confusion with his illustrious nephew of that same name, author of a noted commentary on the Divine Liturgy and the equally celebrated *Life in Christ*. Neilos was the teacher of several illustrious pupils including Demetrios Kydones and the said nephew. Neilos appears to have maintained a neutral position in the early years of the Hesychast Controversy and was on good terms with Barlaam, Akindynos, and Gregoras. Gregoras much appreciated a visit from Neilos in his confinement at the time of the Council of 1351 and even suggested that his 'greatest friend' shared his antipathy to Palamas.[134] Contrary to Gregoras' report, Kabasilas in fact emerged at that time as a vocal and prominent defender of Palamite theology. He was even, according to the anti-Palamite scholar John Kyparissiotes, involved in the redaction of the Tome of 1351.[135]

Neilos wrote relatively little on the Palamite controversy itself, albeit certainly sufficient to demonstrate his commitment to the newly established orthodoxy.[136] His chief efforts were directed against the Latins and it is his main work of this genre, *On the Procession of the Holy Spirit*, that most closely concerns us.[137]

---

[133] *PLP* 10102. Théophile Kislas, *Nilus Cabasilas. Sur le Saint-Esprit* has some excellent introductory material to which much of the material in this paragraph is indebted. See also Giuseppe Schirò, 'Il paradosso de Nil Cabasila' and Atanasije Jevtić, *Études hésychastes*, Chapter 3: 'Rencontre de la scolastique et de l'hésychasme dans l'œuvre de Nilus Cabasilas'.

[134] Gregoras, *History* 22.4 (PG 148 1328B–1329C).

[135] *On the Transgressions of the Palamites* 1.2 (PG 152 677D). This does not square easily with Philotheos Kokkinos' account in which he is the chief drafter and Neilos is not mentioned. Demetrios Kaïmakes (ed.), Φιλοθέου Κοκκίνου δογματικὰ ἔργα I 20.

[136] See Kislas, *Nilus Cabasilas. Sur le Saint-Esprit*, 66–8. The most significant text is that edited by Manuel Candal, 'La "Regla teológica" de Nilo Cabásilas'.

[137] The large work is divided into three parts: five discourses *Against the Conclusions of the Latins*, a *Refutation of the Premises of the Latins*, and a *Refutation of the Syllogisms of the Latins*. The first and third of these have been edited by, respectively, Théophile Kislas, *Nilus Cabasilas. Sur le Saint-Esprit*, 174–416 and Emmanuel Candal, *Nilus Cabasilas et theologia S. Thomae de processione Spiritus Sancti*, 188–385.

Aquinas is a direct target here as a primary defender of the *filioque*, but the treatment is by no means wholly negative. Neilos had long known and admired Aquinas' work. Demetrios Kydones tells us that he had initially welcomed Thomas with unreserved enthusiasm, praising Demetrios' translation and reckoning Thomas an exceptionally valuable teacher. According to Demetrios, Neilos was at one time 'madly in love with' Thomas' works (μανικὸς ἦν ἐραστής) and with Latin theology in general. He knew Thomas not only through Demetrios but also through his own reading—an assertion that implies that he knew Latin. By Demetrios' account, Neilos was initially unconvinced as to the merits of the Palamite distinction, finding plausible arguments both for and against, and turning to embrace it only under imperial and ecclesiastical pressure. Demetrios was appalled by his friend's subsequent disavowal of Thomas in the *On the Procession of the Holy Spirit* and blasts it as a triumph of style over substance. This derivative and vacuous work might, for all its literary flair, be refuted by a child. It will certainly not, he writes, impress the Latins even if its verbal dexterity might play well to the home crowd.[138]

Demetrios doubtless exaggerates here as to the extent of the initial enthusiasm, the depth of the supposed doubts over Palamite theology, and the absoluteness of the later disavowal of Thomas. He also much underestimates the power of Neilos' work. In fact, Neilos may more accurately be regarded as having remained a cautious enthusiast for Thomas—and a moderate Palamite—throughout his career.[139] In the work on the procession of the Spirit, Thomas is certainly attacked in stern terms but this is no straightforward polemic. In practice, Thomas is most often referenced to undermine the Latin positions or to demonstrate his own internal contradictions. He becomes, as it were, a kind of fifth column within the Latin encampment. This is, in short, more a question of appropriation than of simple refutation.

Neilos knew Thomas exceptionally well. He cites the Kydones brothers' translations of the *Summa contra gentiles*, the *Summa theologiae*, and the *De potentia*. His theological methodology emulates that employed by Aquinas in many respects: clear

---

[138] *Apology* I, 390.6–394.88.

[139] John Meyendorff observes that Nilus was consciously trying to 'overcome the dilemma' between Palamism and Thomism, *Byzantine Theology*, 107. This line of thought is pursued in Joost van Rossum's 'Palamism and Church Tradition: Palamism, its Use of Patristic Tradition, and its Relationship with Thomistic Thought', 34–8.

Fragenstellung; forensic use of scripture, patristic authority, and reason; systematic rehearsal of contrary positions and rebuttal of the same; and the furnishing of solutions to the various *aporiae* adduced.[140] The treatise begins with the five discourses *Against the Conclusions of the Latins* and soon lights upon Thomas, taking him as the Latins' 'pre-eminent theologian' (Discourse I.7).[141] But here Thomas is not attacked but used instead to underscore the commonality of Latins and Greeks in respect of the differentiation of names applied to God according to person and according to nature.[142] The second instance also draws on Thomas to bolster the Greek position, taking him to affirm that to emit or to be cause within the Trinity cannot pertain to essence but only to person (I.9).[143] Only at the third mention is anything negative alleged, with Thomas deemed self-contradictory in upholding two who emit but not two emitters, because of the one procession (I.16).[144] The problems of his position are dwelt upon over several sections (I.18–23).[145] But before long, he is again drawn on in support of the Greek case in his assertion that the essence does not beget essence and that the divine nature of the Son is not begotten, either of itself or accidentally (I.42).[146] In the next section, Thomas is hailed as 'interpreter of the theologians', and commended for his exacting amplification and clarification of patristic testimony (in this case, Cyril of Alexandria). Here, Thomas is

---

[140] A favoured formula is ἔνστασις (objection) and λύσις (solution). This Aristotelian terminology was used in systematic form in the neo-Platonic commentary tradition, from where it doubtless percolated through to Neilos. See, for example, 'Elias' of Alexandria (Busse (ed.), *Eliae in Porphyrii isagogen et Aristotelis categorias commentaria*, 80).

[141] The same judgement is repeated in *Against the Conclusions of the Latins* V.20.

[142] Cf. *ST* Iᵃ q.35 a.1–2; q.38 a.1–2.

[143] The Greek here may be rendered, 'The Holy Spirit proceeds from the Father and the Son in as much as they are distinct persons, but not as the creation does in so far as the Father and Son are one in essence.' This appears to be a paraphrase of *ST* Iᵃ q.36 a.4 ad 7: 'Quia spiritus sanctus procedit a patre et filio ut sunt duae personae distinctae, ut dictum est, non autem creatura procedit a tribus personis ut sunt personae distinctae, sed ut sunt unum in essentia.'

[144] *ST* Iᵃ q.36 a.4 ad 7: 'possumus dicere quod pater et filius sunt duo spirantes, propter pluralitatem suppositorum; non autem duo spiratores, propter unam spirationem'. Kislas, loc. cit., mistakenly gives *ST* I 27.5.

[145] This includes a repetition of the paraphrase of *ST* Iᵃ q.36 a.4 ad 7 given in Discourse I.9.

[146] *ST* Iᵃ q.39 a.5 s.c.; ad 2. Kislas, loc. cit., mistakenly gives *ST* I 34.5. Kabasilas also cites Hugh Etherian here in the same regard, noting that he appears right in this instance even if wrong in most other matters.

again marshalled to support the Greek cause, demonstrating that the Son is not begotten of the essence of the Father (I.43).[147] A last citation has him once more approved for treating the creation not as an activity peculiar to any one of the divine hypostases but as a function of the common essence (I.51).[148]

Thomas comes in for some further criticism in the remainder of *Against the Conclusions of the Latins*. He is detected in another bout of self-contradiction in Discourse II.43 and taxed for his temerity in disagreeing with John of Damascus, whom he is acknowledged otherwise to honour, in Discourse V.40–2. The pattern, however, remains one of cautious enthusiasm. This interplay of approbation and repudiation is more than just a tactical move. Thomas is certainly criticized but there no doubt of the powerful authority Neilos deems this 'interpreter of the theologians' to have. Thomas is, in effect, being wrested away from some of his own conclusions and co-opted to support the Greek position in the matter of the *filioque*. This is not a case of straightforward polemic but more a struggle for the appropriation of Aquinas to the cause of Orthodoxy.

The second part of *On the Procession of the Holy Spirit* tackles the scriptural and patristic testimonies adduced by the Latins, and does so very minutely.[149] Thomas' interpretations come in for some rough treatment but again we witness a dynamic of approval and rebuttal. One intriguing instance concerns the potential errancy of patristic testimony. Neilos takes Thomas' partial disavowal of John of Damascus as a precedent for the Greeks' analogous refusal to embrace all aspects of Augustine's avowedly speculative teaching on the Trinity. The commendation of Augustine at the Fifth Ecumenical Council, he argues, no more obliges us to accept the *filioque* than it does the equally commended Gregory of Nyssa's teaching on universal salvation.

The third part of Neilos' *magnum opus* refutes fifteen Latin syllogisms, eight of which derive from *Summa contra gentiles* IV.24. This is a work that makes critical use of Barlaam's anti-logical, anti-Latin writings but remains considerably better disposed towards, and more knowledgeable of, the angelic doctor than ever

---

[147] *ST* Iᵃ q.39 a. 5 ad 1.

[148] This citation is a partial version of the paraphrase of *ST* Iᵃ q.36 a.4 ad 7 given in Discourse I.9 and 22.

[149] Here I rely on Kislas' summary in *Nilus Cabasilas. Sur le Saint-Esprit*, 106–22. Kislas prepared an edition in his unpublished doctoral thesis, 'Nilus Cabasilas et son traité sur le Saint-Esprit'.

was the Calabrian monk.[150] A recurrent tactic in this part is for Neilos to appeal to Thomas' manifest apophaticism in order to expose the weakness of any rational argumentation whatsoever in respect of God. Thomas' frequent protestations of the inadequacies and incapacities of human reason are used to good effect to undermine the very bases of the various Latin syllogisms. In particular, Neilos takes as programmatic Thomas' teaching on the twofold mode of truth in *SCG* I.3.2—some things being accessible to human reason, others definitely not. This teaching is seen to be in continuity with John of Damascus and confirmed by scriptural testimony.[151] Neilos gives us many examples of Thomas' strictures on reason and goes on to upbraid him for his supposedly self-contradictory love of the syllogism, which he is held to 'breathe rather than air'. Neilos finds it deeply ironic that one who expressly notes the inherent weakness of the syllogism should make such profligate use of it.[152]

While some may doubt the extent to which Neilos has succeeded in hoisting Thomas by his own petard, there is no doubt of the value he ascribes to the angelic doctor. His cautious enthusiasm for Aquinas evidently remained undimmed throughout his career. Struck by the success of Thomas in pro-Latin unionist circles, Neilos makes a bid to harness that energy for the Orthodox cause. In Neilos, we have a startling example of the possibilities of an Orthodox reception of Aquinas. Here is a committed Palamite and uncompromising anti-unionist displaying real enthusiasm for Thomas and reaping tangible benefit from that engagement. This instance of suitably critical but deeply positive and constructive reception stands as a useful *point de repère* for this study as a whole.

3.6. NICHOLAS KABASILAS (*c*.1322–*c*.1397/8)

Neilos' illustrious nephew also has a significant part to play in this saga. Nicholas Kabasilas Chamaetos, like many other sons of

---

[150] On the debt to Barlaam, see Kislas, *Nilus Cabasilas. Sur le Saint-Esprit*, 132–41. Kislas is careful to point out the extent to which Neilos has toned down and modified Barlaam's argument.

[151] *Refutation of the Syllogisms of the Latins* §12 (ed. Candal, 194).

[152] *Refutation of the Syllogisms of the Latins* §64–8 (ed. Candal, 238–42).

Thessalonica, became a partisan of John Kantakuzene and, perforce, of the Palamite cause.[153] He is justly celebrated for his *Commentary on the Divine Liturgy* and *On the Life in Christ*. These timeless classics attest to a theological vision of the highest order, one that is uniquely and powerfully Christocentric and sacramental. Unlike most theological productions of the time, Nicholas' works are directed not at monks or specialized theologians, but to the whole people of God. A layman throughout his life, Nicholas epitomizes the very best of Byzantine spiritual writing.[154]

Nicholas' works display a remarkable openness to Latin liturgy and theology. For instance, while giving a robust rebuttal of Latin criticisms of the Greek *epiclesis* (the invocation of the Spirit over the eucharistic gifts) Kabasilas is prepared to discern a form of *epiclesis* in the supplication of the Latin mass, *Supplices te rogamus*.[155] The many references to the Latin rite and Latin liturgical theology in the *Commentary on the Divine Liturgy* attest to a thorough knowledge of and contacts with the Latin world. In this work, he also shows himself perfectly comfortable with scholastic modes of argumentation, tackling the problem of the object of the eucharistic sacrifice in classic *Quaestio* form.[156]

Nicholas' contacts and sympathies with the Latin world are further evidenced by his embrace of elements of Anselm's theory of atonement. This includes the very distinctive idea of sin constituting a 'debt of honour' owed by man to God and the need for a restitution over and above the measure of the original offence:

> To sin is to insult God, as it is said, 'by the transgression of the law, you dishonour God' [Rom. 2:23] and a greater virtue than that of man is required for the indictment (ἔγκλημα) to be cancelled. It is very easy for the least of things to insult the greatest, but then it is impossible to make up in honour (ἀντισηκῶσαι τιμῇ) for the insult suffered by God. [. . .]

---

[153] *PLP* 30531. See also the tremendously valuable article by Yannis Spiteris and Carmelo Conticello, 'Nicola Cabasilas Chamaetos'. Nicholas used by preference the more noble name of Kabasilas which came to him from his mother.

[154] For an evocation of the thrilling beauty of Nicholas' work, there is nothing to beat Myrrha Lot Borodine's *Un maître de la spiritualité byzantine au XIVe siècle, Nicolas Cabasilas*.

[155] *Commentary on the Divine Liturgy* 30 (SC 4bis 190–8).

[156] *Commentary on the Divine Liturgy*, 32 (SC 4bis 202–6). He considers whether the sacrifice be of the bread or of Christ, and if of Christ, in what sense.

For to cancel the indictment and to restore to the injured party the honour taken from him requires a restitution greater than that owed.[157]

In this impossible situation, only Christ through the Cross is able to restore to the Father the honour taken from him, and more.[158] This is precisely the kind of language habitually written off as inadmissibly juridical and legalistic in less nuanced Orthodox critiques of the wickedness of the West. Certainly, any hint of 'satisfaction theory' or substitutionary atonement is widely deemed foreign to Orthodoxy.[159] What, then, to make of the patent use of such language and concepts in Kabasilas?

There are at least two ways in which discussion of this intriguing borrowing can become profitless. The first is to assume that any use of legalistic vocabulary must be explained away: as incompatible with the wider framework of Kabasilas' vision, as aberrant, or even as an interpolation. The second is to exaggerate the significance of that borrowing, taking it as the sign of a mechanical or slavish dependence. Avoiding such blind alleys, it is surely more constructive (and accurate) to read this as fine example of Orthodox reception of a distinctively Latin understanding of redemption. Kabasilas has lighted upon certain striking concepts and themes current in the Latin theology of his time and set these within a broader conception of salvation history extending not only from Fall to redemption but also and simultaneously from creation to deification, deification being communicated to humans principally through participation in the life-giving mysteries of Christ. In adopting certain Latin categories, Kabasilas recognizes that there is nothing intrinsically wrong with

---

[157] *Life in Christ* 4.12–13 (SC 355 272–4). See also 4.14–16 (274–8) and 1.43–53 (116–24). Cf. Anselm, *Cur Deus homo*, 1.11. The possible Anselmian connection was first noted by Wilhelm Gass in 1849, *Die Mystik des Nikolaus Cabasilas*, 78–9. Since then the question has been much pored over: see the summaries in Spiteris and Conticello, 'Nicola Cabasilas Chamaetos', 366–8 and Marie-Hélène Congourdeau, SC 355 (Introduction), 45–6.

[158] *Life in Christ* 4.16 (SC 355 276).

[159] Vladimir Lossky sets up a sharp contrast between Anselm's 'juridical' and overly-rational and the patristic approach, focused on deification. See his 'Redemption and Deification', 99–103. In Lossky's footsteps, Christos Yannaras views Anselm's notion of satisfaction as especially pernicious and commends John Romanides' Τὸ προπατορικὸν ἁμάρτημα with its assertion that the legalism of Augustine, Anselm, and Aquinas constitutes the root cause of the theological deviancy of the Christian West, ' Ὀρθοδοξία καὶ Δύση στὴ Νεώτερη Ἑλλάδα, 65–6, 441 [ET 40, 275–6].

using legal vocabulary and juridical concepts to explore the workings
of the atonement so long these do not constitute an exclusive frame of
reference.[160]

Less important for the purposes of this study is the question of
precisely how Kabasilas became acquainted with Anselm's theories.
There was, so far as we know, no Greek translation of *Cur Deus homo*
available to him—the first such being done by Manuel Kalekas after
Nicholas' death.[161] Sévérien Salaville has suggested that it is Aquinas
who served as a vehicle for some of Anselm's ideas, through the
Kydones translations.[162] But this supposition cannot itself account
for the sense of sin as an insult to God and the debt of honour owed as
a result, distinctly Anselmian notions not countenanced by Thomas.
Nicholas' close ties with the Kydones brothers will certainly have
helped facilitate his knowledge of the Latin thought-world, as will
his intimate association with the monastery of the Xanthopouloi, a
Constantinopolitan house noted for its generous attitude towards
Latins and Latinophiles.[163] But whatever the mechanics of his
encounter with these ideas, the fact remains that he both affirms
and adapts them by incorporating them within his overarching theological vision.

Nicholas' constructive encounter with Latin theology is a recurrent
feature of his work. Jean Gouillard has sketched out a number of
possible parallels between the portraits of the blessed life in the *Life in
Christ* and those given by Augustine and Thomas.[164] He begins with

---

[160] Such vocabulary was by no means foreign to the Fathers. Macarius-Symeon
and Mark the Monk, for example, use the legal term ἔγκλημα (charge, accusation) to
express the indictment laid upon all humans as a consequence of the Fall (Macarius-
Symeon, Collection I 37.6; Mark, *On the Hypostatic Union*, 31(18). See Plested, *The
Macarian Legacy*, 77, 79–80). Both use the term in association with the supposed
'rights' of the Devil, a common theme within patristic treatments of the atonement.
Anselm developed his notion of the 'debt of honour' owed by man to God precisely so
as to counteract any residual notion of the Devil having any 'rights' whatsoever.
Kabasilas was evidently glad to draw on this salutary corrective.

[161] Mercati, *Notizie*, 80, 90.

[162] 'Vues sotériologiques chez Nicolas Cabasilas (XIVᵉ siècle)', 52–5.

[163] Nicholas' close friendship with Demetrios appears to have been life-long,
notwithstanding their theological differences. See Congourdeau in SC 355 (Introduction), 16 n.9. On the monastery of the Xanthopouloi, see Raymond-Joseph Loenertz,
Correspondance de Manuel Calecas, 84–5 and David Balfour, *Politico-historical works
of Symeon, Archbishop of Thessalonica (1416/17 to 1429)*, 279–86. Joasaph, a monk of
the Xanthopouloi, was responsible for copying and disseminating works by both
Nicholas and Demetrios.

[164] 'L'autoportrait d'un sage du XIVe siècle'.

knowledge of God as the essence of beatitude, certainly a theme more commonly associated with Latin than Byzantine writers.[165] Perhaps even more striking is the theme of the desire of an infinite good in a finite nature.[166] Marie-Hélène Congourdeau has detected a further possible parallel with Augustine in the suggestion that God is closer to us than our own soul.[167] Nicholas' three homilies on the Mother of God speak of some acquaintance with contemporary Western developments in Marian theology with their repeated evocations of her complete freedom from all inherited sin.[168]

Kabasilas was a deeply cultured man, well-versed not only in theology but also the natural sciences, philosophy, and poetry.[169] In philosophical terms, his outlook is typically Byzantine in its Christian Aristotelianism, a feature of his intellectual make-up evident not only in his more overtly philosophical works but also in Books VI and VII of the *Life in Christ* with its many resonances with Aristotle's *Ethics*.[170] His

---

[165] *Life in Christ* 2.102 (SC 355 232). This is itself a commonplace: Nicholas introduces it as something 'known to all'.

[166] *Life in Christ* 2.89–90 (SC 355 218); 7.60–1, 66–8 (SC 361 92–4, 184–6). In 2.90, Nicholas speaks at length of the soul's dissatisfaction with things of this world and Christ as its sole desire, in whom alone can it find a resting-place ($\kappa a \tau \acute{a} \lambda \upsilon \mu a$). Similarly, in 7.68, he speaks of the soul's infinite desire finding satisfaction and rest only in God. Such evocations certainly bear comparison with Augustine's famous paean to the heart's restlessness until it finds rest in God (*Confessions* 1.1(1)). Kabasilas' ruminations on the infinite nature of the human faculty of desire in 7.61 also recall Aquinas' observation in I^a–II^{ae} q.2 a.1 arg. 3 that, 'desiderium summi boni, cum nunquam deficiat, videtur esse infinitum'.

[167] *Life in Christ* 7.68 (SC 361 186): 'the Saviour is closer to us than our own soul', cf. *Confessions* 3.6(11): God is 'interior intimo meo'. See her 'Nicolas Cabasilas et le Palamisme', 202 n.52. This article is a particularly pellucid treatment of a complex topic.

[168] Martin Jugie (ed.), *Homélies mariales byzantines* II, 465–510. Her nature is that of Adam before the Fall (*Homily on the Nativity of the Mother of God* 4, 469); she has inherited no trace of the old leaven and is free from ageing and all other forms of corruption (*Homily on the Dormition of the Mother of God* 4, 498). But while Nicholas might certainly have been ready to affirm an 'immaculate conception', this does not imply that he accepted the concomitant theory of the transmission of original culpability through concupiscence.

[169] Nicholas has left works displaying his expertise in all these areas. See Spiteris and Conticello, 'Nicola Cabasilas Chamaetos', 338–41, 345–6.

[170] See Gouillard, 'L'autoportrait d'un sage du XIVe siècle'. Nicholas expressly remarks that his portrait of the life in Christ, the 'life according to correct reason', is in right line with 'what the ancients have spoken of, and many others in their train' (*Life in Christ* 6.3 (SC 361 40); cf. *Nichomachean Ethics* 2.2.2). Gouillard also points out a number of Stoic features in Nicholas' work.

Aristotelianism will certainly have prepared the ground for a positive reception of certain aspects of medieval Latin theology.

Nicholas' philosophical commitments were to put him in a difficult position vis-à-vis the controversies of this time. An instinctively irenic figure, Nicholas avoided controversy wherever possible. He was certainly of the Palamite party, a protégé of John VI and a devoted friend of Palamas, whom he accompanied on his journey to claim his see of Thessalonica. But Kabasilas eschews all mention of the fraught topics of the essence–energies distinction and the character of the light of Thabor. Even his one *opusculum* bearing directly on the controversy, *Against the Ravings of Gregoras*, is largely a personal defence of Palamas, 'the wonder of Thessalonica', and barely touches on the key theological issues at stake.[171] Another *opusculum* would even seem to suggest a degree of unease at some developments within the Palamite camp. This work bears the less than pithy title *Arguments of those who wish to show the uselessness of wisdom gained from reason and solutions to their attempted proofs.*[172]

This defence of the value of secular learning is constructed in good scholastic form with five enumerated arguments followed by solutions thereof. The conclusions are that while reason may not itself be the end goal of human life, this does not mean it is useless. The fact that some have erred through misuse of reason does not show that reason itself is useless. Attacking reason itself rather than the misuses thereof is like attacking Socrates by means of a disquisition on Xerxes' naval mishaps. Nicholas makes a syllogism out of his opponents' position (some have not employed reason to its proper end, such people are foolish, therefore reason is useless) to demonstrate its falsity.

Some recent commentators have detected a critique of Palamas here with John Demetracopoulos going so far as to characterize this as an 'anti-Palamite' treatise.[173] While this short work certainly

[171] Antonio Garzya (ed.), 'Un opuscule inédit de Nicolas Cabasilas'. Nicholas laces the text liberally with classical allusions and defends Gregory from accusations including that of being unread.
[172] Athanasios Angelopoulos (ed.), Νικόλαος Καβάσιλας Χαμαετός. Ἡ ζωὴ καὶ τὸ ἔργον αὐτοῦ, 111–13 (based on one MS) and John Demetracopoulos (ed.), 'Nicholas Cabasilas' *Quaestio de rationis valore*: an anti-Palamite defense of secular wisdom' (based on a wider selection of MSS), 55–7.
[173] See Ioannis Polemis, 'Notes on a short treatise of Nicolas Cabasilas' and John Demetracopoulos, op. cit. In a most valuable contribution to the debate,

detracts from some of the more stringent anti-philosophical remarks in the *Triads* it is by no means inconsistent with Palamas' ultimately positive, if tremendously cautious, approach to philosophy and the outer learning.[174] One might also detect in it a critique of the theological scepticism of critics of Palamas such as Barlaam and Gregoras. Rather than a straightforward attack on Palamas, this text is perhaps better read as a reaction to obscurantist and anti-logical tendencies in Palamite and anti-Palamite circles alike.[175]

Nicholas was similarly cautious and poised in regard to the Latin–Greek schism as to the Palamite controversy. While he has no truck with the *filioque* and is impatient of Latin criticisms of Greek liturgical practices he is in no doubt as to the underlying unity of East and West.[176] Whether in his detection of an implicit *epiclesis* among Latins or his thoughtful embrace of elements of Latin theology, Nicholas is a theologian who inhabits still the common tradition of East and West. This catholic mindset is further revealed in his scrupulous declining of Joseph Bryennios' request that he engage in polemic against the Latins.[177]

Nicholas represents one of the finest flowerings of Byzantine humanism. He was also, and without contradiction, a hesychast, but one whose hesychasm was for all and not geared primarily towards monks. While not a theological Palamite, he shared Palamas' vision of the Christian life as centred on the constant presence of

---

Demetracopoulos gives ample evidence of Nicholas' Aristotelianism and plays down Gouillard's suggestion of a substantial Stoic dimension to his thought. He also suggests (77–83) a number of possible connections with Aquinas, somewhat overstating the case to my mind: there is little here (perhaps excepting the fleetingness of the vision of the divine in this life) that cannot be accounted for by their common Christian Aristotelianism. Lastly, he furnishes (88–9) a useful discussion of the date of this work, plumping for 1354–5 on the basis of its being a relatively early work but exhibiting, as he maintains, knowledge of the translation of the *Summa contra gentiles*. It must be said that if the label 'anti-Palamite' is an exaggeration, so too is Tatakis' depiction of a 'fervent Palamite' (*La philosophie byzantine*, 277) or Meyendorff's perception of a 'total unity of inspiration and purpose' between Nicholas and Gregory (*Byzantine Theology*, 107).

[174] As delineated in Chapter 2, above.

[175] Nicholas is also the author of a short work against the scepticism of Pyrhho. See Spiteris and Conticello, 'Nicola Cabasilas Chamaetos', 338–9.

[176] For his uncompromising position on the *filioque*, see his preface to Neilos' *On the Procession of the Holy Spirit* (PG 149 677–80; Andronikos Demetrakopoulos, ' Ὀρθόδοξος Ἑλλάς, 78–80).

[177] See Spiteris and Conticello, 'Nicola Cabasilas Chamaetos', 323, 351 (Opus 53).

Christ and ordered towards deifying participation in the life of God. In sum, in Nicholas Kabasilas we have a theologian of the highest calibre and of exceptional spiritual acumen who achieves the feat of remaining irreproachably Orthodox but also remarkably open to constructive reception of Latin theology, Aquinas very much included. It is a sophisticated balancing act that few have managed so successfully.

4

Further Readings

Having discussed in the previous chapter the chief figures of the first phase of the Byzantine encounter with Thomas, we now turn to some of the other theologians involved in that encounter, taking the story down to the fall of the City in 1453—a catastrophe regarded by many at the time as tantamount to the end of the world. In the opening sections, several second-tier theologians are dealt with under the simple but not inaccurate headings of 'detractors' and 'devotees'. The discussion then moves to a number of other writers instancing a more complex pattern of reception. These are discussed largely in the context of the burning debates over union with the Latins that dominated the last decades of the Empire, culminating in the Council of Ferrara–Florence (1438-9). The chapter closes with a theologian who managed to be both a devotee and a detractor, a unionist and (later) an anti-unionist: George (Gennadios) Scholarios. As the first Patriarch of Constantinople after the Ottoman takeover, Scholarios stands as both an end and a beginning: one of the last and greatest of Byzantine theologians and also the first to grapple seriously with the aftermath of the final collapse of the Christian Roman Empire. He was also, by his own account, Thomas' most devoted disciple.

4.1. DETRACTORS

For all the positive estimations of Thomas we have uncovered thus far, even in some unexpected quarters, it must never be forgotten that there were great troughs of loathing for the Latins among the Byzantines. This loathing, born of cultural estrangement and economic resentment, had erupted with particular savagery in 1182 with the massacre of a substantial portion of the Latin population of Constantinople. This atrocity was repaid with savage interest in the Latin sack of Constantinople in 1204, an event that stood out even in an age accustomed to violence for its rapaciousness, blood-letting, and desecration. Michael VIII's attempt to impose the Union of Lyons by force after 1274 only deepened Byzantine antipathy to the Latins: the 'new Constantine', the hero of the re-conquest of the City, died in dishonour and was denied Orthodox burial on grounds of his perceived apostasy. The re-conquest also brought with it an acceleration of the process whereby Latin commercial interests took control of an ever-growing share of imperial trade and revenues. This economic stranglehold did little to encourage sympathetic diagnosis of Latin religious errors. Indeed, in such an atmosphere of antipathy and mistrust, it is striking that there are not more figures prepared to condemn Aquinas without equivocation. But there are some and their voices must be heard.[1] The chief exemplars of such a stance are Matthew Panaretos and Kallistos Angelikoudes.

Matthew Angelos Panaretos wrote extensively on the errors of the Latins, composing works on the Roman primacy, the procession of the Spirit, the use of *azymes*, and the fire of purgatory.[2] He was active in the latter half of the fourteenth century, writing most plausibly in the 1350s–60s in reaction to the success of the Greek translations of Thomas and to the pro-Latin policies of John V.[3] His comprehensive treatment of the Latin question earned him designation by Joseph of Methone as one of the authors of the schism and a principal source for Mark of Ephesus.[4] His reputation as a leading anti-unionist writer

---

[1] We know of some detractors only by name. Codex *Urbinatus graecus* 155 (*c.*1436) mentions an Angelos Aeidaros who composed '40 books against Thomas', none of which are known to be extant. Doubtless there were many other opponents (and proponents) of Thomas who have not even left their name. This MS appears prone to some exaggeration: it credits Matthew Panaretos and Kallistos Angelikoudes with, respectively, 34 and 40 'books against Thomas'. Works against Thomas by these authors do survive, but not in anything like such quantities.

[2] *PLP* 21649.

[3] See Andronikos Demetrakopoulos, Ὀρθόδοξος Ἑλλάς, 48–53; Pietro Risso 'Matteo Angelo Panaretos e cinque suoi opuscoli', 8, 91–105; and Carmine Buda, 'Influsso del Tomismo in Bisanzio nel secolo XIV'. Panaretos had long been associated with the run-up to the Council of Lyons, being confused with another Panaretos mentioned by George Pachymeres. Demetrakopoulos noticed a number of serious problems with this identification, but kept him in his 'Thirteenth Century' section. Risso and Buda have shown conclusively that our Panaretos must be a later figure.

[4] *Responsio ad libellum Marci Eugenici* (PG 159 1092B–D).

proved enduring, prompting Patriarch Dositheos of Jerusalem to attempt to publish him in the early eighteenth century, a project that appears to have foundered.[5] Only in the twentieth century were portions of his work edited and published.[6]

Panaretos composed over twenty works against the Latins, two of which are directed specifically against Thomas: one on the procession and one on purgatory. At the end of the treatise on purgatory, a brief note reads:

> This Italian flourished at the time of the pious emperor Andronikos Palaiologos.[7] He had his home in Naples and belonged to the order of the Friar Preachers and wrote much in his own language on the whole of holy scripture, both the Old and the New [Testament] [. . .] these works were unknown in the Church of New Rome and to all the Orthodox until the time of Emperor John Kantakuzene. Towards the end of his reign a native of Thessalonica named Kydones, who knew Latin, translated them all into Greek. Some of these were transcribed by the Emperor Kantakuzene and placed in his library. If God gives me the time, I shall refute these works totally and utterly, both what he has written about the fire of purgatory and about the procession of the Holy Spirit.[8]

The work on the procession is of particular interest. Panaretos sets his sights on the *Ad cantorem Antiochenum*, one of the works translated by Demetrios Kydones. The treatise proceeds in methodical fashion, extracting theses from Thomas and meeting these with antitheses.

[5] See Pietro Risso, 'Matteo Angelo Panaretos e cinque suoi opuscoli', 8, 104–5.
[6] Risso, 'Matteo Angelo Panaretos e cinque suoi opuscoli'; Buda, 'Il tomismo a Bisanzio nel secolo XIV. Una polemica Bizantina del secolo XIV'. Risso gives works on the origins of the schism, the procession, a detailing of twenty-four errors of Latin religious practice, a defence of the addition of hot water to the chalice, and a treatise on azymes. Buda gives the treatise against Thomas on the procession. His work on the Photian Council of 879–80 (*On the Holy and Ecumenical Council which Restored Photios to the Throne of Constantinople and Overcame the Division of the Churches of Old and New Rome*) was published anonymously in William Beveridge's magnificent Συνοδικὸν *sive Pandectae canonum ss. apostolorum, et conciliorum ab ecclesia Graeca receptorum* (II 273–305).
[7] Andronikos II Palaiologos reigned as emperor from 1282 to 1328, although he had been proclaimed as co-emperor from 1261. Panaretos is either simply mistaken in his chronology or is erasing Andronikos' unionist father, Michael VIII, from the record.
[8] Text given in Andronikos Demetrakopoulos, 'Ορθόδοξος 'Ελλὰς, 48–9. See also Giovanni Mingarelli, *Graeci codices manuscripti apud Nanios patricios Venetos asservati*, 299ff (Codex *Nanianus* 130).

Panaretos sets up the debate with an insistence on the insufficiency of reason:

> The supreme and incomprehensible matter of theology not only transcends the human mind but is also inaccessible and unintelligible to the angelic powers; thus our faith is not to be believed on grounds of necessary reasons nor demonstrated by propositions and conclusions. For how should the supernatural be elaborated by means of the natural? But faith has been revealed to human beings by God [. . .].[9]

There is nothing exceptionable here, but one can hardly fail to note the similarity with Thomas' own sentiments expressed in the text that Panaretos had before his eyes:

> Firstly, I want to warn you that in disputations with unbelievers about articles of the faith, you should not try to prove the faith by necessary reasons. This would derogate the sublime nature of the faith, whose truth exceeds not only human minds but also those of angels; we believe in them only because they are revealed by God. (*Ad cantorem Antiochenum* §2)

After this astonishing apparent homage, the treatise begins to dissect the arguments given by Thomas in defence of the reasonableness of the procession of the Spirit from Father and Son, beginning with his assertion that 'every operation of knowledge is followed by some appetitive operation' and proceeding through his 'psychological' image of the Trinity and defence of the divine unity.[10] Panaretos moves through Section 4 of the *Ad cantorem Antiochenum* systematically, grappling with Aquinas' analysis of appetite within thoroughly Aristotelian parameters. He berates Thomas for his reliance on philosophy but is happy to draw on the authority of Anaxagoras to better him in debate. Panaretos judges that Thomas' identification of the intellect, love, and will of God with his essence is functionally Sabellian, precluding the real distinction of the persons. He finds the designation of the persons as 'relations' quite inadequate and scarcely expressive of the unique characteristics of the three hypostases (being unbegotten, begotten, and proceeding). Like Neilos, Panaretos delights in exposing the logical contradictions of Thomas' thought.

---

[9] Buda, 'Il tomismo a Bisanzio nel secolo XIV', 301. Note the explicit denial of the possibility of demonstrative arguments in theology. Panaretos is here closer to Barlaam than he is to either Palamas or Aquinas.

[10] Buda (ed.), 301–2; cf. Aquinas, *Ad cantorem Antiochenum*, §4.

Such operations are, writes Panaretos, quite distinct from the 'im-participable and unapproachable' essence—terminology that confirms his Palamite orthodoxy. Panaretos has left us a fine example of anti-Thomist polemic in the Byzantine scholastic mode. He dissects Thomas' arguments with care and attention, appealing to scripture and the Fathers but also seeking to out-do Aquinas in his command of philosophy and logical argumentation. His denigrations of Thomas for his supposed reliance on sophistries and specious arguments amount to little more than a rhetorical trope. Panaretos is never happier than when exposing Thomas' logical incoherence while simultaneously lambasting him for his reliance on logic. But while Panaretos can be rather testy in his disposal of Thomas, he is a veritable model of reserve and decorum compared to Kallistos Angelikoudes—Thomas' most inveterate Byzantine foe.

Kallistos Angelikoudes is a somewhat shadowy figure, knowledge of whom is complicated by the proliferation of *Kallistoi* in the late fourteenth century.[11] He is certainly to be associated with the additional cognomen Melenikiotes, presumably from the monastery of Melenikion in present-day Bulgaria. Kallistos Angelikoudes has also been plausibly identified with Kallistos Telikoudes and, less convincingly, Kallistos Kataphygiotes, both of whom are represented in the *Philokalia*.[12]

---

[11] *PLP* 145. See also Stylianos Papadopoulos, 'Thomas in Byzanz. Thomas Rezeption und Thomas Kritik in Byzanz zwischen 1354 und 1435', Ἑλληνικαὶ μεταφράσεις θωμιστικῶν ἔργων. Φιλοθωμισταὶ καὶ ἀντιθωμισταὶ ἐν Βυζαντίῳ and Συνάντησις ὀρθοδόξου καὶ σχολαστικῆς θεολογίας ἐν τῷ προσώπῳ Καλλίστου Ἀγγελικούδη καὶ Θωμᾶ Ἀκινάτου; Giovanni Mercati, 'Callisto Angelicudes Meliniceota'; Symeon Koutsas, 'Callistos Angelicoudès. Quatre traités hésychastes inédits'; Ivan Christov, 'Kallistos Angelikoudes' Critical Account of Thomistic and Orthodox Anthropology'; Georgi Kapriev, 'Zwei Modelle mittelalterlicher Philosophie (Thomas von Aquin und Kallistos Angelikudes)'; Ioannis Polemis, 'Notes on Two Texts Dealing with the Palamite Controversy'.

[12] Nikodemos the Hagiorite and Makarios of Corinth (eds.), Φιλοκαλία τῶν ἱερῶν νηπτικῶν (3rd edn.) IV 368–72 and V 4–59. The case for the identification of all three *Kallistoi* is put in Antonio Rigo, 'Callisto Angelicude Catafugiota Meleniceota e l'esicasmo bizantino del XIV secolo. Una nota prosopografica'. While the identification with Telikoudes appears sound, it is not easy to square the great intellectual sophistication of Kataphygiotes with the vehement anti-rationalism of Angelikoudes' tirade against Thomas. This mismatch is only confirmed by the decision of the nineteenth-century Russian translator of the Philokalia, Theophan the Recluse, to omit Kataphygiotes' *Syllogistic Chapters* on grounds of excessive scholasticism. The editor of the original Greek version, Nikodemos the Hagiorite, sides—to add another

Angelikoudes is the author of systematic refutation of the *Summa contra gentiles*.[13] The work is enormous, extracting and attacking no less than 2,000 passages from Thomas over its 641 chapters. It announces its purpose in no uncertain terms: 'Against that which Thomas the Latin writes in heretical fashion and outside the chorus of the holy Church, a clear refutation of his arrogant disregard for holy scripture.'[14] Thomas' *Ursünde* is his reliance on pagan philosophy: time and time again he is reproached for having chosen Aristotle for his master and not heeded scripture or the Fathers and Kallistos finds it deeply suspicious that Thomas should call the Stagirite simply 'the philosopher'.[15] In his wanton use of reason, Thomas has lapsed into the errors of Arius and Mohammed.[16] The *Summa contra gentiles* (Κατὰ Ἑλλήνων) is so full of lies and untruths, so utterly beholden to empty profane wisdom, that it should be recognized as directed not against the pagans but against God's holy Church.[17] Angelikoudes insists on the utter futility of outer learning, even suggesting that such wisdom has a demonic source.[18] In his love for philosophy, Thomas has manifestly fallen prey to the demons.[19] Significantly, this was also the contention of Barlaam the Calabrian.[20] Small wonder, according to Angelikoudes, that Thomas' teaching should be seen to be in such flagrant contradiction with the teachings of the Church in matters of all kinds, from cosmology to anthropology, from the essence–energies distinction to the related matters of the procession of the Holy Spirit and papal primacy.

It is not an edifying work. Podskalsky has aptly characterized it as kind of *Hexenhammer* (witch-hunter's manual) for its relentless and sustained persecution of its subject.[21] And while it certainly serves as a sign of the deep loathing for Latin theology present in certain sections of the Byzantine Church, it defeats itself in its failure to

intriguing possibility—with those who would identify Kataphygiotes with Patriarch Kallistos II Xanthopoulos. Φιλοκαλία τῶν ἱερῶν νηπτικῶν V, 3.

[13] Stylianos Papadopoulos (ed.), Καλλίστου Ἀγγελικούδη κατὰ Θωμᾶ Ἀκινάτου.
[14] §1 (ed. Papadopoulos, 27).
[15] §641 (ed. Papadopoulos, 298–9) and *passim*.
[16] §2–3 (ed. Papadopoulos, 28).
[17] §16–20 (ed. Papadopoulos, 33–5).
[18] §36 (ed. Papadopoulos, 42).
[19] §43 (ed. Papadopoulos, 44).
[20] See Antonio Fyrigos (ed.), *Barlaam Calabro: Opere contro i latini*, A, IV, 8.58–61, 11.94.
[21] Podskalsky, *Theologie und Philosophie*, 211.

take Aquinas seriously and its overblown and merely venomous strictures against all reason and learning. This is not the stance of Gregory Palamas, Philotheos Kokkinos, Neilos Kabasilas, or Mark of Ephesus. If anything, it stands closer to the anti-Latin works of Barlaam the Calabrian. Given its unbalanced and flawed character, it is perhaps not to be lamented that Angelikoudes' tirade has long languished in almost total obscurity.[22]

Among others expressing unease with Aquinas is Makarios, a protégé of Patriarch Kallistos II (Xanthopoulos) of Constantinople and Metropolitan of Ancyra from 1397 to 1405.[23] Makarios was a close associate of Emperor Manuel II, accompanying him on his travels to the courts of Western Europe, even reaching England to spend Christmas of 1400 with Henry IV at Eltham. On his return journey, Makarios began a work on the errors of the Latins which he completed on his return to Constantinople. This work includes a brief sideswipe at Thomas' understanding of the procession of the Holy Spirit.[24] Makarios is also known to have been an opponent of the devoted Thomist Manuel Kalekas.

Another member of Manuel II's inner circle, Demetrios Chrysolaras, re-animated the debate between Neilos Kabasilas and Demetrios Kydones by imaging it in the form of a dramatic dialogue in which the original protagonists are joined by Thomas and himself.[25] Chryso-laras takes Kabasilas' part, with Thomas criticized yet again for his rationalism and love for the syllogism, his views on the procession, and so forth. Chrysolaras strenuously insists that Neilos and Thomas have absolutely nothing in common and that Neilos must certainly be regarded as an opponent of Aquinas. Such protests indicate that Chrysolaras was aware of the positive dimension of Neilos' reception of Thomas and concerned to play down his cautious sympathy for the angelic doctor.

---

[22] In his remarkable survey of anti-Latin writers, Andronikos Demetrakopoulos admitted that he knew nothing whatsoever of Kallistos' life or works. The name alone he had from a passing mention in Dositheos of Jerusalem. Ὀρθόδοξος Ἑλλάς, 161.

[23] *PLP* 16254. Brief notices in Demetrakopoulos, Ὀρθόδοξος Ἑλλάς, 88–9; Jugie, 'Démétrius Cydonès et la théologie latine a Byzance', 401; Papadopoulos, 'Thomas in Byzanz', 292; and Podskalsky, *Theologie und Philosophie*, 216.

[24] Makarios' work was published anonymously in Dositheos of Jerusalem's Τόμος Καταλλαγῆς, 1–205. See especially §59, 99–101.

[25] *PLP* 31156. Brief notices in Demetrakopoulos, Ὀρθόδοξος Ἑλλάς, 87; Jugie, 'Démétrius Cydonès et la théologie latine a Byzance', 399; Papadopoulos, 'Thomas in Byzanz', 294–5; and Podskalsky, *Theologie und Philosophie*, 215–16.

4.2. DEVOTEES

Thomas also had a number of ardent admirers among what we may
call the second tier of Byzantine theologians.[26] These were for
the most part members of the circle of Demetrios Kydones. With
considerably less political influence than their master, they were in a
correspondingly weaker position vis-à-vis the strong anti-Latin and
anti-union currents of the time and some were to have no choice but
to take refuge in the Church of the elder Rome. Of these, the most
theologically engaging is Manuel Kalekas (d. 1410).[27]
  Like his namesake, Patriarch John XIV Kalekas, Manuel was a
decided opponent of Palamite theology. In the 1390s, to demur
from this officially established orthodoxy was to invite trouble. Certainly, his hesitations in the matter of the essence–energies distinction
will have contributed to the failure of the school that he ran for a time
in Constantinople. In any event, Kalekas tells us that he was poor
schoolmaster—unable to impose discipline on his charges and too
soft in collecting fees. He approached Demetrios Kydones in 1391, by
which time the elder statesman was readying himself to leave the City
for good. He was soon established as a close friend and confidant and
was entrusted with preparing the collection of Demetrios' letters
under his supervision.
  But Kalekas was familiar with Demetrios' works long before meeting the man himself. In a work written before 1391, *On Theology* or
On Faith (De fide deque principiis catholicæ fidei), he provides an
elegant and systematic summary of the Christian faith in ten chapters,
woven around patristic testimony.[28] But the treatise also relies heavily
on Thomas, in particular the *Summa contra gentiles* and the *Ad
cantorem Antiochenum*. The treatise moves from the one God to
the three persons and then proceeds to the incarnation, the sacraments, and the last things.
  Kalekas' treatment of the one God offers many parallels with Book
I of the *Summa contra gentiles*, from the argument for a first mover to

[26] Norman Russell provides a fine survey of some of these figures in 'Palamism and
the Circle of Demetrius Cydones', 169–73.
[27] *PLP* 10289. For his biography, see Raymond-Joseph Loenertz, *Correspondance
de Manuel Calecas*, 16–46.
[28] PG 152 429–661.

the various affirmations made of God and the incommensurate nature of names applied to both God and creatures. Like Aquinas, Kalekas treats the Holy Trinity as a matter of revelation by contrast to the philosophically demonstrable existence of the one God.[29] He affirms the Father as the cause of Son and Spirit but centres his attention on the procession of the Spirit through the Son.[30] Large chunks of the chapter on the Trinity come straight from *Summa contra gentiles* IV.[31] The next chapter goes on to present at some length Augustine's teaching on the Spirit as the love of Father and Son.[32]

Kalekas skirts the essence–energies distinction, carefully ruling out the vision of the divine essence but eschewing all mention of uncreated energies distinct from that essence.[33] The divine will, for example, is presented in terms of either the Son (as the 'living and essential energy' of God), or a created effect. When the Cappadocian Fathers speak of knowing God from his energies, one or other of these two options is indicated.[34] Similarly, the divine Wisdom and Word is spoken of as light as a pure act or energy of knowledge, made known in the creation through his gifts and effects.[35] Kalekas is careful not to deny the essence–energies distinction explicitly, opting rather to affirm an altogether different understanding of divine operation.

Kalekas' treatment of the seven sacraments is heavily dependent on *Summa contra gentiles* IV.56 and following chapters.[36] The discussion of the eucharist passes over the *epiclesis*, focusing rather on the words of institution pronounced by the celebrant.[37] It also adopts the

---

[29] PG 152 473C–476A.   [30] PG 152 477A, 508ABC.

[31] See Gouillard, 'Les influences latines dans l'œuvre théologique de Manuel Calécas', 44.

[32] Much of Chapter 5 (PG 152 529A–569A) is taken up with a vindication of Augustine's 'psychological image' of the Trinity, including the presence of an image of the Trinity in the human being. The Holy Spirit is shown to be the love of Father (lover) and Son (beloved) and the love in which God loves himself (545C). Kalekas' knowledge of Augustine is certainly mediated to some degree (he speaks of the Trinitarian doctrine of Augustine 'and those who teach in accordance with him' (545D)) but this does not preclude direct acquaintance with the *De Trinitate* in the Planoudes translation. See Gouillard, 'Les influences latines dans l'œuvre théologique de Manuel Calécas', 40–2.

[33] PG 152 464B.

[34] PG 152 521C–524C.

[35] PG 152 560BC.

[36] Gouillard, 'Les influences latines dans l'œuvre théologique de Manuel Calécas', 44.

[37] PG 152 601A.

theory of transubstantiation: the underlying substance changes while the accidents of bread and wine remain.[38] Kalekas' treatment of the rational basis of the incarnation draws on another work of Thomas: the *Ad cantorem Antiochenum*.[39] The discussions of the atonement and the last things also display a number of distinctly Latin characteristics.

The treatise is discreet about its sources: neither Thomas nor any other recent theologian is ever named, a practice Kalekas maintained even after his conversion. It also treads warily when it comes to the hot topics of the procession and the essence–energies distinction, avoiding any open challenge to the established orthodoxy. Kalekas writes as an Orthodox for the Orthodox, but one who recognizes Thomas as an exceptionally useful guide and teacher in the study and exposition of scripture and the Fathers. Kalekas' treatise is designed to incorporate Aquinas' wisdom and rigour within a presentation of the teachings of the universal Church. And to a great extent it succeeded: this decidedly Thomist work earned the express approbation of the zealously anti-Latin Patriarch of Jerusalem, Dositheos, who pub lished it without attribution in his *Tome of Love against the Latins*. Dositheos commends the work in his introduction as 'highly theological, highly edificatory, highly clear, and highly Orthodox'.[40] Rarely has a Byzantine Thomist found such explicit recognition as a standard-bearer of Orthodoxy.

But Kalekas himself was not to find such enthusiastic acceptance on the part of the Orthodox authorities of his own time. His close association with Demetrios Kydones and his connections with other Latinophiles and with anti-Palamites made him a marked man. As part of a crackdown on the remaining anti-Palamites, he was pressed to affirm the Tome of 1351. This he would not do, and in the autumn of 1396 he elected instead to leave the City and to take refuge in the Genoese colony of Pera. His relocation to Pera gave him the freedom to give full vent to his anti-Palamite proclivities, manifested in his weighty attack on the Tome of the 1351, *De essentia et operatione*. It also saw his reception into the Catholic Church and an acceleration in

---

[38] PG 152 601C–604A.
[39] Specific references in Gouillard, 'Les influences latines dans l'œuvre théologique de Manuel Calécas', 44.
[40] Τόμος Ἀγάπης κατὰ Λατίνων, fifth page of unpaginated preface. The treatise is published simply as Περὶ θεολογίας.

his study of Latin. He went on to translate a number of works from the Latin, including Boethius' *De Trinitate* and Anselm's *Cur Deus homo*.[41] Manuel was also to write extensively on some of the sticking points between East and West, most notably the question of the procession. Having long been drawn to a monastic style of life he joined in 1404 the Order of Preachers on Mytilene where he lived out the remainder of his days.[42]

Kalekas offers a poignant example of the vulnerable position of Latinophiles and anti-Palamites in the last beleaguered years of Byzantium. It should, however, be stressed that it was his anti-Palamism and not his Latin interests that forced him to take refuge in the Roman Church. While his conversion was doubtless sincere enough when it came, there seems little doubt that he would have remained an Orthodox Christian if he could. His one major theological work as an Orthodox, the *De fide deque principiis catholicæ fidei* offers a fascinating example of a thoroughgoing appropriation of Aquinas within the parameters of the Orthodox Church. While its worth is diminished by its rather uncritical mode of reception of Thomas, it is a work that demands recognition, if only because of its enthusiastic propagation by Patriarch Dositheos of Jerusalem.

Kalekas was not the first member of Kydones' circle to join the Order of Preachers. This distinction belongs to Maximos Chrysoberges, who crossed the Golden Horn in 1390 to join the community at Pera.[43] A few years earlier (1385–7), Maximos had been encouraged by Demetrios to persevere in his study of Thomas in a paean of praise for the angelic doctor.[44] Demetrios took a close interest in Maximos' career and introduced him to Manuel II whom he was to accompany during his temporary exile on Lemnos (1387–9). After 1390, Maximos became an enthusiastic proselyte for the Roman Church, seeking to convert his compatriots to his new-found faith. He rather ambitiously attempted to

---

[41] For the Boethius translation, see John Demetracopoulos, 'Manuel Calecas' Translation of Boethius' *De Trinitate*'. The *Cur Deus homo* translation remains unedited.

[42] Manuel had an ἀδελφᾶτον (an associate monastic status conferring, for a price, right of abode and other benefits) at a monastery in Constantinople. In his Letter 51 (ed. Loenertz, 238–40) he complains that he had been forced to leave and that the monks were no longer furnishing him with the share of the revenues to which he was entitled. Manuel also kept up friendly relations with the monks of the monastic house of the Xanthopouloi (Letter 29: ed. Loenertz, 206–7).

[43] *PLP* 31123.

[44] Demetrios Kydones, Letter 333 (Loenertz II 266–8).

convert the firmly anti-unionist Joseph Bryennios by letter from Pavia.[45] He also took on Bryennios and another eminent anti-unionist, Neilos Damylas, in a public debate on Crete in 1400. He produced an oration on the procession of the Spirit and attracted written refutations by both Bryennios and Damylas.[46] But while one can presume that his reading of Thomas played some part in his conversion, his literary remains indicate ample missionary zeal but little theological distinction or palpable use of Thomas.

Maximos was followed into the Dominican order by his younger brother, Andrew (d. 1451) who went on to become Archbishop of Rhodes and, successively, Cyprus.[47] Andrew appears to have applied his knowledge of Thomas to rather greater effect than his elder brother, becoming perhaps the first Greek writer to assert openly and explicitly the absolute incompatibility of Palamite and Thomist teaching in the matter of the essence–energies distinction.[48] His treatise on the question takes Thomas as an unimpeachable and self-validating authority, presenting itself as an *Apodictic Exposition from the Writings of the Most Blessed Thomas concerning the Divine Essence and Energy*.[49] In this work, composed in the immediate run-up to the Council of Ferrara–Florence, Andrew presents Thomas as a 'most divinely-inspired' writer whose teachings are identical with those of the Roman Church as a whole.[50]

Looking at these minor devotees it is apparent that positive reception of Thomas drew some Latinophiles towards Rome. At the same time, several of these were to a greater or lesser extent pushed out of the Church of their birth as a consequence of their inability to affirm the Palamite teachings of that Church. Aquinas is held up by these figures as a vindication of their union with Rome and as a

---

[45] See Joseph Bryennios, Letter 10 (ed. Tomadakes, 309–14).

[46] *Ad Cretenses de processione Spiritus Sancti oratio* (PG 154 1225C). Bryennios' refutation is contained in Eugenios Boulgaris' edition of his complete works (I 407–23). Damylas' contribution is partially edited in the Constantinopolitan periodical Ἐκκλησιαστικὴ Ἀλήθεια (15, 382–3, 391–2 and 16, 7–8, 61–3).

[47] *PLP* 31106. There was another brother, Theodore (*PLP* 31113), also a Dominican and a bishop and heavily involved in negotiations for reunion.

[48] Both Prochoros Kydones and Manuel Kalekas, as we have seen, draw a veil over their use of Thomas in their treatises on the subject although they doubtless shared a sense of the incompatibility of Thomist and Palamite doctrines. Andrew draws on both in this work.

[49] Candal (ed.), 'Andreae Rhodiensis, OP, inedita ad Bessarionem epistula', 344–70.

[50] Candal (ed.), 348.15–16, 360.4–6.

pre-eminent expositor of Latin theology. In this process, he is
increasingly cast as a decisive counterblast to Palamite theology.
We see here a rather complex development whereby anti-Palamite
leanings (possibly fostered by acquaintance with Aquinas) lead to
unionism and thence to a Thomas *redivivus* of a decidedly anti-
Orthodox and anti-Palamite character. The fact that this development took place at a time when Barlaam and Akindynos were
habitually branded as Latin-minded only served to encourage the
association of Thomas with anti-Palamism. But it would be a great
mistake to conflate anti-Palamism with Thomism on the grounds of
such adventitious developments, let alone to suppose that Palamism is
tantamount to anti-unionism and Thomism to unionism. To demonstrate further the falsity of such easy assumptions, we turn now to some
less immediately promising areas for a positive reception of Aquinas.
While it is hardly surprising to find Catholic converts and Byzantine
unionists appropriating Thomas for their own ends, it is considerably
more interesting to find sympathies for Thomas among some of the
most prominent Palamites and anti-unionists of the final decades of
the Empire.

4.3. JOSEPH BRYENNIOS AND MAKARIOS MAKRES

The fifteenth century continues, like the fourteenth, to see Thomas
read and admired even in the most unlikely of quarters. Joseph
Bryennios (*c.*1350–1431/38) is a fine example.[51] We have already
mentioned his lavish praise of Demetrios Kydones and his admiration for Demetrios' translations from the Latin.[52] As an accomplished Latinist himself, Bryennios knew what he was talking about.
A famed preacher, sometime imperial emissary, and renowned monk,
Bryennios was one of the most learned men of his time. He took pride
in listing the contents of his library, which included works on music,
mathematics, and the natural sciences.[53] He was also one of the most

---

[51] *PLP* 3257. On Bryennios' life and times, see Nikolaos Tomadakes, ʽ Ο ᾽Ιωσὴφ
Βρυέννιος καὶ ἡ Κρήτη κατὰ τὸ 1400 and Hélène Bazini, 'Une première édition des
œuvres de Joseph Bryennios: les Traités adressés aux Crétois', 83–7.

[52] See above, p.63.

[53] See his *Testament* (ed. Papadopoulos-Kerameus, 295–6). I have this reference
from Donald Nicol, *Church and Society in the Last Centuries of Byzantium*, 64.

talented and determined opponents of union with Rome. But his firm stance against union did not stop him from drawing intellectual sustenance from Thomas, for all that he disagreed vehemently with his teaching on the procession of the Holy Spirit.[54] Most notably, Bryennios picks up a number of arguments from the *Summa contra gentiles* IV.53 in his own *Dialogue with an Ishmaelite*.[55] He reproduces several of the objections to the suitability of the incarnation adduced by Thomas, adapting, abridging, and adding to them as appropriate. His answers, however, remain very much his own, albeit with occasional borrowings from the defence of the fittingness of the incarnation in *Summa contra gentiles* IV.54–5.[56]

This is by no means a case of any very thoroughgoing dependence on Thomas. Bryennios remains his own man, loudly proclaiming the impossibility of demonstrative argumentation in theology in stridently apophatic terms that might well be taken as directed against Thomas.[57] Bryennios was certainly an inveterate foe of the theological syllogism, declaiming:

Those who subject the dogmas of the faith to chains of syllogistic reasoning strip of its divine glory the very faith they strive to defend. They force us to believe no longer in God but in man. Aristotle and his philosophy have nothing in common with the truths revealed by Christ.[58]

That said, Bryennios was no obscurantist. Indeed, for all his rhetorical denigrations of reason, he is in many respects a typical Byzantine scholastic. This is apparent in the question and answer format of the *Dialogue with an Ishmaelite* in which the Muslim interlocutor requests that Bryennios 'solve my difficulties'.[59] Many other works also adopt a *quaestio* format: the *First Discourse on the Last Judgement*,

[54] See his treatise against Maximos Chrysoberges (Boulgaris I 407–23). Bryennios reveals himself here to be better informed on Thomas than was Maximos himself.

[55] Asterios Argyriou, «'Ιωσὴφ τοῦ Βρυεννίου μετά τινος 'Ισμαηλίτου Διάλεξις».

[56] See Asterios Argyriou, *Macaire Macrès et la polémique contre l'Islam*, 87–8. For correspondences between the respective objections: *SCG* IV.53.3 cf. *Dialexis* (ed. Argyriou) 160.42–4; *SCG* IV.53.5 cf. *Dialexis* 162.72–3; *SCG* IV.53.6 cf. *Dialexis* 167.217–19; *SCG* IV.53.10 cf. *Dialexis* 170.279–80; *SCG* IV.53.11 cf. *Dialexis* 173.357–9; *SCG* IV.53.12 cf. *Dialexis* 173.351–2; *SCG* IV.53.22 cf. *Dialexis* 161.50–1.

[57] *Dialexis* 164.135–43.

[58] Homily 5 (Boulgaris I 84). Cited (and translated) by Kallistos Ware, 'Scholasticism and Orthodoxy: Theological Method as a Factor in the Schism', 21.

[59] *Dialexis* 158.11 (λῦσαι τὰς ἀπορίας μοι).

for example, is cast in the form of thirty-five questions and solutions.[60] In practice, Bryennios' commitment to and estimation of disciplined reasoning chimes closely with that of Aquinas. This consonance is neatly illustrated by his willingness to embrace elements of Thomas' defence of the fittingness of the incarnation in his own *Dialogue with an Ishmaelite*.[61] While there can be no truck with Thomas on matters such as the procession of the Spirit, Bryennios finds him a useful ally in his dialogue with Islam.

In Makarios Makres (*c*.1383–1431) we have a still more remarkable case of anti-unionist esteem for Thomas.[62] This gifted and learned Athonite Hieromonk was a close friend and ally of Bryennios, whom he got to know well during his residence at the Constantinopolitan monastery of Charsianitou in 1421–2.[63] He went on to become Abbot of the Monastery of Pantokrator in Constantinople and Protosynkellos and confessor to Manuel II. He was sent by John VIII Palaiologos as emissary to Pope Martin V in the winter of 1429–30 and died shortly after his return from the papal court. This embassy appears to have brought back a proposal that a reunion council be held in Italy at some future date. Makarios earned some disapprobation for his readiness to consider union and apparent acceptance that the council meet in Italy. He was even to be posthumously rebuked for his Latin sympathies.[64] But Makarios had no great sympathy for the Latin

[60] Boulgaris II 367–8. I have this reference from Martin Jugie, 'Démétrius Cydonès et la théologie latine a Byzance', 397. Jugie exaggerates when he calls him 'un véritable scholastique à la mode occidentale'—'orientale' would be more apposite.

[61] On two occasions, at the beginning and end of the dialogue, the Islamic interlocutor praises Bryennios' shrewdness—his ἀγχινοίας (*Dialexis* 159.21; 194.923). While a veiled allusion to Aquinas through word-play would be impossible to prove, the choice of words is, at the very least, a happy coincidence given the debts to Aquinas evident in this treatise.

[62] *PLP* 16379. On Makres, see especially the excellent introductory materials in Asterios Argyriou, *Macaire Macrès et la polémique contre l'Islam* and Μακαρίου τοῦ Μακρῆ συγγράμματα.

[63] Bryennios was monk of this monastery between 1416 and 1427. On Makarios' sojourn there, see Asterios Argyriou, *Macaire Macrès et la polémique contre l'Islam*, 5, 33.

[64] George Sphrantzes reports (*Chronicon minus* 21.8) that the Patriarch of Constantinople (Joseph II) looked on Makarios as a heretic on these grounds, a charge to which Sphrantzes gives no credence. Vasile Grecu (ed.), *Georgios Sphrantzes Memorii 1401–1477*, 50. Sphrantzes much admired this ἀνὴρ ἄριστος κατά τε λόγον καὶ ἀρετὴν καὶ σύνεσιν. *Chronicon minus* 21.5 (op. cit., 48). The author of the *Eulogy for Makarios Makres* rejects such charges categorically (§122: Argyriou (ed.), *Macaire Macrès et la polémique contre l'Islam*, 232).

Church and had amply proved his Orthodox credentials in his various works bearing largely on the matter of the procession.[65] It is chastening to note that even a willingness to consider the prospect of reunion could generate suspicion in some quarters.

Makarios was the author of a large number of hagiographical works and a series of anti-Islamic writings. It is the latter which concern us most closely. He composed four discourses *Against those Scandalized by the Success of the Infidels* and a related work, the *Defence of Virginity*.[66] In responding to the Islamic critique of celibacy, Makarios makes very substantial use of Thomas' *Summa contra gentiles* in Kydones' translation. Not only, like Bryennios, does he borrow from Thomas' systematic formulation of possible objections, but he also reproduces large chunks of Thomas' arguments in favour of celibacy and follows him in his choice of supporting patristic and scriptural testimonies.[67] Makarios reorganizes, abridges, adapts, and supplements his material but the unacknowledged dependence on Thomas remains very marked. In Makarios, even more clearly than in Bryennios, we see a veiled recognition of the immense value of Thomas' incomparably lucid defence of Christian doctrine and practice on the part of figures known their hostility to the Latin Church.[68] The willingness of such irreproachably anti-Latin figures to embrace Thomas, albeit with great caution and against a common enemy, is quite astonishing. It speaks volumes for the possibilities of a creative Orthodox re-appropriation of Thomas.

---

[65] See, for example, the treatise *On the Procession of the Holy Spirit* edited in Argyriou, Μακαρίου τοῦ Μακρῆ συγγράμματα, 49–63. This is a disciplined and concise treatise enumerating a series of objections to the Latin doctrine on the basis of scriptural and patristic testimony.

[66] Argyriou (ed.), *Macaire Macrès et la polémique contre l'Islam*, 237–51, 258–65, 270–80, 286–300, 307–26. Argyriou makes a good case that the treatise is directed primarily against Islamic critiques of celibacy and an anti-monastic current in Byzantium, rather than against Hussite positions. Makarios had indeed been involved in discussions with the Hussites in the late 1420s but does not appear to engage with any of the Czech Reformers' distinctive arguments against monasticism in this treatise.

[67] *Summa contra gentiles* III.136–7. See the discussion in Argyriou (ed.), *Macaire Macrès et la polémique contre l'Islam*, 86–92. Argyriou delicately admits that this instance 'nous met dans un grand embarras'.

[68] Argyriou aptly remarks that Bryennios' and Makres' borrowings show that 'le mode de pensée rationaliste et aristotélicien de saint Thomas avait acquis, à des degrés divers bien sûr, toutes les couches intellectuelles de la société byzantine'. *Macaire Macrès et la polémique contre l'Islam*, 88.

4.4. MARK OF EPHESUS

Bryennios and Makres are also distinguished as being among Mark Eugenikos' (*c.*1394–1445) guiding lights.[69] As Metropolitan of Ephesus, Mark was the most determinedly anti-unionist member of the Greek delegation at the reunion council of Ferrara–Florence (1438–9).[70] While this council witnessed a level of real theological debate, exchange, and rapprochement far in excess of that achieved at the earlier reunion council of Lyons (1274), it was to prove similarly ephemeral. Mark was the chief spokesman for the Orthodox cause at the council, consistently opposing any sort of compromise with Roman Catholic positions. Mark is celebrated in the East as a 'pillar of Orthodoxy' for his steadfast refusal to sign up to the decree of reunion, *Laetentur caeli*, promulgated by the council and his opposition did much to sink the mooted union. But while Mark, like his esteemed teachers, would have no part in even the slightest surrender to the Latin positions on key matters such as the papacy, *filioque*, and purgatory, he was by no means hostile to Latin theology *per se*.

Mark's approach to theology is distinctly scholastic in the traditional Byzantine mode. He had been very well trained in Aristotelian philosophy and argumentation by John Chortasmenos and continued to draw on that training throughout his tumultuous career.[71] He was, in particular, a forthright advocate of the theological syllogism, producing a set of works based expressly on the syllogism: *Syllogistic Chapters against the Latins on the Procession of the Holy Spirit*; *Ten Syllogisms Demonstrating that there is No Purgatorial Fire*; and *Syllogistic Chapters against the Heresy of the Akindynists concerning the Distinction between the Divine Essence*

---

[69] So Sylvester Syropoulos, *Memoirs* 5.12 (ed. V. Laurent 266). Neither were Mark's teachers in the strict sense, but were certainly great inspirations and guides.

[70] *PLP* 6193. See also Joseph Gill, *Personalities of the Council of Florence*, 55–64, 222–32; Constantine Tsirpanlis, *Mark Eugenicus and the Council of Florence: A Historical Re-evaluation of his Personality*; and, especially, Nicholas Constas, 'Mark Eugenikos'.

[71] On Chortasmenos, see *PLP* 30897 and Herbert Hunger, *Johannes Chortasmenos (ca.1370–ca. 1436/37). Briefe, Gedichte und kleine Schriften*. This astonishingly learned and influential scholar, who also taught Bessarion, went on to become Metropolitan of Selymbria (1431–6/7).

and Energies.[72] Like Palamas and indeed Aquinas he expressly commends and embraces syllogistic reasoning even in the highest realms of theology—so long as proper subservience to the authority of scripture and the Fathers be maintained.

Mark was a systematic thinker, presenting many of his works in the form of *aporiae*, objections, and solutions. He does not hesitate to employ philosophical argumentation where appropriate and can even be found citing Aristotle in support of the doctrine of the procession of the Holy Spirit from the Father alone.[73] Mark also had an exacting knowledge of the patristic tradition and was adept at forensic discussion of issues of textual authenticity, scoring victories over his Latin interlocutors at Ferrara–Florence in a number of disputed readings.

Mark, in other words, was not content to retreat into apophaticism or an appeal to antinomy but perfectly prepared to beat the Latins at their own game, arguing systematically for the Greek position on the basis of scripture, the Fathers (correctly transmitted), and philosophy. Naturally enough, this robust approach led him to take on Thomas directly in some of his works. Mark treats Thomas as the archetypal 'teacher of the Latins' and shows a fair acquaintance with his work in so doing: he certainly knew at least some of Thomas' works at first hand.[74] Eugenikos attacks Aquinas' notion of opposite relations within the Trinity, positing instead the 'contradictory' relations between being uncaused and caused, begetting and proceeding— thereby upholding the irreducibility of the three hypostases.[75] Mark's *Encyclical Letter* in its detailing of the chief differences between Latins and Greeks treats Thomas' teaching as synonymous with that of the Latin Church as a whole.[76] Thus Mark rejects the

---

[72] Edited in, respectively, Louis Petit (ed.), *Marci Eugenici Metropolitae Ephesi opera anti-unionistica*, 60–107 and 114–17; Wilhelm Gass (ed.), *Die Mystik des Nikolaus Cabasilas vom Leben in Christo*, Appendix 2, 217–32.

[73] *Syllogistic Chapters against the Latins on the Procession of the Holy Spirit* §29 (92).

[74] This acquaintance might very well come from his formation at the monastery of St George of the Mangana, where Demetrios Kydones had completed (and had copies made of) his translation of the *Summa contra gentiles* and to which the patron of the translation, John VI, had initially retired. The Mangana remained a centre of cultural and theological activity down to the fall of the City.

[75] *Syllogistic Chapters against the Latins on the Procession of the Holy Spirit* §13, 25 (76–7, 85–9) (cf. *ST* I^a q.36 a.2).

[76] Louis Petit (ed.), *Marci Eugenici Metropolitae Ephesi opera anti-unionistica*, 141–51.

distinction between mediated and unmediated processions main-tained by 'the Latins and Thomas'.[77] 'The Latins and Thomas' are also castigated for their belief in the identity of the divine will and essence and the concomitant understanding of the created nature of the divine operations.[78] Another work on the essence–energies distinction also has Thomas as a chief target but nonetheless makes an intriguing (if ultimately unconvincing) attempt to manipulate Aquinas in support of the distinction between God's essence and power.[79] Thomas, finally, is not neglected in Mark's works on purga-tory, in which he is upbraided for holding the immutability of the will of souls after death.[80]

While Mark could hardly fail to offer some critique of Thomas in his dealings with the Latin positions on the disputed questions be-tween East and West, it is noteworthy that his approach remains temperate and respectful, with even the occasional attempt to recruit Thomas to the Orthodox cause. But what is most significant is that there is, in this supreme and even archetypal defender of Orthodoxy, no trace of any fundamental incompatibility between Latin and Greek theological methodologies. Thomas, and the Latin Church in general, are taken on at their own game. We see here, in other words, a competition between rival scholasticisms, competing in their conclu-sions but perfectly compatible in their approaches to the matter of theology. What we are, however, lacking in this anti-unionist leader is any very significant positive engagement with Thomas. Mark's deeply ingrained Aristotelianism might have pre-disposed him to look with some sympathy on Thomas outside the context of the controverted issues between East and West had he ever had the leisure to do so. But this is a step which he does not appear to have made. For a truly searching engagement with Thomas on the part of a thoroughgoing Aristotelian and anti-unionist we have to turn to the man to whom Mark committed the leadership of those opposed to the Florentine union, George Scholarios.

---

[77] §6.40–2 (149.10–12).   [78] §6.42–7 (149.12–21).

[79] *Syllogistic Chapters against the Heresy of the Akindynists concerning the Distinc-tion between the Divine Essence and Energies* §14 (220); cf. *ST* I[a] q.1 a.1. Mark appears to be using Thomas' notion of passive potency, which he indeed excludes from the divine essence, in order to sustain the more general distinction between power and essence in God. Needless to say, this represents a rather distorted reading of Thomas.

[80] *Second Homily against the Purgatorial Fire* (PO 15 143); cf. *SCG* IV.95.

4.5. GEORGE (GENNADIOS) SCHOLARIOS

George Kurteses Scholarios (*c*.1403–*c*.1472) has the distinction of having been an exceptionally fervent Thomist and a committed Palamite, an advocate of the Florentine union and, later, the leader of the anti-unionist party in the last few years of the Byzantine imperium.[81] He became, as Gennadios II, the first patriarch of Constantinople following the fall of the City to the Ottomans, setting a precedent for the way in which the patriarchate would relate thereafter to its new masters (with, that is, complete obedience). The greatest Orthodox theologian at Byzantium's end, Gennadios was to set the tone for much of the theological and philosophical work produced by Greek scholars in the early Ottoman era.

Scholarios had some of the foremost figures of the age as his teachers: Mark of Ephesus, John Chortasmenos, Joseph Bryennios, and Makarios Makres. But he was also a great autodidact, plunging deeper into the wellsprings of Aristotelian philosophy than almost any Byzantine before him. His love of Latin thought seems to have set in very early, prompting him to seek mastery of the Latin language at the earliest opportunity. George's Latin interests were initially very much governed by his philosophical inclinations. He was thrilled to discover that the Latin commentators on Aristotle drew not only on Greek (largely neo-Platonic) commentators but also on Averroes and Avicenna—producing a much enhanced Aristotelian philosophy in so doing.[82] He appears to have first encountered Thomas thorough his Aristotelian commentaries and philosophical works and was to translate a number of these, including the commentaries on the *De*

---

[81] *PLP* 27304. 'Scholarios', it should be noted, is a name, not a title. The most detailed treatment of Scholarios' life and times is now Marie-Hélène Blanchet's *Georges-Gennadios Scholarios (vers 1400–vers 1472): un intellectuel orthodoxe face à la disparition de l'empire Byzantin*. For a general account, Franz Tinnefeld's 'Georgios Gennadios Scholarios' is *sans pareil*. See also Martin Jugie, 'Scholarios, Georges'; C. J. G Turner, 'The Career of George Gennadios Scholarios'; Joseph Gill, *Personalities of the Council of Florence*, 79–94; Christopher Livanos, *Greek Tradition and Latin Influence in the Work of George Scholarios*; Theodore Zeses, Γεννάδιος Βʹ Σχολάριος. *Βίος-Συγγράμματα-Διδασκαλία*. Scholarios' complete works have long been edited: Louis Petit, Xenophon Sidéridès, and Martin Jugie (eds.), *Oeuvres complètes de Georges Scholarios* (hereafter *OC*). Works of Scholarios are referenced in *OC* and also given the Opus number provided by Tinnefeld, op. cit.

[82] *Dedicatory letter to Constantine Palaiologos OC* VII, 3 (Opus 145a).

anima and the *Posterior Analytics* and the treatise *De esse et essen-tia*.[83] George made Thomas the lynchpin of his teaching at the school of grammar and philosophy he opened in Constantinople at this time.[84] His Latin predilections soon attracted the accusations that he was a 'Latinizer'—a charge he was never to be entirely free from.[85]

Scholarios made a translation of the *De esse et essentia* for a favoured student, Matthew Kamariotes, in which he declared himself to be Thomas' most fervent disciple in either East or West: 'I do not think that any of his disciples has honoured Thomas Aquinas more than I have; nor do I think that any follower of his need have any other Muse.' In saying this, Scholarios is keenly aware that Thomas' value was by no means universally recognized in the West. The Franciscans are singled out for their attraction to the subtleties of more recent teachers (he mentions Francis Mayronis and John (Duns) Scotus). Thomas, he declares, is to be valued above such epigones as the 'most precise and correct', 'the most excellent and learned'—and because he, unlike them, has received the approbation of the Church of Rome, and not only that of the schools. In one note of slight caution, he admits that in 'a few matters' Thomas differs from the teachings of the Orthodox Church but argues that such differences were not of Thomas' making but rather the product of circumstance.[86]

Scholarios was never to depart from this enthusiastic estimation of Thomas although he would often accentuate the note of caution in subsequent works. In an *avis au lecteur* added somewhat later to the same translation, after he had made a name as an opponent of Latin theological errors, Scholarios observes: 'This Thomas, although he was Latin by race and faith, and so differs from us in those things in

---

[83] On Gennadios' encounter with Thomas, see especially Martin Jugie, 'Georges Scholarios et Saint Thomas d'Aquin'; Hugh Barbour, *The Byzantine Thomism of Gennadios Scholarios and his Translation of Armandus de Bellovisu on the* De ente et essentia *of Thomas Aquinas*; Gerhard Podskalsky, 'Die Rezeption der thomistischen Theologie bei Gennadios II Scholarios'; Sévérien Salaville 'Un thomiste à Byzance au XVe siècle: Gennade Scholarios'.

[84] Scholarios also translated works on logic of Peter of Spain, Gilbert de la Porée, and Radulphus Brito. On Brito, see Sten Ebbesen and Jan Pinborg, 'Gennadius and Western Scholasticism: Radulphus Brito's *Ars vetus* in Greek Translation'.

[85] *OC* I, 376–89 (Opus 75): an extensive and pained *apologia* defending himself from this perennial slur.

[86] Prooemium to the translation of Thomas' *De esse et essentia* (Opus 138) *OC* VI, 179–80.

which the Roman Church has in recent times innovated, is, in other respects, wise and profitable for those who read him.' He praises Thomas' exegetical, philosophical, and other works, noting that a great many have been translated. Where Thomas differs from the ancestral faith (ἡ πατρία δόξη), he must be rejected—and Scholarios is at pains to underline his own extensive and well-known contributions to such necessary rebuttal. But Thomas remains of enormous value, as a witness to the universal patristic tradition of Asia and of Europe, of Greek Fathers and Latin—the common inheritance of Christians. As was the case with Demetrios Kydones, Scholarios was not welcoming in a foreign import but recognizing 'one of us'—albeit in unfamiliar Latin garb. Notwithstanding his unfortunate aberrations, Scholarios says, 'we love this divinely-inspired and wise man'.[87]

The fact that Scholarios' love and esteem for Thomas continued undimmed throughout his career helps us to understand how it was that an advocate of union in the lead-up to and during the Council of Ferrara–Florence should have become the leader of the anti-unionist party following Eugenikos' death in 1445. This apparent *volte-face* has long puzzled scholars, leading some from Leo Allatios onwards to question whether the unionist and the anti-unionist were even the same person. But on closer inspection, it seems most plausible to see Scholarios as consistently committed to a true union of the Churches in the right circumstances—a commitment nourished by his lifelong attachment to Thomas.

Scholarios was present at Florence by virtue of the patronage of Emperor John VIII who had conferred on him the positions of Judge General of the Romans, Senator, and Teacher. At Florence, he expressed his hope that the council would indeed produce a true union of Churches, based on dogmatic agreement.[88] He was certainly prepared to subscribe to and support the union that did emerge with apparent enthusiasm so long as it offered a real possibility of tangible military support.[89] Any reservations he may have had at the time he kept to himself. But his commitment to the union seems to have

---

[87] *OC* VI, 177–8.

[88] At Florence, he urged the conclusion of a true dogmatic union and not one based merely on expediency: *That there must be a Union of Dogma and not a Peace of Expediency*, *OC* I, 306–25 (Opus 3). At the time he declared himself convinced that a true dogmatic union was indeed in the offing.

[89] See his oration at Florence on the urgent need to secure help for the fatherland: *Appeal for Help for the Fatherland*, *OC* I, 296–306 (Opus 4). In this speech, he affirms

begun to dim soon after his return from Italy. The evident hostility of the people of Constantinople to the union will also have contributed to his gradual loss of faith in the potential of the council to offer any remedy to God's sundered Church and embattled Empire. We have few works of his from the early 1440s but know that he attempted to maintain a broadly neutral position at this time. In one intriguing work from 1440–2, his *Answer to the Syllogistic Chapters of Metropolitan Mark of Ephesus*, Scholarios demonstrates the logical inadequacies of Mark's syllogisms and lauds the greater sophistication of the Latin theologians but remains cagey as to his own position.[90] This work did not long dampen his friendship with Mark, to whom he sent his *Defence of Aristotle* for approval.[91]

The ignominious defeat of the crusading armies at Varna in 1444 extinguished any real hope that salvation would come from the armies of the West and primed Scholarios to accept Mark's long-standing appeal that he come off the fence and give full vent to his misgivings as to the Florentine union. But even as leader of the anti-unionist faction after Mark's death, Scholarios never gave up his hopes for a true union, nor lost his deep respect and love for Latin theology, nor descended into calling the Latins heretics—for all their regrettable errors. This unusual equanimity in an anti-unionist leader is in large measure attributable to his lifelong devotion to Thomas. Thomas thus serves as a rare thread of continuity in Scholarios' voyage from unionism to anti-unionism.

The anti-unionists achieved a kind of pyrrhic vindication when Constantinople fell to the Turks on 29 May 1453. The union that had been formally promulgated in Constantinople only in December of the previous year had done nothing to assure the survival of the City: indeed some would argue that it hastened its end. After the fall, Scholarios was taken off into captivity—a better fate than that suffered by many of his fellow-countrymen. But he soon came to

---

the orthodoxy of the Latin positions and urges a rapid conclusion of the Council and the swift provision of aid.

[90]　*OC* III, 476–538 (Opus 8).

[91]　*OC* IV, 1–116 (Opus 123). The letter to Mark follows immediately: ibid., 116–18 (Opus 124). The work is a critique of George Gemistos Plethon, questioning his preference for Plato and holding up Aristotle (especially as interpreted by recent Latin scholars) as a more suitable resource for Christian theology. Scholarios evidently saw Plethon as a dangerous innovator and had a suspicion of his adversary's as yet closeted paganism.

the notice of the Sultan, who made him Patriarch of Constantinople, bestowing on him the markers of office just as the Byzantine emperors had done. Gennadios found his office a great burden and achieved little as patriarch. He served only a short term in office (1454–6), with two possible re-instatements in 1463 and 1464–5.[92] His last years were spent at the monastery of St John the Forerunner on Mount Menoikeion. His earthly remains are there still.

Throughout the vicissitudes of his life, Scholarios made sure to have Thomas' works with him whenever possible. In the years following his retirement from the patriarchal throne, when he was subject to periodic displacement at the whim of the Sultan or of other Ottoman potentates, he composed epitomes of the *Summae* for ready portability.[93] In the preface to his abridged version of the *Summa contra gentiles* and the *prima pars* of the *Summa theologiae*, Gennadios gives yet another testimony of his undying love for the angelic doctor. He admits that the author is a Latin and thus bound to adhere to his own ancestral faith where this differs from that of the Orthodox—and such loyalty he regards as only human. Scholarios is careful to limit the points of real difference to two: the procession of the Holy Spirit and the essence–energies distinction. Once again he underlines his own great and sacrificial contributions to the refutation of these Latin errors. But otherwise, Thomas is to be admired and heeded for his astonishing works of theology, exegesis, and philosophy. He is quite simply 'the most excellent expositor and interpreter of Christian theology in those matters in which his Church accords with ours'.[94]

These words epitomize Gennadios' perception of the thoroughgoing congruity between Thomas' teaching and that of the Orthodox. He much regrets the fact that Thomas' unfortunate but

---

[92] Blanchet, *Georges-Gennadios Scholarios*, casts serious doubt on whether these later re-instatements ever happened.

[93] Epitome of the *Summa contra gentiles*, OC V, 1–338 (Opus 139); Epitome of the *first part of the Summa theologiae*, OC V, 338–510 (Opus 140), Epitome of the *prima secundae*, OC VI, 1–153 (Opus 141). The first is more of a potted version whereas the epitomes from the *Summa theologiae* represent a more digested selection. In each case, Scholarios has used the Kydones translation as his source. John Demetracopoulos has detected another abridged version, 'Georgios Gennadios II—Scholarios' *Florilegium Thomisticum*. His early abridgment of various chapters and quaestiones of Thomas Aquinas' *Summae* and his anti-Plethonism'.

[94] OC V, 1–2: ἄριστος τῆς χριστιανικῆς θεολογίας ἐξηγητὴς καὶ συνόπτης, ἐν οἷς καὶ ἡ ἐκκλησία αὐτοῦ τῇ ἡμετέρᾳ ἐκκλησίᾳ συνάδει.

understandable espousal of certain Latin errors might impede his proper recognition and reception among the Orthodox. In a marginal note to his abridged version of the *Prima secundae*, he exclaims:

> If only, most excellent Thomas, you had not been born in the West! Then you would not have been obliged to justify the errors of that Church concerning, for instance, the procession of the Spirit and the distinction between the divine essence and operation. Then you would have been as infallible in theological matters as you are in this treatise on ethics.[95]

Thomas' imprint may be found throughout Scholarios' massive *oeuvre* over and above the quarter of it that bears directly on Thomas. Scholarios was prepared to embrace and promulgate unfamiliar doctrines such as Thomas' teaching on transubstantiation.[96] We also find many and various teachings on the incarnation, creation, predestination, sin, and salvation taken up by Scholarios from Thomas.[97]

Gennadios was certainly no uncritical reader of Thomas.[98] He was also ready to favour other viewpoints from the Latin West over Thomas when he saw fit. A prime example of such discerning reception lies in his adoption of elements of Scotus' teaching on the immaculate conception, teachings that run quite counter to Aquinas.[99] And on the principal matters separating the Churches—the procession and the essence–energies distinction—he is absolutely categorical in his adherence to the Orthodox positions, as amply attested in his

---

[95] *OC* VI, 1. This exclamation (in the margin of *Vaticanus graecus* 433) is paralleled by a similar exclamation in the margin of *Parisinus graecus* 1237. Martin Jugie neatly turns the joke on Scholarios, regretting that he had been born 'on the shores of the Bosphorus and not on the banks of the Tiber or Seine'. 'Georges Scholarios et Saint Thomas d'Aquin', 435.

[96] See his late work *On the Mystical Body of our Lord Jesus Christ*, *OC* I, 123–36 (Opus 90). Here, Scholarios sanctions not only the term μετουσίωσις (126.24, 128.5) but also the accompanying philosophical framework.

[97] See the fine summary in Podskalsky, 'Die Rezeption der thomistischen Theologie bei Gennadios II Scholarios', 309–12. Doubtless there are many more parallels to be found.

[98] *OC* VI, 284.10–14. A note in *Parisinus graecus* 1237 regrets that Thomas is a Barlaamite (that is, unable to confess the essence–energies distinction) but declares him to be in all other respects 'wonderful' (θαυμάσιος). While this marginal comment is not definitely by Gennadios, it certainly reflects his sentiments. See Sévérien Salaville, 'Un thomiste à Byzance au XVe siècle: Gennade Scholarios', 133–4.

[99] See his *Second Treatise on the Rational Human Soul OC* I, 501 (Opus 34) and the *Homily on the Dormition of our Most Holy Lady the Mother of God OC* I, 197–210 (Opus 89). See further, Martin Jugie, 'Georges Scholarios et l'Immaculée Conception'.

many works on those subjects.[100] Martin Jugie's contention that
Scholarios was motivated by sheer embarrassment to confect a 'mitigated Palamism' is an exaggeration based on a rather warped view
of Palamism in the first place. But Jugie was right to suggest
that Gennadios' conception of the real distinction between the divine
essence and operations had something to do with Scotus' *distinctio
formalis a parte rei*, a formal distinction operating between a real and
a conceptual distinction.[101] Gennadios does indeed speak of the
essence–energies distinction as one that exists 'in reality, or rather, so
to say, formally (εἰδικῶς)'.[102] He goes on to speak of the divine operation as formally finite but really infinite, whereas the essence, with
which it is one, is both formally and really infinite.[103] Here, however, we
are dealing not with a watering-down of Palamism but rather a marshalling of Scotus in support of Palamite theology. Gennadios expressly
states that 'many of the Latin doctors are in agreement with Saint
Gregory of Thessalonica' on this matter.[104] Scotus, whom he takes to
be a lesser but still valuable continuator of Thomas, must surely be in
view here. While one may doubt the success or appropriateness of
this use of Scotus to bolster Palamas, there is no doubt as to Scholarios'
conviction that Western theology has much to offer the defence of
the Palamite essence–energies distinction in all its integrity.

Scholarios serves as a fitting conclusion to this chapter as both end
and beginning. The greatest Byzantine theologian and philosopher at
world's end, he helped assure the Church's survival through this most
bitter of times. He had consistently resisted any attempt to secure the
material safety of the Empire through a union of expediency. But he
remained convinced of the underlying unity of the two ecclesial

---

[100] His chief Palamite works are *On a saying of Theodore Graptos*, OC III,
204–28 (Opus 38) and *On the Divine Operations*, OC III, 228–39 (Opus 39).

[101] OC III, xviii–xix (see also 'Palamite, controverse', 1799–1802). Joost van Ros-
sum provides a useful discussion of Gennadios' teaching in relation to Scotus in
'Palamism and Church Tradition: Palamism, its use of Patristic Tradition, and its
Relationship with Thomistic Thought', 38–47. The connection is also pursued in
Sébastien Guichardan, *Le problème de la simplicité divine en Orient et en Occident aux
XIVe et XVe sieècles: Grégoire Palamas, Duns Scot, Georges Scholarios.*

[102] *On a Saying of Theodore Graptos*, OC III, 215.24 (Opus 38).

[103] OC III, 226.5–8.

[104] *Commentary on the* De ente et essentia §94, OC VI, 283.14–16. While much of
this commentary is lifted from Armand de Beauvoir (see Hugh Barbour, *The Byzantine Thomism of Gennadios Scholarios and his Translation of Armandus de Bellovisu
on the* De ente et essentia *of Thomas Aquinas*), these comments are Gennadios' own.

traditions and of the possibility, in God's own time, of a true dogmatic union. Such convictions were nourished largely by his searching and lifelong engagement with Thomas. Thomas functioned for Scholarios as an embodiment of all that united East and West, most especially their shared patristic and philosophical tradition. And while Scholarios' regard for Thomas exceeded that which was current in much of the West, he was well aware of other movements in contemporary Western thought and perfectly capable of disagreeing with his master. A critical, discerning, but devoted disciple of Aquinas, Scholarios stands as the herald of a creative approach to theology based on strict fidelity to ecclesial tradition but nourished, enlivened, and strengthened by close and informed contacts with developments outside the Orthodox world.

Part III

Ottoman Era and Modern Orthodox Readings of Aquinas

5

Responses to Thomas in the Early Modern Period

The Byzantines, as we have seen, stole a march on much of the medieval West in regarding Thomas as the pre-eminent expositor and exemplar of Latin theology. In the years after his death, Thomas' authority was subject to some very strident questioning in the Roman Catholic world.[1] In 1277, propositions associated with Thomas were condemned in both Paris and Oxford.[2] A small flurry of works was generated by these actions, with Franciscan corrections and critiques prompting a series of Dominican counterblasts.[3] This is not, however, to say that Thomas' authority was accepted universally even within his own order: the Oxford condemnations came at the instigation of a Dominican Archbishop of Canterbury, Robert Kilwardby, and were, in a rare sign of mendicant solidarity, confirmed and amplified by his Franciscan successor, John Pecham. Durandus of Saint-Pourçain, also of the Dominican order, offered a robust critique of several of Thomas' positions that found supporters well into the fourteenth century. Aquinas' canonization in 1323, pushed for by his Dominican advocates, cemented his pre-eminent authority within the order, as

---

[1] On Thomas' immediately contested legacy, see Torrell, *Saint Thomas Aquinas: The Person and His Work*, 296–326; John Wippel, 'The Condemnations of 1270 and 1277 at Paris'; 'Thomas Aquinas and the Condemnation of 1277'; and 'Bishop Stephen Tempier and Thomas Aquinas: A Separate Process Against Aquinas?'.

[2] The Paris condemnations were effected by the then Archbishop of Paris, Stephen Tempier, but revoked by his successor following Aquinas' canonization, in so far as they bore upon Thomas. It is a curious fact that the Oxford condemnations, which aim at Aquinas even more directly than their French equivalent, do not appear ever to have been formally revoked.

[3] The key text is William de la Mare's *Correctorium*. See further Mark Jordan, 'The Controversy of the *Correctoria* and the Limits of Metaphysics'.

reflected in the gradual adoption of the *Summa theologiae* as the standard Dominican teaching resource, displacing the *Sentences* of Peter Lombard. But Thomas' followers constituted just one of the competing schools of Western medieval theology. The Franciscans, especially in the shape of John Duns Scotus, posed multiple challenges to many of Thomas' presuppositions and teachings. Further challenges were thrown up by Augustinian theologians such as Thomas Bradwardine and by nominalists including, most notably, William of Ockham. In short, Thomas' whole synthesis of reason and revelation remained a fragile achievement throughout much of the late medieval period.

Gennadios Scholarios was, then, not wholly exaggerating when he claimed in the 1430s that Thomas had no more devoted disciple than himself in all the world. In fact, Thomas' stature in the West only begins to rival that which he enjoyed among the Byzantines from the early sixteenth century onwards. This was the period of the first great commentaries, in particular that of the Dominican Thomas de Vio, Cardinal Cajetan and the beginnings of 'Thomism': the systematic codification and application of Thomas' thought. A strong Spanish Dominican school led by Francisco de Vitoria and Domingo de Soto emerged at a time which also saw Thomas' adoption by the new Jesuit order as their favoured philosopher-theologian. Many writers of that order, such as Luis de Molina and Francisco Suárez, would produce versions of Thomism quite different from and often in competition with those of Aquinas' Dominican commentators. Aquinas was, with Bonaventure, held in great honour at the Council of Trent (1545–63) but the contention, repeated by Leo XIII in *Aeterni Patris*, that the *Summa theologiae* was placed on the altar alongside the scriptures during the Council is little more than a pious fable. Pope Pius V proclaimed Aquinas a Doctor of the Church in 1567 and instigated the publication of his complete works (the 'Piana' edition of 1570–1), confirming and assuring a certain ascendancy (if not yet supremacy) of Thomas in the Catholic theological world.

This chapter offers a survey of Orthodox engagement with Thomas in particular and Latin theology in general during the early modern period. Covering such a long period in two very different thought-worlds, this chapter can offer only a relatively brief treatment of many of its subjects. Matters are also complicated by the fact Thomas is received through multiple mediations, in various versions, and in the company of other scholastic theologians. But while the waters of reception may be muddied by such factors, it is nonetheless possible to discern Thomas' ongoing role within Orthodox theology in this period with some clarity.

Throughout this period, Aquinas remains a regular interlocutor and occasional resource for many Orthodox thinkers, retaining his stature as the pre-eminent exemplar of Latin theology. While the Ottoman era was certainly no golden age of Orthodox theology, it was by no means as jejune and malformed as it has sometimes been presented.[4] The ongoing encounter with Aquinas serves as but one sign of the theological vitality of this neglected and much-maligned era.[5]

5.1. THE GREEK WORLD

Following on from the fall of Constantinople, a number of Greek theologians did what they could to perpetuate Gennadios' legacy. His sometime student, Matthew Kamariotes (d. *c.*1490), continued Gennadios' polemic against Plethon, as did, in turn, his own student, Manuel of Corinth (*c.*1460–*c.*1551), also the author of a number of anti-unionist works. Gennadios' love for Thomas seems largely forgotten in the works of his immediate epigones, none of whom has anything like his searching knowledge and profound admiration. Indeed, Gennadios' delicate balance of anti-unionism and deep sympathy for Latin theology was to remain without posterity for some time. The years following the fall of the City saw a hardening of attitudes against the union of Florence within the Ottoman territories. Doubtless this development was motivated in part by the risk that any signs of rapprochement with the Latins might raise suspicions of disloyalty among the new masters of the Byzantine world. The Council of Constantinople of 1484 formally repudiated the reunion

---

[4] The classic example is the neo-patristic meta-narrative of Fr Georges Florovsky in which the period 1453–1917 is, for the most part, a story of relentless decline and malformation under the influence of one or other variety of Western theology. This is the process he termed, after Oswald Spengler, a 'pseudomorphosis'. See further below pp.175 n.142, 199–200.

[5] On the theology of the period, see Gerhard Podskalsky's indispensable *Griechische Theologie in der Zeit der Türkenherrschaft (1453–1821)*. I owe a great debt to this magnificent work of scholarship.

council, underlining the gulf between the Churches by its insistence that Roman Catholic converts to Orthodoxy be received through re-chrismation rather than, as before, through a simple profession of faith.[6] In this atmosphere, those Greek theologians who made significant use of Thomas in the immediate post-imperial period tended to be unionists based in lands outside of Ottoman control, such as Joseph of Methone (John Plousiadenos) (d. 1500).[7]

Joseph of Methone was a most ardent unionist and is the author of a number of treatises in defence of the Florentine union.[8] He was also keen to give lyrical and musical expression to his beliefs, composing canons in honour of the Council of Ferrara–Florence and also of Thomas Aquinas.[9] It is quite remarkable to hear Thomas praised in the mellifluous cadences of Byzantine hymnography. The following verses will give a flavour:

> As a star out of the West he has illumined
> the Church of Christ
> the musical swan
> and subtle teacher,
> Thomas the all-blessed,
> Aquinas by name,
> to whom we gathered together cry:
> hail, universal teacher!
>
> Among the chorus of the Fathers
> and holy theologians
> as a sublime and subtle theologian
> you, Thomas, have taken your place,
> abiding with them and
> unceasingly theologising,
> father, the uncreated Trinity.

---

[6] The decision regarding reception is given in John Karmires, *Τὰ δογματικὰ καὶ συμβολικὰ μνημεῖα τῆς 'Ορθοδόξου Καθολικῆς ' Εκκλησίας*, II, 987–9.

[7] *PLP* 23385. On his life and times, see especially Manoussos Manoussakas, 'Recherches sur la vie de Jean Plousiadenos (1429?–1500)'.

[8] Many of these are given in PG 159 959–1393. His *Expositio pro Sancta et Œcumenica Synodo Florentina* (ibid. 1109–393) was long mistakenly ascribed to Gennadios Scholarios.

[9] Raffaele Cantarella, ed., 'Canone greco inedito di Giuseppe vescovo di Methone in onore di San Tomaso d'Aquino'. The Canon in honour of the Council is given in PG 159 1096–1101. See further, Kariophiles Mitsakis, 'Byzantine and Modern Greek Parahymnography', 25–7 and Dimitri Conomos, 'Music as Religious Propaganda: Venetian Polyphony and a Byzantine Response to the Council of Florence'.

We also have the *Kontakion*:

> You routed heresies
> with your divine words,
> O Thomas, and illumined the faithful
> with the teaching of right dogma,
> wherefore we honour you,
> greatest of teachers
> of the whole inhabited earth.

And the *Exaposteilarion*:

> Your light-bearing
> and all-holy memory
> today shines forth
> like a star rising in the West
> and illumines the minds
> of all on earth
> with wondrous revelations,
> heartening the faithful
> and freeing them from error.

The canon is constructed with a good deal of the word-play so beloved of the Byzantines, including an acrostic reading 'I, John, hymn you, Thomas, light of the whole world'. One especially ingenious feature of this verse is the rendering of 'Aquinas' in the first verse not by quasi-transliterations such as ἐξ Ἀκινάτου or ντὲ Ἀκουΐνω, but by Ἀγχίνους, an adjective conveying shrewdness, sagacity, and quick-wittedness.[10] As an unabashedly unionist production, the canon has, naturally, never been in liturgical use in the Orthodox Church. While it presents a fascinating instance of synthesis between Byzantine and Latin liturgical and theological traditions, it remains little more than an intriguing hymnographical curiosity.

---

[10] The rendering «τοῦ ἀγχίνου» is found in some MSS of the Greek translations of Aquinas, for example *Parisinus graecus* 1235. See Δημητρίου Κυδώνη, Θωμᾶ Ἀκινάτου: Σούμμα Θεολογική, ἐξελληνισθεῖσα II 15, 26. This form does not, however, carry the same level of wordplay. PLP 7795 gives the following list of renderings: Ἀκουρνᾶτος, ντε Ἀκουΐνω, Ἀκυνᾶτος, Ἀκινάτης, δε Ἀκουΐνου, Ἀκινᾶτος, Ἀκουΐνος, Ἀγχῖνος, ντε Ἀκίνου, ὁ ἐκ τοῦ Ἀγχίνου, δὲ Ἀκίνο, νδὲ Ἀκουΐνο, νδὲ Ἀκῖνο, ὁ ἀπὸ τοῦ Ἀκίνου, δὲ Ἀκίνου, ντεκουΐνω, ντὲ Ἀκυΐνο, ὁ ἐξ Ἀκινάτου, Ἀκυινάτης, ὁ Ἀκίνου, ὁ ἐξ Ἀκυΐνου, and Ἀγχίνους.

With unionism a practical dead-end after the fall of the Empire and the Council of 1484, subsequent Greek unionist engagement with Thomas (in figures such as John Matthew Karyophylles and Leo Allatios), must fall outside the scope of this book. In any event, as we move into the sixteenth century, the Orthodox encounter with Thomas begins to play out against a different background as the question of union is subsumed into the more complex dynamics of the Western European Reformation.

Aquinas crops up in the fascinating exchange between Patriarch Jeremiah II Tranos of Constantinople (1536–95) and the Tübingen theologians concerning the *Confessio Augustana* of 1530.[11] Philip Melanchthon had already sent his Greek version of the Confession to Jeremiah's predecessor, Joasaph II, but this does not appear ever to have reached its addressee. Jeremiah did receive the copy sent to him in 1573 by Jacob Andreæ and Martin Crusius and wrote back in friendly terms in 1576, expressing his hopes for union but also furnishing an extensive counterblast to the Confession. Jeremiah composed, with a number of collaborators, three replies making extensive use of various unattributed sources. The replies serve as valuable statement of the Orthodox faith, and were given canonical status at the Council of Jerusalem of 1672. As the correspondence continued, the Patriarch became wearied by the Protestants' stubborn refusal to conform to the sacred traditions guarded by the Orthodox Church; his exhortations that they give up 'every unwonted innovation' fell on deaf ears.[12] He appears to have given up hope of any practical consequence emerging from the exchange and, in 1581, closed his third letter with a plea that the German professors cease to bother him on matters of doctrine, and write back, if at all, only for friendship's sake.[13]

---

[11] Jeremiah served as Patriarch from 1572–9, 1580–4, and 1587–95. On this fascinating exchange, see Ernst Benz, *Wittenberg und Byzanz*; Dorothea Wendebourg, *Reformation und Orthodoxie*; Georges Florovsky, 'An Early Ecumenical Correspondence. Patriarch Jeremiah II and the Lutheran Divines'; George Mastrantonis, *Augsburg and Constantinople*. See also the superb contribution of Christian Hannick and Klaus-Peter Todt, 'Jérémie II Tranos'.

[12] *Acta et Scripta Theologorum Wirtembergensium et Patriarchae Constantinopolitani, D. Hieremiae*, 263. Also given in Karmires, Τὰ δογματικὰ καὶ συμβολικὰ μνημεῖα τῆς ᾿Ορθοδόξου Καθολικῆς ᾿Εκκλησίας II, 475.

[13] *Acta et Scripta Theologorum Wirtembergensium*, 370 [= Karmires II, 489].

Jeremiah was no unthinking traditionalist or theological obscurantist. The *Second Letter to the Tübingen Theologians*—amazingly—makes positive reference to Aquinas in relation to the essence–energies distinction in reproducing an anti-Latin syllogism framed by Mark of Ephesus.[14] Like Mark before him, he is careful to condemn not the theological syllogism *per se* but only meddling or excessively intrusive syllogisms.[15] The pious use of reason is, he affirms, specifically commended by the Fathers.[16] While he remains cautious about the scope and value of human reason, he explicitly affirms that 'true philosophy', philosophy properly subordinated to scriptural proofs, 'never contradicts theology'.[17]

In addition to the explicit reference to Aquinas, the impact of Latin theology is also evident in the Patriarch's treatment of the sacraments. The enumeration of seven sacraments (and only seven) reflects the enumeration that had become standard in the West though the labours of Peter Lombard and Aquinas.[18] Furthermore, the *First Letter* also clearly distinguishes between the 'matter' and 'form' of a sacrament in terms established as normative by Thomas.[19] It also asserts that the sacraments, composed of matter and form, have an 'efficient, or rather, instrumental cause' and goes on to specify that the priest may be described as this 'instrumental cause' (ὀργανικὸν αἴτιον).[20] Such concepts and terminology are inescapably rooted in Western scholasticism and more particularly in the scholasticism of Thomas Aquinas.[21] On closer inspection, this whole

---

[14] *Acta et Scripta Theologorum Wirtembergensium*, 204–5 [= Karmires II, 437–8]. This intriguing comment in his *Second Letter to the Tübingen Theologians* is remarked on by Podskalsky, *Griechische Theologie in der Zeit der Türkenherrschaft*, 110 and by Wendebourg, *Reformation und Orthodoxie*, 345 n.92. Neither notice the precise dependence on Mark's *Syllogistic Chapters against the Heresy of the Akindynists* §14 (220).

[15] «Τοὺς περιέργους συλλογισμούς». *Acta et Scripta Theologorum Wirtembergensium*, 235 [= Karmires II, 457].

[16] Ibid.

[17] *Acta et Scripta Theologorum Wirtembergensium*, 213 [= Karmires II, 443].

[18] Not that the Byzantines had any *a priori* objection to the sevenfold taxonomy—which is also found in Joseph Bryennios and Symeon of Thessalonica.

[19] *Acta et Scripta Theologorum Wirtembergensium*, 77–8 [= Karmires I, 388–9]. Cf. Aquinas, *ST* III^a q.60 a.6–7. Here, Thomas builds on and brings greater precision to William of Auxerre's pioneering use of the Aristotelian terminology of matter and form in sacramental theology.

[20] *Acta et Scripta Theologorum Wirtembergensium*, 77 [= Karmires I, 388–9].

[21] Cf. Aquinas, *ST* III^a q.64.

section is revealed to reproduce a treatise on the sacraments by the fourteenth-century anti-Palamite and anti-unionist writer, George Lapithes.[22] This treatise had circulated as part of a collection of Cypriot synodal decrees, in which form it may have reached the Patriarchal archives in Constantinople.[23] The reply continues seamlessly with another unattributed borrowing: Symeon of Thessalonica's brief catechism on the seven sacraments. This neat conjunction serves as a fine demonstration of the essential compatibility, in practice, of Latin scholasticism and Orthodoxy.[24]

Jeremiah's replies to the Protestants of Tübingen evidence a remarkable openness to Latin theology in general and to Thomas in particular. He also makes it clear that on many important points, Old and New Rome form a united front.[25] All this came hand-in-hand with noticeably friendly relations with the then Pope, Gregory XIII, founder (in 1576) of the Greek College of St Athanasius in Rome and instigator of a new papal *Ostpolitik* expressly geared to the union of the Orthodox with Rome.[26] The Patriarch welcomed this new college and was even involved in a number of projects and discussions regarding reunion during his first patriarchate and subsequent exile. Ultimately, however, he maintained a strict position on the cardinal points separating the Churches and demonstrated his commitment to the unchanging truths of Orthodoxy in his rejection of the Pope's reform of the calendar. His elevation of the Metropolitanate of Moscow to the status of a Patriarchate in 1589 was certainly intended as a counter to Roman Catholic expansionism in Eastern Europe. He died shortly before the conclusion of the Union of Brest (1596), an agreement by which substantial numbers of Christians in the

---

[22] *PLP* 14479. Lapithes (*fl.* 1340s) knew Latin and would have had no need to rely on Byzantine translations of Western theological texts. A resident of Lusignian Cyprus, he was well-placed to engage directly with Latin theology.

[23] The treatise was incorrectly ascribed to Gennadios Scholarios by Martin Jugie and included in the collected works, *OC* IV 190–7. See further, Jean Darrouzès, 'Textes synodaux chypriotes' and Dorothea Wendebourg, 'Mysterion und Sakrament. Zu einigen frühen Zeugnissen scholastischer Einflüsse auf die griechische Theologie'.

[24] *Acta et Scripta Theologorum Wirtembergensium*, 78–9 [= Karmires I, 389–90]. Cf. Symeon of Thessalonica, *De sacramentis* PG 177B–180D. See Dorothea Wendebourg, 'Mysterion und Sakrament', 276 n.31.

[25] *Acta et Scripta Theologorum Wirtembergensium*, 369 [= Karmires II, 488].

[26] The new college used the *Summa theologiae* as its chief theological text, presenting it as a 'way in' to the study of the Greek patristic tradition. See the statutes given in Émile Legrand, *Bibliographie hellénique (XVIIe siècle)* III, 502ff.

Polish-Lithuanian Commonwealth entered into communion with Rome. This is a development that Jeremiah would certainly have deplored.

Other Orthodox theologians at this time showed a similar capacity to maintain a strict conception of Orthodoxy alongside a positive embrace of Latin scholasticism. Of these the prime examples are Gabriel Severos (1540–1616) and Maximos Margounios (1549–1602). A native of Monemvasia, Severos was a well-connected and well-educated man who had studied in Padua and went on to be consecrated Metropolitan of Philadelphia in 1577.[27] He attained a certain scholarly fame, being gratefully acknowledged by the English Hellenist Sir Henry Savile for his assistance in Savile's magnificent 1612 edition of the complete works of Chrysostom. Severos spent most of his episcopal career in Venice, where he had charge of the substantial Greek community of the Serene Republic. His small flock in Philadelphia remained unshepherded.

Gabriel's episcopal consecration was performed in Constantinople by Patriarch Jeremiah, whom he assisted in the preparation of his first reply to the Tübingen theologians. Severos may well have been responsible for the Latin scholastic dimension of this first letter. His own sacramental theology is very much like that of George Lapithes: an adaptation to Byzantine use of a distinctly Latin and Aristotelian approach. In his own treatise on the sacraments, Severos insists on the sevenfold taxonomy of the sacraments and interprets the mysteries in terms of form, matter, and causality.[28] He also goes further than Lapithes (as reproduced in the replies of Jeremiah) in embracing the term 'transubstantiation' and in speaking of the indelible character of the sacraments of baptism, ordination, and chrismation.[29] It is beyond doubt that Severos's views on the sacraments were shaped to some extent by his reading of Aquinas,

---

[27] On Severos, see Émile Legrand, *Bibliographie hellénique (XVe et XVIe siècles)* II, 142–51; Martin Jugie in *DTC* 6, 977–84; Gerhard Podskalsky, *Griechische Theologie in der Zeit der Türkenherrschaft*, 118–24.

[28] Published in Venice in 1600 as Συνταγμάτιον περὶ τῶν ἁγίων καὶ ἱερῶν μυστηρίων and also in the Συνταγμάτιον περὶ τῶν ὀφφικίων, κληρικάτων καὶ ἀρχοντικίων τῆς τοῦ Χριστοῦ ἁγίας ἐκκλησίας published by Patriarch Chrysanthos (Notaras) of Jerusalem in 1715.

[29] In regarding chrismation as indelible, Severos would seem to distance himself from the then official policy of the Patriarchate of Constantinople that Roman Catholics be received by chrismation.

whose work he possessed in a manuscript copy once owned by Gennadios Scholarios.[30] Severos also wrote a series of works on the schism, defending the faith and ritual of the Orthodox Church and serving as a rejoinder to the anti-Greek polemics of the Jesuits Cardinal Bellarmine and Antonio Possevino. Severos composed a work on the five 'general and principal' differences between East and West (procession, papacy, azymes, purgatory, and the blessedness of the saints).[31] While Severos uses the essence–energies distinction to criticize the Latin position on the procession (for mistakenly equating the Holy Spirit with the undifferentiated energy of the Holy Trinity), he evidently does not regard the distinction itself as a cardinal difference.

Severos had something of a rival in the shape of Maximos Margounios.[32] Like Severos, Margounios was a graduate of Padua, long-term resident of Venice, and an absentee bishop.[33] Margounios was a prolific author and a talented translator (from Latin into Greek and *vice versa*).[34] He was also the owner of a spectacular library. Many of his Latin books found their way to the monastery of Iviron on Mount Athos after his death. The collection includes published editions of the *Summa theologiae* of Alexander of Hales, the Venetian edition of the *Opera omnia* of Thomas Aquinas (1593–4), and works by dozens of other Latin authors down to a complete set of the works of Alphonsus Tostado.[35]

Margounios' chief claim to fame is a remarkable attempt to find a way out of the impasse of the *filioque* question. He expresses the

---

[30]   Émile Legrand, *Bibliographie hellénique (XVe et XVIe siècles)* II, 151.

[31]   This text was printed in 1627 by Nikodemos Metaxas in Constantinople on the first Orthodox-controlled press in the City. Metaxas also printed works of Maximos Margounios and Meletios Pegas.

[32]   On Margounios see Émile Legrand, *Bibliographie hellénique (XVe et XVIe siècles)* II, xxiii–lxxvii; Louis Petit, 'Margounios, Maxime' in *DTC* 9, 2039–44; Deno Geanakoplos, *Byzantine East and Latin West: Two Worlds of Christendom in Middle Ages and Renaissance*, 165–93; Gerhard Podskalsky, *Griechische Theologie in der Zeit der Türkenherrschaft*, 135–51.

[33]   In Margounios' case, the absence from his see of Kythera (on Crete) was involuntary: the Venetian authorities refused him the necessary permission. Severos, by contrast, was never disposed to take up residence in Philadelphia (Asia Minor), doubting the ability of the Christian community there to maintain a Metropolitan.

[34]   Examples of his translation include John of Damascus' *Against the Manicheans* and various other works of the Byzantine Aristotelian tradition.

[35]   A list of the works held at Iviron is given by Deno Geanakoplos, *Byzantine East and Latin West: Two Worlds of Christendom in Middle Ages and Renaissance*, 183–93.

conviction that the faith of Latins and Greeks is essentially the same, but that this unity has been obscured through a confusion of the categories of temporal and eternal procession. He demonstrated this conviction in a series of works, including a detailed commentary on Augustine's *De Trinitate*.[36] While sticking resolutely to the traditional Orthodox position on procession from the Father alone according to hypostasis, he allows that the Spirit proceeds from the Father and the Son in terms of the communication of God's gifts to the world. He will even concede that the recitation of the Creed with the *filioque* is permissible, so long as it is rightly understood as denoting temporal procession. Gabriel Severos denounced him to the authorities in Constantinople as a dangerous Latinizer. The Holy Synod, however, exonerated him from any taint of heresy and he and Severos were, eventually, reconciled. Rome, for its part, wanted him hauled before the Inquisition for his suspicious views on the Trinity and his attacks on the Jesuits and Franciscans, but Venice gave him her protection.

Margounios makes reference to Aquinas on a number of occasions. He criticizes Thomas' contention that the Spirit could not be distinguished from the Son if he did not proceed from him, at least in so far as this contention implies procession according to essence.[37] But he also approves what Thomas has to say in the matter of consubstantiality.[38] In a treatment of the historical development of the *filioque* he draws explicitly on the wisdom and authority of Aquinas.[39] Thomas is certainly a figure of huge significance for Margounios, and one whom he regards as a potential ally even in the highly controverted matter of the *filioque*. Margounios emerges, then, as yet another example of a strictly Orthodox writer willing to make suitably critical but ultimately positive use of Aquinas.

A more critical response to Aquinas may be found in Meletios Pegas (1549–1601). A friend of both Severos and Margounios, Meletios was one of the great luminaries of his age. Meletios reigned as

---

[36] *Elucidatio librorum divi Augustini* De Trinitate. Edited in Giorgio Fedalto, *Massimo Margunio e il suo commento al De Trinitate di S. Agostino (1558).*

[37] *Elucidatio librorum divi Augustini* De Trinitate18.2 (ed. Fedalto, 247). Cf. *ST* I^a q.36 a.2.

[38] *Elucidatio librorum divi Augustini* De Trinitate14.26 (ed. Fedalto, 218). Cf. *ST* I^a q.41 a.3 ad.2.

[39] See Fedalto (ed.), *Massimo Margunio e il suo commento al De Trinitate di S. Agostino (1558)*, 95–6. Margounios cites *ST* I^a q.36 a.3 ad.2 in an unedited treatise on the procession of the Spirit.

Patriarch of Alexandria from 1590 to 1601.[40] He was a close associate
of Patriarch Jeremiah II and served as *locum tenens* of the see
of Constantinople for a brief period from 1597 to 1598. Like Margounios, Meletios was a Cretan and an alumnus of Padua. He was a man
of profound scholarship and wide-ranging contacts, as amply
illustrated by his voluminous correspondence.[41] His writings and
activities show him to have been a great defender of Orthodoxy. He
wrote against both Luther and Calvin (while maintaining friendly
contacts with many eminent Protestants) but devoted his chief
polemical efforts towards the Roman Catholics. Meletios distinguished himself by his ardent agitation against the Union of Brest
and by his many works on questions such as papal primacy, the
necessity of communion in both kinds, the non-existence of purgatory, and the unacceptability of the reformed calendar. But even in
this inveterate foe of Latin religious errors and papal machinations of
all varieties, we find an unusual familiarity with the Latin patristic
tradition and a close knowledge of Latin scholasticism.

Meletios was, in particular, a great devotee of Augustine who
figures prominently in his major catechetical work, *Orthodox
Doctrine* ('Ορθόδοξος διδασκαλία). First published in 1596 in Vilnius,
this manual, composed in demotic Greek, spends a great deal of time
defending Augustine from any possible misapprehension as regards
Trinitarian theology. Augustine's statements on the Spirit as the
mutual love of Father and Son are deemed perfectly correct, so long
as they are not taken to impinge on the single procession according
to hypostasis. References to the Paraclete as the common gift of
Father and Son are, in similar vein, to be understood as referring to
temporal procession only.[42] It is very remarkable indeed to find an
Orthodox catechesis revolving to such an extent around the correct
interpretation of Augustine. Gennadios Scholarios is esteemed as an
exceptionally lofty authority, a valuable indication of his ongoing
authority, but Gennadios' great love, Aquinas, comes in for some
harsh words for his treatment of the procession.[43] There is, it may

[40] See especially Gerhard Podskalsky, *Griechische Theologie in der Zeit der Türkenherrschaft*, 128–35. Podskalsky provides, as ever, an exemplary bibliography.
[41] See Émile Legrand (ed.), *Lettres de Mélétius Pigas antérieures à sa promotion au
Patriarcat*. These early letters give a fine idea of his range: correspondents include
Theodore Beza, Martin Crusius, Francis Portus, and Queen Margaret of Navarre.
[42] 'Ορθόδοξος διδασκαλία, 114ff.
[43] 'Ορθόδοξος διδασκαλία, 126.

be noted, no sign in this treatise of the Palamite essence–energies distinction.

Meletios shows an indirect debt to Thomas in his taking-up of the term 'transubstantiation', as seen in his *On the Immaculate Mysteries* (Περὶ τῶν ἀχράντων μυστηρίων) (1594) but he deliberately refrains from adopting the attendant philosophical framework.[44] By this time, the term had become a kind of shibboleth, serving as an effective way to exclude any Protestant interpretation of the eucharist. But Meletios also distances himself categorically from Aquinas' suggestion that communion in one kind might suffice.[45] His composite work *Discourse on the question as to which is the True Catholic Church* [. . .]. *And against the Rule of the Pope* was published as *Against the Rule of the Pope* (Κατὰ τῆς ἀρχῆς τοῦ Πάππα) by Dositheos of Jerusalem in his *Tome of Joy* (1705). In this work, Augustine again emerges as a great favourite, with the *City of God* particularly in view. The treatise adopts classic Latin scholastic methodology, enumerating seven propositions and proceeding, after an initial response, to rebut them one by one.[46]

Meletios' nephew, Cyril Lukaris (1570/2–1638), succeeded him as Patriarch of Alexandria from 1601 to 1620 and went on to occupy, with several interruptions, the see of Constantinople from 1620 to 1638.[47] A giant of his time, Cyril has a certain notoriety as the 'Protestant' or 'Calvinist' Patriarch, labels arising from the profoundly Calvinist character of his *Confession of Faith* (1629). But such labels hardly do justice to the achievements of this great man, one whose stature so worried the Sultan that he ended up having him strangled. Roman Catholicism was ever Cyril's great bane. His struggles began in earnest when he was sent by Meletios to Poland-Lithuania in 1596 to oppose the Union of Brest and continued to the end of his days. The Jesuits proved to be a perpetual thorn in his side and it was

---

[44] Περὶ τῶν ἀχράντων μυστηρίων, 103.

[45] Περὶ τῶν ἀχράντων μυστηρίων, 134, 137, 143–4.

[46] Κατὰ τῆς ἀρχῆς τοῦ Πάππα, 582–95. Note that scholasticism was by this time an inescapable feature of both Catholic and Protestant theology. Meletios' fondness for Augustine will also have provided common ground with Western theologians of all stamps.

[47] See Émile Legrand, *Bibliographie hellénique (XVIIe siècle)* IV, 161–521; Klaus-Peter Todt, 'Kyrillos Lukaris'; and Gerhard Podskalsky, *Griechische Theologie in der Zeit der Türkenherrschaft*, 162–80.

Catholic-sponsored machinations in Constantinople that secured his grisly demise.

In the context of such battles, it is no surprise that Cyril tended to shun Latin theology in all its manifestations and to look rather to the Reformers for succour and inspiration. He fostered very friendly relations with Protestant theologians and states, the latter (above all England and Holland) being of vital importance in his dealings with the Sublime Porte. In theological terms, it is the Dutch Calvinists with whom he developed most sympathy, embracing many of their doctrines with evident sincerity. His *Confession* stands as the starkest statement of such affinities, but a zeal for the Reform is evident in many of his works and letters. The *Confession* proclaims, *inter alia*, the primacy of scripture over tradition, justification by faith, and the predestination of the elect while renouncing such things as transubstantiation, prayers for the dead, and icon-veneration. It makes for chastening reading.

Fighting for the survival of the Orthodox Church against a powerful Catholic onslaught, it is perhaps not to be wondered at that Cyril veered heavily towards Protestantism. But Cyril's enthusiasm for the Reformers was to prove a *hapax phenomenon* without real posterity. On the contrary, his *Confession* was, as we shall see, to foster a reaction in which the employment of Roman Catholic sources was to become virtually normative within Orthodox theology. Aquinas, naturally, was to figure prominently in this backlash. But before proceeding to study this reaction further, some mention must be made of Cyril's intellectual legacy.

In his powerful and effective resistance to Catholic expansionism, Cyril placed special emphasis on education. He was especially concerned with higher learning, as seen in his reorganization of the Patriarchal Academy in Constantinople. In 1624 or thereabouts, Cyril appointed the eminent Athenian Aristotelian Theophilos Korydaleus (*c.*1574–1646) as head of the Academy. Korydaleus brought the neo-Aristotelianism of Padua into the heart of the Greek thought-world. Rejecting the Christian Aristotelianism of the Byzantine and Latin traditions alike, Korydaleus fostered the study of Aristotle's texts and methodology as a discrete discipline, distinct from any possible religious application or synthesis. While always technically subordinating his conclusions to revealed truth, Korydaleus was committed to the divorce of philosophy from theology. His commentaries on Aristotle were to form the bedrock of higher learning in much of Orthodox world down to the late eighteenth century.

Korydaleus regarded Latin scholasticism as an illegitimate hybrid of philosophy and theology. He shared a loathing for Catholicism with Lukaris and partook to some degree of his patron's Protestant sympathies. His theological standpoint is attested in his *Dogmatic Letter* and *Solutions of Arguments relating to the Procession of the Holy Spirit*.[48] The *Dogmatic Letter* (1640) makes it plain that only the Orthodox Church has guarded the apostolic faith. This faith is communicated by the Fathers and ecumenical councils but always and only in conformity with scripture. The Roman Church's deviation from the truth is squarely associated with the scholasticism of Aquinas, Scotus, Bellarmine, and Lombard, with their 'modern innovations' and 'excessive curiosity'.[49] Scholastic approaches to the eucharist serve as glaring examples of such unwonted prying. Korydaleus, for his part, is content to insist on the mysterious nature of the sacrament.[50] He was also known for taking a firm stance against the notion of transubstantiation.[51] The *Solutions* go on to refute Aquinas' argument as to the necessity of opposite relations for the distinction of persons, noting that this contention is peculiar to him and that it had not been accepted by many papists, especially Scotus.[52] But while Korydaleus' anti-scholasticism dovetailed well with Cyril's wider agenda, it was to have little impact in Orthodox theological circles.

The reaction to Cyril's frankly Protestantizing agenda was swift to take hold. Councils in 1638 and 1642 repudiated his *Confession* and theologians of a more Catholic stamp came into the ascendancy. George Koressios (after 1566–*c*.1660) is a fine example: a forthright and vigorous anti-unionist Palamite with a searching knowledge of

---

[48] *Solutions of Arguments relating to the Procession of the Holy Spirit*, 1077 (cf. 1079).

[49] *Dogmatic Letter*, 1073.

[50] *Dogmatic Letter*, 1075–6.

[51] Gerhard Podskalsky argues that this was largely on philosophical grounds. *Griechische Theologie in der Zeit der Türkenherrschaft*, 197–8.

[52] Korydaleus is right to assert that Scotus saw no necessity in specifically *opposed* relations, relations of inverse correspondence (such as Son of the Father/Father of the Son) but held that properly understood relations could themselves be constitutive of distinction within the Godhead.

Latin scholasticism.[53] Koressios was famed as a doctor, philosopher, and theologian.[54] He had shown himself a keen polemicist in days as a teacher in Pisa with his attacks on the theories of Galileo. That same warring spirit was also to animate many of his later works against Catholics, Protestants, and straying Orthodox. Koressios became an official spokesman of the see of Constantinople with the title 'Theologian of the Great Church'. As such he engaged in public debates in Constantinople with the Dutch Calvinist Antoine Leger, sometime chaplain to the Dutch embassy and a confidant of Lukaris.

Koressios produced a vast oeuvre, little of which has ever been published. It includes medical works, a great deal of theological polemic, commentaries on Aristotle, and liturgical compositions. His theological work is marked by a thoroughgoing immersion in the Latin Fathers and in medieval Western scholasticism. This expertise is most amply displayed in his weighty *Enchiridion* on the procession of the Spirit and the essence–energies distinction, published by Dositheos of Jerusalem in his *Tome of Reconciliation*.[55] Koressios is well acquainted with and makes use of a stunning range of writers in this systematic and scholarly treatise. In addition to Aquinas these include Peter Lombard, Albert the Great, Alexander of Hales, Peter Aureol, Durandus, Hervaeus, William of Ockham, Francis Mayronis, James of Viterbo, Thomas of Strasbourg, Bellarmine, Suárez, and Molina. Aquinas receives special attention, being one of the few writers for whom Koressios gives detailed textual references. Thomas is typically the first cited authority from the scholastics on a given issue. His *Commentary on the Sentences* I d.11 q.1 a.4, for example, is taken to evidence the Latin acceptance of two principles of procession in the generation of the Spirit.[56] His account of real distinction between the divine hypostases in *Commentary on the Sentences* I d.12 q.1 a.2 is seen to be confirmed by 'Bonaventure, Giles of Rome, Albert, Hervaeus, and

---

[53]   See Émile Legrand, *Bibliographie hellénique (XVIIe siècle)* III, 255–72; Anthimos Papadopulos, «Γεώργιος Κορέσσιος» Raymond Vancourt, 'Georges Coressios. Quelques aspects de sa doctrine sur la grâce et la predestination, d'après des documents inédits'; Gerhard Podskalsky, *Griechische Theologie in der Zeit der Türkenherrschaft*, 183–90; Nikos Stoupakes Γεώργιος Κορέσσιος (1570 ci–1659/60): Η ζωή, το έργο του και οι πνευματικοί αγώνες της εποχής του.

[54]   See, for example, the preface to Dositheos of Jerusalem's *Τόμος Καταλλαγῆς*.

[55]   ' *Εγχειρίδιον περὶ τῆς ἐκπορεῦσις τοῦ ἁγίου πνεύματος*

[56]   ' *Εγχειρίδιον*346.

other scholastics'.[57]*De potentia* q.8 a.3 is also mentioned in this same context. Thomas is the chief source cited for the West's lamentable failure to acknowledge the Palamite essence–energies distinction and its attendant downgrading of all divine operations *ad extra* to created status. 'Thomas', he writes, 'divides the operations into those that are immanent and those that proceed outwards, that is to say interior and exterior operations.' This indeed faithfully reflects Thomas' position as stated in the *Summa theologiae* (I^a q.14 pr.). Koressios goes on to state, accurately, that Thomas affirms the former, including intellect and will, to be uncreated. But the exterior operations, including justifying grace and all divine operations effecting human salvation, are seen to be created.[58] This last assertion is, to say the least, a rather unsubtle take on Thomas' account of divine operation *ad extra*.

Thomas also appears in a short work also directed against the Catholic understanding of the procession of the Spirit, the *Dialogue with a Friar*.[59] Here, Koressios very consciously and carefully addresses the question with due attention paid to the respective authorities of East and West. In the latter category we find Anselm, Peter Lombard, and Thomas. Koressios avers that Thomas' assertion that Father and Son cause the Spirit to proceed as one God carries the inference that the Spirit is not God but a creature. Thomas, of course, explicitly precludes such a conclusion in all his works on the subject.[60]

Koressios shows himself more amenable to some of the teachings associated with Thomas and his disciples outside the context of the anti-Catholic polemics of the *Enchiridion*. He was certainly a great champion of transubstantiation (including its philosophical underpinnings) and attacked both Korydaleus and Lukaris for holding Protestant views on the subject. His debate with Leger also saw him defending transubstantiation as an indubitably Orthodox doctrine. Subsequent anti-Protestant works find him embracing a broadly Thomist account of predestination, justification, and grace.[61] But

---

[57] ᾽ *Εγχειρίδιον*377.   [58] ᾽ *Εγχειρίδιον*393.
[59] *Διάλεξις μετά τινος τῶν φράρων.*   [60] *Διάλεξις*, 3.
[61] Here I rely on the judgement of Raymond Vancourt, 'Georges Coressios. Quelques aspects de sa doctrine sur la grâce et la predestination, d'après des documents inédits', 87–95. Vancourt unearths some remarkable teachings in various unedited texts, most notably a treatise on predetermination and grace. These include a developed notion of the created effects of grace, both actual and habitual. This aspect of the uncreated divine operation is deemed a 'passive grace'. This may plausibly be

Vincent Damodos greatly exaggerated when he claimed, a century later, that Koressios 'bases all his teaching on Thomas Aquinas from whom he has taken everything theological that he has written. For he followed the teachings of the Thomists, from whom he was instructed in the scholastic method.'[62] His debts to Thomas are not quite so large, nor as uncritical. Aquinas certainly looms large in Koressios' work, but explicit references are invariably given solely for purposes of correction.

Meletios Syrigos (1585–1663) stands as a still more implacable adversary of Cyril's programme, and one similarly steeped in Latin scholarship.[63] Syrigos composed a powerful demolition of the *Confession*, subjecting each chapter to a comprehensive dissection and rebuttal.[64] He devotes a very lengthy section to the eucharist and to the defence of transubstantiation. Giving a recital of patristic citations (from Justin, Ambrose, Chrysostom, John of Damascus, and Theophylact of Ochrid), he argues that all the various terms used by 'our teachers of old', whether 'making, or changing, or transforming, or transelementation', are recapitulated and confirmed in the term 'transubstantiation'.[65] An attack on transubstantiation is seen as tantamount to an attack on the whole tradition of the Church. Meletios also produced a revised version of Peter Mogila's distinctly Catholicizing *Confession* that gained canonical status at the Synods of Jassy (Iaşi) (1642) and Jerusalem (1672).[66]

Nicholas Koursoulas (*c.*1602–52) deserves mention for the counterpoise he offered to Korydaleus' neo-Aristotelianism.[67] An alumnus of the Greek College in Rome and a bishop *manqué* (two candidacies

---

interpreted as an adaptation of Palamite teaching along Thomist lines in terms reminiscent of Theophanes of Nicaea (cf. below pp.92–3).

[62] See George Metallinos, *Παράδοσῃ καὶ ἀλλοτρίωσῃ*, 75 (cited in Christos Yannaras, ᾽*Ορθοδοξία καὶ Δύσῃ στὴ Νεώτερῃ Ἑλλάδα*, 138). Damodos himself was deeply indebted to Thomas. See below, pp.162–4.

[63] See Gerhard Podskalsky, *Griechische Theologie in der Zeit der Türkenherrschaft*, 207–13.

[64] *Κατὰ τῶν καλβινικῶν κεφαλαίων, καὶ ἐρωτήσεων Κυρίλλου του Λουκάρεως, Ἀντίρρησις*. See Émile Legrand, *Bibliographie hellénique (XVIIe siècle)* II, 458–72.

[65] *Κατὰ τῶν καλβινικῶν κεφαλαίων*, 137.

[66] See below, p.174.

[67] See Émile Legrand, *Bibliographie hellénique (XVIIe siècle)* V, 261–8; Sergios Raftanes (ed.), *Σύνοψις τῆς ἱερᾶς θεολογίας, φιλοπονηθεῖσα εἰς ὠφέλειαν τῶν ὀρθοδόξων φιλομαθῶν, ι-λβ* (ix–xxxii); Gerhard Podskalsky, *Griechische Theologie in der Zeit der Türkenherrschaft*, 242–4.

having failed), he spent much of his life as a monk, spending his last years on Athos. He produced a number of commentaries on Aristotle but his most important work is his *Synopsis of Sacred Theology*, a systematic presentation of the faith in the tradition of John of Damascus' *Exact Exposition of the Christian Faith* or John Kyparissiotes' *Elementary Exposition of Theological Texts*. The *Synopsis* stands as a re-affirmation of scholasticism, whether Byzantine or Latin in form, and as a plain rebuttal of Korydaleus' projected divorce of philosophy from theology. It is also a sign of the ongoing legacy of Gennadios Scholarios, whom he regards as a very great authority.

The *Synopsis* opens with a fascinating defence of the scholastic method. Koursoulas allows a distinction between the rhetorical and dialectical method of the Fathers and the more forensic approach of the scholastics. But while the latter are certainly of less consequence that the former, the scholastic method is not to be rejected, *pace* Luther, Calvin, and other heretics. Nor is it anything new: Koursoulas denies that scholastic theology began in Paris four hundred years previously and traces the scholastic method right back to the catechetical school of Alexandria, to teachers such as Pantaeus, Clement, and Origen. Scholasticism has, he argues, always been at the Church's disposal. It is characterized by its 'method, order, differentiation of questions and arguments, formulation of syllogisms' and other qualities but remains geared to the essential simplicity of the truth. He is careful to note that he is not necessarily endorsing the conclusions of the schoolmen. Some conclusions he finds useful, others wholly unacceptable. But the scholastic method itself he regards as indispensable.

Koursoulas presents his own work in impeccably scholastic form, dividing it into questions, objections, and responses. A thorough familiarity with Latin scholasticism is evident throughout, not least in the forceful defence of the immaculate conception of the Blessed Virgin.[68] He also provides a lengthy consideration of that most stereotypical of scholastic questions, the nature of angels.[69] This discussion revolves largely around the competing opinions of Thomas Aquinas and Duns Scotus, with Averroes and Aristotle

---

[68] Σύνοψις τῆς ἱερᾶς θεολογίας, φιλοπονηθεῖσα εἰς ὠφέλειαν τῶν ὀρθοδόξων φιλομαθῶν, 335–42. Koressios and Syrigos, by contrast, oppose this teaching.

[69] Σύνοψις τῆς ἱερᾶς θεολογίας, 260–321.

also brought into the discussion. Other conversation partners in the work include William of Ockham. Koursoulas treats his sources in suitably critical and sophisticated fashion. On issues such as the procession of the Spirit, for example, he can have no truck with any of them, for all that he appreciates the reasonableness of their positions. He devotes particular attention to Thomas' claim that double procession is essential in order to maintain the distinction of persons within the Godhead, a claim he rejects only after very careful consideration.[70] The schoolmen emerge, in short, as valuable but never unimpeachable authorities. In Koursoulas, then, we encounter the intriguing phenomenon of a handbook of Orthodox theology based in large measure around a conversation with medieval Western scholasticism. It is a remarkable feat, and one which awaits emulation.

Few other Orthodox writers of the period are quite so explicit about their debts to the Catholic West. Koursoulas is, however, perfectly typical of the time in that the reaction against both Protestantism and neo-Aristotelianism brought with it a thorough utilization of Catholic sources. This pattern is very much in evidence in the imposing figure of Patriarch Dositheos II (Notaras) of Jerusalem (1641–1707).[71] Dositheos was a great defender of Orthodoxy against the intense proselytizing efforts of both Catholics and Protestants. As Patriarch of Jerusalem from 1669 until his death, he was a vigorous champion of the rights of the Orthodox in the Holy Land, above all in the Holy Sepulchre—a bitterly contested space then as now. Perceiving with great acumen the power of the printing press, Dositheos became a spectacularly prolific editor. His publishing achievements are best embodied in his monumental and beautifully produced volumes of anti-Latin literature: the *Tome of Reconciliation* (1694), the *Tome of Love* (1698), and the *Tome of Joy* (1705).[72]

Dositheos played a prominent role in the anti-Cyrilline reaction, producing his own *Confession of the Orthodox Faith* as a direct counter to Cyril's and seeing it canonized at the Council of Jerusalem

---

[70] Σύνοψις τῆς ἱερᾶς θεολογίας, 252–6.
[71] See Konstantinos Sathas, Νεοελληνικὴ Φιλολογία, 379–83; Gerhard Podskalsky, *Griechische Theologie in der Zeit der Türkenherrschaft*, 282–95; and Klaus-Peter Todt, 'Dositheos II. von Jerusalem'.
[72] Τόμος Καταλλαγῆς; Τόμος Ἀγάπης; Τόμος Χαρᾶς.

in 1672. Roman Catholic sources are very much in evidence in the *Confession.*[73] Its most obvious recognizable debt to Thomas lies in the explicit affirmation of transubstantiation, including the attendant philosophical language of substance and accidents (§17).[74] Dositheos had subsequently to defend this doctrine against the powerful assaults of a prominent disciple of Korydaleus, John Karyophylles, and had his views vindicated (and those of his opponent condemned) at the Council of Constantinople in 1691. Latin affinities are also evident in Dositheos' affirmation of the seven sacraments (as opposed to Cyril's two) and of the indelible character of the sacraments of baptism and ordination. The treatment of free will in §3 has some striking similarities with the teaching of the Jesuit Thomist Luis de Molina.[75] The presentation of the fate of souls after death in §18 all but admits the existence of purgatory.[76] His list of the canonical books of scripture also appears partly modelled on that of Trent.[77]

The issue of precisely how Dositheos came to embrace such elements of Roman Catholic teaching is less significant than the fact of his having done so. We know, for example, that he possessed an anthology of texts from Thomas in manuscript form.[78] But while such reading-matter may plausibly have helped shape his views on a matter such as transubstantiation, this teaching was by now so entrenched in Orthodox theological writing that Thomas is most likely only an indirect source. Other connections with Western sources (such as the Council of Trent) may be more direct but,

---

[73] John Karmires (ed.), *Τὰ δογματικὰ καὶ συμβολικὰ μνημεῖα τῆς Ὀρθοδόξου Καθολικῆς Ἐκκλησίας*II, 747–73. Note that this edition takes in a number of additions and clarifications introduced by Dositheos in his 1690 edition of the text. These changes serve to underline the distinction between the Orthodox and Roman Catholic faiths, asserting that there is no human head of the Church, that communion must be in both kinds, and that there are three rather than two canonical Books of Maccabees.

[74] Karmires II, 761–4.

[75] Karmires II, 748–9.

[76] Karmires II, 764–8. Not that this was unusual: Gabriel Severos and Elias Meniates, for example, admit the existence of a state of purification that seems scarcely dissimilar from what the Latins call purgatory. See further Timothy Ware, *Eustratios Argenti*, 143–8. Ware concludes his discussion with the rueful reflection, 'One cannot but feel that Orthodox theologians have sometimes been over-anxious to discover differences between themselves and Rome.'

[77] Karmires II, 769–70.

[78] See Klaus-Peter Todt, 'Dositheos II. von Jerusalem', 705 n.169.

again, the precise mechanisms of such encounter remain less significant than the fact of their existence.

Such connections are more than accidental. Dositheos certainly draws on Catholic sources in the battle against Protestantism but this is not simply a case of fighting fire with fire. There is in this *Confession* a tangible sense of the united witness of Greek East and Latin West standing against the dangerous novelties of the Reformation. When Dositheos speaks of the 'Catholic Church', he does not mean this in a purely confessional sense, referring only to the Eastern Churches, but to the shared tradition of the universal Church from which the Latins have of late, regrettably, deviated. But this deviation does not mean that all Latin works subsequent to the schism are to be abhorred. Dositheos gives ample demonstration in his *Confession* of the ongoing value of post-schism Latin theology for the expression of Orthodox theology. The value of such a positive estimation of the potentialities of Roman Catholic theology is accentuated by the fact that Dositheos was fervently opposed to any sort of accommodation with the Roman Catholic Church, amply meriting his popular title of 'scourge of the Latins' (λατινομάστιξ).[79]

Dositheos' bitter struggles in the Holy Land and elsewhere were typical of a general deterioration in relations between Orthodox and Catholics in the late seventeenth and early eighteenth centuries. The formerly widespread practice of limited concelebration and *communicatio in sacris* became a rarity in this period. In addition to the competition over the Holy Places, aggressive and often clandestine proselytism, the Venetian occupation of the Peloponnese (1685–1718), and the schism in Antioch (1724) conspired in various ways to end the pattern of cooperation and mutual recognition that had previously been common practice.[80] But this breakdown in relations did little to change the predominantly Latin-leaning character of Orthodox theology at this time.

Elias Meniates (1669–1714) is a fine case in point.[81] His hugely successful *Rock of Scandal* did much to underline the gravity of the

---

[79] Timothy Ware, *Eustratios Argenti*, 31.

[80] The phenomenon of *communicatio in sacris* and its decline is elegantly detailed in Ware, *Eustratios Argenti*, 16–42 and, idem, 'Orthodox and Catholics in the Seventeenth Century: Schism or Intercommunion?'

[81] See Konstantinos Sathas, Νεοελληνικὴ Φιλολογία, 394–7; Gerhard Podskalsky, *Griechische Theologie in der Zeit der Türkenherrschaft*, 319–23.

split between East and West in the popular consciousness.[82] Written in the demotic, the book traces the history of the schism back to the time of Patriarch Photios in the late ninth century. The blame for the schism between Rome and Constantinople that occurred at that time is placed squarely on the shoulders not of the Patriarch but of the power-hungry Pope Nicholas I. Subsequent popes share much of the guilt for the perpetuation of the split. The second part of the work deals with the five principal issues separating East and West: papacy, procession, azymes, purgatory, and the blessedness of the saints. Needless to say, it is the papacy that constitutes the eponymous 'rock of scandal' (*Πέτρα σκανδάλου*).

Meniates was also well known as an exceptional preacher, a talent which earned him the sobriquet of a 'new Chrysostom'. In his oratory, Meniates shows easy familiarity with both Greek and Latin Fathers, displaying, like so many Orthodox theologians of this period, a special attachment to Augustine. A collection of his sermons first published in 1716 (another very popular publication, frequently reprinted) reveals a profound indebtedness to Western sources, most especially the *Art of Rhetoric* (1681) of the Cretan Catholic Francis Skouphos.[83] The sermons breathe freely of the air of the Counter-Reformation, drawing on figures such as Segneri, Bossuet, Bourdaloue, and Massillon.[84] Meniates makes use of Latin scholastic arguments against the Lutherans and Calvinists and adopts the doctrine of transubstantiation with its philosophical underpinnings. He was also a great advocate of the immaculate conception. In Meniates we have yet another instance of that intriguing phenomenon whereby strict confessional boundaries in no way inhibit positive and conscious reception of non-Orthodox sources.

But there are also, of course, Orthodox theologians who strive to avoid such positive reception as best they can. One such is Eustratios Argenti (*c.*1687–*c.*1758), certainly among the ablest theologians and polemicists of our period.[85] Argenti composed a series of works

[82] First published in 1718, the work was reprinted five times in the eighteenth century alone.
[83] *Διδαχαὶ εἰς τὴν Ἁγίαν καὶ Μεγάλην Τεσσαρακοστὴν καὶ εἰς ἄλλας Κυριακὰς τοῦ ἐνιαυτοῦ καὶ ἐπισήμους ἑορτάς.*
[84] So Gerhard Podskalsky, *Griechische Theologie in der Zeit der Türkenherrschaft*, 321.
[85] See Timothy Ware, *Eustratios Argenti*; Gerhard Podskalsky, *Griechische Theologie in der Zeit der Türkenherrschaft*, 331–5.

against Roman Catholic positions on the use of unleavened bread, the necessity of the *epiclesis*, purgatory, and the papal claims. He has relatively little to say about the *filioque*. Roman Catholic errors in these various areas are sufficiently grave as to render their sacraments invalid. His is a resolutely Cyprianic ecclesiology: outside the (Orthodox) Church there is no salvation. Argenti's uncompromising ecclesiology helped pave the way for the decision of the Patriarchs of Constantinople, Alexandria, and Jerusalem in 1755 that all converts to Orthodoxy be thereafter (re-)baptized.

Argenti demonstrates an impressive command of Greek and Latin patristic testimony. He shares in the general enthusiasm for Augustine we find among Orthodox theologians of this period. Argenti is also very familiar with more recent developments in Western theology although he finds much to deplore. In his *Treatise against Azymes*, he follows Korydaleus in characterizing Latin scholasticism as the root cause of the schism between East and West. He sees this phenomenon as the enslavement of theology to Aristotelian philosophy and asserts that all the errors of the Latins have arisen from this misbegotten alliance. He names Peter Lombard as the pioneer of this heresy and reserves special venom for Aquinas denouncing him as that 'corrupter of theology'. For some unknown reason he believes Aquinas to have lived some 350 years after the turn of the millennium. Argenti laments the fact that certain 'modern Orthodox theologians', whom he refrains from naming, have followed after the scholastics 'like young bullocks'. Instead of nonsensical discussions about 'matter' and 'form', we had far better simply affirm the mysterious nature of the sacraments.[86] In fact, the Latin scholastics are deficient in both philosophy and theology. They misunderstand and misuse Aristotle in order to explain the immaterial by means of the material.[87]

But while Latin scholasticism comes in for some global condemnation, with Aquinas attracting special censure, Argenti's own writing has many scholastic features. Much of the discussion in his *Treatise against Azymes* is framed in terms of propositions and demonstrations, textual commentary, appeal to authority, and reasoned argumentation. There is nothing especially apophatic about his work in

---

[86] Σύνταγμα κατὰ ἀζύμων, 171–2. Cited in Ware, *Eustratios Argenti*, 110.
[87] Σύνταγμα κατὰ ἀζύμων, 173. While he will use the term 'transubstantiation' he strictly avoids its philosophical underpinnings.

practice. Argenti is also not above claiming particular Latin theologians as his allies. At one point in this treatise he gives a long list of authorities who, he claims, side with the Orthodox position against that of the Council of Trent in holding that the words of institution do not accomplish the eucharistic consecration. These include Pope Innocent III, Francis Titelman, Bruno the Carthusian, Peter of Aquila, and Richard Simon.[88] He will also often find common ground with the Roman Catholics against the Protestants. Take, for example, the shared belief in the need for the consecration of the elements before the communion of the faithful. This he presents as the practice of 'the Church in the East and, in orthodox fashion, the West'.[89] Even for this profoundly anti-Latin figure, convinced of the invalidity of Roman Catholic sacraments and of the utterly pernicious nature of Latin scholasticism, the Catholic West remains possessed of some redeeming, even orthodox, features.

Argenti's preoccupation with the religious errors of the West precluded his paying much attention to the seismic intellectual developments in the West conventionally (if tendentiously) referred to as the 'Enlightenment'. Perhaps the first Orthodox thinker to get his hands burnt by this development was Methodios Anthrakites (c.1660–after 1736). After a fine education in the West, Anthrakites embarked on a teaching career which evidently involved some use of contemporary philosophy. His bishop, Zossimos of Achrida, had him hauled before the Home Synod in Constantinople in August of 1723 for his various novel opinions.[90] He was accused of adopting methods and doctrines inimical to proper Greek education, including a broadly Cartesian account of mind with the intellect deemed sufficient for the apprehension, judgement, and knowledge of truth. He was also believed to have succumbed to the 'atheistic' heresy of the Quietist Miguel de Molinos, whom he had translated.[91] All this is presented in stark contrast to the 'ancient tradition of our people', its philosophy embodied in the Peripatetics and its theology in scripture and the Fathers. It is remarkable to note that deviation from Aristotelianism might be regarded as grounds for synodal

---

[88] Σύνταγμα κατὰ ἀζύμων, 97–8.   [89] Σύνταγμα κατὰ ἀζύμων, 98.
[90] Mansi, *Sacrorum conciliorum nova et amplissima collectio* 37, 231–45.
[91] The Roman Catholic Church was also cracking down on the Quietists at this time.

condemnation. In any event, Anthrakites was removed from the priesthood and his works consigned to the pyre. The burning of Anthrakites' works makes it difficult to judge the extent to which he did indeed champion the philosophy of the Enlightenment. His Quietist leanings alarmed the synod quite as much as his modernism. But whatever the real character of his work, the Anthrakites affair serves as an indicator that things were moving on in the West. The intellectual predominance of Thomism in its various forms was coming under great pressure with the emergence of new philosophical practices and theories increasingly independent of any theological reference point. The Greek world was certainly not immune to such developments. Vincent Damodos (1700–52) is the first Orthodox thinker we know to have seriously confronted and given currency to Enlightenment ideas.[92] Descartes, in particular, is treated critically but with great sympathy. Scholasticism, by contrast, comes in for some harsh criticism.

In the prooemium to his *Dogmatic Theology*, Damodos lashes out at scholastic theology as a muddle of sublime questions and prying speculations which seems to value disputatiousness above all else.[93] Such theology is both 'fruitless and useless', more concerned with controversy and argument than with the pursuit of the truth. In stark contrast stands the patristic tradition of Orthodox theology. But it is always much easier to dismiss Western theology than to do without it entirely. He goes on to admit that he will, in practice, be presenting scholastic opinions on various subjects that aid comprehension of divine matters. Such sympathy is evident in his treatment of the sacraments in terms of form, matter, efficient and final cause, and his embrace of the doctrine of transubstantiation with its philosophical substratum.[94] On closer inspection, it becomes clear that his strictures on scholasticism apply more to the perceived wrangling of some

---

[92] See Gerhard Podskalsky, *Griechische Theologie in der Zeit der Türkenherrschaft*, 337–42; George Metallinos, *Παράδοση καὶ ἀλλοτρίωση*, 45–84; Vasiliki Bobou-Stamate, *Βικέντιος Δαμοδός. Βιογραφία—Ἐργογραφία* 1700–54.

[93] The prooemium is given in Vasiliki Bobou-Stamate, *Βικέντιος Δαμοδός*, 397–9. Damodos also produced a potted version in demotic Greek, George Metallinos (ed.), *Βικεντίου Δαμοδού Θεολογία δογματικὴ κατὰ συντομίαν ἥ τε συνταγμάτιον θεολογικόν*.

[94] What he does not mention is that the categories of his compendium and much of its material are borrowed from the *Opus de theologicis dogmatibus* of the Jesuit historical theologian Denys Petau (Petavius).

contemporary theologians than to the actual teachings of the great scholastics, above all Aquinas. Aquinas is a recurrent resource in the *Dogmatic Theology*, for all that he is often detected in error on the issue dividing East and West.

Away from the contentious issues dividing East and West, Damodos could be remarkably free in his approbation of Aquinas. His *Outline of Metaphysics* has Thomas as one of its chief guiding lights.[95] Hailing him as 'the supreme Latin theologian', Damodos makes no secret of his high esteem and appeals frequently to Thomas' authority on a wide range of issues.[96] He approves, for instance, of Thomas' assertion that the knowledge of God is the cause of things.[97] Similarly, he appeals to *ST* I^a q.62 a.3 with its teaching on the simultaneous creation of the angelic and material worlds.[98] He affirms a direct continuity between Aquinas and John of Damascus in the matter of the antecedent and consequent will of God, declaring this teaching to be the common view 'of the theologians and of Thomas Aquinas'.[99] Aquinas serves, for Damodos, as a pre-eminent theological authority in substantial agreement with the patristic tradition.

Only rarely in the *Outline of Metaphysics* is there a hint of disapproval, and this in relation not so much to Thomas himself but to his squabbling epigones. Damodos is very much alive to the distinction between Thomas and Thomism. He is, for instance, critical of the teaching of the Thomists on predestination and reprobation, in particular the contention that God's will is the sole basis not only of predestination but also of reprobation. But while he notes that the Thomists base their understanding on *ST* I^a q.32 a.3 it is not so much Thomas himself as later Thomists that are in his sights here. In this instance, the Thomists are deemed in opposition to 'all other scholastic theologians, Augustine, and Scripture'.[100] On several other matters, Thomist (and indeed Scotist) arguments are rejected but Thomas himself emerges relatively unscathed. Damodos stands,

---

[95] Vasiliki Bobou-Stamate (ed.), Βικέντιος Δαμοδός. Συνταγμάτιον τῆς Μεταφυσικῆς.

[96] Συνταγμάτιον τῆς Μεταφυσικῆς, 30.8.

[97] Συνταγμάτιον τῆς Μεταφυσικῆς, ibid. Cf. *SCG* I 49; *ST* I^a q.14 a.8.

[98] Συνταγμάτιον τῆς Μεταφυσικῆς, 42.1ff.

[99] Συνταγμάτιον τῆς Μεταφυσικῆς, 33.9ff. Cf. *ST* I^a q.19 a.6 ad 1. Damodos cites the *Exact Exposition of the Orthodox Faith* 2.29. This is, although Damodos does not admit it, precisely the same passage Thomas had cited.

[100] Συνταγμάτιον τῆς Μεταφυσικῆς, 38.21ff.

in short, as a fine example of a suitably critical but largely positive Orthodox appropriation of Aquinas and one that, crucially, distinguishes between his teaching and that of his less impressive successors.

Damodos' works remained unpublished until recent years but his interaction with the Enlightenment was to bear spectacular fruit in the life and work of his sometime student, Eugenios Boulgaris (1716–1806).[101] Boulgaris was a tower of learning and by many estimations the foremost Orthodox theologian of the eighteenth century. Uncompromisingly Orthodox and a great student of the Fathers, Boulgaris was nevertheless deeply impressed by the philosophy of the Enlightenment. He corresponded with Voltaire and lectured on Wolff, Leibniz, and Locke. In 1753 he was appointed head of the new Academy on Mount Athos established by Patriarch Cyril V. Boulgaris' openness to modern philosophy soon ran into opposition on the Holy Mountain and elsewhere and the Academy was, eventually, forced to close. Boulgaris went on to grace the courts of Frederick the Great of Prussia and Catherine the Great of Russia. Catherine was to create him Archbishop of Cherson.

Boulgaris' theological work, which makes up only a small part of his vast oeuvre, is grounded in the Fathers, both Latin and Greek, and decidedly anti-Catholic. He attacks the *filioque* with gusto and zealously champions the essence–energies distinction. His anti-Latin credentials are further bolstered by his editing and publishing of the works of Joseph Bryennios and Mark of Ephesus. In his *Against the Latins*, he characterizes the West's plethora of theological schools as a sure sign of its Babylonian confusion, contrasting this with the pristine unity of the patristic witness.[102] Elsewhere, he laments the heavily philosophical orientation of Latin theology and its abandonment of the Fathers for the opinions of such as 'Aquinas, Scotus, Durandus, Vasquez, Suárez, and others'.[103]

That said, he expressly affirms the great utility (but not necessity) of the scholastic method for theology, with its precision, systematic

---

[101]   See Daniel Stiernon, 'Eugène Boulgaris' and Gerhard Podskalsky, *Griechische Theologie in der Zeit der Türkenherrschaft*, 344–53.

[102]   Βιβλιάριον κατὰ Λατίνων, cited in Gerhard Podskalsky, *Griechische Theologie in der Zeit der Türkenherrschaft*, 346. See also Legrand, *Bibliographie hellénique (XVIIIe siècle)*, 453–4 ('ouvrage de la plus extraordinaire rareté'); and Daniel Stiernon, 'Eugène Boulgaris', 747–8 (Opus 12).

[103]   *Zapiska* 92. Cited Daniel Stiernon, 'Eugène Boulgaris', 794.

approach, and use of philosophy in due obedience to faith. He regards John of Damascus as the founder of this method, and Peter Lombard as his pioneering continuator in the West.[104] Scholastic authorities are constant companions in Boulgaris' great but apparently incomplete *Theological Compendium* (Θεολογικόν).[105] This work adopts a thoroughgoing scholastic methodology with the whole panoply of questions, objections, responses, and distinctions. Aquinas is by far the most frequently cited Latin scholastic. The long treatment of the angels, for example, follows him in most respects.[106] For example, he commends Thomas' bold assertion that there are far more bodiless angels than material beings, referring to *ST* I^a q.50 a.3 and finding this position to be amply supported by patristic testimony.[107] But the treatment of Thomas is never slavish: he is roundly denounced for his position on the essence–energies distinction whereas Duns Scotus and others are applauded for affirming the real distinction between the divine essence and energies.[108] On the other hand, the Thomists are approved, and the Scotists found to be in error, for holding that the incarnation was conditional upon the Fall. The Thomist position is found to be in closer accordance with the witness of scripture and the Fathers.[109]

Among Boulgaris' many students was the conservative theologian Athanasios Parios (1721–1813). Athanasios had an instinctive antipathy to the European Enlightenment, recognizing its dangers for Orthodox theology and for the security of the Greek people within the Ottoman Empire. He attacked Voltaire and Rousseau for their unrealistic notions of freedom and equality. He also confronted the dangerous and politically subversive nationalism of Adamantios Koraes, another, very different, student of Boulgaris. Athanasios recognized that the *Theological Compendium*, while inspired by

[104] Θεολογικόν 1.4, 17–22.
[105] See Daniel Stiernon, 'Eugène Boulgaris', 746–7 (Opus 11). Boulgaris repudiated the Θεολογικόν in his old age, advising one student against trying to publish it. He does not give his reasons, but these are plausibly related more to the incompleteness of the work than any blanket rejection of its scholastic character.
[106] Θεολογικόν 3.1, 324–68.
[107] Θεολογικόν 3.1, 342.
[108] Θεολογικόν 1.6, 90–2. Duns Scotus is allied here with, among others, Durandus, Francis Mayronis, James of Viterbo, and Marsilius of Inghen. Thomas' stance is said to be shared by Bonaventure, Giles of Rome, Peter Aureol, Henry of Ghent, and others.
[109] Θεολογικόν 4.16, 556–7.

Latin scholasticism, was free from Roman Catholic error. But he still found it unsatisfactory and so produced an improved version in the shape of his *Epitome or Summary of the Divine Dogmas of the Faith*.[110] The *Epitome* nonetheless draws its structure, main themes, and a great deal of its material straight from the *Theological Compendium*.

In his prologue, Athanasios loudly proclaims his intention to distance himself from disputatious scholastic theology and to follow rather the surer testimony of scripture and the holy Fathers.[111] But in practice, the *Epitome* is considerably less removed from scholasticism than the prologue might suggest. A few pages later, Athanasios describes, with perfect equanimity, the division of theology into scholastic and positive theology. Positive theology refers to the proclamation of the dogmatic truths in the rhetorical manner of the Fathers. Scholastic theology, with its argumentation and strict methodology, exists to support and articulate those truths. In a footnote, Athanasios traces the genealogy of scholasticism from John of Damascus through to Peter Lombard and Thomas Aquinas. John was the first to gather the scattered words of the Fathers into one book while Peter Lombard imitated him in arranging these words under distinct headings. Thomas Aquinas, for his part, 'brought the scholastic form to perfection by composing a theological synopsis in three parts which, it is said, Demetrios Kydones translated into Greek'.[112]

The *Epitome* is also divided into three parts covering theology, creation, and incarnation. The pattern is very much that of the *Summa theologiae*, proceeding after preliminary considerations from the one God (whose existence Athanasios demonstrates by means of an Aristotelian apodictic syllogism drawn from John of Dasmascus) through to the Trinity, creation (split into invisible and visible), and the incarnate dispensation (with additional sections on sacraments and ethics). In his preliminary section, Athanasios deals with the opening question of the *Summa theologiae*: 'whether theology is necessary' (*ST* Iᵃ q.1 a.1). His answer reproduces much of Eugenios' treatment of the question, including the admission of the

---

110 ᾽ *Ἐπιτομὴ εἴτε συλλογὴ τῶν θείων τῆς πίστεως δογμάτων*. The prologue also recognizes Theodoret as the first to have provided a summary version of orthodox dogma. Ibid., viii.

111 ᾽ *Ἐπιτομὴ εἴτε συλλογὴ τῶν θείων τῆς πίστεως δογμάτων*iii–xiv.

112 ᾽ *Ἐπιτομὴ εἴτε συλλογὴ τῶν θείων τῆς πίστεως δογμάτων*Prolegomena 2, 6; cf. *Θεολογικόν*, Prolegomena 4, 17–22.

utility (if not necessity) of scholastic theology.[113] The treatment of the essence–energies distinction also follows Boulgaris very closely, including a discussion of the various merits of Thomist and Scotist takes on the question.[114] Athanasios will often strengthen what Boulgaris has to say about the errors of Aquinas on this issue and goes so far as to name Thomas and Bonaventure as 'great enemies of our Church' for their opposition to the essence–energies distinction. The treatment remains, nonetheless, closely modelled on the source: a sifting of scholastic positions and not in any way a rejection of scholasticism *per se*. The treatment of the sacraments offers further signs of deep scholastic affinities, not least a remarkably enthusiastic embrace of the doctrine of transubstantiation with all its trappings. In one extraordinary passage, he marvels at the extraordinary divine dispensation that permits the existence of a substance without accidents, and accidents without substance.[115] Rarely has Latin scholasticism excited such fervent enthusiasm in a canonized Orthodox writer of determinedly conservative stamp.

Athanasios was a leading figure of the renewal movement referred to as the *Kollyvades*, the name deriving from their objections to the common practice of memorializing the dead (with a blessing of boiled wheat or *kollyva*) on Sunday, the day of the Resurrection. Most importantly, they pursued a conscious process of Orthodox *ressourcement*, gathering and publishing many patristic and Byzantine works, with particular emphasis on the Hesychast tradition. Athanasios planned a complete edition of Palamas, a task he was unable to bring to fruition.[116] Other great figures associated with this movement include the compilers of the *Philokalia* (1782): Makarios (Notaras) of Corinth (1731–1805) and Nikodemos the Hagiorite (1749–1809).[117] Makarios was the driving force behind the initial

---

[113] Ἐπιτομὴ εἴτε συλλογὴ τῶν θείων τῆς πίστεως δογμάτων Prolegomena 3, 9–15; cf. Θεολογικόν, Prolegomena 2, 13 and 4, 19. In Boulgaris' text, which Athanasios follows closely, only John of Damascus and Peter Lombard are mentioned.

[114] Ἐπιτομὴ εἴτε συλλογὴ τῶν θείων τῆς πίστεως δογμάτων 1.4 ('On the simplicity of God'), 59–68; cf. Θεολογικόν, 1.6 ('On the simplicity of God'), 85–95.

[115] Ἐπιτομὴ εἴτε συλλογὴ τῶν θείων τῆς πίστεως δογμάτων 3.2.3, 367–8.

[116] He handed the task over to Nikodemos the Hagiorite, whose own efforts were stymied by the declaration of the Austrian authorities that Palamas' work constituted subversive material. See Elia Citterio, 'Nicodemo Agiorita', 924 (Opus 9).

[117] Makarios has tended to be somewhat overshadowed by his co-editor in contemporary scholarship. Gerhard Podskalsky gives a typically complete bibliography in *Griechische Theologie in der Zeit der Türkenherrschaft*, 372–4. On Nikodemos, see

collection of materials that comprise the *Philokalia* and was also responsible for publishing Athanasios' *Epitome*.[118] The *ressourcement* pursued by Makarios and Nikodemos was by no means limited to materials from the Christian East. Their *Treatise on Frequent Communion* (1783) displays many affinities with Counter-Reformation sources on the same topic.[119] More concretely, Nikodemos published Greek adaptations of Counter-Reformation works including Lorenzo Scupoli's *Combattimento spirituale* and Giovanni Pietro Pinamonti's version of the *Spiritual Exercises* of Ignatius Loyola.[120] In neither case does he give any indication of the true source of the material. As *Unseen Warfare* (1796), Scupoli's work has become a minor classic of Orthodox spirituality. The *Spiritual Exercises* (1800) never came close to such 'bestseller' status. Nikodemos' own work on confession, the *Exomologetarion* (1794), displays manifold borrowings from Paolo Segneri.[121] Lastly, the collection of canons, the *Pedalion* (1800), is demonstrably beholden to various Western collections and conceptions of canon law.[122] Not that any of this is necessarily a bad thing: Nikodemos' engagement with Western sources and concepts in no way diminishes the fervour and robustness of his vision and presentation of the Orthodox faith.

While there is little in Nikodemos (and less in Makarios) to connect him directly with Thomas, their openness to Roman Catholic sources is typical of a long Latin-leaning phase of Orthodox theology beginning in earnest with the reaction to Cyril Lukaris. In this period, Gennadios Scholarios' synthesis of Byzantine and Latin

---

especially Elia Citterio, 'Nicodemo Agiorita' and *L'orientamento ascetico-spirituale di Nicodemo Aghiorita*; Podskalsky, op. cit., 377–82; and Kallistos Ware, 'St Nikodimos and the *Philokalia*'.

[118] The *Philokalia* is itself to some extent a product of the anthologizing spirit of scholasticism.

[119] Elia Citterio, 'Nicodemo Agiorita', 926–97 (Opus 11). The text is given in the fine study of Hieromonk Patapios and Archbishop Chrysostomos, *Manna from Athos: The Issue of Frequent Communion on the Holy Mountain*. Note the scholastic methodology in Part IV of this work containing responses to thirteen objections against the practice of frequent communion, 133–74. Actual connections with specific Counter-Reformation sources remain to be demonstrated, cf. ibid., 39 n.40.

[120] Elia Citterio, 'Nicodemo Agiorita', 927 (Opus 12), 928 (Opus 13), 943–55.

[121] Elia Citterio, 'Nicodemo Agiorita', 932–3 (Opus 17), 945–6.

[122] Elia Citterio, 'Nicodemo Agiorita', 934–5 (Opus 19), 969–72. Christos Yannaras, ' Ὀρθοδοξία καὶ Δύση στὴ Νεώτερη Ἑλλάδα, 201–9 [ET 131–7], launches a fierce attack on the legalistic and merely punitive character of the *Pedalion* and *Exomologetarion*, faults he attributes squarely to Nikodemos' Western dalliances.

scholasticism is, in all essentials, vindicated. While there are few in this period quite so openly devout in their admiration of the angelic doctor, Gennadios' anti-unionist but otherwise pro-Latin stance achieved normative status in this period. While Aquinas is, naturally, encountered in the company of other scholastic theologians and through various mediations, he remains in the days of the Ottoman Empire, as in the Byzantine, a prominent interlocutor and recurrent resource for Orthodox theology.

5.2. THE RUSSIAN WORLD

With the demise of the Byzantine Empire, the Grand Duchy of Moscow emerged as the most powerful Orthodox Christian state in the world. Moscow grew into a great Empire in the early modern period but at the outset controlled only a small portion of the territories it was later to acquire. Many Orthodox Christians of Russian tradition lived under Catholic rule in Poland-Lithuania, a vast territory encompassing much of what is now Belorussia and the Ukraine. Kiev itself, while never regaining the glory it had before succumbing to the Tartar yoke in 1240, became an important theological centre in the seventeenth century and was to govern the pattern of theological endeavour in Moscow for many generations to come. This Kievan school, as it became known, was decidedly Thomist in orientation and attained a kind of institutionalization in this period. In this respect the Thomist inheritance in early modern Russian world was more pronounced than in the Greek. It must, however, be acknowledged that this was a Thomism of a distinctly derivative variety that generated little of the theological creativity or sense of actual dialogue with Aquinas that we have discovered in the Greek world. That said, this period serves as a crucial backdrop to later developments in the Russian theological sphere and some account must therefore be given of its contours.

Russian acquaintance with Latin theology goes back long before the ascendancy of the Kievan school. The swift repudiation of the Florentine union in Moscow did not hinder, and may even have encouraged, theological contacts across the confessional divide. Dynastic alliances may also have helped: Ivan III's marriage to the Byzantine princess Zoë in 1472 was arranged through the papal court.

Zoë herself was a Roman Catholic (although she converted to Orthodoxy on her marriage) and was accompanied to Moscow by a papal legate and a retinue including the Greek unionist Trachaniotes brothers. These brothers later formed part of the circle associated with Gennady, Archbishop of Novgorod from 1484 to 1504. This was a circle that also included at least one Dominican. Gennady patronized a series of translations from the Latin including much of the Vulgate and two treatises against the Jews. He himself translated the liturgical treatise *Rationale divinorum officiorum* of William Durandus of Mende. Gennady was a prime mover in what became known as the faction of the 'possessors', those Churchmen who defended ecclesiastical ownership of property and exercise of power, notably in the treatment of heretics. The possessors borrowed much from the West, including a version of the spurious *Donation of Constantine* and, regrettably, some of the methods and justifications of the Spanish Inquisition.[123]

But the non-possessors, those who saw power and property as inimical to authentic Christian piety, also had Latin connections. These connections are most auspiciously displayed in Maxim the Greek (1470–1556).[124] This extraordinary figure, the foremost scholar and most venerated monk of his time, came to Moscow in 1518 after a dazzling career that took him from Corfu to Florence, Venice, and Athos. In Florence, the young Michael Trivolis fell under the spell of two very different figures: Marsilio Ficino and the Dominican revivalist preacher Girolamo Savonarola. From Ficino, he imbibed a lifelong love of Plato, from Savonarola, an antipathy to worldliness in the Church and to moral laxity of all kinds. It was doubtless under Savonarola's spell that he entered the Dominican

---

[123] See Donald Treadgold, *The West in Russia and China. Volume I: Russia 1472–1917*, 3–8 and Dimitri Obolensky, *Byzantium and the Slavs*, 86. Kievan Rus' had also had many connections with Latin Christianity; see Francis Dvornik, 'The Kiev State and Its Relations with Western Europe'.

[124] On Maxim, the seminal work remains Élie Denissoff, *Maxime le Grec et l'Occident*. Denissoff demonstrated conclusively that Maxim is to be identified with Michael Trivolis. See also Dimitri Obolensky, *Six Byzantine Portraits*, 201–19; Donald Treadgold, *The West in Russia and China. Volume I: Russia 1472–1917*, 12–19; Gerhard Podskalsky, *Griechische Theologie in der Zeit der Türkenherrschaft*, 89–97. Maxim is also mentioned in Denissoff's slim volume, *L'Église russe devant le thomisme*, 53–4. This elegant work argues for the Russian Church's adoption of Thomism in its battle against communism and presents Thomas as a bridge figure between East and West.

order, being professed in 1502 at the monastery of San Marco once headed by the fiery preacher himself.[125] But his Dominican days were to prove short and by 1505 or 1506 he had become a monk of the Athonite monastery of Vatopedi, assuming the name Maximos under circumstances veiled in obscurity.

After ten years on Athos, Maximos was sent to Moscow at the behest of Basil III. He was brought in as an expert translator and soon found himself siding with the non-possessors over their better-placed rivals, a move that led to his spending the majority of his years in Russia in monastic imprisonment. Maxim (to use the Slavic form of his name) compared the landholding Russian monasteries un-favourably to the Dominican, Carthusian, and Franciscan Orders with their firm commitment to apostolic poverty.[126] As he puts it:

> Thus the Latins, although in many ways they have yielded to temptation and invented certain strange doctrines, having been tempted by their own great learning in the Greek sciences, nevertheless have not finally fallen away from faith, hope, and love for Jesus Christ, and therefore those among them who have dedicated themselves to the monastic life assiduously order their service to God according to his holy command-ments, since their harmony of belief, brotherly love, non-possessorship, silence, lack of concern for worldly things, and care for salvation ought to be imitated by us, so that we should not show ourselves worse than they.[127]

Such observations were not well received.

Maxim also provided a detailed and affirmative description of the life and organization of the Dominican order for his Russian audi-ence, without ever mentioning his own former membership.[128] Maxim was certainly a foe of Latin deviations from Orthodoxy but was careful to limit these to the *filioque*, purgatory, and the use of azymes. He was remarkably open on the question of primacy, regarding the pre-schism popes as legitimate successors of Peter.[129] His anti-papal strictures are directed not at the notion of primacy

---

[125] Maxim furnished his Russian audience with a brief *Life of Savonarola*. Deniss-off, ibid. 423–8, gives the text in translation.

[126] Dimitri Obolensky, *Six Byzantine Portraits*, 216.

[127] Translation from Donald Treadgold, *The West in Russia and China. Volume I: Russia 1472–1917*, 16.

[128] Élie Denissoff, *Maxime le Grec et l'Occident*, 249–52.

[129] Élie Denissoff, *Maxime le Grec et l'Occident*, 376.

itself but at its abuse in the hands of such miscreants as Alexander VI.[130] He even has some good words for the Inquisition.[131]

Maxim's coyness about his Dominican past may explain the puzzling fact that he never so much as mentions Aquinas, whose works he will certainly have known. He mentions Albert the Great and Duns Scotus, but only to disparage them. Denissoff makes the plausible suggestion that the omission of Thomas is a matter of tact: if one cannot safely praise him, better to honour him in silence.[132] The subservience of theology to philosophy in the West is a recurring theme in Maxim's work but his criticism appears directed principally at later scholastic developments, especially the Nominalism of Bologna and the Averroist Aristotelianism of Padua.[133] Never a word does he utter against Aquinas. Maxim is also convinced of the vital importance and sacred character of philosophy in due obedience to theology and holds up the work of John of Damascus as paradigmatic of good Christian philosophy—much as Aquinas had done.

But whatever his actual allegiances to Thomas, Maxim remained something of an anomaly in the Russia of his time. As a Greek, he would always be an outsider and a representative of a culture that still claimed superiority over the rough northern realm of Muscovy. His situation was not helped by his frankly avowed conviction that the Metropolitanate of Moscow was in an irregular canonical situation pending recognition of its independence by Constantinople. His Western sympathies and interests in classical philosophy will also have won him few friends. But in the end it was not his Greekness or his Latin leanings that sealed his downfall but his taking-up of the cause of the non-possessors.

Maxim embodies much of what was best in the Byzantine world: a generosity of vision operating on broad cultural, philosophical, and theological horizons within the strict parameters of Orthodoxy. His vision was doubtless a little too broad, a little too catholic, for most Russians of his time and his immediate impact was to be minimal. But he stands as the herald of much that was to come. For that legacy, we must turn from Muscovy to the Polish-Lithuanian Commonwealth

---

[130] See his *Life of Savonarola* in Élie Denissoff, *Maxime le Grec et l'Occident*, 428.
[131] Élie Denissoff, *Maxime le Grec et l'Occident*, 376.
[132] Élie Denissoff, *Maxime le Grec et l'Occident*, 260.
[133] Gerhard Podskalsky, *Griechische Theologie in der Zeit der Türkenherrschaft*, 95; Élie Denissoff, *Maxime le Grec et l'Occident*, 254–5.

and to the foundation of the Kievan school under the towering figure of Peter Mogila (1596–1646).[134]

Born in the year of the Union of Brest, Mogila spent much of his life fighting against it.[135] A well-connected and well-educated scion of a princely family, Peter pulled all the strings he could to hold back the spread of Uniatism and to improve the lot of the Orthodox in the lands of the Catholic Commonwealth. Peter secured a number of concessions for the Orthodox from King Vladislav IV including his own election as Metropolitan of Kiev and all Rus' in 1632. Peter devoted much of his energy to education, establishing in 1631 an Orthodox college at the Kiev Pechersk Lavra. The following year, the college merged with a school founded somewhat earlier by the Orthodox Brotherhood of Kiev and went on to achieve Academy status in 1658. The pattern of education laid down by Peter was based squarely on Western models and conducted largely in Latin. While unimpeachably Orthodox in dogma, its theological teaching was heavily dependent on Latin scholastic sources. Kiev had known theologians of markedly Latin stamp before, such as Kyrill Trankvillion-Stavrovetsky and Kassian Sakovich, but this institutionalization of Latin scholasticism was a new departure.[136] In its dual character, both Latin and Orthodox, the Academy encompassed and to some extent integrated the diverse cultural and religious currents of seventeenth-century Ukraine.

---

[134] See Georges Florovsky, *Ways of Russian Theology* I, 64–78. Florovsky's analysis of Mogila remains essential reading, but must be balanced by other assessments including Francis Thomson, 'Peter Mogila's Ecclesiastical Reforms and the Ukrainian Contribution to Russian Culture: A Critique of Georges Florovsky's Theory of the Pseudomorphosis of Orthodoxy' and Ihor Ševčenko, 'The Many Worlds of Peter Mohyla'. Thanks to Nadieszda Kizenko for these references. See also Frank Sysyn, 'Peter Mohyla and the Kiev Academy in Recent Western Works' and Gerhard Podskalsky, *Griechische Theologie in der Zeit der Türkenherrschaft*, 229–36. We also find a rather more sympathetic account of Mogila and the Kievan school in Florovsky's sometime colleague Anton Kartashev's *Ocherki po istorii russkoy tserkvi* II, 281–91. The last Over-Procurator of the Holy Synod, Kartashev was a founding father and long-term professor of the Institut St-Serge in Paris.

[135] A comparison may be made here with a fellow Ukrainian, Kyrill Stavrovetsky, author of the *Zertsalo bohosloviia* (*Mirror of Theology*) (1618), a work that draws extensively on Anselm and Aquinas. Unlike Mogila, Stavrovetsky's Latin theological sympathies led him to accept the *Unia* in 1626.

[136] Both men composed theological works of distinctly Thomist character and were eventually to embrace the *Unia*, being pushed to do so by the condemnation of their works in Moscow. See Georges Florovsky, *Ways of Russian Theology* I, 60–1.

Peter's theological vision is encapsulated in his *Orthodox Confession*, composed as a conscious counterblast to that of Cyril Lukaris. In a revised version prepared by Meletios Syrigos, this *Confession* was adopted by the Councils of Jassy (Iași) (1642) and Jerusalem (1672) as an authoritative statement of Orthodox faith.[137] It takes the form of a catechism explicitly structured around the three theological virtues: faith, hope, and charity. It is based directly on Roman Catholic exemplars including the catechism of Trent and the doctrinal syntheses of the Jesuits Peter Canisius and Robert Bellarmine with Thomas' *Summae* certainly in the background.[138] It also deals with the three theological virtues, the four cardinal virtues, and the various mortal and venial sins. The treatment of the sacraments employs a structure of matter, form, and priestly intention.[139] The doctrine of transubstantiation is, naturally, a given.[140] Mogila adapted his material so as to exclude egregious Roman errors, such as the *filioque*, while Meletios adapted it still further by, for example, denying the existence of purgatory and removing the assertion that the words of institution effect the consecration and emphasizing rather the *epiclesis*, the invocation of the Holy Spirit. But the fact remains that it is, as Kallistos Ware puts it, 'still the most Latin document ever to be adopted by an official council of the Orthodox Church'.[141]

The official adoption of Mogila's *Orthodox Confession* marks a high-water point of the Latin-leaning reaction to Lukaris and serves as a potent confirmation of the acceptability and utility of Latin scholasticism within Orthodox theology. The document may indeed be profoundly Latin but it was also recognized as perfectly Orthodox. Peter's Latin, or Occidental Orthodoxy, if we may so dub it, was to have a determinative influence on the subsequent pattern of theological endeavour throughout the Russian world. Its ascendancy was not immediate: the Council of Moscow in 1690 repudiated Peter's

---

[137] John Karmires, Τὰ δογματικὰ καὶ συμβολικὰ μνημεῖα τῆς ᾿Ορθοδόξου Καθολικῆς᾿ ἘκκλησίαςII, 593–686.

[138] Peter's own library was richly supplied with Jesuit commentaries on Thomas, including those of Philip de Gamaches, Diego Ruiz de Montoya, and Adam Opatowczyk (Opatavius). See Liudmila Charipova, *Latin Books and the Eastern Orthodox Clerical Elite in Kiev, 1632–1780*, 77, 82–3. The library of the Kievan Academy itself was destroyed by fire in 1780, along with its catalogue.

[139] Karmires II, 635.

[140] Karmires II, 638–9. In an interesting twist on Trent, the transubstantiation of the elements is said to take place after the recitation of the epiclesis.

[141] Kallistos Ware, *The Orthodox Church*, 97.

teaching on the words of institution while the Leikhoudes brothers provided for a brief period in the 1680s–1690s a Greek-oriented intellectual counterweight to the Kievan school. But from the early eighteenth century, the Kievan pattern came to dominate theological education in Kiev and Moscow alike.[142]

Among the most prominent figures of the early years of the Academy is Joasaph Krokovsky (d. 1718), sometime Rector and later Metropolitan of Kiev. Krokovsky taught theology on the basis of Aquinas and Scotus and exhibited an enthusiastic cultic devotion to the doctrine of the immaculate conception. The finest representative of the school is Dimitri of Rostov (1651–1709). A Saint of the Orthodox Church, Dimitri made known in Russia the hagiographical advances of the West, in particular the immense achievement of the *Acta sanctorum* produced by the Bollandist Fathers. He was certainly well-versed in Aquinas and his theological and spiritual works bear unmistakable traces of his Western learning. Stephan Javorsky (1658–1722) was perhaps the most prominent agent of the Kievan school in Moscow. A former Rector of the Academy, he became guardian of the patriarchal throne under Tsar Peter who greatly valued his Western learning and leanings. Javorsky's chief work is his *Rock of Faith* (*Kamen' Very*) (1713), a monumental rejection of Protestantism in all its guises. Like Mogila, Javorsky bases his work in large measure on Catholic sources, notably Robert Bellarmine and Martin Becanus. Javorsky brought with him to Moscow a number of

---

[142] This dominance is the key moment in Florovsky's saga of pseudomorphosis: 'From the cultural and historical points of view, Kievan learning was not a mere passing episode but an event of unquestionable significance. This was the first outright encounter with the West. One might even have called it a free encounter had it not ended in captivity, or more precisely, surrender. But for this reason, there could be no creative use made of the encounter. A scholastic tradition was developed and a school begun, yet no spiritually creative movement resulted. Instead there emerged an imitative and provincial scholasticism, in its literal sense a *theologica scholastica* or "school theology". This signified a new stage in religious and cultural consciousness. But in the process theology was torn from its living roots. A malignant schism set in between life and thought. Certainly the horizon of the Kievan erudites was wide enough. Contact with Europe was lively, with word of current searchings and trends in the West easily reaching Kiev. Still, the aura of doom hovered over the entire movement, for it comprised a "pseudomorphism" of Russia's religious consciousness, a "pseudomorphosis" of Orthodox thought.' *Ways of Russian Theology* I, 85. Note, however, the sense of wasted opportunity: Florovsky has no objection to Western theology *per se* but only to the aping of such theology by the Orthodox. See below, pp.199–200.

eminent teachers from the Kievan Academy, including Theophylact Lopatinsky (d. 1742), a thoroughgoing Thomist.

The dominance of Latin theology underwent a partial setback through the labours of Theophan Prokopovich (1681–1738). An alumnus of the Academy himself, Prokopovich was to turn sharply against its Latin scholastic orientation and, as Rector, instituted a curriculum based rather on German Lutheran models. Latin, however, remained the primary language of instruction as indeed it was in Lutheran schools of the time. He attracted the patronage of Tsar Peter and became the principal theorist of the subordination of the Church to the state. Javorsky fell from grace for his opposition to the Tsar's reforms and Theophan was able to secure the suppression of the *Rock of Faith*. Prokopovich bequeathed a Protestant tincture to theological education in Russia for some decades to come, as witnessed in the widely circulated *Orthodox Doctrine* (1765) of Metropolitan Platon Levshin (1737–1811) or Bishop Theophylact Gorsky's *Ortodoxae orientalis ecclesiae dogmata* (1784). This Protestant tincture did not, however, entail any diminution in the deeply scholastic character of theological endeavour in the period and nor did it lead to the displacement of Latin as the primary language of theological instruction.

A very different challenge came in the shape of the Hesychast revival associated with Paissi Velichkovsky (1722–94). Paissi studied for some years at the Kievan Academy but left it disillusioned at the prominence given to the Greek classics. Paissi embraced the monastic life, eventually settling in what is now Romania. As Abbot of the Niamets Monastery, he supervised the translation of a Slavonic version of the *Philokalia*, the *Dobrotolubiye*.[143] First published in 1793, the *Dobrotolubiye* had a swift impact in Russia, far greater than that of the *Philokalia* in the Greek lands, inspiring and informing a remarkable spiritual revival. But neither Prokopovich nor Velichkovsky was able to alter fundamentally the pattern of Orthodox theological education in Russia which remained shaped by the Latin and broadly Thomist orientation of Kiev well into the nineteenth century. It is to that century that we now turn.

---

[143] Paissi's *Dobrotolubiye* is best regarded as an independent text from that of the published Greek version but based on many of the same sources and source-collections.

6

Readings of Aquinas
in Modern Orthodox Thought

The various challenges of Protestantism, the scientific revolution, and the Enlightenment all posed grave threats to the Thomist ascendancy of the early modern period. Bitter theological disputes between Jesuits and Dominicans also served to sap the strength and prestige of the Thomist schools. Far more deadly, however, was the turmoil spawned by the French Revolution which had a devastating impact on Catholic theology in general and the Thomist tradition in particular. The seventeenth to nineteenth centuries therefore see a gradual decline in the intellectual predominance of Thomas, a decline that becomes positively precipitate into the nineteenth century. The Orthodox world was not insensitive to such developments, hence the relative paucity of engagement with Thomas for much of the nineteenth century: for if the Catholics were not talking about Thomas, there would seem little reason for the Orthodox to do so. Where we do catch a glimpse of an encounter with Thomas this tends to be at a distinct remove within the context of the enduring legacy of the Kievan school. The Kievan school continued to shape Orthodox theological education well into the nineteenth century and generated a counter-movement in the shape of the Slavophiles. This counter-movement was to be of inestimable importance for the subsequent development of Orthodox thought, most especially through its promotion of an East–West theological polarity. It is only at the end of the nineteenth century that we begin to see signs of a re-emergence of sustained Orthodox attention to Thomas in response to the Thomist revival generated in Catholic circles by the papal encyclical *Aeterni Patris*. In the twentieth century, Orthodox interest in Thomas was to attain an intensity unseen since the Byzantine era. But in stark contrast with the Byzantine era, twentieth-century Orthodox readings of Thomas have been resoundingly negative and all too often in thrall to some kind of paradigm of opposition between East and West. An examination of the Orthodox response to Aquinas during this time must, therefore, be undertaken within the broader context of the East–West dialectic characterizing so much modern Orthodox theology. Before undertaking such an examination, however, some account must be made of the relatively fallow period in the Orthodox reception of Aquinas preceding the intriguing developments of the twentieth century.

6.1. IMPERIAL RUSSIA 1812–1900

The tumultuous and terrifying experience of the Napoleonic wars instilled a spirit of instinctive conservatism at the heart of the Russian Empire, as throughout much of Europe. One sign of this conservatism was the scuppering of a programme of biblical translations into Russian, once a pet project of Tsar Alexander I. Philaret Drozdov (1782–1867), the greatest Russian theologian and Churchman of his age, had his *Catechism* withdrawn from circulation in 1824 on the grounds that he had employed Russian (as opposed to Church Slavonic) scriptural translations. As Metropolitan of Moscow from 1826, Philaret spent much of his episcopal career battling with Nikolai Protasov (1798–1855), Over-Procurator of the Holy Synod from 1836–55. Deeply suspicious of the vernacular, Protasov worked to re-affirm the normative character of the Latin-leaning Kievan tradition and to extinguish utterly the Protestantizing legacy of Theophan Prokopovich. The Jesuit-educated Protasov encouraged the re-publication and wide dissemination of Stephan Javorsky's *Rock of Faith* and of the *Confessions* of Peter Mogila and Dositheos of Jerusalem. Philaret was something of an obstacle to this programme, not only because of his grounding in the Lutheran scholasticism favoured by Prokopovich but also, and more importantly, because of his commitment to a more distinctively biblical and patristic pattern of theological education—and to theological education in Russian.

Protasov oversaw the publication of a new version of Philaret's catechism in 1839, ensuring its close conformity with the teaching of Mogila's *Confession.* Thus the *Longer Catechism* has additional sections on tradition (§16–24) and predestination (§121–5) lacking in the suppressed version and also omits that version's preface dealing with natural theology.[1] The *Longer Catechism* adheres to Mogila's structure, based around the three theological virtues. Other points of contact with the Kievan school include aspects of its teaching on the atonement including an emphasis on the satisfaction of God's justice and Christ's acquisition of a 'fund of infinite merit' enabling him to grant forgiveness of sins (§208).[2]

Even in its adapted form, Philaret's *Longer Catechism* did not quite satisfy Protasov. More to his taste were drier, more conservative texts such as the *Dogmatic Theology* (1849) of Anthony Amfiteatrov (1815–79) and, especially, the *Orthodox Dogmatic Theology* (1849–53) of Makary Bulgakov (1816–82). These works are classic expressions of nineteenth-century Russian scholastic theology and exemplify the enduring legacy of the Kievan school—even if now presented in the vernacular. But state sanction is rarely a great motor of theological creativity, and these tomes are no exception. They have little of Philaret's apostolic zeal or spirit of theological enquiry and present Orthodox theology as a closed system. While at one time a fertile meeting-ground of Eastern and Western theological traditions, the Kievan school of Orthodox theology was, by the mid-nineteenth century, little more than a handmaiden of imperial conservatism.

A fruitful challenge to Russian scholasticism, whether broadly of the Thomist or the Lutheran variety, came in the shape of Slavophile theology. The Slavophile movement emerged in opposition to the Westernizers, those who saw Russia's future primarily in terms of an emulation of Western European models. Nurtured by German Idealism and Romanticism, the Slavophiles looked back rather to Russia's past for the tools with which to resist creeping Westernization, one prominent sign of which was the dominance of the scholastic tradition in the theological schools. Ivan Kireevsky (1806–56), treats scholasticism as a most insidious and stultifying phenomenon. Its task, he declares, was 'not only to combine theological concepts into a rational system, but also to provide them with a rationalistic,

---

[1] Platon Levshin's *Orthodox Doctrine* had given particular prominence to the theme of natural knowledge, devoting Part I to the theme (the other two parts dealing with Gospel faith and divine law respectively).

[2] These teachings saw him severely criticized in several works of the fiercely anti-Catholic Metropolitan Anthony Khrapovitsky (1863–1936) who considered that Philaret had succumbed to the non-Orthodox teachings of Anselm and Aquinas on such matters.

metaphysical basis'. It is intriguing to see how rationality elides with 'rationalism' in Kireevsky's thinking. Scholasticism has nothing to do with theology proper and is concerned only with the 'posing of arbitrary problems based on improbable assumptions and the analysis of all possible arguments for and against them'. He continues:

> This endless, tiresome juggling of concepts over seven hundred years, this useless kaleidoscope of abstract categories spinning unceasingly before the mind's eye, was bound in the end to blind it to those living convictions that lie above the sphere of rationalistic understanding and logic—convictions to which people do not attain through syllogisms, but whose truth, on the contrary, people can only distort, if not utterly destroy, through syllogistic deduction.[3]

This profitless logic-chopping dominated the European intellectual arena until the sixteenth century, when its hold was broken by the advent of the 'fresh uncontaminated air of Greek thought' with the Byzantine exodus after the fall of Constantinople in 1453. This fresh air—albeit, as we have seen, hardly as free of scholasticism as Kireevsky would have us believe—is seen to have inspired the modern philosophy of Descartes, Spinoza, and Leibniz, although all of these are seen to remain tainted by scholastic rationalism.[4] What Kireevsky proposes as a counter to the enduring hold of scholasticism is a theology based on the collective wisdom and living tradition of the Slav peoples and nurtured by a return to the patristic and ascetic inheritance of the Church.

Alexei Khomiakov (1804–60) fully shared Kireevsky's anti-scholastic animus. He singles out the eucharist as the single most sorry case of scholastic blindness and vanity, whether of the Protestant or the Catholic variety. Whereas the East properly confesses the essentially mysterious nature of the sacraments, the West squabbles in a hopeless attempt to define the indefinable:

> One reasons on the basis of the physical substance of the sacrament, distinguishing this from its accidents as if it were possible, thanks to the insights of Peter Lombard and Thomas Aquinas, to tell the difference. The other denies the possibility of the presence of Christ in the sacrament on the grounds that this body, according to the testimony of the holy apostles, resides in heavenly glory at the right hand of the Father,

---

[3] *On Spiritual Unity: A Slavophile Reader*, 207–8. Kireevsky names Aristotle the 'soul' of scholasticism and John Scotus Eriugena as its earliest Christian exponent.

[4] *On Spiritual Unity: A Slavophile Reader*, 208–10.

as if they knew what heaven, glory, and the right-hand of the Father were.[5]

Excessive rationalism is a defect common to all Western confessions, whether supplemented by papal authoritarianism or Protestant individualism. This is yet one further instance of Khomiakov's insistence that Protestantism and Catholicism are simply two sides of the same coin.[6] By contrast, Khomiakov proposes an ecclesiology founded on the innately conciliar nature of the Slavs with their natural instinct towards wholeness, unity, and freedom. Such conciliarity is seen as the polar opposite and antidote to the excessive rationalism of the West typified by Peter Lombard and Thomas Aquinas.

It is significant that it is the Slav and not the Byzantine past that is evoked here. Khomiakov's thought involved a good dose of esotericism, particularly visible in the rather peculiar opposition he proposed between two great principles of world-history, the freedom-loving 'Iranian' and the necessity-driven 'Kushite' principle. Christianity, while Iranian by nature, has been infected and subverted by the authoritarian Kushite principle from the time of Constantine onwards. This Kushite inheritance is manifest in the formalism of the Byzantine era as well as in the sorry history of the Western Church. Russia must throw off not only her Western but also her Byzantine shackles. Only then will the purity of her properly Iranian Orthodoxy be fully manifest.[7]

The fact that the whole Slavophile world-view was conditioned by Western sources, whether the eternal opposites of Schlegel, the quasi-mystical conception of freedom and knowledge in Schelling, or the union-in-communion ecclesiology of Möhler, proved no impediment to a deeply anti-Western conceptualization of Orthodoxy. Indeed, Slavophile theology represents the emergence of something rather new: a dialectic construct of Orthodoxy. Orthodoxy is defined by the Slavophiles not so much for what it is, but for what it is not—that is, as non-Western. Naïve appeals to a mythical Slavic past cannot obscure the fact that this is a theology of opposition, a conception of Orthodoxy governed precisely by that which it proposes to reject. Having equated

---

[5] *L'Église latine et le protestantisme au point de vue de l'Église d'orient*, 140.
[6] See Kallistos Ware, *The Orthodox Church*, 1.
[7] A forerunner of Samuel Huntingdon's 'Clash of Civilisations' approach, Khomiakov's theory is developed at length in his extensive *Notes on World History*. See Robert Bird's introduction to *On Spiritual Unity: A Slavophile Reader*, 16.

scholasticism with rationalism and presented this as the defining feature of Western theology (and of the Western-leaning theology of the Russian Theological Academies) the only truly Orthodox theology, for the Slavophiles, is one that is anti-scholastic and anti-rational, in short a species of anti-Thomism. Reacting to the rather decayed scholasticism of nineteenth-century Russia, the Slavophiles produce a simulacrum of Orthodox theology in which the age-old rational and scholastic dimension is simply missing. Certainly, they did a great service in re-affirming (at least in theory) the mystical, ascetic, and patristic inheritance of the Church—but they also left a great deal out.

The Slavophile vision lived on in some of Russia's greatest literary figures, most notably Fyodor Dostoevsky, but had practically no impact on the theology of the ecclesiastical schools: these remained dominated by scholastic models down to the Revolution, albeit with a greater emphasis on historical context from the late 1860s onwards, doubtless fuelled by contemporary German scholarship. Attempts by figures such as Alexander Bukharev (Archimandrite Theodore) (1822–71) to encourage a more explicit engagement with the distinctive issues of modernity also failed to make the slightest impression in official theological circles.

Of more immediate impact, if still very much on the margins of academic theology, was the extraordinary figure of Vladimir Soloviev (1853–1900). Soloviev shares much with the Slavophiles: a strong mystical streak, a grounding in German Idealism, and a deep, if eclectic, interest in Church tradition.[8] But Soloviev had never been wholly convinced by easy oppositions between Russian Orthodoxy and the West. He certainly critiqued the rationalism of the West in his earlier works, contrasting it with the more contemplative and spiritual tradition of the East. But his instincts were always towards harmony, not opposition, and he argued for the uniting of Western logical form with Eastern spiritual content. He refused, therefore, any wholesale rejection of scholasticism, for all that he would vigorously criticize certain developments within it, notably Nominalism. Aquinas is treated relatively benignly by Soloviev, being clearly favoured over Abelard or Ockham.[9] Further traces of positive engagement with

---

[8] On the dogmatic as opposed to esoteric dimensions of Soloviev's thought, see Brandon Gallaher, 'The Christological Focus of Vladimir Solov'ev's Sophiology'.

[9] Soloviev's chief bone of contention is that within medieval scholasticism lay a tendency towards recognition of the autonomy of the human reason, a recognition

Aquinas have been detected in the area of theological aesthetics.[10] Soloviev continued to share with the Slavophiles a sense of Russia's special destiny but he looked to the fulfilment of that destiny not in antithesis to the West but in the re-integration of the fractured Christian tradition. That re-integration (which he believed achieved to some extent in his own person) necessarily presupposed a serious Orthodox re-appraisal of Aquinas.

Soloviev was able to inspire an interest in theology well beyond ecclesiastical confines, dazzling audiences with a heady vision of Christianity as the culmination of a cosmic process whereby the pre-eternal divine humanity is gradually discerned and proclaimed. This primordial Godmanhood (*bogochelovechestve*) is revealed not only in Christ but also as Sophia (Wisdom).[11] Soloviev tells us that he was privileged to have three visions of this eternal and somehow feminine principle, one of which took place in the domed Reading Room of the British Library. Soloviev is also justly famed for his various works on Christian unity. He urges that the plenitude of Christianity requires the positive reception of the distinctive insights of Orthodoxy, Roman Catholicism, and Protestantism in the interests of a greater synthesis.[12] Responding to Leo XIII's call for a return to Aquinas in *Aeterni Patris* and certain Russian writers' call for a return to the Eastern Fathers, Soloviev affirms that each of these systems has a perfection of logical form that gives it a monumental quality and an approximation to truth greater than any abstract philosophical system.[13] But he found any traditional theology, whether Thomist or patristic, ultimately insufficient for the needs of the modern world.

For all his sometimes rather *sui generis* speculations, Soloviev is a thinker worthy of the most serious attention. While sensibly sceptical

that would give rise to the Enlightenment, *et cetera*. See further his *The Philosophical Principles of Integral Knowledge*, 44 and *The Crisis of Western Philosophy: Against the Positivists*, 13–18.

[10] See Vladimir Wozniuk, *The Heart of Reality: Essays on Beauty, Love, and Ethics by V. S. Soloviev*, introduction.

[11] *Lectures on Divine Humanity*.

[12] Soloviev's intuition of the distinctive charisms of the three chief Christian traditions is given vivid form in his apocalyptic *Tale of the Antichrist* (1899). In this narrative, the only persons to resist the blandishments of a seemingly ideal leader of a united European Union are Pope Peter II, the Elder John, and a certain Professor Pauli.

[13] *Kritika otvlechennykh nachal* [*Critique of Abstract Principles*], 349 (his doctoral thesis). Cited in Paul Vallière, *Modern Russian Theology. Bukharev, Soloviev, Bulgakov: Orthodox Theology in a New Key*, 138.

as to the limits of reason, Soloviev was committed to the elaboration of an all-encompassing Christian metaphysics. Hans Urs von Balthasar hailed him as 'perhaps second only to Thomas Aquinas as the greatest artist of order and organisation in the history of thought'.[14] This is both an exaggeration and an understatement: Soloviev sought a global synthesis far beyond anything envisaged by Thomas but he also fell correspondingly short of achieving it.

Soloviev's instinct for synthesis manifested itself in a very salutary opposition to the dialectical Orthodoxy of the Slavophiles, attacking those 'who suppose the Orthodoxy or religion of the Greco-Russian Church in opposition to the Western communions to be the very essence of our national identity'.[15] True orthodoxy precludes national particularity and the differences between Orthodoxy and Catholicism do not constitute a division in their essential unity of faith and piety.[16] The purely negative and oppositional construct of Orthodoxy is a 'pseudo-orthodoxy' and amounts to little more than a faith constituted by anti-papalism.[17] Oppositional theologizing was not, of course, going to disappear overnight, even at the urgings of such profound and prophetic figures as Soloviev. Indeed such dialectical theologizing, with Aquinas as its chief object, was to dominate Orthodox theology for much of the twentieth century. But before turning to this triumph of dialectical Orthodoxy, we shall now review developments in the Greek world from the War of Independence down to the cusp of the 1960s.

6.2. GREEK ORTHODOX THEOLOGY 1821–1960

The Greek theological sphere was somewhat muted in the nineteenth century and produced little to rival its eighteenth-century achievements. The War of Independence gave birth to a small Greek state but had a very damaging effect on the intellectual life and possibilities of Orthodox Christians remaining under Ottoman rule. The ethnic question dogged theological debate in the early years of the new Greek state,

---

[14] *The Glory of the Lord: A Theological Aesthetics* III, 284.
[15] *La Russie et l'Église universelle*, 14–15.
[16] *La Russie et l'Église universelle*, 16–17.
[17] *La Russie et l'Église universelle*, 18–20.

with endless arguments between Athens and Constantinople as to the admissibility of ethnic criteria in ecclesiastical organization. The University of Athens was established in 1837 on German lines but higher training in theology generally entailed study in Germany, with the Protestant or Catholic character of the chosen German institution tending to remain indelibly stamped on its graduates.

In the course of the nineteenth century, the greater scale and superior resources of Russian theology became very evident. The theological compendia of Platon Levshin, Anthony Amfiteatrov, and Makary Bulgakov were all widely circulated in Greek translation, with Platon's going through at least six editions between 1782 and 1884. These Russian tomes inspired the production of similar works in Greece, such as Antonios Moschopoulos' *Epitome of Dogmatic and Ethical Theology* (1851) and, especially, Nicholas Damalas' *On First Principles, Epistemological and Ecclesiastical, of Orthodox Theology* (1865).[18]

A professor of the University of Athens trained in German Protestant universities, Nicholas Damalas (1842–92) was very much a product of the German theological and philosophical culture of his day. His book attempts, in dialogue with Schleiermacher, to establish Orthodox theology on a scientific basis. Theology is defined as 'the science of Christian religion', this religion being understood as the relationship between God and human beings restored by Christ on the Cross, reconciling us with God the Father.[19] Damalas takes Clement and Origen of Alexandria as the fathers of the scientific approach to the Christian religion with John of Damascus also a great guiding light.[20] Theology is the work of human reason submitted to the authority of scripture as understood in the Church.[21] Theology is human, the Church, founded in the will of God, divine.[22] When it comes to the ecclesiastical principles of theology, Damalas orders his material under three headings: Trinity, man, and the Church. Much of this section is oppositional with constant references made to the various errors of the Latin and Protestant Churches. For all that he sets out to present Orthodoxy as the unchanging continuation of the ancient Church, Damalas' theology is shaped by German philosophy

---

[18] Ἐπιτομὴ Δογματικῆς καὶ Ἠθικῆς Θεολογίας (Moschopoulos). Περὶ Ἀρχῶν Ἐπιστημονικῶν τε καὶ Ἐκκλησιαστικῶν τῆς Ὀρθοδόξου Θεολογίας (Damalas).
[19] *On First Principles*, 18.
[20] *On First Principles*, 23, 13.
[21] *On First Principles*, 24.
[22] *On First Principles*, 31.

and has a distinct Protestant bias. He gives great emphasis to scripture and justification by faith and is rather spare in his treatment of the sacraments. He returns again and again to the errors of Trent, and deliberately downplays the authority of the Latin-leaning confessions of Dositheos of Jerusalem and, especially, Peter Mogila.[23]

Damalas is typical of a hardening attitude towards Roman Catholic theology in the nineteenth century as also evidenced in the *Encyclical of the Four Patriarchs* of 1848 which points to the false primacy of the Pope as the source of all the errors of the Latins. These errors are restated in the *Encyclical of Anthimos VII* in 1894 and supplemented with arguments against the immaculate conception and the declaration of papal infallibility.

It should not, of course, be imagined that nineteenth-century Greek theology was solely the preserve of official pronouncements and university professors. The period also witnessed the emergence of a strong current of scripture-based revivalism in the missionary figures Kosmas Phlamiatos, Christophoros Panayiotopoulos, Ignatios Lambropoulos, Apostolos Makrakis, and Eusebios Matthopoulos. Makrakis is the most vivid figure here, a firebrand preacher who denounced abuses in the Church with prophetic zeal. He was also a scathing critic of the theology of the University of Athens, attacking its 'pseudo-theology' with some venom. Through his preaching, the foundation of various associations, and the establishment of his own theological school in Athens, Makrakis agitated for a return to a more obviously scriptural and patristic mode of theological education. Such calls won many sympathizers, despite the patent impracticality of his calls for the speedy restoration of the Byzantine Empire. He was also a direct inspiration for the *Zoe* movement established in 1907 by his follower, Eusebios Matthopoulos.

But Greek academic theology remained on its scholastic and Germanic trajectory for many years to come. The opening of the twentieth century saw the appearance of Zikos Rhosis' *Dogmatic System* (1903) and, most significantly, Christos Androutsos' *Dogmatics of the Orthodox Eastern Church* (1907).[24] The work of Christos Androutsos (1869–1935) demonstrates a profound knowledge of Orthodox and

---

[23] He treats these confessions as valuable catechetical resources but not as possessing any dogmatic or ecumenical authority. *On First Principles*, 49–50. More to his taste is the somewhat Protestant-friendly *Confession* of Metrophanes Kritopoulos, protégé of Cyril Lukaris.

[24] Rhosis, Σύστημα Δογματικῆς τῆς Ὀρθοδόξου Καθολικῆς Ἐκκλησίας; Androutsos, Δογματικὴ τῆς Ὀρθοδόξου Ἀνατολικῆς Ἐκκλησίας.

Western theological and philosophical traditions. The book lies to
some extent within the Latin-leaning tradition of Orthodox theology,
as illustrated by its positive but cautious affirmation of transubstantiation, but also has many points of contact with modern German
philosophy.[25] Overall, it stands as a great defence of the rational
coherence of Orthodox dogma and perhaps the finest fruit of the
Athenian scholastic tradition.

Androutsos was also the author of a substantial work on ethics, the
System of Ethics (1925), that followed in the path marked out by Kant
in basing ethics largely on reason and will.[26] A rather different
account was provided in Vasilios Antoniades' (1851–1932) *Handbook of Ethics According to Christ* (1927) which tallies more obviously
with Aquinas (whom he refers to frequently) in treating ethics primarily in terms of virtue and humanity's return to God in Christ.[27]
Antoniades was a professor of the theological school at Halki, the
chief theological centre of the Patriarchate of Constantinople. Halki
itself was traditionally somewhat more in sympathy with Roman
Catholic theology than was the University of Athens. Antoniades
was also one of the first Greek theologians to recognize the significance of Leo XIII's retrieval of Thomas, his acute interest in Thomas
being evident in his earliest published work in 1890 dealing with
Aquinas' political theology.[28] But Antoniades is a *rara avis* among
Greek Orthodox theologians of this period, none of whom display
anything like his interest in and appreciation of the angelic doctor.

The University of Athens continued to be dominated by the systematic and scholastic approach well into the post-war period, as witnessed
in the *Dogmatics* (1959–61) of Panayiotis Trembelas (1886–1977).[29]
This massive work of great erudition deliberately expands the range of
Androutsos, adding a historical and analytical dimension Trembelas
deemed lacking in the earlier work. While irreproachably Orthodox and

[25] Transubstantiation is dealt with in Δογματικὴ τῆς Ὀρθοδόξου Ἀνατολικῆς
Ἐκκλησίας, 351–4. Androutsos appeals to the authority of the confessions of Peter
Mogila and Dositheos of Jerusalem, and notes the term's first introduction by
Gennadios Scholarios. Androutsos generated some criticism for his views on the
eucharist, most notably from Constantine Dyobouniotes.
[26] Σύστημα Ἠθικῆς.
[27] Ἐγχειρίδιον κατὰ Χριστὸν Ἠθικῆς (2 vols.).
[28] *Die Staatslehre des Thomas ab Aquino.*
[29] Δογματικὴ τῆς Ὀρθοδόξου Καθολικῆς Ἐκκλησίας. Kallistos Ware's review of the
French translation remains essential reading, as does Christos Yannaras' lively but one-
sided discussion in ' Ὀρθοδοξία καὶ Δύση στὴ Νεώτερη Ἑλλάδα334–47 [ET 207–16].

teeming with patristic citations, the work owes much, like all the manuals, to Western models and concepts—with a leaning towards Protestant sources but also containing many Latin scholastic elements such as the distinction between the 'matter' and 'form' of the sacraments. Like Androutsos, Trembelas inhabits a Germanic thought-world, and one that does not appear appreciably changed in the fifty years intervening between their respective works. In its scholastic, systematic, and confessional character, it is a typical product of the prevailing mode of Orthodox theological endeavour in the preceding centuries. But seemingly unbeknownst to Trembelas, Orthodox theology had undergone some startling developments in the early twentieth century including a serious re-evaluation of scholasticism in general and Aquinas in particular. To examine these developments, we must turn back to the Russians.

6.3. PAVEL FLORENSKY AND SERGIUS BULGAKOV

Soloviev's powerful vision of all-encompassing unity found very capable exponents in Pavel Florensky (1882–1937) and Sergius Bulgakov (1871–1944). Both aimed to give a more obviously ecclesial and patristic character to the theology of the divine wisdom, downplaying but not entirely dispensing with the more esoteric currents in Soloviev's approach. In his masterwork, *The Pillar and Ground of the Truth* (1914), Florensky emphasizes the iconographic, liturgical, and ascetic traditions of the Church as the seed-bed of sophiology. Bulgakov, moving at this time from Marxism via Idealism to Orthodoxy, subverts the basic premises of Marxism in his *Philosophy of Economy* (1912) by proposing *Sophia* as the transcendent subject of the economy, as of all human activity. Subsequent works, from his *Unfading Light* (1917) to the masterworks of his Parisian period, emphasize the dogmatic foundations of sophiology through a close engagement with scripture, the Church Fathers, and modern philosophy.

Florensky inherited the Slavophile distrust of rationality and dismissive attitude towards scholasticism. He is at pains to point out that the theological disputes of the late Palaiologan era were 'far from scholastic arguments over useless niceties of abstract thought, but rather the most profound analysis of the very conditions of the existence of culture'.[30] Theology is a living and experiential reality that defies the objectification and rational analysis of the scholastics. Florensky expresses the guiding theme of *The Pillar and Ground of the Truth* thus: 'Living religious experience as the sole legitimate way to gain knowledge'.[31] He goes on to expose the utter insufficiency of human reason. Confronted with the primordial antinomy of the Trinity, one must either accept the absurdity and insanity of mere logic (whether mathematical or theological), or recognize the grounding of logic and reason in supra-logical and antinomical rationality: 'Either the Triune Christian God or the dying in insanity'. A merely rational faith is a very horrid thing.[32] None of this entails the rejection of reason or system but rather the recognition of the paradoxical and provisional character of knowledge.

Florensky's finely poised understanding of reason enables him to engage with Thomas and Thomism in a sophisticated fashion. He commends the ontological understanding of truth in the 'semi-Thomist' John Gratiadei of Ascoli seeing here an approximation to the Russian understanding.[33] He attacks Aquinas' contention of the identity of essence and existence (including reason) in God, seeing in this a 'scarlet thread' that leads to Spinoza's definition of substance as 'that which is in itself and is conceived through itself'—in other words, 'the self-proving Subject'.[34] Discussing the Holy Spirit, Florensky cites Mark of Ephesus' criticism of the distinction between mediate and immediate procession made by 'Thomas and the Latins' as a sign of Orthodox resistance to Latin attempts to rationalize dogma.[35] More positively, he makes use of Aquinas in support of Georg Cantor's understanding of absolute infinity.[36] In his lucid discussion of identity in scholastic philosophy, he finds much to admire in Thomas' treatment of unity and difference. But he goes on to lament the tendency he detects in Suárez to reduce numerical

---

[30] *The Trinity—St Sergius Lavra and Russia.* Thanks to Robert Bird for a copy of his translation.

[31] *The Pillar and Ground of the Truth,* 5.

[32] *The Pillar and Ground of the Truth,* 47–8.

[33] *The Pillar and Ground of the Truth,* 15. John Gratiadei of Ascoli (d. 1341) was a Dominican commentator on Aristotle.

[34] *The Pillar and Ground of the Truth,* 34–5. Cf. Aquinas *SCG* I 80; Spinoza, *Ethics* I, definition 3.

[35] *The Pillar and Ground of the Truth,* 88–9. Cf. Mark Eugenikos, *Syllogistic Chapters against the Latins on the Procession of the Holy Spirit* §6.40–2 (149.10–12).

[36] *The Pillar and Ground of the Truth,* 354.

unity to generic unity and to construct individual identity by contraction from a general concept: humans are thus, in this analysis, no more than singular instances of the human genus. Florensky finds that this tendency has led to individualism and the denial of the idea of the person.[37] In one last reference, he finds Thomas' natural and moral explanations of the significance of the sky-blue colour of the garments of the High Priest a little lacklustre.[38]

Florensky treats Aquinas with respect and even some deference. He is very ready to contradict him, and to trace back to him certain negative currents in the later history of European thought, but in Florensky's delicate and subtle theological sensibility there is little room for animus or blanket denunciation. We find in Florensky something rather like the attitude of Nicholas Kabasilas or Theophanes of Nicaea or Gennadios Scholarios: a confident Orthodoxy capable of disciplined but constructive reception of Western theology. A somewhat less delicate take on the character and possibilities of Western scholasticism is furnished by Sergius Bulgakov.

Bulgakov is a figure who defies easy categorization. Mystic, prophet, hierophant, economist, philosopher, patristician, and scriptural scholar—he was all of these, and more. Certainly Orthodoxy's most constructive theologian of the twentieth century, Bulgakov articulated a compelling but often rather mystifying vision of the world in God and God in the world, a vision in which *Sophia* becomes the link-piece of a vast theological synthesis uniting Trinitarian theology, Christology, pneumatology, cosmology, ecclesiology, and Mariology. *Sophia* is God revealed *ab intra* and *ad extra*, God's self-bestowal within the Trinity and upon the world. She is the principle of unity and co-inherence in God, and between God and the world.

Needless to say, there is little in this potted summary that would suggest any great affinity between Bulgakov and Aquinas. Indeed, Aquinas emerges as something of a *bête noire* for Bulgakov. In an essay on 'The Eucharistic Dogma' (1930), Bulgakov homes in on Aquinas as the classic exponent of Western eucharistic theology. He notes that the Council of Trent and the Roman Catechism have given canonical and obligatory status to Aquinas' teaching and that Protestant teachings on

---

[37] *The Pillar and Ground of the Truth*, 365–6. This would seem to be a somewhat reductionist reading of Suárez and one which lays rather too much at his door.

[38] *The Pillar and Ground of the Truth*, 47–8. Cf. Aquinas *ST* Iª–IIae q.102 a.4 ad 5, a.5 ad 10.

the eucharist can only be understood as a rejection and overcoming of this doctrine. 'In other words, the whole of Western eucharistic theology is a positive or negative Thomism.' And this is not simply a matter of external Church relations: 'The influence of Aquinas' doctrine also spread to the East; recent Orthodox theology concerning this question is still under the indirect and insufficiently understood influence of Thomism, an influence that must be completely overcome.'[39]

Bulgakov proceeds to a close examination of Aquinas' teaching and its philosophical underpinnings, concluding that it represents the enslavement of theology to philosophy—and to a very particular and outmoded philosophy at that. Even in purely philosophical terms, transubstantiation is 'an outright coercion of reason, a completely unnecessary and unjustified archaism'.[40] To make this 'rationalistic, groundless determination' a matter of faith strikes Bulgakov as patently absurd.[41] Bulgakov allows that many Orthodox theologians have given credence to the theory of transubstantiation, especially when criticizing Protestantism. But he does not think Orthodoxy has yet 'said its word' on the matter. To do so it must 'return to the theology of the Fathers (one thousand years into the past), to the patristic doctrine, and to use it as a true guide, to unfold it creatively and apply it to our time'.[42] Warming to his theme, Bulgakov perceives the rationalism of the Latin West to be encapsulated in Thomas' doctrine of transubstantiation. In the recesses of such hubristic investigations lay 'the rationalism that was just beginning to raise its head and would lead to the humanistic Renaissance'. The only exit from the stifling confines of scholasticism is, he reiterates, a return to the Fathers: 'By relying on the patristic doctrine, we can exit the scholastic labyrinth and go out into the open air, although an exertion of thought will be necessary to assimilate the patristic doctrine. Such, in general, is the path of Church tradition: it is always not only conservative but also creative.'[43]

Bulgakov's brisk treatment of Aquinas has many affinities with Slavophile theology: the rejection of scholasticism, the assumption that the Western confessions are variants of a single theme, and the appeal to the patristic past. There is also much that anticipates later

---

[39] Sergius Bulgakov, 'The Eucharistic Dogma', 69. This article was originally published in 1930 in the Russian émigré journal *Put'* (*The Way*).
[40] 'The Eucharistic Dogma', 76–7.
[41] 'The Eucharistic Dogma', 79.
[42] 'The Eucharistic Dogma', 82.
[43] 'The Eucharistic Dogma', 83.

developments in the theology of the Russian Diaspora: the assault on the pernicious 'influence' of Western theology on the Christian East and the call for a creative reaffirmation of the patristic tradition. Georges Florovsky would address the same questions under the headings of 'pseudomorphosis' and 'neo-patristic synthesis'.

This is by no means the only treatment of Aquinas in the whole Bulgakovian corpus, but is perhaps the most typical. We also encounter sustained discussions of Thomas in *The Comforter* and *The Bride of the Lamb*, the second and third volumes of Bulgakov's 'greater trilogy'. In *The Comforter* (1936), Bulgakov attacks Aquinas' argument for the *filioque* on the basis of opposite relations as a logical *non sequitur*. Aquinas' Trinitarian theology represents an impersonal account of relationality that has afflicted Catholic theology ever since.[44] He also notes with some justice the way in which Orthodox discussions of the procession have been straitjacketed into Western modes and structures. Bulgakov argues that at Ferrara–Florence, Mark of Ephesus' strenuous defence of the Orthodox position was conducted largely within the parameters of Thomism. While seeking to counter and outdo Thomas, Mark finds himself debating on entirely Latin grounds and, in the end, 'only parodies Aquinas'.[45]

The Bride of the Lamb contains Bulgakov's most detailed treatment of Thomas and Thomism.[46] Published posthumously in 1945, it represents Bulgakov's most mature and developed discussion of a figure whom he continues to regard as paradigmatic of Western theology. Bulgakov is well aware of competing versions of Thomism, paying particular attention to the Molinist controversy. This controversy had long pitted Dominican Thomists against Jesuit Thomists on the complex matter of the proper understanding of the relationship between divine grace and human freedom. Bulgakov takes the controversy down to its recent resurgence in the respective positions

---

[44]   *The Comforter*, 122–3.
[45]   *The Comforter*, 113–17.
[46]   A number of other works also mention Aquinas. His lack of any developed discussion of the icon is deemed typical of Catholic neglect of this essential topic, *L'Icône et sa vénération*, 113 n.20. Cf. *The Lamb of God*, 260: the art of the iconographer is far more profound than scholastic theology. Thomas' Christology is deemed to suppress the Chalcedonian duality of natures in referring the humanity to the divine hypostasis, *Du Verbe incarné*, 136. This reference to Aquinas is missing from the English translation. In a rare positive note he allows, in one early work, for an apophatic dimension in Thomas owing to the legacy of the Areopagite, *La Lumière sans déclin*, 140, 393 n.91.

of the Dominican Reginald Garrigou-Lagrange (representing a strict Thomism) and the Jesuit Adhemar d'Alès (representing a mitigated Molinism, allowing somewhat more scope to human free will). But in no case do such disputes impinge upon the essential of unity of Thomism which remains united in its basic premises. The apparent differences are, Bulgakov observes, 'fictitious'.[47]

Looking more closely at what Thomism actually is, Bulgakov pinpoints Thomas' fatal flaw as subservience to Aristotle. The impersonal prime mover of the Stagirite is Thomas' real starting-point.[48] Thomas' admission of the philosophical possibility of the world's eternity (as opposed to the revealed truth of its creation) is a sure sign of this reliance, which ends up producing an account that is a makeshift compromise between Aristotle and Moses.[49] The *Summa theologiae* might well add a layer of dogmatics to the Aristotelian foundations but the whole remains conditioned by its philosophical presuppositions.[50] Enlarging on the weaknesses of Aquinas' theory of Ideas, Bulgakov argues that in it 'we have a Platonism that is supplemented by Aristotelianism, and this combination is mechanically, inorganically, brought into Christian theology'.[51] Bulgakov finds Aquinas a deeply un-sophiological thinker, with a woefully deficient account of God, the created world, and human freedom. Through identifying itself so thoroughly with Thomas, Catholic theology shares in all his limitations and errors. It is no surprise, therefore, that it should find itself at a complete 'dead end'.

6.4. THE RISE OF THE NEO-PATRISTIC PARADIGM

Bulgakov's pugnacious and deeply unflattering treatment of Aquinas is the most sustained Orthodox engagement with the angelic doctor since the Byzantine era. The attention Bulgakov lavishes on the topic

---

[47] *The Bride of the Lamb*, 205–12. Garrigou-Lagrange is Bulgakov's most frequently cited contemporary Thomist, described as 'a major representative of contemporary Thomism', ibid., 206. Étienne Gilson's *The Philosophy of St Thomas Aquinas* earns only a footnote, ibid., 58 n.25.

[48] *The Bride of the Lamb*, 19–20.

[49] *The Bride of the Lamb*, 20–1. Bulgakov also claims that Aquinas' world-view is pantheistic in tendency, 57. Neo-Thomism avoids pantheism only by failing to follow through the logic of its own presuppositions, ibid., 220.

[50] *The Bride of the Lamb*, 23.   [51] *The Bride of the Lamb*, 26.

is itself a sign of the strength of a resurgent Thomism in the early twentieth century, albeit the Thomism of Garrigou-Lagrange rather than that of Gilson or Maritain. With his newly re-acquired predominance, Thomas becomes a convenient whipping-boy for Bulgakov, a one-man representative of Catholic theology whom he can berate and belabour at will. Thomas becomes the embodiment and progenitor of the rationalism, impersonalism, and determinism of a West diametrically opposed to Orthodoxy. In so far as he has infiltrated the theology of the Christian East, Thomas represents an 'influence that must be completely overcome', and overcome through a creative retrieval of the Fathers.

An almost identical approach to Aquinas is found in Vladimir Lossky (1903–58). Lossky and Bulgakov are not often presented as being of one mind. Lossky was one of the chief torchbearers of the campaign against Bulgakov's sophiology, contributing to its condemnation by sections of the Russian Church in 1935 and savaging it in print in a pamphlet entitled *Spor o Sofii* (*The Sophia Controversy*) (1936).[52] But the ferocity of this debate should not obscure the great similarities between the two men. These similarities become very apparent when one compares their attitude to Aquinas.

Lossky was privy to some most exciting developments in the Thomist revival of the early twentieth century. As a student of the Sorbonne from 1924, Lossky had direct exposure to Étienne Gilson's compelling account of authentic Thomism as a living and properly Christian philosophy centred on the fundamental issues of human existence and a far cry from any sort of static systematization. Gilson fired in Lossky a passion for medieval theology that inspired and informed his doctoral work on Meister Eckhart. Gilson penned a warm and moving portrait of Lossky as the preface to the posthumously published form of the work, *Théologie négative et connaissance de Dieu chez Maître Eckhart*. Lossky, for his part, maintained an abiding affection and respect for Gilson throughout his all too short life, admiring his 'existentialist' retrieval of the 'authentic Thomism of S. Thomas and his immediate predecessors, a thought rich with new perspectives which the philosophical herd, giving in to the natural tendency of the human understanding, was not slow in conceptualizing, and changing into

---

[52] See Rowan Williams, *Sergii Bulgakov: Towards a Russian Political Theology*, 172–81.

school Thomism, a severe and abstract doctrine, because it has been detached from its vital source of power'.[53]

Such sentiments did not, however, deter Lossky from an all-out assault on Aquinas along distinctly Bulgakovian lines. For Lossky, it is not transubstantiation but the *filioque* that most aptly represents the rationalist excesses of Western theology. With Augustine as its progenitor and Aquinas as its supreme exponent, the doctrine of the *filioque* is decried as a wholly unwarranted intrusion into the mystery of the Trinity that has led inexorably to modern secularism:

> By the dogma of the Filioque, the God of the philosophers and savants is introduced into the heart of the Living God, taking the place of the *Deus absconditus, qui posuit tenebras latibulum suum.* The unknowable essence of the Father, Son, and Holy Spirit receives positive qualifications. It becomes the object of natural theology: we get 'God in general', who could be the god of Descartes, or the god of Leibnitz, or even perhaps, to some extent, the god of Voltaire and of the dechristianized Deists of the eighteenth century.[54]

In his masterly *Essai sur la théologie mystique de l'Eglise d'Orient,* Lossky grandly contrasts the mystical and experiential foundations of Orthodox theology with the ratiocinations of Latin theology—with Thomas typically the chief exemplar.[55] Other works of Lossky's relatively spare corpus adhere to this basic pattern. Thomas' archetypical teaching on the procession of the Holy Spirit is confirmed as woefully impersonal, notwithstanding the best efforts of Gilson to suggest otherwise.[56] His understanding of the Trinity in terms of

---

[53] Vladimir Lossky, Review of Eric Mascall, *Existence and Analogy*, 195. See also the positive remarks on Gilson in his 'The Theological Notion of the Human Person'.

[54] Vladimir Lossky, 'The Procession of the Holy Spirit in Orthodox Trinitarian Doctrine', 88. In his views on the genesis of the *filioque*, Lossky owes something to Basil Bolotov, 'Thesen über das "Filioque". Von einem russischen Theologen'. Lossky, however, categorically denies Bolotov's contention that the distinctive approaches and conclusions of East and West represent mere *theologoumena*, questions of legitimate theological disagreement that offer no real impediment to the reunion of the Churches. Ibid., 72–3. In treating the *filioque* as the matter of a profound division between East and West, Lossky is more in tune with the thought of Lev Karsavin. Karsavin, author of the seminal *Vostok, zapad, i russkaia idea* (*East, West, and the Russian Idea*), embraced a mitigated Slavophilism in which Russia's special destiny is seen to lie in a re-affirmation of her Greek Orthodox identity.

[55] See, for example, *Essai sur la théologie mystique de l'Église d'Orient*, 24, 56, 90 [ET 26, 57, 95].

[56] 'The Theological Notion of the Human Person', 121–2. This deficiency is attributed in part to Thomas' dependence on Boethius, ibid., 116.

relations of opposition reveals an inadmissible essentialism in which the persons are subsumed by the nature.[57] Thomas is seen to be irredeemably rationalist even in his Dionysian inheritance, retaining nothing (in stark contrast to Palamas) of the truly apophatic theology of the Areopagite but reducing such theology to a question of simple negation.[58] Aquinas' account of the vision of God is unfavourably contrasted with a Dionysian-Palamite account in his *The Vision of God*. In this work, based on lectures given in 1945–6, Lossky expresses great sympathy for those scholastic theologians who would question the compatibility of Thomas' account of the beatific vision with patristic testimony, going into some detail regarding the controversy involving Gabriel Vasquez, Francisco Suárez, Diego Ruiz de Montoya, and Denys Petau (Petavius).[59] In one rare positive reference to Aquinas, Lossky allows that he was no Averroist, just as Palamas was no Messalian.[60]

All this brings Lossky to the conclusion that between the positive rationalizing approach of the West (represented by Augustine and Aquinas) and the negative mystical approach of the East (represented by the Cappadocian Fathers, Dionysius, and Palamas) there is really no common ground at all:

> The difference between the two conceptions of the Trinity determines, on both sides, the whole character of theological thought. This is so to such an extent that it becomes difficult to apply, without equivocation, the same name of theology to these two different ways of dealing with divine realities.[61]

For Lossky, as for Bulgakov, only a creative return to the Fathers offers a real alternative to a Western theology characterized by rationalism and

---

[57] 'The Procession of the Holy Spirit in Orthodox Trinitarian Doctrine', 76.

[58] 'The Theology of Light in the Thought of St Gregory Palamas', 53. Cf. also, 'Apophasis and Trinitarian Theology', 26.

[59] *The Vision of God*, 9–20 ('The Tradition of the Fathers and Scholasticism'). Lossky concludes that this Western controversy shows the serious difficulties faced by Latin scholasticism when confronted with the question of the vision of God.

[60] 'The Theology of Light in the Thought of St Gregory Palamas', 49 n.5. Cf. idem, *The Vision of God*, 126.

[61] 'The Procession of the Holy Spirit in Orthodox Trinitarian Doctrine', 80. In contrasting the Trinitarian theologies of East and West, Lossky is quite frank about his debt to Theodore de Régnon's *Études de théologie positive sur la Sainte Trinité*, appealing to his authority for the contrast between the Latin emphasis on essence and the Greek accent on person, ibid., 78 n.10. Cf. *Essai sur la théologie mystique de l'Église d'Orient* 56–7 [ET 57–8].

impersonalism, and responsible for many of the ills of the modern world.[62] As the chief exemplar and exponent of this deficient form of theology Aquinas is, predictably, a figure of the greatest opprobrium for these two otherwise rather opposed theologians.

In both Lossky and Bulgakov the Orthodox tradition is held up in stark opposition to the Thomist West. Both are, of course, responding to the success and strength of the Thomist revival of the late nineteenth and early twentieth centuries, a retrieval that had manifested the possibility for creative and effective re-expressions of Thomas' theology. In proposing a creative retrieval of the Orthodox tradition as a counterpoise to the Catholic retrieval of Thomas, Lossky and Bulgakov find themselves playing catch-up with the West, a predicament all too familiar to Orthodox theologians through the ages.

Where Lossky and Bulgakov differ is in their very different takes on the precise nature of the tradition that is to be creatively re-affirmed. Bulgakov's version is inextricably connected with the theology of the divine Wisdom. As a moderately coherent summation and creative extension of the patristic tradition up to and expressly including Palamas, Bulgakov's sophiology is itself a form of 'neo-patristic synthesis'. Lossky's version of Orthodox tradition operates on a distinctly Dionysian-Palamite axis with a marked emphasis on apophatic theology and mystical experience. Lossky was also concerned to disassociate Orthodox theology utterly from the (predominantly Germanic) mystical and philosophical currents that he perceived to be the true root of Russian sophiology. The neo-Thomisms addressed are also different in character: that of Garrigou-Lagrange in Bulgakov and that of Gilson in Lossky. But these and other minor differences do not detract from the fact that both present us with a version of patristic Orthodoxy which is anti-Western, anti-rationalist, anti-scholastic, and, of course, anti-Thomist.

The Slavophile roots of this dialectical stance vis-à-vis the West are not hard to discern, for all that both Bulgakov and, especially, Lossky shed much of the Russian particularism of their theological forebears. A rather different and considerably subtler position is adopted by Fr Georges Florovsky.[63] Widely regarded in Orthodox circles as the

[62] This theme of creative fidelity to the patristic tradition is also a feature of Lev Karsavin's work, as indeed of many other Russian Orthodox writers of the period.

[63] My understanding and appreciation of Florovsky has been greatly assisted by numerous exchanges and discussions with Matthew Baker and Brandon Gallaher, both of whom have furnished me some valuable materials and references. My sincerest thanks to both. It has also been a great boon to find myself working on

most authoritative theologian of the twentieth century, Florovsky's name is indelibly associated with the notion of a 'neo-patristic synthesis', a term of his own coinage. He and Lossky are often lumped together as the primary exponents of this programme of creative retrieval. But in reality his vision of what a neo-patristic synthesis might look like is very different from that of Lossky. Palamas and, especially, Dionysius loom rather less large in his vision which is centred more obviously on Athanasius and the Cappadocian Fathers. More to the point, Florovsky's proposed synthesis explicitly embraces the Latin Fathers, above all Augustine, in a manner that would be quite unthinkable for Lossky.

Florovsky is also associated with Lossky as an opponent of Bulgakov's sophiology. But while Florovsky was implacably opposed to Bulgakov's speculations on the divine wisdom, he maintained the greatest respect and love for the man himself and became embroiled in the dispute only with the greatest reluctance. The controversy evidently caused him a good deal of pain and suffering, poisoning his relations with much of the Russian émigré community in Paris and precipitating his eventual emigration to the United States. Bulgakov had done a great deal for Florovsky, encouraging his shift from philosophy to theology through the simple but effective mechanism of appointing him to teach patristics at the Institut St-Serge, the chief theological institution of the Russian Diaspora. Florovsky was to repay that trust by perpetuating Bulgakov's vision of a creative retrieval of patristic tradition as a means of tackling the distinctive questions of the modern era—albeit often in ways scarcely congenial to his sometime Dean.

But Florovsky is to be sharply distinguished from both Lossky and Bulgakov in his approach to Thomas and Thomism. In Florovsky, there is little trace of the blanket criticism of the rationalistic, scholastic, Thomist West indulged in by his fellow Russian theologians. He can be positively scornful of any suggestion that East and West are clearly delineated and opposing categories: 'The antithesis of "West and East" belongs more to the polemical and publicistic phraseology than to sober historical thinking.'[64] Florovsky took Lossky to task on

Florovsky in his beloved Princeton, with easy access to his archive and the occasional serendipitous discovery of Florovsky ephemera.

[64] Review of Lev Zander's *Vision and Action*, 191. Zander's problem, according to Florovsky, is that he takes 'divided Christendom' as an 'inevitable and ultimate fact of history' about which nothing at all can be done, ibid., 188.

precisely this score. Commenting on the treatment of Augustine and the Cappadocians, he observes:

> [Lossky] probably exaggerates the tension between East and West even in the patristic tradition. A 'tension' there obviously existed, as there were 'tensions' inside the 'Eastern tradition' itself, e.g., between Alexandria and Antioch. But the author seems to assume that the tension between the East and the West, e.g., between the Trinitarian theology of the Cappadocians and that of Augustine, was of such a sharp and radical character as to exclude any kind of 'reconciliation' and overarching synthesis.[65]

Florovsky's address at the opening of St Vladimir's Seminary, New York, expresses the same point of view with even greater emphasis, arguing that East and West are manifestly 'offsprings of the same root' sharing the same Hellenic and Roman parentage. They are to be regarded as sisters or, better, Siamese twins—dangerously and tragically separated and incomplete without the other: 'neither is self-explanatory, neither is intelligible when taken separately'. The envisaged neo-patristic synthesis is explicitly geared to the reintegration of East and West.[66]

What we do find in Florovsky are some very sustained discussions of the wholly baneful and pernicious effects of Western theology and philosophy on Russian theology from early Muscovy down to modern times. This is the master-theme of his greatest work, *Ways of Russian Theology* (1937).[67] This extraordinary *mythistorema* details the tragic story of the steady displacement of Russian theology from its proper patristic and Byzantine foundations.[68] But while there

---

[65] Review of *The Mystical Theology of the Eastern Church*, 207.

[66] 'The Legacy and Task of Orthodox Theology'.

[67] Nikolai Berdiaev aptly claimed that the book was incorrectly titled and should rather be called *The Waywardness of Russian Theology*. Review of *Puti russkogo bogosloviya*, 53. Florovsky's approach also stands in marked contrast to the accounts of the period in Anton Kartashev's *Ocherki po istorii russkoy tserkvi* (2 vols.) or Basil Zenkovsky's *Istoriya russkoy filosofii* (2 vols.) (Paris 1948–50). Both of these writers are willing to regard Russian engagement with Western sources and models as positively beneficial.

[68] The designation 'mythistorema' comes to me from George Seferis' great poem-cycle of that name. The term (also used of the novel in Modern Greek) combines elements of 'myth' and 'history' in a manner that fits Florovsky rather well. With his full consciousness of the impossibility of impartiality and frequent evocation of mythic themes such as lost purity and the 'Russian soul', this is in fact a rather post- (rather than pre-) modern take on the practice of history.

are endless criticisms of this process of steady malformation or 'pseudomorphosis', and precious few bright spots, this tale of woe should not be read as an attack on Western theology *per se.*[69]

Florovsky's approach to Western theology in its own terms is intrinsically bound up with his understanding of Christian Hellenism. He gives perhaps the clearest treatment of this in the as-yet unpublished preface to his treatise *In ligno crucis. The Patristic Doctrine of the Atonement.* 'Hellenism means philosophy [...] and philosophy means simply {the vocation} of the human mind to apprehend the ultimate Truth, now revealed and consummated in the Incarnate Word.'[70] Without suggesting for a moment that classical Greek philosophy was anything but fallible and contingent, Florovsky detects a permanent value in the conversion of the Hellenic mind to the service of the Church effected by the Church Fathers. This conversion has had a decisive and far-ranging impact:

> Christian Hellenism is much wider than one is prepared to realize. St Augustine and even St Jerome were no less Hellenistic than St Gregory of Nyssa and St John Chrysostom. St Augustine introduced Neoplatonism into Western theology. Pseudo-Dionysios was influential in the West no less than in the East, from Hilduin up to Nicholas of Cusa. And St John of Damascus was an authority both for the Byzantine Middle Ages and for Peter Lombard and Thomas Aquinas. Thomism itself is surely Hellenistic.

This recognition of the Hellenistic character of Thomas and Thomism is a striking confirmation of the analogous assessments of Demetrios Kydones and Gennadios Scholarios. Florovsky does allow that 'Medieval scholasticism was perhaps overburdened with unreformed philosophy' but finds in the Protestant rejection of even such partially digested Hellenism a rejection of philosophy itself. Naturally, the Protestants soon found they could not do without philosophy altogether and an Aristotelian scholasticism was revived among the second generation of Reformers. But something had been lost in the breach—the spirit of metaphysical enquiry. A deep distrust of philosophy settled in, generating a desire to eliminate metaphysics from

---

[69] For a trenchant critique of the notion of pseudomorphosis see Dorothea Wendebourg, '"Pseudomorphosis"—ein theologisches Urteil als Axiom der kirchen- und theologiegeschichtlichen Forschung'.

[70] Florovsky Archive, Princeton University, Box 3, Folder 4. The material signified thus {} belongs to the version of 1948, a revision of an earlier version dated 1940.

Christian doctrine and producing 'the break-away from the Patristic tradition in modern theology'. This is a phenomenon Florovsky sees not only in Protestantism but also in some Catholic circles. The inclusion of Thomas and Thomism under the banner of Christian Hellenism allows for some very positive estimations thereof. Here again, Florovsky finds fault with Lossky's reading and defends an authentically apophatic current in Thomist thought remarking that, 'Lossky dismisses the Thomistic versions of the "negative theology" probably too easily'. He gives Charles Journet's *The Dark Knowledge of God* as a fine example. Elsewhere, Florovsky notes with regret the extent to which Aquinas is so little known in the East, remarking that many Orthodox may even be rather disappointed to find in Thomas a tangible mystical and apophatic dimension founded on his immersion in the Greek Fathers.[71]

Discussing Lossky's work with Archimandrite Sophrony (Sakharov) in a letter of 1958, he cautions, 'With respect to the Western (Roman) theology, I myself prefer cautious judgments. First, we should not over-generalize and lump all "Latin" theology together. In particular, Duns Scotus deserves more attention that he is paid under the hypnosis of Thomism.' He goes on to critique Lossky's genealogy of the *filioque* (rooted, that is, in papism).[72]

A slight Scotist preference is also noticeable in an intriguing discussion of Scotus' argument for the absolute necessity of the incarnation—regardless of the Fall. Florovsky finds support in Maximus the Confessor for Duns Scotus' conjecture and finds against Aquinas' conclusion that the Incarnation is to be seen as consequent upon human sin.[73] This is a fine example of the creative possibilities Florovsky saw for Orthodox engagement with Western medieval theology—with Aquinas and Scotus especially in mind. As he puts it at the conclusion of his *Ways of Russian Theology*:

---

[71] Florovsky Archive, Princeton University, Box 3, Folder 11 (Typescript of a lecture on 'The Vision of Unity').

[72] Arximandrit Sofronii (Saxarov), *Perepiska s Protoiereem Georgiem Florovskim*, 79–81. Thanks to Matthew Baker for this reference. Archimandrite Sophrony (1896–1993) had been closely connected with Vladimir Lossky and was preparing to give a talk in his memory. On Archimandrite Sophrony, see further, Nikolai Sakharov, *I Love, Therefore I Am: The Theological Legacy of Archimandrite Sophrony*.

[73] 'Cur Deus Homo? The Motive of the Incarnation'. We may now add the testimony of Isaac the Syrian in favour of Scotus—albeit in a text that would have been inaccessible to Florovsky.

The Orthodox thinker can find a more adequate source for creative awakening in the great systems of 'high scholasticism', in the experience of the Catholic mystics, and in the theological experience of later Catholicism than in the philosophy of German Idealism or in the Protestant critical scholarship of the nineteenth and twentieth centuries, or even in the 'dialectical theology' of our own day.[74]

This 'creative re-awakening' is no by-water in Florovsky but an intrinsic part of his vision for the accomplishment of his neo-patristic synthesis. In the same crescendo moment of the *Ways*, he argues that freedom from Western 'pseudomorphosis' should not entail estrangement from the West. On the contrary:

the entire Western experience of temptation and fall must be creatively examined and transformed [. . .] Only such a compassionate co-experience provides a reliable path towards the reunification of the fractured Christian world [. . .] It is not enough to refute or reject Western errors or mistakes—they must be overcome through a new creative act.[75]

This 'new creative act' is described as 'a historiosophical exegesis of the Western religious tragedy' that is to replace the 'old "polemical theology"'. Enduring and reliving this experience 'precisely as one's own' will require great sensitivity:

In this newly sought Orthodox synthesis, the centuries-old experience of the Catholic West must be studied and diagnosed by Orthodox theology with greater care and sympathy than has been the case until now.[76]

Florovsky's vision of a 'neo-patristic synthesis', then, expressly includes a sustained and sympathetic engagement with Western theology. While this 'new creative act' is chiefly a retrieval of patristic tradition designed to assert anew the truth of Orthodoxy, there is no doubt that high scholasticism has much to offer the Orthodox theologian.

Florovsky goes on to make the vitally important point that Orthodox theology is part and parcel of a universal tradition of theological enquiry. Its task is not to disassociate itself from that tradition but to freely participate in it. This long passage deserves to be cited at length:

[74] *Ways of Russian Theology* II, 303.
[75] *Ways of Russian Theology* II, 301.
[76] *Ways of Russian Theology* II, 302–3.

The encounter with the West has yet another dimension. During the Middle Ages, a very elaborate and complex theological tradition arose and flourished in the West, a tradition of theology and culture, of searching, acting, and debating. This tradition was not completely abandoned even during the bitterest confessional quarrels and altercations of the Reformation. [...] Russian theology, as a discipline and as a subject of instruction, was born precisely in that tradition. Its task is not to abandon that tradition, but to participate in it freely, responsibly, consciously, and openly. The Orthodox theologian must not, and dares not, depart from this universal circulation of theological searching. After the fall of Byzantium only the West continued to elaborate theology. Although theology is in essence a catholic endeavour, it has been resolved only in schism. This is the basic paradox of the history of Christian culture. The West expounds theology while the East is silent, or what is still worse, the East thoughtlessly and belatedly repeats the lessons already learned in the West.[77]

Florovsky's abhorrence of Orthodox parroting of Western lessons (also known as 'pseudomorphosis') does not equate to a wholesale rejection of Western theology. On the contrary, Orthodox and Western theologies are seen to be inextricably connected.[78] Only through a frank and searching encounter with Western theology, argues Florovsky, will Orthodox theology find its distinctive and authentic voice.

All this is a far cry from the straightforwardly oppositional accounts of Lossky or Bulgakov. Thomas Aquinas is recognized as a representative of a shared tradition of Christian Hellenism and, through various mediations, as a shaping force in the development of Russian Orthodox theology. Florovsky's 'neo-patristic synthesis' necessarily entails a critical but sympathetic study of Thomas and the Thomist tradition from which he explicitly avers there is much to be learned. East and West are not opposites here but rather potential allies.

Florovsky is, it may be admitted, something of a hero of this study. That said, there is much that remains problematic in his achievement, not least the hellenocentrism of his patristic canon and the assumption of the possibility of 'a positive reconstruction of the original Patristic doctrine'.[79] Is he not a little too sanguine in evoking a

---

[77] *Ways of Russian Theology* II, 303.

[78] Florovsky is also one of the relatively few to acknowledge openly the debts of the Orthodox theologian to Western scholarship, ibid., 303–4.

[79] Revised preface to *In ligno crucis*. Florovsky describes this work on the patristic doctrine of the atonement as 'a pointer to toward what one may describe as a neo-patristic synthesis'.

univocal patristic doctrine that can be 'positively reconstructed'? Florovsky was also afflicted with a spirit of Romanticism that led to some peculiar culture-bound musings on the Russian soul and on the beneficent effects of Russian Freemasonry.[80] There remains in him a residual sense of opposition between Orthodoxy and the West, for all his recognition of their intricate interconnectedness and shared parentage. One may also regret the lack of apparent appreciation of the long tradition of Byzantine scholasticism that inspired and informed Latin scholasticism and that in turn underpinned the remarkably positive reception of Aquinas in the Byzantine world. But such criticisms do not detract from the fact that Florovsky presents one of the most affirmative and constructive accounts of Western medieval theology since the Byzantine era and one which offers some profoundly helpful pointers towards a possible Orthodox re-appropriation of Aquinas.

6.5. EAST AND WEST IN MODERN ORTHODOX THOUGHT

The subtlety of Florovsky's treatment of Latin scholasticism has rarely been appreciated, still less his call for a creative appropriation of that tradition. Lossky's rather more antithetical account of the eternal opposition between East and West has proved of greater impact, to such an extent that Florovsky is often conflated with Lossky as a theologian of East–West antithesis. Lossky's approach has, in fact, more in common with that of Bulgakov, representing a current of oppositional theology going back to the Slavophiles. Indeed, the paradigm of antithesis became virtually normative within the theology of the Russian Diaspora, receiving perhaps its clearest and most erudite expression in the retrieval of Palamas effected by John Meyendorff (1926–92).[81] Within this paradigm, Aquinas is invariably the

---

[80] Florovsky is perhaps the only modern Orthodox theologian to have anything good to say about Freemasonry, crediting it with a revival in national consciousness and mystical interest: 'The Russian soul recovered itself through Freemasonry from the alien customs and dissipations in St Petersburg [...] Psychologically, Slavophilism is an offshoot of the Freemasonry of Catherine's reign (as it certainly did not derive from any rustic country customs)'. *Ways of Russian Theology* I, 149.

[81] See above, pp.31–4.

archetypal representative of the West, the 'other side'. This paradigm was also to be adopted by and prosper in the post-war Greek world. Perhaps the most acutely polarized account of East and West is that offered by the Greek Orthodox theologian John Romanides (1927–2001). Often associated with Yannaras as a prime mover of what is sometimes called 'neo-Orthodoxy', Romanides staged a rebellion against the scholastic dominance of academic theology in post-war Greece.[82] Steeped, like Yannaras, in the theology of the Russian Diaspora, Romanides exploded onto the Greek theological scene with an all-out assault on Augustine. Much extending Lossky's criticism of Augustine, John Romanides traces virtually all the ills of the modern West back to the Bishop of Hippo. He observes a sharp distinction between, on the one hand, Augustine and the 'Franco-Latin' theologians that followed him and, on the other, 'the Biblical and Patristic line of thought'. The Fathers of the Church, all of whom are to be regarded as expressly Palamite, offer a wholly different world-view to that of the West. The deficient and overly philosophical theology of the West has, in turn, given rise to challenges and questions, in shapes such as Darwin, Nietzsche, and Freud, to which it has no satisfactory answer.[83] Only the biblical-patristic tradition of Roman Orthodoxy offers a solution to the woes of the modern world.[84]

Augustine is reprimanded especially for his rationalist approach to the divine mystery and his pernicious doctrine of original sin. Thomas Aquinas is the chief representative of the 'Franco-Latin' theologians who have, in practice, done little more than work out the implications of Augustine's theology. The notion of God as *actus*

---

[82] The 'neo-Orthodox' moniker emerged in left-wing critiques of the early 1980s and was not intended as a compliment.

[83] Romanides expresses his world-view in a nutshell in the opening pages of *An Outline of Orthodox Patristic Dogmatics*. His critique of Augustine is outlined at length in his dissertation of 1957 Τὸ Προπατορικὸν Ἁμάρτημα. Augustine's pernicious doctrine of original sin is contrasted with the very different notion of ancestral sin formulated in the ante-Nicene Fathers. Seraphim Rose offers a pertinent defence of Augustine's place in the Orthodox *pleroma* in *The Place of Blessed Augustine in the Orthodox Church*. Perhaps the best survey of Augustine's reception by the Orthodox is provided by George Demacopoulos and Aristotle Papanikolaou in their 'Augustine and the Orthodox: The "West" in the East'.

[84] Romanides puts forward a striking and original vision of Roman Orthodoxy, the shared tradition of East and West lost by the elder Rome under Frankish pressure. For an English language version of this thesis, see his *Franks, Romans, Feudalism and Doctrine*.

purus, for example, has its roots, we are told, in Augustine's confusion of essence and energy and his unwonted probing of the divine essence.[85] Aquinas is definitely the chief epigone of this primal error, and avoids pantheism only through the notion of created grace, thereby breaking the connection between God and the world.[86] Romanides admits to a fascination with Aquinas in his youth, when he had studied under a Dominican teacher, but he evidently came to regard Thomas with something close to loathing.[87]

Unsurprisingly, Romanides was a staunch critic of the scholastic current in modern Orthodox theology and nursed a particular antipathy towards Trembelas.[88] In contrast to such admittedly uninspiring presentations of Orthodoxy, Romanides offered a fresh and exciting theological vision that has found many sympathizers in the Orthodox world.[89] But for all his invigorating insights and his salutary emphasis on the mystical and ascetic dimensions of Orthodoxy, his global rejection of Augustine and all subsequent 'Franco-Roman' theology leaves us with an impossibly simple situation in which the biblical-patristic-Palamite tradition stands in stark and splendid isolation from the philosophical-Augustinian-scholastic West. This straitened version of Orthodoxy is conditioned by Western categories. It is a theology of reaction in which Orthodoxy is defined by way of negatives: *not* Augustinian, *not* scholastic, *not* essentialist, *et cetera*. There are, furthermore, signs of what might waggishly be called Western 'pseudomorphosis'. The account of Augustine, for example, may be traced back via Lossky to the East–West Trinitarian taxonomy of Theodore de Régnon. Romanides' assaults on Western rationalism

---

[85] *An Outline of Orthodox Patristic Dogmatics*, 5.

[86] *Τὸ Προπατορικὸν Ἁμάρτημα*, 42–4. Aquinas is also attacked for his notions of evil (22), *eudaimonia* (32, 100), and divine punishment (120).

[87] 'The Theologian in the Service of the Church in Ecumenical Dialogue'. Lecture in honour of Fr Georges Florovsky given at St Vladimir's Seminary, 23 May 1980.

[88] John Romanides, Letter of 8 August 1957 to Georges Florovsky. Florovsky Archive, Princeton University, Box 22, Folder 4. Romanides comments on the first volume of Trembelas' *Dogmatics* that it was written to show off the author's 'panacademic brilliance'. Romanides finds Trembelas to be, in fact, in 'ignorance of patristic, scholastic, and protestant theology'.

[89] George Metallinos, one of his ablest defenders, credits him with having 'brought about a true cut and break with our scholastic past which had operated as a Babylonian Captivity of our theology'. Eulogy for Protopresbyter John Romanides, cited by George Dragas in his preface to *An Outline of Orthodox Patristic Dogmatics*, xiv. Similar sentiments may be found in Metropolitan Hierotheos (Vlachos) of Naupaktos.

also recall Karl Barth, with whom he shared an antipathy to the *analogia entis* and a general distrust of scholasticism.[90]

Romanides' theology amounts to a rejection of the place of reason and philosophy in theology and its supersession by a rather subjective and selective account of Orthodox tradition. That account, with its emphasis on the pre-Nicene Fathers and the great mystics and ascetics, contains much worthy of the utmost admiration but must be recognized as only part of a greater whole. All this is far removed from the position of Florovsky who unambiguously recognized Augustine as a Father of the Church and for whom Latin scholasticism had an indispensable part to play within his proposed neo-patristic synthesis.[91] More to the point, Romanides presents us with a reconstruction of Church tradition that simply does not tally with historical reality. Orthodox theology has a long history of creative and constructive involvement with Western theology that cannot be overlooked or dismissed.

Christos Yannaras presents a considerably more sophisticated but essentially analogous form of anti-Westernism. He regards Romanides' work with something close to veneration, writing that *The Ancestral Sin* 'is and will remain not only the definitive landmark of the theological revolution of the 1960s but also the purest measure of ecclesiastical Orthodoxy'.[92] Yannaras is less fixated on Augustine than is Romanides and focuses on Aquinas as his chief target. His views on Thomas and the devastating consequences of Kydones' translations have already been discussed and need not be laboured much further.[93] Aquinas is, for Yannaras, the archetypal representative of Western rationalism, individualism, and legalism and a key figure in the West's relentless march towards secularism and nihilism.[94] But such taxonomies of Westernism

---

[90] Not to be outdone, Romanides also rejects the notion of *analogia fidei*. See his discussion of Barth in *Τὸ Προπατορικὸν Ἁμάρτημα*, 23 n.1.

[91] 'Augustine is a Father of the Church Universal, and we must take his testimony into account, if we are to attempt a true ecumenical synthesis.' 'The Doctrine of the Church and the Ecumenical Problem', 156. Not that he agreed with all aspects of Augustine's teaching, notably on sin and grace or the failure to recognize the essence–energies distinction. The authority of the Fathers is never infallible. As Florovsky wrote to A. F. Dobbie Bateman, 'They are guides and witnesses, no more. Their "vision" is of authority, not necessarily their words.' Brandon Gallaher (ed.), 'Florovsky on Reading the Life of St Seraphim', 62.

[92] ' *Ὀρθοδοξία καὶ Δύση στὴ Νεώτερη Ἑλλάδα* 444 [ET 278].

[93] See above, pp.2–3.

[94] Yannaras cites not an Eastern but a Western source for his intuition: 'Heidegger has assured us that Descartes represents the natural end result of Western scholasticism.' 'Orthodoxy and the West', 286. Yannaras' account of Heidegger is presented

need not detain us much further, save to recognize that Yannaras' account of Orthodoxy and the West is not without its subtleties. The East–West division is not one of competing blocs but, like the line between good and evil in Solzhenitsyn, cuts through the human heart: 'There is no entity called the West "confronting" Orthodoxy; the West is "within us" and Orthodoxy is the common nostalgia of all who perceive the falling away of both East and West.'[95] Yannaras also writes off much of the theology of the Russian Diaspora as structured and determined by its relationship with the West. It is a 'theology of dialogue'. This mode of theologizing in constant dialogue with the West brings with it a risk of complete marginalization:

> If we continue to theologize dialectically with the West, we shall perhaps come in a short time to represent no more than an interesting, some-what exotic, aspect of the Western theoretical worldview, or a narrowly confessional doctrine which belongs to the sphere of 'archaeology of ideas'. This is, I believe, where the ecumenical dialogue is inevitably leading us; all of us have, I think, personal experience, at conferences and encounters, of the fact that Orthodox views ring out beautifully as poetical notes, deeply moving but completely utopian, having no actual reality within our own Churches today.[96]

Yannaras' own response to this danger was to propose a reformulation of the existential event with an accent on person and *eros*. In constant dialogue with Heidegger, Yannaras asserts in Dionysian and Palamite terms the apophatic character of knowledge and the foundation of human freedom and uniqueness in the essence–energies distinction. It is a bold and brilliant vision which, notwithstanding its flaws, deserves the most serious attention.

Yannaras' approach has much in common with the narrative articulated by Philip Sherrard in *The Greek East and Latin West*, published in 1959.[97] In his foreword, Sherrard frankly admits that his account of the schism is not primarily historical, but conditioned by

---

most fully in his *On the Absence and Unknowability of God: Heidegger and the Areopagite*. As one might except, Aquinas again appears in this work as a pivotal player in the decline of the West.

[95] Commencement Address at the Holy Cross Greek Orthodox School of Theology, Brookline MA, 21 May 2011. Yannaras expresses similar sentiments in the preface to the English translation of his *Orthodoxy and the West*.

[96] Yannaras, 'Orthodoxy and the West', 296–8.

[97] Yannaras says very little of his connection with Philip Sherrard, with whom he was at one time on close terms.

principles of a non-historical order drawn from the matrix of the Christian tradition. It is history *sub specie aeternitatis*. The fissure between Greek East and Latin West, in other words, is a matter much more of metaphysics than of what Fernand Braudel called the 'flotsam' of history.[98] 'This is not to say', Sherrard writes, 'that historical facts are ignored, but only that they tend more to serve as illustration than to form the basis of the study.' Much the same may be said of Yannaras' approach to history. Having set his cards on the table with admirable candour, Sherrard proceeds to an analysis of the Western decline and traces a 'curious inner dialectic' in Western thought from Augustine through Aquinas to Descartes in which reason is divorced from revelation and elevated to wholly autonomous status.[99] This process entailed a gradual separation of God from the world in which God became dispensable in the Western mindset. This process is deemed responsible for the subsequent ills of Western society, most notably in the devastation now afflicting the ecological sphere. In sharp contrast stands the tradition of the Greek Fathers, interpreted largely in Dionysian and Palamite terms and with an accent on the intuitive knowledge of the spiritual intellect (*nous* or heart), mystical experience, and the participatory relationship between the creation and its Creator. Philip Sherrard, however, maintained a guarded respect for Aquinas, and a sympathy for certain aspects of his theology (such as analogy) that prevents his theology from lapsing into the merely polemical.

A similar sense of opposition between the rationalistic West and the mystical, experiential East is found in Sherrard's close friend Zissimos Lorentzatos, articulated most clearly in his famous essay on George Seferis, 'The Lost Centre' (1962).[100] Like Sherrard, Lorentzatos pinpoints the mystical tradition as the defining characteristic of the Greek spiritual tradition. That tradition may have been 'consistently ignored and deformed' by the rationalistic and humanistic West (especially since 1821) but it remains a living reality. This is not to say that mysticism is the exclusive preserve of the Greeks (he is well aware of the great Syrian mystics) but that the Greeks have been 'the

---

[98] *The Mediterranean and the Mediterranean World in the Age of Philip II* (volume II), 1243.
[99] *The Greek East and Latin West*, 139–64.
[100] «Τὸ Χαμένο Κέντρο». ET in *The Lost Center and Other Essays in Greek Poetry* (tr. Kay Cicellis). Yannaras pays warm tribute to Lorentzatos in ' Ὀρθοδοξία καὶ Δύση στὴ Νεώτερη Ελλάδα, 430–5.

main vehicle of the great tradition of Christian mysticism'. Where the West has produced great mystics, such as Eckhart 'who outweighs all the other Western mystics put together', these could not 'possibly have existed had it not been for the diffusion and transfusion of our own mystical tradition from the *sketes* and cells of the East to the mist-shrouded monasteries of Ireland, to say nothing of the great Slavic tradition of the *startsi* at a later period'. Lorentzatos saw many signs of a kind of underground stream of mystical inspiration in the Western literary canon, above all in W. B. Yeats and William Blake— both of whom he translated into Greek. Sherrard, also a great devotee of Blake and Yeats, aptly christened Lorentzatos' underground tradition 'the Orthodoxy of the West'.[101]

The 1960s witnessed an astonishing theological revival in Greece conducted in large measure under the banner of a return to the Fathers and expressly concerned with the theological and philosophical concerns of the day.[102] This return to the Fathers was not a wholly new phenomenon: theologians such as Hamilcar Alivisatos (1887–1969) of the University of Athens had done much to foster a spirit of patristic revival (coupled with devoted ecumenical engagement) from at least the 1940s. John Romanides paid special tribute to Alivisatos in the prologue to his own distinctly anti-Western version of patristic retrieval in 1957, a work that certainly had an impact on the coming generation.[103]

The key figure in the formation of the new wave of younger theologians was Demetrios Koutroubis (1921–83), a lay theologian with no academic or ecclesiastical position. At regular salons in his ramshackle home just outside of Athens, Koutroubis played the role of Socrates to a vibrant circle of young Greek thinkers, among them Christos Yannaras.[104] Koutroubis had spent some years in the Jesuit order and brought with him on his return to Greece from France something of the fire of the patristic *ressourcement* urged by the French Jesuits Henri de Lubac and Jean Daniélou. He introduced this new generation to the riches of the Russian Orthodox Diaspora, beginning with a set of articles in 1960 on the Palamite retrieval of John Meyendorff and the masterly work of Myrrha Lot-Borodine on

[101] Philip Sherrard, «Σήσιμος Λορεντζάτος: τα κρίσιμα χρόνια» in Ἀντὶ Χρυσέων, 60–1.
[102] Norman Russell gives a useful survey of this revival in 'Modern Greek Theologians and the Greek Fathers'.
[103] Τὸ Προπατορικὸν Ἁμάρτημα, xiii–xiv.
[104] See Yannaras, ' Ὀρθοδοξία καὶ Δύση στὴ Νεώτερη Ἑλλάδα 464–73 [ET 290–7].

Nicholas Kabasilas, both published just the previous year.[105] Koutroubis was also instrumental in circulating of the works and ideas of Georges Florovsky, Vladimir Lossky, Alexander Schmemann, Sergius Bulgakov, Paul Evdokimov, and others. In 1964, Koutroubis founded with Elias Mastroyiannopoulos, leader of the *Zoe* brotherhood, the journal *Synoro* (*Frontier*) which did much to further the progress of Russian Diaspora theology into the Greek world, including their 'European disciples', to use Yannaras' term, Olivier Clément, Kallistos Ware, and Philip Sherrard.[106]

Koutroubis himself was quite free of any sort of animus against the West and had the highest regard for its religious traditions, reserving special veneration for the Marian shrine at Walsingham, England. His articles are peppered with affirmative references to Western writers, from Jacques Maritain and Louis Bouyer to the Anglican biblical scholar Sir Edwyn Hoskyns ('the foremost contemporary interpreter of scripture').[107] Koutroubis also welcomed the Second Vatican Council with considerable enthusiasm and the genuine hope.[108] He was, however, prepared to see in the West a great decline '*after* the death of the great scholastics'. In successive generations, the systems of these men were elevated to autonomous and all-sufficient status and theology became a merely self-serving enterprise.[109] He is also content to accept Meyendorff's discernment of two competing world-views in the debate between Barlaam and Palamas, humanist-philosophical and biblical-ecclesial. The dominance of the former strand in the West has, he claims, led through the Renaissance, the anarchy of Protestantism, Cartesianism, and German Idealism, to the parlous situation of the modern world in which Communists and Capitalists alike operate on the Nietzschean assumption that 'God is dead' and that man is free to do what he wills with his life. The East's relative freedom from this saga of decline is down in large measure to the theology of Gregory Palamas.[110]

---

[105] These articles are given in collected volume of Koutroubis' works, Ἡ χάρις τῆς θεολογίας, 157–211.

[106] ' Ορθοδοξία καὶ Δύση στὴ Νεώτερη Ελλάδα469 [ET 294].

[107] Ἡ χάρις τῆς θεολογίας 23, 91, 226–7.

[108] Ἡ χάρις τῆς θεολογίας, 257–72.

[109] Ἡ χάρις τῆς θεολογίας, 174. Emphasis mine. Koutroubis also stood firmly against the scientific approach to theology that still reigned in the theological schools. See the alternative vision of theology expressed in Ἡ χάρις τῆς θεολογίας, 15–27.

[110] Ἡ χάρις τῆς θεολογίας, 168–9.

Another member of the Koutroubis circle, Vasileios Gontikakis, has enlarged on some of the differences between Orthodoxy and the West, most notably in his best-known work, *Hymn of Entry*. The book as a whole stands as a marvellous portrait of Orthodoxy painted in brilliant liturgical and patristic colours. But while for the most part a very positive and affirmative work, it does contain some severe criticisms of the West, intended to help explain Athonite reluctance to engage in the ecumenical arena. Gontikakis, then Abbot of the Monastery of Stavronikita, notes that the doctrine of papal infallibility 'sums up the impudence of all heresies' and 'marks the acme of human self-assurance and alienation from the mystery of the Church'. It is a sign of the pride that lies at the root of all heresies. In this respect, The Roman Catholic deviation from Orthodoxy is similar to that of the various Protestant denominations.[111] Gontikakis expresses great sympathy for the separated Church of Rome: 'The whole tragedy of Roman Catholicism is not something foreign to the feeling and care of the Orthodox Church. It is painful for the Orthodox, a matter that concerns us personally.'[112]

Also a member of the Koutroubis circle, and an important figure in the Palamite revival in modern Greece, Panayiotis Nellas (1936–86) put forward a staunchly Orthodox theological vision (on a Cappadocian–Palamite axis) and fully cognizant of the debt owed by Orthodox theologians to the Russian Diaspora and to the patristic *ressourcement* of the Roman Catholic *nouvelle théologie*.[113] Other representatives of the Palamite revival such as Panayiotis Chrestou (1917–96) and George Mantzarides tread a similar line to Nellas. All three take Palamas as archetypical of an Orthodoxy clearly contradistinguished from Western theology—but do so without egregious polemics.

The patristic revival of the 1960s also shaped theologians such as Nikos Nissiotes (1925–86) and Metropolitan John Zizioulas. Adopting a critical but deeply constructive approach to Western theology, Nissiotes and Zizioulas have both impacted decisively on the ecumenical arena, offering vibrant articulations of the Orthodox tradition forged in dialogue with (and frequently in opposition to)

---

[111] *Hymn of Entry*, 99.   [112] *Hymn of Entry*, 56.
[113] Nellas paid homage to the *Sources chrétiennes* project by establishing a smaller-scale Greek equivalent, Ἐπὶ τὰς πηγὰς (*To the Sources*). In 1982 he founded the journal *Synaxi* as a successor to *Synoro*.

Western philosophy and theology. In Zizioulas' masterpiece, *Being as Communion*, Aquinas makes occasional appearances as the representative of precisely the opposite ontology to that articulated in the book. In identifying God's essence with his existence and thereby privileging nature over person, Aquinas is found to be worlds away from recognizing the ontological primacy of the person of the Father.[114] His notion of opposite relations is quite unacceptable to the author who finds it devoid of ontological content.[115] Zizioulas is suspicious of the psychological model of the Trinity articulated by Aquinas, regarding such models as based on a false assumption concerning the relation between knowledge and love.[116] Zizioulas treats Aquinas with respect, recognizing the importance of his work of systemization along lines established by John of Damascus and Origen.[117] He also recognizes that Aquinas' theology of the Trinity was motivated by a concern to uphold the dignity of the Son.[118] This is, in short, a spare and subtle treatment of Aquinas devoid of hostility but quite convinced of the vast gulf separating him from the worldview of the Greek Fathers.

The frankly polemical theology of Yannaras and Romanides is, in sum, perhaps best regarded as an extreme expression of the widely held assumption of East–West opposition within the much-lauded theological revival of 1960s Greece.[119] While rarely expressed quite as forcefully as in 'neo-Orthodoxy', the East–West paradigm remains deeply entrenched in Greek Orthodox theology and Aquinas definitely *persona non grata*. Few are the writers prepared to question the essential otherness of East and West, fewer still prepared to integrate Aquinas into an Orthodox world-view.

---

[114] 'The West, as the study of the trinitarian theology of Augustine and Thomas Aquinas witnesses, had no difficulty in maintaining the *Filioque* precisely because it identified the being, the ontological principle, of God with his substance rather than with the person of the Father.' *Being as Communion*, 41 n.35. Cf. *Communion and Otherness*, 151.

[115] *Being as Communion*, 220 n.28. Zizioulas allows that Augustine, by contrast, does have an authentic understanding of relation, at least in respect of the relation between Creator and creature.

[116] *Being as Communion*, 104. Cf. *Lectures in Christian Dogmatics*, 71.

[117] *Lectures in Christian Dogmatics*, 2.

[118] *Being as Communion*, 210 n.5.

[119] One must also note that Yannaras has been subject to some fierce criticism by, among others, Pantelis Kalaitzides and Stavros Zoumboulakis. See, for example, the latter's «Τό σύνορο καί ὁ Χρῆστος Γιανναρᾶς».

6.6. BEYOND DICHOTOMY?

It would be wrong to suggest that modern Orthodox theology is wholly in thrall to the paradigm of opposition. Even Lossky, the chief proponent of this paradigm was, according to Olivier Clément, moving towards a more nuanced account of the *filioque* issue in his last years, pursuing a line of enquiry emerging out of Gregory of Cyprus' notion of the eternal manifestation of the Spirit through the Son.[120] Clément takes this as a sign of Lossky's emergence from his militant phase, 'où il ne pouvait annoncer sans dénoncer'. John Meyendorff makes the same point, writing that, 'As a controversialist and apologist, Vladimir Lossky was sometimes intransigent and harsh. However, in the last years of his life one sees him developing more and more that serene wisdom which made his personality so engaging.'[121] Lossky had indeed been prone to massive generalizations on, for example, the East's utter rejection of such Western themes as the imitation of Christ, the Spirit as the mutual love of Father and Son, or the dark night of the soul. Clément also reports a softening in Lossky's stance on sophiology and an intention to pursue further the commonalities between East and West exemplified in Eckhart.[122] Clément's intimation of a less militantly oppositional Lossky only sharpens the poignancy of his early death.[123]

Olivier Clément (1921–2009), himself a theologian of distinction, was also a friend and admirer of Paul Evdokimov (1901–70) with whom he shared a remarkably open and generous approach to Western theology, philosophy, and culture. Neither have a great

---

[120] *Orient-Occident: Deux passeurs, Vladimir Lossky et Paul Evdokimov*, 83–4. Clément sees in such Byzantine developments a conscious integration of themes from Augustine and Aquinas into Orthodox Trinitarian theology in the late thirteenth and early fourteenth centuries. He is, however, mistaken in suggesting Aquinas had been translated by that time. Clément also reports that Lossky would use the *Summa theologiae* in his dogmatics lectures as an example of how *not* to approach theology, 18–20.

[121] Preface to Vladimir Lossky, *The Vision of God*, 5.

[122] *Orient-Occident: Deux passeurs, Vladimir Lossky et Paul Evdokimov*, 91–3. Lossky had, in 1944, trekked some distance through war-torn France to attend Bulgakov's funeral—a sign of sure respect and perhaps some regret.

[123] Lossky himself was a charming but utterly uncompromising ecumenical interlocutor. See the affectionate portrait given by Eric Mascall, *Saraband: The Memoirs of E. L. Mascall*, 186–9.

deal to contribute on Aquinas, saving Evdokimov's distinctly Bulgakovian take on the deficiencies of Western eucharistic theology.[124] But
with their eschewal of polemic both served as effective witnesses to the
creative possibilities of a non-oppositional presentation of Orthodoxy.
Evdokimov was also one of the few theologians of the Russian Diaspora
to carry the torch of sophiology into the post-war period, maintaining it
to be the 'glory of modern Orthodox theology'.[125]

Lev Gillet (1893–1980), who wrote under the pen name 'A Monk of
the Eastern Church', was himself an embodiment of the underlying
unity of East and West, moving from the Benedictine order through
Greek Catholicism and into the Orthodox Church without ever
disowning any part of that heritage. In the opening pages of his
*Orthodox Spirituality: An Outline of the Orthodox Ascetical and
Mystical Tradition*, he declares that, 'The whole teaching of the
Latin Fathers may be found in the East, just as the whole teaching
of the Greek Fathers may be found in the West.' The book goes on to
draw on Aquinas as an authority on mystical experience—a rare
reference indeed in modern Orthodox literature.[126]

A similar generosity of vision is evident in the work of Kallistos
Ware, Metropolitan of Diokleia, perhaps the most unimpeachably
balanced and nuanced expositor of the Orthodox tradition in modern
times. Ware had also cited Aquinas with approval on the mystical life,
in a passage concerning the outpouring of the soul's glory onto the
body at the resurrection, a passage he found reminiscent of the
Macarian writings.[127] Ware's inimitable subtlety is perhaps at its
most apparent in an article on 'Scholasticism and Orthodoxy: Theological Method as a Factor in the Schism'. The article was composed
as a response to Yannaras' article, 'Orthodoxy and the West' and to
Gerald Bonner's subsequent criticism. Without accusing either party,
he gives the following salutary warning:

> It is misleading and unhelpful to pose the question starkly in black and
> white, contrasting 'East' and 'West' as two independent and self-contained

---

[124] 'The Eucharist—Mystery of the Church', in idem, *In the World, of the Church: A Paul Evdokimov Reader*.
[125] *L'Orthodoxie*, 87.
[126] *Orthodox Spirituality: An Outline of the Orthodox Ascetical and Mystical Tradition*, viii, 68. Aquinas is especially commended for his teaching on the spiritual senses.
[127] 'The Transfiguration of the Body', 29.

worlds, as two opposed and mutually exclusive blocs; for this is to ignore our original kinship in a shared past.[128]

Ware does, however, ascribe to scholasticism a role in the parting of ways between Greek East and Latin West. Recognizing that Aquinas may well have made more extensive use of the Areopagite than did Palamas, he avers:

> But the Latins analysed Patristic texts, arguing, questioning, and distinguishing, in a way that most Greeks did not. Theology became a 'science' for the medieval Latins, in a way that it never was for the early Greek Fathers and their Byzantine successors.[129]

Similarly, while acknowledging the important mystical side to Thomas, he observes that mystical experience was never the criterion of theology it became for Palamas.[130] Ware doubts the depth and extent of Thomas' apophaticism and questions whether his approach to the Fathers conforms to Florovsky's notion of a theology *ad mentem Patrum*.[131]

But Ware does not make the mistake of falling into any sort of anti-rationalist stance, arguing that logic and clear thinking are vital theological tools, within their proper limits. Appeal to the mysterious must never become an 'excuse for muddle and mystification'. Orthodox strictures against scholasticism, as expressed by Joseph Bryennios, Symeon of Thessalonica, and others, are to be regarded not as assaults on reason *per se* but on the improper and excessive use of reason. That said, he does not hold it to be proven that Aquinas did in fact use reason in such a fashion, or employ philosophy in a fundamentally different way from the Cappadocian Fathers or John of Damascus.[132] Noting the enthusiasm of many Byzantines for Aquinas, Ware is quick to note that not all of these were unionist and that, conversely, there was no systematic animosity against the Latin West in the Palamite party. As for those Byzantines who felt Latin scholasticism to be overly conformed to this world, rather than the next, he closes by asking, 'How far were those Byzantines right?'[133] How far indeed.

---

[128] 'Scholasticism and Orthodoxy: Theological Method as a Factor in the Schism', 16.
[129] Op. cit., 18.
[130] Op. cit., 20.
[131] Op. cit., 22. This notion was itself a counterpoise to Leo XIII's call in *Aeterni patris* for a theology *ad mentem sancti Thomae Aquinatis*.
[132] Op. cit., 24.
[133] Op. cit., 25–7.

The Romanian Orthodox tradition may also provide some important pointers towards a mode of Orthodox theology comfortable with its Latin heritage and chary of self-definition vis-à-vis the West. This self-consciously Latin expression of Eastern Christianity has as its most accomplished and significant spokesman Dumitru Stăniloae (1903–93), certainly one of the twentieth-century's foremost (if neglected) theologians. As well as translating and compiling a much-extended Romanian version of the *Philokalia*, Stăniloae also produced a three-volume *Orthodox Dogmatic Theology*, demonstrating that there was life yet in the genre of Orthodox dogmatics.[134] In its structure and some of its content (such as the treatment of the seven sacraments), this work relies to some extent on earlier manuals—Stăniloae himself had translated Androutsos in his youth. But it is also a product of the neo-patristic revival and indeed arguably the closest thing to a neo-patristic synthesis yet achieved. Stăniloae's treatment of Trinitarian theology follows the line laid out by Florovsky, as opposed to Lossky, by deliberately encompassing Augustine. Stăniloae makes much of the intuition of the Holy Spirit as the bond of love between Father and Son, an intuition also adopted by Gregory Palamas. Stăniloae insists on the proper place of reason in theological endeavour and refuses, in contradistinction to Lossky or Yannaras, to single out apophaticism as the exclusive defining characteristic of Orthodox theology. Stăniloae insists rather on the interdependence of the cataphatic and apophatic ways.[135] There is, however, little in Stăniloae to suggest any great sympathy with Aquinas or indeed with post-patristic Western theology in general.

The categories of East and West have also been subject to the withering gaze of David Bentley-Hart. In typically bracing fashion, he bears down on what he calls the 'myth of the schism', tearing apart pious certainties and historical platitudes with such gusto that one is left wondering whether there was ever any real difference between East and West at all.[136] His work on Trinitarian theology adopts the same rumbustious approach, finding the distinction between Greek East and Latin West to be 'artificial'.[137] This 'take no prisoners' style

---

[134] As a consciously patristic renewal of the genre of Orthodox dogmatics, Stăniloae's work bears comparison with Justin Popović's (1894–1979) *Dogmatika Pravoslavne tserkve*. Popović's work is, however, quite explicitly anti-Western.

[135] See Ion Bria's preface to Stăniloae's, *The Experience of God. The World: Creation and Deification*, ix and ibid., 99, 123.

[136] 'The Myth of Schism'.

[137] 'The Mirror of the Infinite: Gregory of Nyssa on the *Vestigia Trinitatis*', 116.

may well impede recognition of the undoubted merits of his acutely perspicacious theological vision. His astonishing *Beauty of the Infinite*, certainly a work of importance, blazes a trail in forging a theological aesthetics emerging out of his own reading of Thomas and developed with reference to a dizzying array of sources, including many Greek patristic and modern Orthodox. Regrettably, there is no perceptible continuity with the long tradition of Orthodox engagement with Aquinas. This virtuoso work operates, in short, too far outside the traditional frameworks of Orthodox theology to have much hope of effecting a serious rethinking of Aquinas in that world.

A still more radical take on Aquinas is evident in the work of Stelios Ramphos, one of the most vibrant and original thinkers in modern Greece. As we saw in the introduction, Ramphos presents Aquinas as a paradigm of the kind of theology the Orthodox world most desperately needs: rational, engaged with the world, and affirmative of the body. Aquinas is, for Ramphos, a synecdoche for all that the Orthodox world has rejected in its unfortunate espousal of Hesychasm. He expresses his profound admiration for many aspects of Aquinas' theology, for example his exegesis of scripture, doctrine of the spiritual senses, and anthropology.[138] Most of all he applauds Thomas' marshalling of Aristotle and his Arabic commentators in the interests of a rationally coherent defence of the faith.[139] But while Ramphos has performed a service of inestimable worth in highlighting the virtues of Aquinas from a broadly Orthodox perspective, he remains beholden to the old supposition of eternal opposition between East and West. The difference is that the sympathies are reversed: the West, in the shape of Aquinas, being not the villain but the hero of the piece. The weaknesses of the dichotomous approach remain very much in evidence: Ramphos overplays the differences between East and West, finds no place for the long history of Orthodox encounter with Thomas, and produces a simplified and insufficiently nuanced account of Palamite theology. This inability to move beyond dichotomy greatly limits the potential impact of Ramphos' remarkably enthusiastic embrace of Aquinas.

[138] See *Τὸ ἀδιανόητο τίποτα*, 132 (allegorical exegesis), 134–5 (spiritual senses), 217 (anthropology). See also his ʿ *Ο καημὸς τοῦ ἑνός* Κεφάλαια τῆς ψυχικῆς ἱστορίας τῶν Ἑλλήνων.
[139] *Τὸ ἀδιανόητο τίποτα*, 462.

In the final analysis, it must be admitted that the words of Rudyard Kipling still hold largely true for modern Orthodox theology: 'East is East and West is West, and never the twain shall meet.'[140] Aquinas, where he is mentioned at all, is still routinely treated as an archetype of the West against which East must set its face. Only rarely has the idea that he might have something to offer the Orthodox world been seriously entertained and then very much outside the mainstream of modern Orthodox theology. Still more seldom has there been any recognition of the very real role Aquinas has already played in the articulation of Orthodox theology. Orthodox theologians today find themselves worlds away from the discerning and constructive appropriation of Aquinas characteristic of so much Orthodox theological endeavour in the Byzantine and early modern periods. The final chapter will consider the reasons behind this strange dissimilarity.

The time has now come to reflect on where this long journey has brought us. In keeping with the 'exercise in multiple perspective' with which this book opened, the last chapter will not confine itself solely to re-iterating the chief conclusions reached but will open up two further perspectives. The first additional perspective concerns the contribution Orthodox readings of Aquinas might make to the image and understanding of Thomas himself. The second relates to the possibility of breaking thorough the East–West dichotomy to an Orthodox re-appropriation of Aquinas.

---

[140] *The Ballad of East and West*, 1.

7

New Perspectives

The aim of this study has been to open up a fresh set of perspectives on Aquinas, the Orthodox reception of Aquinas, and Orthodoxy itself. In imitation of an Orthodox icon, it has striven to operate at a level beyond the presentation of appearances and to inculcate a dynamic sense of the multifaceted reality of the centuries-long encounter between Orthodoxy and Aquinas, confounding or at least nuancing many of the stereotypes and assumptions that beset this field of study. Pre-eminent among those stereotypes ripe for rejection is the hoary assumption of theological dichotomy between Christian East and West. Taking as its starting-point the supposed archetypes of East and West, Gregory Palamas and Thomas Aquinas, this book opened with a sketch of a very 'Eastern' Thomas, a devoted student of the Greek Fathers, a pioneer in the use of material from the later ecumenical councils, and an enthusiastic propagator of near-contemporary Byzantine exegetical sources. This Thomas, far from being an innovator in theological methodology was, rather, the heir to a long tradition of Byzantine scholasticism—albeit one who took that tradition to new heights of lucidity and sophistication. Palamas, for his part, has been depicted as one who shared fully in that same tradition of Byzantine scholasticism, being steeped in Christian Aristotelianism and expressly committed to the defence of the proper place of reason within the theological sphere. This is a Palamas prepared to build bridges across the Greek–Latin divide even in the dread matter of the *filioque*, a Byzantine theologian who maintained extensive contacts across the Latin world and who was willing and able to assimilate distinctively Latin Fathers such as Augustine into his theological purview. Palamas approached the Latin tradition with a hermeneutic of orthodoxy being convinced, like Aquinas, of the underlying catholicity and harmony of East and West. In all these respects, Palamas emerges as rather more 'Western' than many of his adversaries.

The chief opponents Gregory faced in the course of the Hesychast controversy—Barlaam, Akindynos, and Gregoras—all expressed bitter hostility towards the Latins and profound suspicion of the claims of reason and rational demonstration in theology. Indeed it is a great irony that while Palamite theology emerged victorious in the Byzantine world, it is often the anti-rational and anti-Latin rhetoric of Palamas' enemies that has held sway in subsequent Orthodox discourse. A prominent example is the invective of Kallistos Angelikoudes against Aquinas, more obviously indebted to Barlaam than to Palamas. There is nothing anti-rational or intrinsically anti-Latin about the theology of St Gregory Palamas.

The widespread assumption that there was a clear-cut confrontation between Palamism and Thomism in the Byzantine world is certainly overdue for revision. There was no such confrontation. Aquinas was, as we have seen, embraced with enthusiasm by Palamites and anti-Palamites alike, as indeed he was by unionists and anti-unionists. There was emphatically no default setting of either opposition or enthusiasm towards Aquinas among any of the many and various competing parties of the late Byzantine world.

The only sustained attempt to marshal Aquinas against Palamite theology came after the Hesychast controversy had been definitively settled. In this belated episode, Prochoros Kydones departed significantly from the angelic doctor on the pivotal issue of the character of the light of the Transfiguration. On this key matter, it is the leading Palamite after Gregory's death, Patriarch Philotheos Kokkinos, who emerges as closer to Thomas than was Prochoros. Prochoros' infidelity to Aquinas is also exposed by another arch-Palamite, the Monk-Emperor John Kantakuzene. Such instances leave the notion of a battle between Palamism and Thomism in late Byzantium in ruins.

This study has, naturally, paid due attention to those Byzantines for whom the encounter with Aquinas proved a catalyst for personal submission to the claims of the elder Rome—figures such as Demetrios (but not Prochoros) Kydones, Manuel Kalekas, and Maximos Chrysoberges. The association between admiration for Thomas and conversion to Roman Catholicism is doubtless an unsurprising one. But it is important to note that enthusiasm for Aquinas in such figures was invariably motivated in large measure by intra-Byzantine concerns: unionism and, especially, anti-Palamism. Over the latter half of the fourteenth century, anti-Palamism became an increasingly untenable position for a member of the Orthodox Church, leaving some with no option but to jump ship altogether. Such figures were, in short, as much pushed towards Thomas as they were propelled by him into the Roman Catholic Church. It was only by this curious and quasi-accidental process that anti-Palamism become associated with Thomism. The two positions are, at root, quite unrelated.

The passage of some Byzantine anti-Palamites to Roman Catholicism is, however, of less intrinsic significance and interest than the intriguing phenomenon of Palamite admiration for the angelic doctor. Far from being instinctive opponents of Aquinas, many committed Palamites embraced and made constructive use of him. Here we may recall John Kantakuzene, Neilos Kabasilas, and Theophanes of Nicaea. This capacity for critical but essentially positive reception of Aquinas remained an established feature of the Byzantine theological sphere down to its last days. Prominent anti-unionists and Palamites such as Makarios Makres, Joseph Bryennios, Mark of Ephesus, and, above all, Gennadios Scholarios all treated Thomas with respect and appropriated aspects of his work in support of their own theological endeavours. This critical but constructive mode of reception remained and remains open to Orthodox theologians to emulate—even if few have chosen to do so of late. But before enlarging further on the subsequent history and possibilities of such a mode of encounter, a further perspectival shift is in order. What, we may ask, does this study reveal about Thomas himself?

7.1. A BYZANTINE THOMAS

The reception history of Aquinas in the Orthodox world offers a perspective on Thomas rarely accounted for in contemporary scholarship. The very suggestion of an 'Eastern' Thomas is likely to be unfamiliar to many readers. Similarly surprising may be the sheer extent of Byzantine acquaintance and engagement with Aquinas. The Byzantines were vastly better informed about Latin theology than were the Latins about developments in the Greek world. What is perhaps even more remarkable is the consistency with which Aquinas has been recognized by the Orthodox as the principal authority and spokesman of Latin theology. This is an understanding that became established in the wake of the first translations and has endured to the present day in devotees and detractors alike. By contrast, Thomas' stature in the West has been subject to peaks and troughs of roller-coaster proportions. Only relatively fleetingly has he been ascribed in the West the kind of normative and authoritative status that he has long enjoyed in Eastern eyes. Whether by approbation or critique, the East has honoured Thomas far more consistently than has been the case in the West.

This study has also presented a Thomas in decided sympathy with the Greek world. His mastery of classical Greek philosophy and grounding in the Greek Fathers have won him recognition as an embodiment of a Christian Hellenism in figures as diverse as Demetrios Kydones, Gennadios Scholarios, and Georges Florovsky. Thomas' appeal to so many Orthodox writers across the centuries owes much to his Greek inheritance. This Greek dimension to Aquinas is rarely at the forefront of contemporary Thomistic studies.

Thomas has also been recognized by many Orthodox readers as a profoundly traditional theologian, theologizing from within the scriptural, patristic, and conciliar tradition of the Church. Again, the deeply traditional dimension of Thomas' work is not always sufficiently appreciated in contemporary scholarship. Thomas is valued by many Orthodox principally as a figure of synthesis and summation and not as the herald of a new theological dawn. He is received positively by virtue of his continuity and affinity with a long tradition of Byzantine scholasticism going back to the Christological debates of the fifth century and recapitulated in John of Damascus. Thomas' limpid and systematic methodological approach won him respect across the Orthodox theological spectrum. Even where his teachings failed to elicit the slightest sympathy, his method has been admired and emulated. Orthodox commentators have often discerned a natural progression between the Damascene and the angelic doctor. Like the Damascene, Aquinas has been widely received by the Orthodox as an exemplar of the proper and disciplined use of reason within theology—always, that is, in due subservience to revelation.

Some of the most sophisticated Orthodox readings of Aquinas have discerned in Aquinas a bridge figure, a theologian of the Church universal embracing East and West alike. For all his regrettable errors in respect of certain dogmatic matters, he has been received by figures such as John Kantakuzene, Neilos Kabasilas, Theophanes of Nicaea, and Gennadios Scholarios as an embodiment of the underlying congruity of the Greek and Latin instantiations of the Christian tradition. Such readings have tangible ecumenical implications.

This study of the Orthodox reception of Aquinas certainly serves to underpin some of the developments associated with the 'New Image of Thomas' outlined in Chapter 1. But it also goes beyond such welcome developments in building up a distinctly Byzantine image of Thomas. We have here a figure admired not so much for his own brilliancy but for his mastery of and fidelity to Greek patristic and philosophical sources, a figure received not as the voice of a new and superior theological methodology but as a fresh articulation of a shared tradition. A picture emerges here, in a nutshell, of a Byzantine Aquinas, as much at home on the shores of the Bosphorus as by the banks of the Tiber or the Seine. The Byzantine Aquinas deserves attention.

7.2. TOWARDS AN ORTHODOX RE-APPROPRIATION OF AQUINAS

The Orthodox reception of Aquinas has been subject to a great many developments over time. The most startling of these is evident in the contrast between Byzantine and twentieth-century readings. As we have seen, theologians of the Byzantine era studiously refrained, with very rare exceptions, from positing any sort of substantial methodological or theological gap between Aquinas and Orthodoxy. Critiques of Aquinas tend to be limited to the specific issues of contention between Greeks and Latins and do not fan-out into global confrontations between East and West, still less into metaphysical stand-offs between personalism and essentialism, mysticism and rationalism, apophaticism and cataphaticism, or Palamism and Thomism. Such dichotomies are very much the preserve of the modern Orthodox mindset and do not accurately reflect the Byzantine legacy.

Between the surprisingly positive Byzantine and largely negative modern Orthodox approaches to Thomas lies a long period often seen as a theological 'dark ages', a period of 'Babylonian captivity' or 'pseudomorphosis'. It has been a concern of this book to demonstrate that this was an era far removed from the common caricature of sterility and malformation and was, in fact, possessed of theologians of the highest calibre capable of sophisticated dialogue with and constructive embrace of Latin scholasticism. Aquinas is a figure of special interest and attention within this wider process of interaction, enthralling and stimulating many of the finest minds of the period. Even the less inspiring products of the encounter between Latin scholasticism and Orthodoxy, such as the theological manuals of the nineteenth and early twentieth centuries, are not to be simply written off as products of an 'arid' scholasticism, as if intellectual rigour, the careful use of sources, and systematic method were somehow foreign to Orthodoxy.

It is only with the Slavophiles in the early nineteenth century that an expressly reactive definition of Orthodoxy begins to take hold, shaped and inspired by German Idealism and Romanticism. Such oppositional theologizing became virtually normative in the twentieth century in the aftermath of the Russian Revolution. Indeed it is worth noting that the most oppositional phase of Orthodox theology was conditioned to some extent by vulnerability, the consequence of the collapse of a whole polity, and the attendant experience of emigration. Set adrift in a sea of Catholic and Protestant disinterest, it is perfectly understandable that so many Russian Orthodox theologians should have accentuated the differences between East and West, if only to get Orthodoxy taken seriously. Such conscious accentuation of difference was also very much the product of the shift of the focus of Orthodox theological endeavour from the seminaries, academies, and universities of Russia to the ecumenical and academic arenas of the West. One aspect of this oppositional strategy has been the elevation of Palamas to the status of an anti-Aquinas in response to the success of neo-Thomism. This strategy did indeed prove modestly successful in getting Orthodoxy noticed and has set the tone for theological endeavour across much of the Orthodox world ever since. The oppositional mode of Orthodox self-definition was perpetuated by the experience of the Cold War during which East and West functioned as axiomatic geopolitical opposites. In a bipolar world, nothing seems more natural than dichotomy. In our own globalized and multipolar world we may be better positioned to adopt a less dichotomous approach.

Reflecting on the reception history explored in this volume, it becomes clear that any sort of wholesale rejection of Aquinas and all he stands for is more the exception than the rule. While there are certainly voices prepared to denounce him at any given time, the Byzantine and early modern response to Thomas does not conform to the dominant modern narrative of East–West opposition. Despite its acutely vulnerable political and economic situation, Byzantium did not, even in its last decades, succumb to any reactive form of anti-Western self-definition. Even Mark of Ephesus could quote Thomas with approval while Gennadios Scholarios appropriates Aquinas with a sense of confidence in the Orthodox theological tradition quite incommensurate with the actual political situation of Orthodox Christians in the rapidly expanding Ottoman Empire. A certain confidence is also evident in the theological productions of the Ottoman era notwithstanding the irksomeness of the *Turkokrateia* and the pressures posed by Protestant missions and Catholic expansionism.

The oppositional theologizing that has dominated Orthodox discourse in the twentieth century is, then, a sign of weakness rather than strength—in Plato's words, a 'failing of the wing'.[1] A self-confident Orthodoxy has no need of a caricature of the West against which to model itself in reaction. A self-confident Orthodoxy need not fear the corrupting 'influence' of the West, nor be afraid to learn from and embrace the best of the West—Aquinas in particular. A self-confident Orthodoxy can afford to be generous.

The abandonment of the hackneyed East–West dichotomy is perhaps more to the ultimate purpose of this book than any specific insights or models or doctrines that might be drawn from Aquinas by the Orthodox. The very recognition that Aquinas might have something to offer is of more immediate moment than the precise nature of that offering. That said, some remarks on the possibilities for an Orthodox re-appropriation of Aquinas are in order.

By an 'Orthodox appropriation' I mean something akin to the approach of Gregory Palamas to the Latin West or of Thomas Aquinas to the Greek East, as delineated in the opening chapters of this book. For all its glaring errors, each recognizes the essential catholicity of the other's tradition and approaches it according to a hermeneutic of orthodoxy. Gennadios Scholarios serves as another useful paradigm: a fervent anti-unionist and devoted Palamite steeped in Thomas and profiting immensely from that immersion. And

---

[1] Plato, *Phaedrus*, 248c; cf. Plotinus, *Enneads*, 4.8.1.

Gennadios is hardly the only anti-unionist Palamite to have found much to admire in Aquinas: similar sentiments may be found in Neilos Kabasilas and Theophanes of Nicaea. The point is that there is no contradiction between an uncompromising Orthodoxy and a positive but discerning appropriation of Aquinas.

An Orthodoxy that refuses to have any truck with Aquinas is not only impoverished by that refusal but also untrue to itself. From his first emergence into the Byzantine world, Thomas has a exercised a profound impact on Orthodox theology, not only directly in such shining instances as Scholarios but also, by various mediations, throughout the long Latin-leaning phase of Orthodox theology and down to the academic theology of recent times. The Orthodox encounter with Thomas has, assuredly, been peppered with instances of capitulation to the claims of Rome and, more insidiously, with merely iterative and imitative forms of reception. But such examples hardly do justice to the long history of the Orthodox encounter with Aquinas. To disown this fruitful encounter is to disown a hefty part of the tradition of Orthodox theology.

The largely negative take on Aquinas in recent Orthodox theology has certainly had its upside. It has tended to go hand-in-hand with a welcome re-affirmation of the patristic tradition, with the accent on its mystical and ascetic dimensions. All this is profoundly salutary and its importance must not be underestimated. But there is a very grave risk that in this process of re-affirmation and retrieval such essential elements of the Orthodox experience may be taken to stand for the whole. Mysticism has an essential role to play within Orthodox theology, but so does reason. The apophatic and cataphatic ways are not opposites, but complementary and interdependent: pure apophaticism, if such a thing were possible, is tantamount to obfuscation. Asceticism, too, is a vital and distinctive manifestation of Orthodox tradition but it is not, and has never been, the sole reference point for Orthodox theology. Modern Orthodox theology too often presents a rather partial account of itself, one that fails to do justice to its own substantial scholastic inheritance, an inheritance going back almost a thousand years before 1354 and which enabled many Byzantines to recognize Thomas as one of their own.

An Orthodox re-appropriation of Thomas offers the promise that scholasticism need not remain forever a pejorative term in Orthodox circles. It offers a potential resource for the articulation of Orthodox theology of inestimable worth and utility, one which many

Orthodox theologians have been only too happy to employ in the past if not often in the present. Such an appropriation would serve to explode the very human and time-bound construct of an East–West dichotomy and to demonstrate the fundamental congruity and, so to say, consanguinity of Greek and Latin theological traditions. Such an appropriation would, in so doing, enable Orthodoxy to be true to itself, true to its inherent catholicity and to an orthodoxy neither occidental nor oriental but 'one in Christ Jesus'.

Bibliography
Main Bibliography

Primary Sources

Andrew of Rhodes
Candal, E., 'Andreae Rhodiensis, OP, inedita ad Bessarionem epistula', *OCP* 4 (1938), 329–70.

Anthimos of Athens
Dyobuniotes, K., «Ἀνθίμου Ἀθηνῶν λόγος ἀνέκδοτος περὶ τῶν τοῦ Ἁγίου Πνεύματος προόδων», Ἐπετηρὶς ᾿ Ἑταιρείας Βυζαντινῶν Σπουδῶν 7 (1930), 30–41.

Athanasios of Paros
Makarios of Corinth, Ἐπιτομὴ εἴτε συλλογὴ τῶν θείων τῆς πίστεως δογμάτων (Leipzig 1806).

Athanasius of Alexandria
Opitz, H.-G., *Athanasius Werke* 2.1 (1935), 1–42. [*De decretis*]

Barlaam the Calabrian
Fyrigos, A., *Barlaam Calabro: Epistole a Palamas* (Rome 1975).
——*Opere contro i Latini* (*Studi e Testi* 347 and 348; Vatican 1998).

Demetrios Kydones
Blum, W. (tr.), *Furcht vor dem Tod: Die Schrift des Demetrios Kydones „Über die Verachtung des Todes"* (Münster 1973).
Cammeli, G., *Démétrius Cydonès. Correspondance* (Paris 1930).
Candal, M., 'Demetrio Cidonio y el problema trinitario palamitico', *OCP* 28 (1962), 75–120. [= *De personarum proprietatibus in Trinitate ad Constantinum Asanem*]
Deckelmann, H., *Demetrii Cydonii De Contemnenda Morte* (Leipzig 1901 (repr. 1987)).
Kalamakes, D., Ἀνθολόγιον ἐκ τῶν ἔργων Αὐγουστίνου Ἱππῶνος ἐξελληνισθὲν ὑπὸ Δημητρίου τοῦ Κυδώνη (Athens 1996).
Loenertz, R.-J., *Démétrius Cydonès. Correspondance* (2 vols.) (*Studi e testi* 186 and 208; Vatican City 1956, 1960).

Tinnefeld, F. (tr.), *Demetrios Kydones: Briefe* (5 vols.) (*Bibliothek der griechischen Literatur* 12, 16, 33, 50, 60; Stuttgart 1981–2003).

Δημητρίου Κυδώνη, Θωμᾶ Ἀκυινάτου: Σούμμα Θεολογική, ἐξελληνισθεῖσα (*Corpus Philosophorum Graecorum Recentiorum* II 15 (G. Leontsinis and A. Glycophrydi-Leontsini), 16 (P. Demetracopoulos), 17a (P. Demetracopoulos and M. Brentanou), 17b (S. Sideri and P. Photopoulou), 18 (E. Kalokairinou (Athens 1976–2002). [= *Summa theologiae* II^a II^ae 1–79]

Dositheos II (Notaras) of Jerusalem
Τόμος Καταλλαγῆς (Jassy 1694).
Τόμος Ἀγάπης κατὰ Λατίνων (Jassy 1698).
Τόμος Χαρᾶς (Râmnicu-Vâlcea 1705).

Elias Meniates
Πέτρα σκανδάλου (Leipzig 1718).
Διδαχαὶ εἰς τὴν Ἁγίαν καὶ Μεγάλην Τεσσαρακοστὴν καὶ εἰς ἄλλας Κυριακὰς τοῦ ἐνιαυτοῦ καὶ ἐπισήμους ἑορτάς (Venice 1716).

Eugenios Boulgaris
Θεολογικόν (Venice 1872).
Βιβλιάριον κατὰ Λατίνων (Constantinople 1756).

Eustratios Argenti
Σύνταγμα κατὰ Ἀζύμων (Leipzig 1760).

Gabriel Severos
Συνταγμάτιον περὶ τῶν ἁγίων καὶ ἱερῶν μυστηρίων (Venice 1600).
Chrysanthos (Notaras) of Jerusalem, Συνταγμάτιον περὶ τῶν ὀφφικίων, κληρικάτων καὶ ἀρχοντικίων τῆς τοῦ Χριστοῦ ἁγίας ἐκκλησίας (Bucharest 1715).

George Koressios
Διάλεξις μετά τινος τῶν φράρων in the collected volume of texts dealing with the procession and the papacy published by Nikodemos Metaxas (Constantinople 1627). [Του Μακαριωτάτου πατρός ημών Μελετίου Αρχιεπισκόπου Αλεξανδρείας [. . .]]
Ἐγχειρίδιον περὶ τῆς ἐκπορεύσις τοῦ ἁγίου πνεύματος, in Dositheos of Jerusalem, Τόμος Καταλλαγῆς, 276–410.

George (Gennadios) Scholarios
Gill, J., *Orationes Georgii Scholarii in Concilio Florentino habitae* (Rome 1964).

Petit, L., X. Sidéridés and M. Jugie, *Oeuvres complètes de Georges Scholarios* (8 vols.) (Paris 1928–36). [= OC]

Gregory Akindynos
Hero, A., *Letters of Gregory Akindynos* (Dumbarton Oaks Texts 7; Washington, DC 1983).

Gregory Palamas
Chrestou, P. (*et al.*), Γρηγορίου τοῦ Παλαμᾶ συγγράμματα (5 vols.) (Thessalonica 1962–92).
Meyendorff, J., *Grégoire Palamas. Défense des saints hésychastes* (*Spicilegium Sacrum Lovaniense. Études et documents* 30; Louvain 1973). [= *Triads*]
Sinkewicz, R., *Saint Gregory Palamas, The One Hundred and Fifty Chapters* (*Studies and Texts* 83; Toronto 1988). [= *Capita*]

Jeremiah II (Tranos)
Acta et Scripta Theologorum Wirtembergensium et Patriarchae Constantinopolitani, D. Hieremiae (Wittenberg 1584). [ET G. Mastrantonis, *Augsburg and Constantinople: The correspondence between the Tubingen theologians and Patriarch Jeremiah II of Constantinople on the Augsburg Confession* (Boston 1982)]

John Chortasmenos
Hunger, H., *Johannes Chortasmenos (ca. 1370–ca. 1436/37). Briefe, Gedichte und kleine Schriften. Einleitung, Regesten, Prosopographie* (Wiener Byzantinische Studien 7; Vienna 1969).

John of Damascus
Holl, K., *Die Sacra Parallela des Johannes Damascenus* (Texte und Untersuchungen 16; Leipzig 1897).
Kotter, B., *Die Schriften des Johannes von Damaskos* (5 vols.) (Patristische Texte und Studien 7, 12, 17, 22, 29; Berlin 1969–88).

John VI Kantakuzenos
Voordeckers, E. and F. Tinnefeld, *Iohannis Cantacuzeni. Refutationes duae prochori cydonii et disputatio cum Paulo Patriarcha Latino epistulis septem tradita* (CCSG 16; Turnhout 1987).
Soteropoulos, Ch., ' Ἰωάννου ΣτΚαντακουζηνοῦ Κατὰ ' ΙουδαίωνΛόγοι Ἐννέα (Athens 1990).

John Kyparissiotes
Candal, M., 'Juan Ciparisiota y el problema trinitario palamítico', *OCP* 25 (1959), 127–64.

John Plousiadenos (Joseph of Methone)
Cantarella, R., 'Canone greco inedito di Giuseppe vescovo di Methone in onore di San Tomaso d'Aquino', *Archivum Fratum Praedicatorum* 4 (1934), 145–85.

Joseph Bryennios
Argyriou, A., «' Ἰωσὴφ τοῦ Βρυεννίου μετά τινος ' Ἰσμαηλίτου Διάλεξις ' Ἐπετηρὶς ' Ἐταιρείας Βυζαντινῶν Σπουδᾶδ (1967), 141–95.
Boulgaris, E., ' Ἰωσὴφ Μοναχοῦ τοῦ Βρυεννίου Τὰ Εὑρεθέντα (3 vols.) (Leipzig 1768, 1784).
Papadopoulos-Kerameus, A., *Varia Graeca Sacra* (St Petersburg 1909), 295–6. [= *Testament*]
Tomadakes, N., «Ἐκ τῆς βυζαντινῆς ἐπιστολογραφίας. Ἰωσὴφ μοναχοῦ τοῦ Βρυεννίου Ἐπιστολαὶ Λ' καὶ πρὸς αὐτὸν Γ'», Ἐπετηρὶς ' Ἐταιρείας Βυζαντινῶν Σπουδῶν 46 (1983–6), 283–362.

Kallistos Angelikoudes
Koutsas, S., 'Callistos Angelicoudès. Quatre traités hésychastes inédits. Introduction, texte critique, traduction et notes', Θεολογία 67 (1996), 109–56, 316–60, 518–29, 696–755; 68 (1997), 454–88.
Papadopoulos, S., Καλλίστου Ἀγγελικούδη κατὰ Θωμᾶ Ἀκινάτου (Athens 1970).

Makarios Makres
Argyriou, A., *Macaire Macrès et la polémique contre l'Islam* (*Studi e Testi* 314; Vatican City 1986).
——Μακαρίου τοῦ Μακρῆ συγγράμματα (Βυζαντινὰ Κείμενα καὶ Μελέται 25; Thessalonica 1996).

Manuel Kalekas
Demetracopoulos, J. A., 'Manuel Calecas' Translation of Boethius' *De Trinitate*', *Synthesis Philosophica* 39 (2005), 85–118.
Dositheos II of Jerusalem, Τόμος Ἀγάπης κατὰ Λατίνων (q.v.), 413–90. [Περὶ θεολογίας=De fide deque principiis catholicæ fidei (PG 152 429–661)]
Loenertz, R.-J., *Correspondance* (*Studi e Testi* 152, Vatican City 1950).

Mark of Ephesus
Gass, W., *Mystik des Nikolaus Cabasilas vom Leben in Christo*, Appendix 2, 217–32). [= *Syllogistic Chapters against the Heresy of the Akindynists concerning the Distinction between the Divine Essence and Energies*]
Petit, L., *Marci Eugenici Metropolitae Ephesi opera anti-unionistica*, 10/2 (Rome 1977). [= PO 17]

Matthew Angelos Panaretos
Beveridge, W., Συνοδικὸν sive Pandectae canonum ss. apostolorum, et conciliorum ab ecclesia Graeca receptorum (II 273–305) (Oxford 1672). [= On
the Holy and Ecumenical Council which Restored Photios to the Throne
of Constantinople and Overcame the Division of the Churches of Old
and New Rome]
Buda, C., 'Il tomismo a Bisanzio nel secolo XIV. Una polemica Bizantina
del secolo XIV', Archivio Storico per la Calabria e la Lucania 26 (1957),
291–323; 27 (1958), 3–33.
Risso, P., 'Matteo Angelo Panaretos e cinque suoi opuscoli', Roma e l'oriente
8 (1914), 91–105, 162–79, 231–7, 274–90; 9 (1915), 112–20, 202–6;
10 (1915), 63–77, 146–64, 238–51; 11 (1916), 28–35, 76–80, 154–60.

Maximos Margounios
Fedalto, G., Massimo Margunio e il suo commento al De Trinitate di
S. Agostino (1558) (Brescia 1968).

Meletios Pigas
Dositheos II of Jerusalem, Τόμος Χαρᾶς (q.v.), 553–609. [Discourse on the
question as to which is the True Catholic Church [...]. And against the
Rule of the Pope, published as Κατὰ τῆς ἀρχῆς τοῦ Πάππα]
Legrand, E., Lettres de Mélétius Pigas: antérieures à sa promotion au Patri-
arcat (Bibliothèque grecque vulgaire 9; Paris 1902).
Ὀρθόδοξος διδασκαλία (Vilnius 1596; second edition 1769).
Renaudot, E., Gennadii Patriarchae Constantinopolitani Homiliae de
Eucharistia (Paris 1709), 100–49. [= second part of Περὶ τῶν ἀχράντων
μυστηρίων]

Meletios Syrigos
Ἀντίρρησις κατὰ τῶν καλβινικῶν κεφαλαίων και ἐρωτήσεων Κυρίλλου του
Λουκάρεως (Bucharest 1690).

Neilos Damylas
Ἐκκλησιαστικὴ Ἀλήθεια 15th Year (1895-6) 382-3, 391-2; 16th Year
(1896-7), 7-8, 61-3.

Neilos Kabasilas
Candal, E., Nilus Cabasilas et theologia S. Thomae de processione Spiritus
Sancti (Vatican City 1945).
——'La "Regla teológica" de Nilo Cabásilas', OCP 23 (1957), 240–56.
Kislas, T., 'Nilus Cabasilas et son traité sur le Saint-Esprit' (Diss. University
of Strasbourg 1998).
——Nilus Cabasilas. Sur le Saint-Esprit (Paris 2001).

Nicholas Kabasilas
Angelopoulos, A., Νικόλαος Καβάσιλας Χαμαετός: Ἡ ζωή καὶ το ἔργον αὐτοῦ (Thessalonica 1970), 111–13.
Bornert, R. et al., *Explication de la Divine Liturgie* (SC 4 bis; Paris 1967).
Congourdeau, M.-H., *La Vie en Christ* (SC 355, 361; Paris 1989, 90).
Demetracopoulos, J. A., 'Nicholas Cabasilas' *Quaestio de rationis valore*: An Anti-Palamite Defense of Secular Wisdom', Βυζαντινὰ 19 (1998), 77–83.
Garzya, A., 'Un opuscule inédit de Nicolas Cabasilas', *Byzantion* 24 (1954), 521–32.
Jugie, M., *Homélies mariales byzantines* II (PO 19; Paris 1926), 465–510.

Nicholas Koursoulas
Σύνοψις τῆς ἱερᾶς θεολογίας, φιλοπονηθεῖσα εἰς ὠφέλειαν τῶν ὀρθοδόξων φιλομαθῶν (2 vols.) (Zakynthos 1862).

Nikephoros Gregoras
Bekker, I. and L. Schopen, *Nicephori Gregorae historiae Byzantinae* (3 vols.) (*Corpus scriptorum historiae Byzantinae* 6, 7, 8; Bonn 1829–55).

Nikodemos the Hagiorite
With Makarios of Corinth:
Φιλοκαλία τῶν ἱερῶν νηπτικῶν (Venice 1782; 3rd edn. Athens 1957–63).
Patapios, Hieromonk and Archbishop Chrysostomos, *Manna from Athos*: *The Issue of Frequent Communion on the Holy Mountain in the Late Eighteenth and Early Nineteenth Centuries* (Oxford 2006). [ET of Περὶ συνεχοῦς μεταλήψεως (*Treatise on Frequent Communion*) (Venice 1783)]
Ἀόρατος πόλεμος (Venice 1796). [= Lorenzo Scupoli, *Combattimento spirituale*]
Γυμνάσματα πνευματικά (Venice 1800). [= Pietro Pinamonti's version of the *Spiritual Exercises* of Ignatius Loyola]
Ἐξομολογητάριον (Venice 1794).
Πηδάλιον τῆς νοητῆς νηός (Leipzig 1800).

Philotheos Kokkinos
Kaïmakes, D., Φιλοθέου Κοκκίνου δογματικὰ ἔργα (volume I) (*Thessalonian Byzantine Writers* 3; Thessalonica 1983).

Photios of Constantinople
Laourdas, B. and L. Westerink (eds.), *Photii Patriarchae Constantinopolitani Epistulae et Amphilochia* (6 vols.) (Leipzig 1983–8).

Prochoros Kydones
De essentia et operatione 1–2 (PG 151 1191–1242 [attributed to Akindynos]);
6 (M. Candal, 'El libro VI de Prócoro Cidonio [sobre la luz tabórica]', *OCP*
20 (1954), 247–96).
Hunger, H., *Prochoros Kydones, Übersetzung von acht Briefen des Hl. Augustinus* (Wiener Studien 9; Vienna 1984).
——*Prochoros Kydones' Übersetzungen von S. Augustinus, De libero arbitrio I 1–90, und Ps.-Augustinus, De decem plagis Aegyptiorum* (Wiener Studien 14; Vienna 1990).
Nikitas, D., *Boethius, De topicis differentiis καὶ οἱ βυζαντινὲς μεταφράσεις τοῦ Μανουὴλ ᾿Ολοβώλου καὶ τοῦ Προχόρου Κυδώνη*(*Corpus philosophorum Medii Aevi*. Philosophi Byzantini 5; Athens, Paris, Brussels 1990).
Tinnefeld, F., 'Ein Text des Prochoros Kydones in Vat. gr. 609 über die Bedeutung der Syllogismen für die theologische Erkenntnis', in A. Schoors and P. van Deun (eds.), *Philohistôr: Miscellanea in honorem Caroli Laga septuagenarii* (Louvain 1994), 520–3.

Slyvester Syropoulos
Laurent, V., *Les «Mémoires» du grand Ecclésiarque de L'Église de Constantinople Sylvestre Syropoulos sur le concile de Florence (1438–1439)* (Concilium Florentinum: Documenta et Scriptores 9; Paris 1971).

Theodoret of Cyrrhus
Ettlinger, G., *Theodoret of Cyrus, Eranistes: Critical Text and Prolegomena* (Oxford 1975).

Theophanes of Nicaea
Jugie, M., *Theophanes Nicaenus. Sermo in sanctissimam Deiparam* (*Lateranum*. Nova series 1; Rome 1935).
Polemis, I., *Θεοφάνους Νικαίας Ἀπόδειξις ὅτι ἐδύνατο ἐξ ἀϊδίου γεγενῆσθαι τὰ ὄντα καὶ ἀνατροπὴ ταύτης* (*Corpus Philosophorum Medii Aevi*. Philosophi Byzantini 10; Athens 2000).
Soteropoulos, Ch., *Θεοφάνους Γ΄ ἐπισκόπου Νικαίας περὶ Θαβωρίου φωτός, λόγοι πέντε* (Athens 1990). [Accessed via the *TLG*]

Theophilos Korydaleus
Zoernickau, A., *Tractatus Theologici Orthodoxi de Processione Spiritus Sancti a Solo Patre* II (Königsberg 1775), 1069–76, 1076–80. [= *Dogmatic Letter* and *Solutions of Arguments relating to the Procession of the Holy Spirit*]

Theophylact of Ochird
Gautier, P., *Theophylacte d'Achrida: Discours, traités, poésies* (Thessalonica 1980).

Vincent Damodos
Bobou-Stamate, V., Βικέντιος Δαμοδός. Συνταγμάτιον τῆς Μεταφυσικῆς (Ioannina 2002).
Metallinos, G., Βικέντιου Δαμοδόυ Θεολογία δογματικὴ κατά συντομίαν ἤ τε συνταγμάτιον θεολογικόν (Athos 2008).

Secondary and Modern Sources

Alcalay, C., 'Le _parisinus graecus_ 135: un hommage à Jean Cantacuzène? Étude historique d'un livre de Job du XIVe siècle', _Byzantion_ 78 (2008), 404–80.
Alexander, P., 'Church Councils and Patristic Authority: The Iconoclastic Councils of Hiereia (754) and St Sophia (815)', _Harvard Studies in Classical Philology_ 63 (1958), 493–505.
Androutsos, C., Δογματικὴ τῆς Ὀρθοδόξου Ἀνατολικῆς Ἐκκλησίας (Athens 1907).
——Σύστημα Ἠθικῆς (Athens 1925).
Angelou, A., '"Who am I?" Scholarios' Answers and the Hellenic Identity', in Φιλέλλην, _Studies in Honour of Robert Browning_ (ed. Constantinides et al.) (Venice 1996), 1–19.
Antoniades, V., _Die Staatslehre des Thomas ab Aquino_ (Leipzig 1890).
——Ἐγχειρίδιον κατὰ Χριστὸν Ἠθικῆς (2 vols.) (Constantinople 1927).
Antonova, C., _Space, Time, and Presence in the Icon: Seeing the World with the Eyes of God_ (Farnham 2010).
——'On the Problem of "Reverse Perspective": Definitions East and West', _Leonardo_ 43 (2010), 464–9.
Balthasar, H. Urs von, _The Glory of the Lord: A Theological Aesthetics_ III (Edinburgh 1986).
Barber, C. and D. Jenkins, _Medieval Greek Commentaries on the Nicomachean Ethics_ (Leiden 2009).
Barbour, H., _The Byzantine Thomism of Gennadios Scholarios and his Translation of Armandus de Bellovisu on the_ De ente et essentia _of Thomas Aquinas_ (Studi Tomistici 53; Vatican City 1993).
Bardy, G., 'La littérature patristique des "Quaestiones et Responsiones" sur l'Écriture sainte', _Revue Biblique_ 41 (1932) 210–36, 341–69, 515–37; 42 (1933) 14–30, 211–29, 328–52.
Barnes, M. R., 'De Régnon Reconsidered', _Augustinian Studies_ 26 (1995), 51–79 'Augustine in Contemporary Trinitarian Theology', _Theological Studies_ 56 (1995), 237–50.
Beck, H.-G., 'Der Kampf um den thomistischen Theologiebegriff in Byzanz', _Divus Thomas_ 13 (1935), 3–22.
——_Vorsehung und Vorherbestimmung in der theologischen Literatur der Byzantiner_ (OCA 114; Rome 1937).
——_Kirche und theologische Literatur im Byzantinischen Reich_ (Munich 1959).

—'Humanismus und Palamismus' [with responses by Schirò and Meyendorff], *Actes du XIIe Congrès international des études byzantines: Rapports III* (Ochrid 1961), 1–26.

—*Geschichte der orthodoxen Kirche im byzantinischen Reich* (Göttingen 1980).

Benakis, L., 'Commentaries and Commentators on the Logical Works of Aristotle in Byzantium', in *Gedankenzeichen* (Festschrift Klaus Oehler) (Tübingen 1988), 3–12.

—'Commentaries and Commentators on the Works of Aristotle (except the Logical Ones) in Byzantium', in *Historia Philosophiae Medii Aevi* (Festschrift Kurt Flasch) (Amsterdam 1991), 45–54.

—'Lateinische Literatur in Byzanz. Die Übersetzungen philosophischer Texte', in Φιλέλλην, *Studies in Honour of Robert Browning* (ed. C. Constantinides et al.) (Venice 1996), 35–42.

—«Ἡ Παρουσία τοῦ Θωμᾶ Ἀκινάτη στό Βυζάντιο», in *Ζῶ δὲ οὐκετι ἐγώ, ζῆ ἐν ἐμοὶ Χριστὸς* (Festschrift Archbishop Demetrios of America) (Athens 2002).

Bentley Hart, D., *The Beauty of the Infinite* (Grand Rapids, MI 2004).

—'The Mirror of the Infinite: Gregory of Nyssa on the *Vestigia Trinitatis*', in S. Coakley (ed.), *Re-thinking Gregory of Nyssa* (Oxford 2004), 111–32.

—'The Myth of Schism', in F. Murphy (ed.), *Ecumenism Today: The Universal Church in the 21st Century* (Aldershot 2008), 95–106.

Benz, E., *Wittenberg und Byzanz. Zur Begegnung und Auseinandersetzung der Reformation und der Östlich-orthodoxen Kirche* (Marburg 1949).

Berdiaev, N., Review of G. Florovsky, *Puti russkogo bogosloviya*, *Put'* 53 (1937), 53–65.

Bird, R. and B. Jakim, *On Spiritual Unity: A Slavophile Reader* (Hudson, NY 1998).

Blanchet, M.-H., *Georges-Gennadios Scholarios (vers 1400–vers 1472): un intellectuel orthodoxe face à la disparition de l'empire Byzantin* (Paris 2008).

Bobou-Stamate, V., Βικέντιος Δαμοδός. Βιογραφία—Ἐργογραφία 1700–1754 (Athens 1998).

Bolotov, B., 'Thesen über das „Filioque". Von einem russischen Theologen', *Revue internationale de théologie* 6 (1898), 681–712.

Boulnois, M.-O., *Le paradoxe trinitaire chez Cyrille d'Alexandrie: herméneutique, analyses philosophiques et argumentation théologique* (Paris 1994).

Bouvy, E., 'Saint Thomas: Ses traducteurs byzantins', *Revue Augustinienne* 16 (1910), 401–8.

Bradshaw, D., *Aristotle East and West* (Cambridge 2004).

Buda, C., 'Influsso del Tomismo in Bisanzio nel secolo XIV', *BZ* 49 (1956), 318–31.

Bulgakov, S., *Du verbe incarné* (tr. C. Andronikof) (Lausanne 1982); (tr. B. Jakim) *The Lamb of God* (Grand Rapids, MI 2008).

—— *Le buisson ardent* (tr. C. Andronikof) (Lausanne 1987); *The Burning Bush* (tr. T.A. Smith) (Grand Rapids, MI 2009).

—— *La lumière sans déclin* (tr. C. Andronikof) (Lausanne 1990).

—— 'The Eucharistic Dogma', in B. Jakim (tr.), *The Holy Grail and the Eucharist* (Hudson, NY 1997), 76–83.

—— *L'icône et sa veneration* (tr. C. Andronikof) (Lausanne 1996).

—— *The Bride of the Lamb* (tr. B. Jakim) (Grand Rapids, MI 2002).

—— *The Comforter* (tr. B. Jakim) (Grand Rapids, MI 2004).

Candal, E., 'Fuentes Palamíticas. Diálogo de Jorge Facrasí sobre el contradictorio de Pálamas con Nicéforo Grégoras', *OCP* 16 (1950), 303–57.

Cañellas, J., *La résistance d'Akindynos à Grégoire Palamas: enquête historique, avec traduction et commentaire de quatre traités édités récemment* (Louvain 2006).

Catoire, A., 'Philosophie byzantine et philosophie scolastique. Simples notes', *EO* 12 (1909), 193–201.

Christov, I., 'Kallistos Angelikoudes' Critical Account of Thomistic and Orthodox Anthropology', *Synthesis Philosophica* 39 (2005), 73–83.

Citterio, E., *L'orientamento ascetico-spirituale di Nicodemo Aghiorita* (Alexandria 1987).

—— 'Nicodemo Agiorita', in G. and V. Conticello (eds.), *La théologie byzantine et sa tradition* (vol. 2) (q.v.), 905–78.

Clément, O., *Orient-Occident: Deux passeurs, Vladimir Lossky et Paul Evdokimov* (Geneva 1985).

Congar, Y., 'Neuf cents ans après: Notes sur le 'Schisme oriental', in *L'Église et les églises, 1054–1954: Neuf siècles de douloureuse séparation entre l'Orient et l'Occident* (Festschrift Lambert Beauduin) (Chevetogne 1954) I, 3–95.

Congourdeau, M.-H., 'Notes sur les Dominicains de Constantinople au début du 14 siècle', *REB* 45 (1987), 175–81.

—— 'Frère Simon le Constantinopolitain, OP (1235?–1325?)', *REB* 45 (1987), 165–74.

Conomos, D., 'Experimental Polyphony, "According to the ... Latins" in Late Byzantine Psalmody', *Early Music History* 2 (1982), 1–16.

—— 'Music as Religious Propaganda: Venetian Polyphony and a Byzantine Response to the Council of Florence', in J. Behr et al. (eds.), *Abba: The Tradition of Orthodoxy in the West* (Festschrift Kallistos Ware) (Crestwood, NY 2003), 111–34.

Constas, N., 'Mark Eugenikos', in G. and V. Conticello (eds.), *La théologie byzantine et sa tradition* (vol. 2) (q.v), 411–64.

Conticello, G. and V. (eds.), *La théologie byzantine et sa tradition* (vol. 2) (Turnhout 2002).

Daley, B., 'Boethius' Theological Tracts and Early Byzantine Scholasticism', *Mediaeval Studies* 46 (1984), 158–91.

Damalas, N., *Περὶ Ἀρχῶν Ἐπιστημονικῶν τε καὶ ' Ἐκκλησιαστικῶν τῆς Ὀρθοδόξου Θεολογίας* (Leipzig 1865).

Darrouzès, J., 'Textes synodaux chypriotes', *REB* 37 (1979), 5–122.

——Review of Zeses (q.v.), *REB* 39 (1981) 350–1.

Delacroix-Besnier, C., *Les dominicains et la chrétienté grecque aux XIVe et XVe siècles* (*Collection de l'École française de Rome*, 23; Rome 1997).

Demetracopoulos, J., *Αὐγουστῖνος καὶ Γρηγόριος Παλαμᾶς. Τὰ προβλήματα τῶν Ἀριστοτελικῶν κατηγοριῶν καὶ τῆς Τριαδικῆς ψυχοθεολογίας* (Athens 1997).

——«*Ὁ αντιπληθωνισμός τού Γεωργίου Γενναδίου Σχολαρίου ως ρίζα τού φιλοθωμισμού του και ο αντιχριστιανισμός τού Γεωργίου Πλήθωνος Γεμιστού ως ρίζα τού αντιαριστοτελισμού του*», *Λακωνικά* 37 (2000) 5–8 and 38 (2001) 3–5. [Abridged version of 2002 article]

——'Georgios Gennadios II—Scholarios' *Florilegium Thomisticum*. His early abridgment of various chapters and quaestiones of Thomas Aquinas' *Summae* and his anti-Plethonism', *Recherches de théologie et philosophie médiévales* 69 (2002), 117–71.

——'Georgios Scholarios—Gennadios II's Florilegium Thomisticum II (*De Fato*) and its anti-Plethonic Tenor', *Recherches de théologie et philosophie médiévales* 74 (2007), 301–76.

——'Demetrius Cydones' Translation of Bernardus Guidonis' List of Thomas Aquinas' Writings and the Historical Roots of Byzantine Thomism', in A. Speer and D. Wirmer (eds.), *1308: Eine Topographie historischer Gleichzeitigkeit* (Berlin 2010), 827–82.

Demetracopoulos, P., 'Demetrius Kydones' Translation of the Summa Theologica', *JÖB* 32 (1982), 311–19.

Demetrakopoulos, A., ' *Ὀρθόδοξος ' Ἑλλ*(Leipzig 1872).

Demos, R., 'The Neo-Hellenic Enlightenment (1750–1821)', *Journal of the History of Ideas* 19 (1958), 523–41.

Denissoff, E., *L'Église russe devant le thomisme* (Paris 1936).

——*Maxime le Grec et l'Occident: Contribution à l'histoire de la pensée religieuse et philosophique de Michel Trivolis* (Paris 1943).

Dennis, G., 'Reality in the Letters of Demetrius Cydones', in *Porphyrogenita* (Festschrift Julian Chrysostomides, ed. C. Dendrinos et al.) (Aldershot 2003), 401–10.

Divry, É., *La transfiguration selon l'orient et l'occident: Grégoire Palamas, Thomas d'Aquin: vers un dénouement oecuménique* (Paris 2009).

Dondaine, A., 'Contra Graecos. Premiers écrits polémiques des Dominicains d'Orient', *Archivium Fratrum Praedicatorum* 21 (1951), 320–446.

Dörries, H., 'Eratopokriseis', *Reallexikon für Antike und Christentum* 6 (1966), 347–70.

Dvornik, F., 'The Kiev State and Its Relations with Western Europe', *Transactions of the Royal Historical Society* (Fourth Series) 29 (1947), 27–46.

Ebbesen, S. and J. Pinborg, 'Gennadius and Western Scholasticism: Radulphus Brito's Ars vetus in Greek Translation', *Classica et Mediaevalia* 33 (1981–2), 263–319.

Evdokimov, P., *L'Orthodoxie* (Neuchâtel 1959).

——*In the World, of the Church: A Paul Evdokimov Reader* (New York 2001).

Fahey, M. and J. Meyendorff, *Trinitarian Theology East and West: St Thomas Aquinas—St Gregory Palamas* (Patriarch Athenagoras Memorial Lectures; Boston, MA 1977).

Flogaus, R., 'Der heimliche Blick nach Westen: zur Rezeption von Augustins *De trinitate* durch Gregorios Palamas', *JÖB* 46 (1996), 275–97.

——*Theosis bei Palamas und Luther: ein Beitrag zum ökumenischen Gespräch* (Göttingen 1997).

——'Palamas and Barlaam Revisited: A Reassessment of East and West in the Hesychast Controversy of 14th Century Byzantium', *SVQ* 42 (1998), 1–32.

——'Inspiration—Exploitation—Distortion: The Use of St Augustine in the Hesychast Controversy', in G. Demacopoulos and A. Papanikolaou (eds.), *Orthodox Readings of Augustine* (New York 2008), 63–80.

Florensky, P., *The Trinity—St Sergius Lavra and Russia* (New Haven, CT 1995).

——*The Pillar and Ground of the Truth* (Princeton, NJ 1997).

——*Beyond Vision: Essays on the Perception of Art* (Chicago, IL 2006).

Florovsky, G., 'The Legacy and Task of Orthodox Theology', *Anglican Theological Review* 31 (1948), 65–71.

——'The Doctrine of the Church and the Ecumenical Problem', *Ecumenical Review* 2 (1950), 152–61.

——Review of L. Zander, *Vision and Action* (London 1952), in *Ecumenism I: A Doctrinal Approach* (Vaduz 1989) [*CW* XIII], 185–92.

——Review of V. Lossky, *Mystical Theology of the Eastern Church* (London 1957), *The Journal of Religion* 38 (1958), 207–8.

——'St Gregory Palamas and the Tradition of the Fathers', *Sobornost* 4.4 (1961), 165–76.

——*Collected Works* (Belmont, MA/Vaduz 1972–89). [= *CW*]

——'Patriarch Jeremiah II and the Lutheran Divines', in *Christianity and Culture* (Belmont, MA 1974) [*CW* II], 143–55.

——'*Cur Deus Homo?* The Motive of the Incarnation', in *Creation and Redemption* (Belmont, MA 1976) [*CW* III], 163–70.

—— *Ways of Russian Theology* (2 vols.) (Belmont, MA 1979; Vaduz 1987).
[*CW* V and VI]

—— *The Byzantine Fathers of the Sixth to Eighth Century* (Vaduz 1987). [*CW* IX]

—— 'The Tragedy of Christian Divisions', in *Ecumenism I: A Doctrinal Approach* (Vaduz 1989) [*CW* XIII], 28–33.

Gallaher, B., 'Florovsky on Reading the Life of St Seraphim', *Sobornost*/ECR 27.1 (2005), 58–70.

—— 'The Christological Focus of Vladimir Solov'ev's Sophiology', *Modern Theology* 25 (2009), 617–46.

Gass, W., *Die Mystik des Nikolaus Cabasilas vom Leben in Christo* (Leipzig 1899).

Geanakoplos, D., *Byzantine East and Latin West: Two Worlds of Christendom in Middle Ages and Renaissance* (New York 1966).

—— *Interaction of the 'Sibling' Byzantine and Western Cultures in the Middle Ages and Renaissance (330–1600)* (New Haven, CT 1976).

Gemeinhardt, P., *Die Filioque-Kontroverse zwischen Ost- und Westkirche im Frühmittelalter* (Berlin 2002).

Gigante, M., 'La cultura Latina a Bizanzio nel secolo XIII', *La parola del passato* 82 (1962), 32–51.

Gill, J., *The Council of Florence* (Cambridge 1959).

—— *Personalities of the Council of Florence* (Oxford 1964).

—— *Byzantium and the Papacy 1198–1400* (New Brunswick, NJ 1979).

Gillet, L., *Orthodox Spirituality: An Outline of the Orthodox Ascetical and Mystical Tradition* (London 1945).

Glycofrydi-Leontsini, A., 'La traduzione in Greco delle opere di Tomasso d'Aquino', *Nicolaus* 3 (1975), 423–8.

—— 'Demetrius Cydones as a Translator of Latin Texts', in *Porphyrogenita* (Festschrift Julian Chrysostomides, ed. C. Dendrinos et al.) (Aldershot 2003), 175–85.

Gontikakis, V., *Hymn of Entry* (New York 1984). [ET of Εἰσοδικόν· Στοιχεῖα λειτουργικῆς βιώσεως τοῦ μυστηρίου τῆς ἑνότητος μέσα στὴν Ὀρθόδοξη Ἐκκλησία (Athos 1974)]

Gouillard, J., 'Les influences latines dans l'œuvre théologique de Manuel Calécas', *EO* 37 (1938), 36–52.

—— 'L'Autoportrait d'un sage du XIVe siècle', *Actes du XIVe Congrès international des études byzantines* II (Bucharest 1971), 103–8.

Graumann, T., *Die Kirche der Väter: Vätertheologie und Väterbeweis in den Kirchen des Ostens bis zum Konzil von Ephesus (431)* (Tübingen 2002).

Grumel, V., 'Grégoire Palamas, Duns Scot et Georges Scholarios devant le problème de la simplicité divine', *EO* 34 (1935), 84–96. [Review of S. Guichardan, *Le problème de la simplicité divine en Orient et en Occident aux XIVe et XVe siècles: Grégoire Palamas, Duns Scot, Georges Scholarios; étude de théologie comparée* (Lyon 1933)]

Halleux, A. de, 'Palamisme et Scolastique: exclusivisme dogmatique ou pluriformité théologique?', *Revue Théologique de Louvain* 4 (1973), 409–22.

Haney, J., *From Italy to Muscovy: The Life and Works of Maxim the Greek* (Munich 1973).

Hannick, C. and K.-P. Todt, 'Jérémie II Tranos', in G. and V. Conticello (eds.), *La théologie byzantine et sa tradition* (vol. 2) (q.v.), 551–612.

Hussey, M. E., 'The Palamite Trinitarian Models', *SVQ* 16 (1972), 83–9.

Ierodiakonou, K., (ed.) *Byzantine Philosophy and its Ancient Sources* (Oxford 2002).

—— 'The Anti-Logical Movement in the Fourteenth Century' in idem (ed.), *Byzantine Philosophy and Its Ancient Sources* (q.v.), 219–36.

—— 'The Byzantine Reception of Aristotle's *Categories*', *Synthesis Philosophica* 39 (2005), 7–31.

Ivánka, E. von, *Plato christianus: Übernahme und Umgestaltung des Platonismus durch die Väter* (Einsiedeln 1964).

Jevtić, A., *Études hésychastes* (Lausanne 1995).

Journet, C., 'Palamisme et thomisme, à propos d'un livre récent', *Revue Thomiste* 60 (1960), 429–52.

Jugie, M., 'Georges Scholarios et l'Immaculée Conception', *EO* 17 (1915), 527–30.

—— 'Démétrius Cydonès et la théologie latine a Byzance', *EO* 27 (1928), 385–402.

—— 'Écrits apologétiques de Gennade Scholarios à l'addresse des musulmans', *Byzantion* 5 (1930), 296–316.

—— 'Georges Scholarios et Saint Thomas d'Aquin', in *Mélanges Madonnet* I (Paris 1930), 423–40.

—— 'Palamas, Grégoire' and 'Palamite, Controverse', *DTC* 11 (Paris 1932), 1735–1818.

—— *Theologia dogmatica christianorum orientalium ab ecclesia dissidentium* (vol. 2) (Paris 1933).

—— 'La polémique de Georges Scholarios contre Pléthon: nouvelle édition de sa "correspondence"', *Byzantion* 10 (1935), 517–30.

—— 'L'Unionisme de Georges Scholarios', *EO* 36 (1937), 65–86.

—— *Le schisme byzantin* (Paris 1941).

Kapriev, G., 'Transzendentalien und Energien. Zwei Modelle mittelalterlicher Philosophie (Thomas von Aquin und Kallistos Angelikudes)', in *Die Logik des Transzendentalen* (Festschrift Jan Aertsen) (Berlin 2003), 433–53.

—— 'Kydones, Demetrios' and 'Kydones, Prochoros', in D. Berger and J. Vijgen (eds.), *Thomisten-Lexikon* (Bonn 2006), 346–58.

Karmires, J. (tr.), *Σούμμα θεολογική Α΄, τεύχη α΄-β΄* (Athens 1935, 1940).

—— *Τὰ δογματικὰ καὶ συμβολικὰ μνημεῖα τῆς 'Ορθοδόξου Καθολικῆς 'Εκκλησίας* (2 vols.) (Athens 1952–3).

Karpozilos, A., 'St Thomas Aquinas and the Byzantine East (*De essentia et operatione*)', *Ekklesiastikos Pharos* 52 (1970), 129–47.

Karsavin, L., *Vostok, zapad, i russkaia idea* (Petrograd 1922).

Kartashev, A., *Ocherki po istorii russkoy tserkvi* (2 vols.) (Paris 1959).

Khomiakov, A., *L'Église latine et le protestantisme au point de vue de l'Église d'orient* (Paris 1872).

——*Polnoe sobranie sochinenii Alekseia Khomiakova* (8 Vols.), ed. F. Samarin (Moscow 1900–11). [Vols. V–VII = *Notes on World History*]

Kianka, F., 'The Apology of Demetrius Cydones: A Fourteenth-Century Autobiographical Source', *Byzantine Studies* 7 (1980), 51–71.

——'Demetrius Cydones. Intellectual and Diplomatic Relations between Byzantium and the West' (Diss. Fordham University 1981).

——'Demetrius Cydones and Thomas Aquinas', *Byzantion* 52 (1982), 264–86.

——'A Late Byzantine Defence of the Latin Church Fathers', *OCP* 49 (1983), 419–25.

——'Byzantine-Papal Diplomacy: The Role of Demetrius Cydones', *International History Review* 7 (1985), 175–213.

——'The Letters of Demetrios Kydones to Empress Helena Kantakouzene Palaiologina', *Dumbarton Oaks Papers* 46 (1992), 155–64.

——'Demetrios Kydones and Italy', *Dumbarton Oaks Papers* 49 (1995), 99–110.

Kolbaba, T., 'The Orthodoxy of the Latins in the Twelfth Century', in A. Louth and A. Casiday (eds.), *Byzantine Orthodoxies: Papers from the Thirty-Sixth Spring Symposium of Byzantine Studies* (Aldershot 2006), 199–214.

Koutroubis, D., *Ἡ χάρις τῆς θεολογίας* (Athens 1995).

Krumbacher, K., *Geschichte der Byzantinischen Literatur von Justinian bis zum Ende des Oströmischen Reiches* (Munich 1897).

Kuhlmann, J., *Die Taten des einfachen Gottes. Eine römisch-katholische Stellungnahme zum Palamismus* (Würzburg 1968).

Lemerle, P., 'L'Orthodoxie byzantine et l'oecuménisme médiéval: Les origines du "schisme" des Églises', *Bulletin de l'Association Guillaume Budé* (1965), 228–46.

——*Le premier humanisme byzantin* (Paris 1971).

Lévy, A., *Le créé et l'incréé: Maxime le confesseur et Thomas d'Aquin: aux sources de la querelle palamienne* (Paris 2006).

Likoudis, J., *Ending the Byzantine Greek Schism: The 14th c. Apologia of Demetrios Kydones for Unity with Rome* (New Rochelle, NY 1983).

Lison, J., 'L'Esprit comme amour selon Grégoire Palamas: Une influence augustinienne?', *Studia Patristica* 32 (1937), 325–31.

Livanos, C., *Greek Tradition and Latin Influence in the Work of George Scholarios* (Piscataway, NJ 2006).

Loenertz, R.-J., 'Les établissements dominicains de Péra-Constantinople', *EO* 34 (1933), 333–4.

——'Autour du traité de fr. Barthélemy de Constantinople contre les Grecs', *Archivum Fratrum Praedicatorum* 6 (1936), 361–71.

Loenertz, R.-J., *Les recueils de lettres de Démétrius Cydonès* (*Studi e Testi* 131; Vatican City 1947).

——'Fr Philippe de Bindo Incontri, O.P. du convent de Pera, inquisiteur en Orient', *Archivum Fratrum Praedicatorum* 18 (1948), 265–80.

——'Le chancelier impérial à Byzance au XIVe et au XIIIe siècle', *OCP* 26 (1960) 275–300.

——'Démétrius Cydonès I: De la naissance à l'année 1373', *OCP* 36 (1970), 47–72.

——'Démétrius Cydonès II: De 1373 à 1375', *OCP* 37 (1971), 5–39.

Lorentzatos, Z., *The Lost Center and Other Essays in Greek Poetry* (tr. K. Cicellis) (Princeton, NJ 1980).

Lossky, V., *Essai sur la théologie mystique de l'Église d'Orient* (Paris 1944). [ET *Mystical Theology of the Eastern Church* (London 1957)]

——'The Theology of Light in the Thought of St Gregory Palamas' in idem, *In the Image and Likeness of God*. [ET of 'La théologie de la lumière chez saint Grégoire de Thessalonique', *Dieu Vivant* 1 (1945), 94–118]

——'The Procession of the Holy Spirit in Orthodox Trinitarian Doctrine' in idem, *In the Image and Likeness of God*. [ET of *La procession du Saint-Esprit dans la doctrine trinitaire orthodoxe* (Paris 1948). Also in *Eastern Churches Quarterly* 7.2 (1948), 31–52]

——Review of Eric Mascall, *Existence and Analogy* (London 1949), *Sobornost* 3.7 (1950), 295–7.

——'Redemption and Deification', in idem, *In the Image and Likeness of God*. [ET of 'Rédemption et déification', *Messager de l'Exarchat du Patriarche russe en Europe occidentale* 15 (1953), 161–70]

——'The Theological Notion of the Human Person', in idem, *In the Image and Likeness of God*. [ET of 'La notion théologique de la personne humaine', *Messager de l'Exarchat du Patriarche russe en Europe occidentale* 24 (1955), 227–35]

—— 'Apophasis and Trinitarian Theology', in idem, *In the Image and Likeness of God*. [ET of *L'Apophase et la théologie trinitaire* (Paris 1956)]

——*Théologie négative et connaissance de Dieu chez Maître Eckhart* (Paris 1960).

——*The Vision of God* (London 1964).

——*In the Image and Likeness of God* (New York 1974).

Lössl, J., 'Augustine's *De Trinitate* in the 150 Chapters of St Gregory Palamas', *Augustinian Studies* 30 (1999), 61–82.

——'Augustine in Byzantium', *JEH* 51 (2000), 267–95.

Lot Borodine, M., *Un Maître de la spiritualité byzantine au XIVe siècle: Nicolas Cabasilas* (Paris 1958).

Louth, A., *St John Damascene: Tradition and Originality in Byzantine Theology* (Oxford 2002).

——'Some Recent Works by Christos Yannaras in English Translation', *Modern Theology* 25 (2009), 329–40.

Manoussakas, M., 'Recherches sur la vie de Jean Plousiadénos (Joseph de Méthone) (1429?–1500)', *REB* 17 (1959), 28–51.

Marshall, B., 'Action and Person: Do Palamas and Aquinas Agree about the Spirit?', *SVQ* 39 (1995), 379–408.

——'*Ex occidente lux*? Aquinas and Eastern Orthodox Theology', *Modern Theology* 20 (2004), 23–50.

Mascall, E. L., *The Openness of Being: Natural Theology Today* (London 1971). [Gifford Lectures 1970–1]

——*Saraband: The Memoirs of E. L. Mascall* (Leominster 1992).

Mercati, G., 'Callisto Angelicudes Meliniceota', in *Bessarione* 31 (1915).

——*Notizie di Procoro e Demetrio Cidone, Manuela Caleca e Theodore Meliteniota ed altri appunti per la storia della teologia e della letteratura bizantina del secolo XIV* (Vatican City 1931).

Metallinos, G., Παράδοση καὶ ἀλλοτρίωση (Athens 1986).

Meyendorff, J., 'Le thème du 'retour en soi' dans la doctrine palamite du XIVe siècle', *Revue de l'histoire des religions* 145 (1954), 188–206.

——'Humanisme nominaliste et mystique chrétienne à Byzance au XIVe siècle', *Nouvelle Revue Théologique* 89 (1957), 905–14.

——*Introduction à l'étude de Grégoire Palamas* (Paris 1959).

——'Projets de concile oecumenique en 1367: un Dialogue inédit entre Jean Cantacuzène et le légat Paul', *Dumbarton Oaks Papers* 14 (1960), 147–77.

——*Byzantine Theology: Historical Trends and Doctrinal Themes* (New York 1974).

——'The Mediterranean World in the Thirteenth Century, Theology: East and West', *The 17th International Byzantine Congress: Major Papers* (New York 1986), 669–82. [Revised versions in J. Chrysostomides (ed.), *Kathēgētria* (Festschrift Joan Hussey) (Camberley 1988) and the collected volume *Rome, Constantinople, Moscow: Historical and Theological Studies* (New York 1996), 73-86]

Michelson, P., 'Slavophile Religious Thought and the Dilemma of Russian Modernity 1830–1860', *Modern Intellectual History* 7 (2010), 239–67.

Mitsakis, K., 'Byzantine and Modern Greek Parahymnography', in D. Conomos (ed.), *Studies in Eastern Chant* 5 (New York 2001), 9–76.

Moschopoulos, A., ' Ἐπιτομὴ Δογματικῆς καὶ ' Ἠθικῆς Θεολογίας (Athens 1851).

Moutsopoulos, E., 'L'Hellénisation du Thomisme au XIVe siècle', *Annuaire Scientifique de la Faculté de Philosophie de l'Université d'Athènes* 24 (1975), 131–6.

——'Thomisme et Aristotélisme à Byzance', *JÖB* 32 (1982), 301–10.

Nicol, D. M., 'Byzantine Requests for an Oecumenical Council in the Fourteenth Century', *Annuarium historiae conciliorum* 1 (1969), 69–95.

——*Church and Society in the Last Centuries of Byzantium* (Cambridge 1979).

——*The Reluctant Emperor: A Biography of John Cantacuzene, Byzantine Emperor* (Cambridge 1996).

Obolensky, D., *Six Byzantine Portraits* (Oxford 1988).

Oehler, K., 'Aristotle in Byzantium', *Greek Roman and Byzantine Studies* 5 (1964), 133–46.

Oehler, K., *Antike Philosophie und byzantinisches Mittelalter; Aufsätze zur Geschichte des griechischen Denkens* (Munich 1969).

Panofsky, E., 'Die Perspektive als symbolische Form', in *Vorträge der Bibliothek Warburg* 25 (1925), 258–330. (Also published as *Die Perspektive als symbolische Form* (Leipzig/Berlin 1927). [ET: *Perspective as Symbolic Form* (New York 1991)]

Papadakis, A., 'Gennadius II and Mehmet the Conqueror', *Byzantion* 42 (1972), 88–106.

——'Byzantine Perceptions of the Latin West', *Greek Orthodox Theological Review* 36 (1992), 231–42.

Papadopulos, A., «Γεώργιος Κορέσσιος», *Ἀθήνα* 46 (1935), 191–208.

Papadopoulos, S., ' Ἑλληνικαὶ μεταφράσεις θωμιστικῶν ἔργωνΦιλοθωμισταὶ καὶ ἀντιθωμισταὶ ἐν Βυζαντίῳ (Athens 1967).

——Συνάντησις ὀρθοδόξου καὶ σχολαστικῆς θεολογίας ἐν τῷ προσώπῳ Καλλίστου Ἀγγελικούδη καὶ Θωμᾶ Ἀκινάτου (Thessalonica 1970).

——'Thomas in Byzanz. Thomas Rezeption und Thomas Kritik in Byzanz zwischen 1354 und 1435', *Theologie und Philosophie* 49 (1982), 264–86.

Pelikan, J., *The Spirit of Eastern Christendom 600–1700* (Chicago, IL 1974).

Plested, M., *The Macarian Legacy: The Place of Macarius-Symeon in the Eastern Christian Tradition* (Oxford 2004).

——'Wisdom in St Maximus the Confessor', *Studia Patristica* 42 (2006), 205–9.

Podskalsky, G., 'Die Rezeption des der thomistischen Theologie bei Gennadios II Scholarios', *Theologie und Philosophie* 49 (1974), 305–23.

——*Theologie und Philosophie in Byzanz. Der Streit um die theologische Methodik in der spätbyzantinischen Geistesgeschichte (14./15. Jahrhundert)* (Munich 1977).

——*Griechische Theologie in der Zeit der Türkenherrschaft: die Orthodoxie im Spannungsfeld der nachreformatorischen Konfessionen des Westens (1453–1821)* (Munich 1988).

——Review of R. Flogaus, *Theosis bei Palamas und Luther: ein Beitrag zum ökumenischen Gespräch* (Göttingen 1997), *BZ* 91 (1998), 118–20.

——*Von Photios zu Bessarion: Der Vorrang humanistisch geprägter Theologie in Byzanz und deren bleibende Bedeutung* (Schriften zur Geistesgeschichte des östlichen Europa 25; Wiesbaden 2003).

Polemis, I., 'Notes on a Short Treatise of Nicolas Cabasilas', *REB* 51 (1993), 155–60.

——*Theophanes of Nicaea: His Life and Works* (Wiener Byzantinistische Studien 20; Vienna 1996).

——'An Unpublished Anti-Latin Treatise of Manuel Moschopoulos', *JÖB* 46 (1996), 251–64.

—— 'Notes on Two Texts Dealing with the Palamite Controversy', in *Realia Byzantina* (Festschrift Apostolos Karpozilos, ed. S. Kotzabassi and G. Mavromatis) (Byzantinsches Archiv 22; Berlin 2009), 207–12.

Popović, J., *Dogmatika Pravoslavne tserkve* (3 vols.) (Belgrade 1932, 1935, 1978).

Raby, J., 'Mehmed the Conqueror's Greek Scriptorium', *Dumbarton Oaks Papers* 37 (1983), 15–34.

Rackl, M., 'Demetrius Kydones als Verteidiger und Übersetzer des heiligen Thomas von Aquin', *Der Katholik* 1 (1915), 21–40.

—— 'Die ungedruckte Verteidigungsschrift des Demetrios Kydones für Thomas von Aquin gegen Neilos Kabasilas', *Divus Thomas* 7 (1920), 303 17.

—— 'Die griechische Übersetzung der Summa Theologiae des hl. Thomas von Aquin', *BZ* 24 (1923–4), 48–60.

—— 'Die griechischen Augustinusübersetzungen', in *Miscellanea Francesco Ehrle. Scritti di storia e paleografia* I (Rome 1924).

—— 'Der hl. Thomas von Aquin und das trinitarische Grundgesetz in byzantinische Beleuchtung', *Xenia Thomistica* III (1925), 363–89.

—— 'Thomas von Aquin im Werturteil eines byzantinische Theologen', in A. Lang (ed.), *Aus der Geisteswelt des Mittelalters* II (Festschrift Martin Grabman) (Munster 1935), 1361–72.

Ramplius, S., *Ὁ καημὸς τοῦ ἑνός Κεφάλαια τῆς ψυχικῆς ἱστορίας τῶν Ἑλλήνων*(Athens 2000).

—— *Ἱλαρὸν φῶς τοῦ κόσμου* (Athens 2006).

—— «*Τὸ μηδέν σαν μακρόβιος ἐπιθανάτιος ρόγχος»* in *Η Καθημερινή*, 14 December 2008.

—— *Τὸ ἀδιανόητο τίποτα: Φιλοκαλικὰ ριζώματα τοῦ νεοελληνικοῦ μηδενισμοῦ. Δοκίμιο φιλοσοφικῆς ἀνθρωπολογίας* (Athens 2010).

Regnon, T. de, *Études de théologie positive sur la Sainte Trinité* (4 vols.) (Paris 1892–98).

Rhosis, Z., *Σύστημα Δογματικῆς τῆς Ὀρθοδόξου Καθολικῆς Ἐκκλησίας* (Athens 1903).

Rigo, A., 'Callisto Angelicude Catafugiota Meleniceota e l'esicasmo bizantino del XIV secolo. Una nota prosopografica', in N. Kautchtschischwili *et al.* (eds.), *Nil Sorskij e l'esicasmo. Atti del II Convegno internazionale di spiritualità russa* (Magnano 1995), 251–68.

—— *Gregorio Palamas e oltre: studi e documenti sulle controversie teologiche del XIV secolo bizantino* (Florence 2004).

Romanides, J., 'Notes on the Palamite Controversy and Related Topics', *Greek Orthodox Theological Review* 9 (1963–4), 225–70.

—— *Franks, Romans, Feudalism and Doctrine* (Boston, MA 1982).

—— *Τὸ προπατορικὸν ἁμάρτημα* (Athens 1989²).

—— *An Outline of Orthodox Patristic Dogmatics* (Rollinsford, NH 2004).

Rose, S., *The Place of Blessed Augustine in the Orthodox Church* (Platina, CA 1996²).

Rossum, J. van, 'Palamism and Church Tradition: Palamism, its Use of Patristic Tradition, and its Relationship with Thomistic Thought' (Diss. Fordham University 1985).

Russell, N., *Cyril of Alexandria* (London 2000).

—— 'Palamism and the Circle of Demetrius Cydones', in *Porphyrogenita* (Festschrift Julian Chrysostomides, ed. C. Dendrinos et al.) (Aldershot 2003), 153–74.

—— 'Modern Greek Theologians and the Greek Fathers', *Philosophy and Theology* 18 (2006), 77–92.

—— 'Prochoros Cydones and the Fourteenth-Century Understanding of Orthodoxy', in A. Louth and A. Casiday (eds.), *Byzantine Orthodoxies: Papers from the Thirty-Sixth Spring Symposium of Byzantine Studies* (Aldershot 2006), 75–91.

—— 'Theosis and Gregory Palamas: Continuity or Doctrinal Change?', *SVQ* 50.4 (2006) 357–79.

Ryder, J., *The Career and Writings of Demetrius Kydones: A Study of Fourteenth-Century Byzantine Politics, Religion and Society* (Leiden 2010).

Sahas, D., *Icon and Logos: Sources in Eighth-Century Iconoclasm* (Toronto 1986).

Sakharov, N., *I Love, Therefore I Am: The Theological Legacy of Archimandrite Sophrony* (New York 2002).

Sakharov, S., *Perepiska s Protoiereem Georgiem Florovskim* (Tolleshunt Knights 2008).

Salaville, S., 'Le traité "du mépris de la mort" de Démétrios Cydonès traduit en français par Ménard en 1686', *EO* 22 (1923), 26–49.

—— 'Un thomiste à Byzance au XVe siècle: Gennade Scholarios', *EO* 23 (1924), 129–36.

—— 'Philosophie et théologie ou Épisodes scolastiques à Byzance de 1059 à 1197', *EO* 29 (1930), 132–56.

—— 'Vues sotérilogiques chez Nicolas Cabasilas (XIVe siècle)', *Études Byzantines* 1 (1943), 5–57.

Sathas, K., Νεοελληνικὴ Φιλολογία (Athens 1868).

Schirò, G., 'Il paradosso de Nil Cabasila' in *Studi bizantini e neoellenici* 9 (1957), 362–88.

—— 'Grigorio Palamas e la scienza profana', *Le millénaire du Mont Athos 963–1963* II (Venice 1963), 6–36.

Schönborn, C. von, 'Immanente und ökonomische Trinität. Zur Frage des Funktionsverlustes der Trinitätslehre in der östlichen und westlichen Theologie', *Freiburger Zeitschrift für Philosophie und Theologie* 27 (1980), 247–64.

Setton, K., 'The Byzantine Background to the Italian Renaissance', *Proceedings of the American Philosophical Society* 100 (1956), 1–76.

Ševčenko, I., 'Intellectual Repercussions of the Council of Florence', *Church History* 24 (1955), 291–323.

——'Society and Intellectual Life in the Fourteenth Century', *Actes du XIVe Congrès international des études byzantines* I (Bucharest 1971), 69–92.

——'The Many Worlds of Peter Mohyla', *Harvard Ukrainian Studies* 8 (1984), 9–40.

Sherrard, P., *Greek East and Latin West* (Oxford 1959).

——«Σήσιμος Λορενζάτος: τα κρίσιμα χρόνια», in ' Ἀντὶ ΧρυσέωῆFestschrift Zissimos Lorentzatos) (Athens 1995), 49–61.

Sinkewicz, R., 'The Doctrine of the Knowledge of God in the Early Writings of Barlaam the Calabrian', *Mediaeval Studies* 44 (1982), 181–242.

Slipyj, J., 'San Tommaso e la scienza teologica e filosofica nell'oriente', *Angelicum* 46 (1969), 3–15.

Soloviev, V., *Kritika otvlechennykh nachal* (Moscow 1880).

——*La Russie et l'Église universelle* (Paris 1889).

——*Lectures on Divine Humanity* (ET London 1948; Hudson, NY 1995).

——*The Crisis of Western Philosophy: Against the Positivists* (ET Hudson, NY 1996).

——*The Philosophical Principles of Integral Knowledge* (ET Grand Rapids, MI 2008).

Spiteris, Y., *Cabasilas: teologo e mistico bizantino. Nicola Cabasilas Chamaętos, e la sua sintesi teologica* (Rome 1996).

——and G. Conticello, 'Nicola Cabasilas Chamaetos', in G. and V. Conticello (eds.), *La théologie byzantine et sa tradition* (vol. 2). (q.v.), 315–95.

Stăniloae, D., *Teologia dogmatică ortodoxă* (3 vols.). (Bucharest 1978) [ET (vol. 1): *The Experience of God* (2 vols.) (Boston 1994, 2000)]

Stiernon, D., 'Bulletin sur le palamisme', *REB* 30 (1972), 231–341.

——'Eugène Boulgaris', in G. and V. Conticello (eds.), *La théologie byzantine et sa tradition* (vol. 2) (q.v.), 721–837.

Stoupakes, N., *Γεώργιος Κορέσσιος* (1570 ci–1659/60): *Η ζωή, το έργο του και οι πνευματικοί αγώνες της εποχής του* (Chios 2000).

Tatakis, B., *La philosophie byzantine* (Paris 1949).

Thomson, F., 'Peter Mogila's Ecclesiastical Reforms and the Ukrainian Contribution to Russian Culture: A Critique of Georges Florovsky's Theory of the Pseudomorphosis of Orthodoxy', *Slavica Gandensia* 20 (1993), 67–119.

Tinnefeld, F., 'Intellectuals in Late Byzantine Thessalonike', *DO* 57 (2003), 153–72.

——'Georgios Gennadios Scholarios', in G. and V. Conticello (eds.), *La théologie byzantine et sa tradition* (vol. 2) (q.v.), 477–541.

Todt, K.-P., 'Kyrillos Lukaris', in G. and V. Conticello (eds.), *La théologie byzantine et sa tradition* (vol. 2) (q.v.), 617–51.

Tomadakes, N., ' Ο ' Ἰωσὴφ Βρυέννιος καὶ ἡ Κρήτη κατὰ 1400 (Athens 1947).

Treadgold, D., *The West in Russia and China I: Russia, 1472–1917* (Cambridge 1973).

Trembelas, P., Δογματικὴ τῆς Ὀρθοδόξου Καθολικῆς Ἐκκλησίας (Athens 1959–61).

Tsirpanlis, C., *Mark Eugenicus and the Council of Florence: A Historical Re-evaluation of his Personality* (Thessalonica 1974).

Turner, C. G., 'The Career of George Gennadios Scholarios', *Byzantion* 39 (1969), 420–55.

Turyn, A., *Codices Graeci Vaticani saeculis XIII et XIV scripti annorumque notis instructi* (Vatican City 1964).

Tyn, T., 'Prochoros und Demetrios Kydones: der byzantinische Thomismus des XIV Jahrhunderts', in W. Eckert (ed.), *Thomas von Aquino: Interpretation und Rezeption* (Mainz 1964), 837–912.

Vancourt, R., 'Georges Coressios. Quelques aspects de sa doctrine sur la grâce et la predestination, d'après des documents inédits', *Orientalia Christiana* 32 (1933), 40–95.

Ven, P. Van den, 'La patristique et l'hagiographie au concile de Nicée de 787', *Byzantion* 25–27 (1955–7), 325–62.

Ware, K. T., 'The Transfiguration of the Body', *Sobornost* 4.8 (1963), 420–33 [reprinted in A. M. Allchin (ed.), *Sacrament and Image* (London 1967), 17–32].

——*Eustratios Argenti* (Oxford 1964).

——'Orthodox and Catholics in the Seventeenth Century: Schism or Inter-communion', in D. Baker (ed.), *Schism, Heresy and Religious Protest* (Studies in Church History 9; Cambridge 1972), 259–76.

——'Scholasticism and Orthodoxy: Theological Method as a Factor in the Schism', *ECR* 5 (1973), 16–27.

——'St Nikodimos and the *Philokalia*', in D. Conomos and G. Speake (eds.), *Mount Athos the Sacred Bridge: The Spirituality of the Holy Mountain* (Oxford/Bern 2005), 69–121.

Wendebourg, D., *Geist oder Energie. Zur Frage der innergöttlichen Veranker-ung des christlichen Lebens in der byzantinischen Theologie* (Munich 1980).

——'From the Cappadocian Fathers to Gregory Palamas: The Defeat of Trinitarian Theology', *Studia Patristica* 17 (1982), 194–7.

——'Mysterion und Sakrament. Zu einigen frühen Zeugnissen scholastischer Einflüsse auf die griechische Theologie', in *Unser ganzes Leben Christus unserm Gott überantworten* (Festschrift Fairy von Lilienfeld) (Göttingen 1982), 272–94.

——*Reformation und Orthodoxie* (Göttingen 1986).

——'"Pseudomorphosis"—ein theologisches Urteil als Axiom der kirchen- und theologiegeschichtlichen Forschung', in R. Taft (ed.), *The Christian East: Its Institutions and its Thought: A Critical Reflection* (Rome 1996), 565–89. [ET: '"Pseudomorphosis": A Theological Judgement as an Axiom in the History of Church and Theology', *The Greek Orthodox Theological Review* 42 (1997), 321–42]

Williams, A. N., *The Ground of Union: Deification in Aquinas and Palamas* (New York 1999).

Wozniuk, V., *The Heart of Reality: Essays on Beauty, Love, and Ethics by V.S. Soloviev* (Notre Dame, IN 2003).

Wulff, O., 'Die umgekehrte Perspektive und die Niedersicht. Eine Raumanschauungsform der altbyzantinischen Kunst und ihre Fortbildung in der Renaissance', in *Kunstwissenschaftliche Beiträge* (Festschrift August Schmarsow) (Leipzig 1907), 1–40.

Yannaras, C., 'Orthodoxy and the West', *ECR* 3 (1971), 286–300.

—— ' Ὀρθοδοξία καὶ Δύση στὴ Νεώτερη Ἑλλάδα (Athens, 1992). [ET P. Chamberas and N. Russell, *Orthodoxy and the West* (Brookline, MA 2006)]

—— *On the Absence and Unknowability of God: Heidegger and the Areopagite* (tr. H. Ventis) (London 2005).

Zenkovsky, B., *Istoriya russkoy filosofii* (2 vols.) (Paris 1948–50).

Zeses, Th., Γεννάδιος Β' Σχολάριος. Βίος-Συγγράμματα-Διδασκαλία (Thessalonica 1980).

Zizioulas, J., *Being as Communion: Studies in Personhood and the Church* (New York 1985).

—— *Communion and Otherness* (London 2006).

—— *Lectures in Christian Dogmatics* (London 2008).

Zoumboulakis, S., «Τό σύνορο καί ὁ Χρῆστος Γιανναρᾶς», in idem, Χριστιανοί στον δημόσιο χῶρο. Πίστη ἤ πολιτιστική ταυτότητα (Athens 2010), 45–64.

Thomas and Thomism:
A Select Bibliography

Primary

Thomas Aquinas
Sancti Thomae Aquinatis, Doctoris Angelici, Opera Omnia: iussi impensaque Leonis XIII, P.M., edita (Rome 1882–). [This and other modern editions accessed at the splendid corpusthomisticum.org]

Secondary

Backes, I., *Die Christologie des heilige Thomas von Aquin und die griechischen Kirchenväter* (Paderborn 1931).

Bardy, G., 'Sur les sources patristiques grecques de saint Thomas', *Revue des sciences philosophiques et théologiques* 12 (1923), 493–502.

Bataillon, L.-J., 'Les sermons de Saint Thomas et la *Catena aurea*', in A. Maurer (ed.), *St Thomas Aquinas 1274–1974. Commemorative Studies* (Toronto 1974), 67–75.

—— 'Saint Thomas et les pères: de la *Catena* à la *Tertia pars*', in *Ordo sapientiae et amoris: image et message de Saint Thomas d'Aquin à travers les récentes études historiques, herméneutiques et doctrinales* (Festschrift J.-P. Torrell) (Fribourg 1993), 15–36.

Benson, R. and G. Constable (eds.), *Renaissance and Renewal in the Twelfth Century* (Cambridge, MA 1982).

Berger, D., *Thomismus: grosse Leitmotive der thomistischen Synthese und ihre Aktualität für die Gegenwart* (Cologne 2001).

Brett, E., *Humbert of Romans: His Life and Views of Thirteenth-Century Society* (Toronto 1984).

Chenu, M.-D., *Introduction à l'étude de saint Thomas d'Aquin* (Montreal 1950).

Colish, M., 'St Thomas Aquinas in Historical Perspective: The Modern Period', *Church History* 44 (1975), 433–49.

—— 'Haskins's Renaissance Seventy Years Later: Beyond Anti-Burckhardtianism', *Haskins Society Journal* 11 (1998), 1–15.

—— *Remapping Scholasticism* (Toronto 2000).

Congar, Y., 'Valeur et portée œcuménique de quelques principes herméneutiques de saint Thomas d'Aquin', *Revue des sciences philosophiques et théologiques* 57 (1973), 611–26.

——'"Ecclesia" et "populus (fidelis)" dans l'ecclésiologie de S. Thomas', in A. Maurer (ed.), *St Thomas Aquinas 1274–1974: Commemorative Studies* (Toronto 1974), 159–73.

Constable, G., *The Reformation of the Twelfth Century* (Cambridge 1996).

Conticello, G., 'San Tommaso ed i Padri: la *Catena aurea super Ioannem*', *Archives d'histoire doctrinale et litteraire du moyen âge* 65 (1990), 31–92.

——'Théophylacte de Bulgarie, source de Thomas d'Aquin (*Catena aurea in Ioannem*)', in *Philomathestatos* (Festschrift Jacques Noret, ed. B. Janssens et al.) (Leuven 2004), 63–75.

Cross, R., 'Perichoresis, Deification, and Christological Predication in John of Damascus', *Mediaeval Studies* 62 (2000), 69–124.

——*The Metaphysics of the Incarnation: Thomas Aquinas to Duns Scotus* (Oxford 2002).

Dauphinais, M. and M. Levering (eds.), *Reading John with St Thomas Aquinas: Theological Exegesis and Speculative Theology* (Washington, DC 2005).

Davies, B., *The Thought of Thomas Aquinas* (Oxford 1993).

——*Aquinas: An Introduction* (London/New York 2002).

Elders, L., 'Thomas Aquinas and the Fathers of the Church', in I. Backus (ed.), *The Reception of the Church Fathers in the West* (Leiden 1997), 337–66.

Emery, G., 'Le photinisme et ses précurseurs chez Saint Thomas', *Revue Thomiste* 95 (1995), 371–98.

——*Trinity in Aquinas* (Ypsilanti, MI 2003).

——*The Trinitarian Theology of Saint Thomas Aquinas* (Oxford 2007).

——*Trinity, Church, and the Human Person: Thomistic Essays* (Naples, FL 2007).

Emery, K. and J. Wawrykow, *Christ among the Medieval Dominicans* (Notre Dame, IN 1998).

Fabro, C., *La nozione metafisica di partecipazione secondo S. Tomaso d'Aquino* (Milan 1939).

Geenen, G., 'Saint Thomas et les Pères', in idem 'Thomas d'Aquin', *DTC* 15.1 (1946), 738–61.

——'En marge du Concile de Chalcédoine. Les textes du Quatrième Concile dans les œuvres de Saint Thomas', *Angelicum* 29 (1952), 43–59.

——'Le fonte patristiche come 'autorità' nella teologia di San Tomaso', *Sacra Doctrina* 77 (1975), 7–67.

Geiger, L.-B., *La participation dans la philosophie de S. Thomas d'Aquin* (Paris 1953).

Ghellinck, J. de, *Le mouvement théologique du XIIe siècle* (Brussels 1969).

Gilson, É., *Le Thomisme. Introduction à la philosophie de saint Thomas d'Aquin* (Paris 1944⁵).

——*Wisdom and Love in St Thomas Aquinas* (Milwaukee 1951).

Grabmann, M., *Thomas von Aquin. Eine Einführung in seine Persönlichkeit und Gedankenwelt* (Kempten 1912).

—— *Die Geschichte der scholastischen Methode, nach den gedruckten und ungedruckten Quellen* (2 vols.) (Freiburg in Breisgau 1909, 1911).

Hankey, W., *God in Himself: Aquinas' Doctrine of God as Expounded in the Summa theologiae* (Oxford 1987).

Haring, N., 'The "Liber de Differentia naturae et personae" by Hugh Etherian and the letters addressed to him by Peter of Vienna and Hugh of Honau', *Mediaeval Studies* 24 (1962), 1–34.

Henle, R. J., *Saint Thomas and Platonism* (The Hague 1956).

Hoping, H., *Weisheit als Wissen des Ursprungs: Philosophie und Theologie in der 'Summa contra gentiles' des Thomas von Aquin* (Freiburg im Breisgau 1997).

Iribarren, I., *Durandus of St Pourçain: A Dominican Theologian in the Shadow of Aquinas* (Oxford 2005).

Jordan, M., 'The Controversy of the *Correctoria* and the Limits of Metaphysics', *Speculum* 57 (1982), 292–314.

—— 'Theological Exegesis and Aquinas's Treatise "Against the Greeks"', *Church History* 56 (1987), 445–56.

—— *The Alleged Aristotelianism of Thomas Aquinas* (Toronto 1992).

—— *Rewritten Theology: Aquinas after his Readers* (Oxford/Malden, MA 2006).

Kerr, F., *After Aquinas: Versions of Thomism* (Oxford/Malden, MA 2002).

—— 'Recent Thomistica' (I–IV), *New Blackfriars* 83 (2002), 245–51; 84 (2003) 148–55; 85 (2004), 628–41; 87 (2006), 651–9.

Kremer, K., *Die neuplatonische Seinsphilosophie und ihre Wirkung auf Thomas von Aquin* (Leiden 1966).

Leclercq, J., 'Tradition patristique et monastique dans l'enseignement de S. Thomas sur la vie contemplative', in *S. Tommaso fonti e riflessi del suo pensiero* (Studi Tomistici 1; Rome 1974), 129–53.

Levering, M., *Scripture and Metaphysics: Aquinas and the Renewal of Trinitarian Theology* (Oxford/Malden, MA 2004).

Little, A., *The Platonic Heritage of Thomism* (Dublin 1949).

Lubac, H. de, 'À propos de la formule: "diversi, sed non adversi"', in *Mélanges Jules Lebreton* II, *Recherches de science religieuse* 40 (1951–2), 27–40.

Maritain, J., *Distinguer pour unir; ou, Les degrés du savoir* (Paris 1932).

—— *Science et Sagesse* (Paris 1935).

Mascall, E. L., 'Guide-Lines from St Thomas for Theology Today', in A. Maurer (ed.), *St Thomas Aquinas 1274–1974: Commemorative Studies* (Toronto 1974), 489–501.

Milbank, J. and C. Pickstock, *Truth in Aquinas* (London/New York 2000).

Morard, M., 'Une source de saint Thomas d'Aquin: Le deuxième concile de Constantinople (553)', *Revue des sciences philosophiques et théologiques* 81 (1997), 21–56.

—'Thomas d'Aquin, lecteur des conciles', *Archivum franciscanum histor-icum* 98 (2005), 211–365.

Nieuwenhove, R. van and J. Wawrykow (eds.), *The Theology of Thomas Aquinas* (Notre Dame, IN 2005).

O'Meara, T., *Thomas Aquinas: Theologian* (Notre Dame, IN 1997).

Pasnau, R. and C. Shields, *The Philosophy of Aquinas* (Boulder, CO 2004).

Pegis, A., *Saint Thomas and the Greeks* (Milwaukee, WI 1939).

Pera, C., *Le fonti del pensiero di S. Tommaso d'Aquino nella Somma teologica* (Turin 1979^2).

Picavet, F., *Esquisse d'une histoire générale et comparée des philosophies médiévales* (Paris 1907^2).

Roy, L., *Lumière et sagesse: la grâce mystique dans la théologie de saint Thomas d'Aquin* (Montreal 1948).

Santeler, J., *Der Platonismus in der Erkenntnislehre des heiligen Thomas von Aquin* (Innsbruck 1939).

Slipyj, J., 'S. Tommaso e la scienza teologica e filosofica nell'oriente', *Angel-icum* 46 (1969), 3–15.

Somme, L.-C., *Thomas d'Aquin, la divinisation dans le Christ* (Geneva 1998).

Stump, E., *Aquinas* (London 2003).

Torrell, J. P., 'Thomas d'Aquin (saint)', *DS* 15 (1991), 718–73.

—*Saint Thomas Aquinas* (Volume I: *The Person and his Work*; Volume II: *Spiritual Master*) (Washington, DC 1996, 2005).

—*Recherches thomasiennes: études revues et augumentées* (Paris 2000).

—(tr.) *Somme Théologique. IIIa, q. 1–26: Le Verbe incarné* (Paris 2002).

—*Aquinas's Summa: Background, Structure, & Reception* (Washington, DC 2005).

—'Saint Thomas et l'histoire: état de la question et pistes de recherches', *Revue Thomiste* 105 (2005), 355–409.

—*Nouvelles recherches thomasiennes* (Paris 2008).

Velde, R. te, *Aquinas on God: The 'Divine Science' of the* Summa theologiae (Aldershot 2006).

Velecky, C., 'Following the Fathers', Appendix 3 of idem (ed.), *Summa Theologiae: Volume 6—The Trinity (I^a a.27–32)* (Cambridge 2006^2).

Weinandy, T. et al. (eds.), *Aquinas on Doctrine: A Critical Introduction* (London/New York 2004).

—*Aquinas on Scripture: An Introduction to his Biblical Commentaries* (London/New York 2005).

Wippel, J., 'The Condemnations of 1270 and 1277 at Paris', *The Journal of Medieval and Renaissance Studies* 7 (1977), 169–201.

—'Thomas Aquinas and the Condemnation of 1277', *The Modern School-man* 72 (1995), 233–72.

—'Bishop Stephen Tempier and Thomas Aquinas: A Separate Process Against Aquinas?' *Freiburger Zeitschrift für Philosophie und Theologie,* 44 (1997), 117–36.

General Index

Abelard, Peter 182
Aeidaros, Angelos 109n
aesthetics (theological) 183, 218
Aeterni Patris (1879) 11–12, 20n, 32n,
        138, 177, 183, 216n
Akindynos, Gregory 30n, 55, 58, 59,
        74, 76n, 77, 77n, 90, 96,
        120, 221
Albert the Great 22, 51n, 152, 172
Alcalay, Caroline 86n
d'Alès, Adhemar 193
Alexander I (Tsar) 178
Alexander of Hales 146, 152
Alexander VI (Pope) 172
Alexandria, Alexandrian theology
        155, 199
Alivisatos, Hamilcar 210
Allatios, Leo 129, 142
d'Alverny, Marie-Thérèse 16n
Amadeus of Savoy 1n
Ambrose of Milan 69, 154
Amfiteatrov, Anthony 179, 185
analogia entis 207
analogia fidei 207n
Anastasius of Sinai 17, 48–9, 52–3
Anaxagoras 111
ancestral sin, *see* original sin
Ancyra 89n, 114
Andreæ, Jacob 142
Andronikos II Palaiologos 110
Andronikos III Palaiologos 43n
Androutsos, Christos 186–8, 217
Angelikoudes, Kallistos 109n, 109,
        112–14, 221
angels 91, 111, 155, 163, 165
Anselm of Canterbury 21n, 71, 101–3,
        118, 153, 173n, 179n
Anslem of Havelberg 15n
Anthimos of Athens 68n
Anthrakites, Methodios 52n, 161–2
Antioch, Antiochene theology
        46, 199
Antoniades, Vasilios 187
Antonova, Clemena 9n
Apollinarius 48n

apophatic theology 20, 30n, 41n, 45–6,
        50, 53, 55, 57, 100, 121, 125, 160,
        192n, 196–7, 201, 208, 216, 217,
        224, 227
Aquinas, Thomas *passim* (*see also*
        Thomism)
    angels 111, 163, 165
    apophaticism 20, 100, 192n, 196,
        201, 216
    baptism 27, 82–3
    Byzantines, contemporary 21–8
    canonization 137n, 137
    celibacy 123
    Christology 19, 20, 79–84, 192n
    creation 92–3, 98n, 99, 132, 163,
        166, 193
    deification 13
    divine will 126, 153
    Ecumenical Councils 18–19, 27,
        220, 223
    essence and energies 32, 92–3, 95,
        113, 126, 132, 132n, 143, 153,
        165, 206
    eucharist, transubstantiation 25, 26,
        27, 116–17, 132, 149, 157
    exegetical works 12, 17, 19, 129,
        131
    Fathers (Greek) 15–21, 24, 26, 27,
        80, 129, 220, 223, 224
    Fathers (Latin) 26, 129
    Fathers (general) 17–18, 24, 80, 113,
        216, 223
    grace 153, 206
    Greek language 22, 24, 25, 27
    hermeneutic of orthodoxy 24,
        25, 28, 220, 226
    incarnation 121, 122, 166, 201
    liturgy 12n, 20, 27
    mediated and unmediated
        processions 125–6
    papal primacy 22, 25, 26n, 27
    philosophy 71, 111, 112,
        113, 131
    Plato, Platonism, neo-Platonism 13,
        14, 20, 70, 71n, 81, 193

Index Locorum

.

Printed and bound by CPI Group (UK) Ltd, Croydon, CR0 4YY